FOLKLORE:

Selected Essays

Richard M. Dorson

F O L K L O R E :

Selected Essays

Indiana University Press

BLOOMINGTON / LONDON

Published in Canada by Fitzhenry & Whiteside Limited, Don Mills, Ontario

Library of Congress catalog card number: 72–76944

ISBN: 0–253–32320–7

Manufactured in the United States of America

For Ron, Roland, Jeff, Linda

who sometimes keep me from thinking

about folklore

CONTENTS

FOLKLORE:

Selected Essays

INTRODUCTION

Folklore and Other Fields

FOLKLORE IS AT ONCE an independent discipline and an intimate associate of sister disciplines in the humanities and the social sciences. Possessing its own scholarly methods and concepts, folklore requires an apprenticeship and a special aptitude the same as does any other field of learning. The qualified folklorist belongs to a separate guild of folklore societies, just as the scholar in other areas attends the professional meetings and reads the esoteric journals of his subject. Yet by the nature of his materials the student of folklore interacts closely with other academic guilds. In reverse, members of other guilds are frequently attracted to and find themselves immersed in folklore collections and treatises.

The composition of the Folklore Institute at Indiana University can illustrate the cross-disciplinary character of folklore studies. Indiana University was the first American institution of higher learning to initiate a doctoral degree program in folklore. An interdepartmental committee was empowered to award such a degree in 1949, and four years later conferred its first Ph.D. in folklore. The day came, in 1963, when the committee blossomed into an independent department with its own faculty. Some of the fifteen members of this faculty hold full appointments in folklore, some hold joint appointments with other departments, and some, who are budgeted wholly in other departments but whose teaching and research interests lie strongly in folklore areas, receive the title Fellows of the Folklore Institute.

Three of these joint appointments unite folklore with anthropology, English, and history. These fields have always intersected at certain points with the realm of the folklorist. Eminent anthropologists such as Franz Boas and Melville Herskovits encouraged their students in the field to collect the oral literature of American Indians and tribal Africans in order to appreciate the full measure of their cultures. Courses on "Folklore and cultural anthropology" and "Anthropological folklore" are taught in the institute.

Professors of English literature—and here one immediately thinks of the hallowed names of Harvard's Francis James Child and George Lyman Kittredge—have demonstrated a fondness for the ballad and other aesthetic products of the folk imagination. Folklore itself may qualify as literature, in the case of artistically pleasing tales, ballads, oral epics, and oral romances. And authors of novels, short stories, plays, and poems have often found inspiration in folklore. A standard course in the institute is "Folklore in its literary relations."

Historians in Europe, Asia, and Africa have shown greater sympathy for the folklore approach than those in the United States, but the tide is turning. With the acceptance of oral history, black history, and ethnic history into the thinking of American historians, they have begun to recognize the values of tape-recorded interviews and oral historical traditions as sources of information that can complement written records. In particular such sources contribute to the history of the common man. A seminar on "The folk in American history" at Indiana University introduces folklore concepts to students in history and historical concepts to students in folklore.

Music and folklore form another firm academic partnership within their common province of ethnomusicology. Today ballad scholars acknowledge that tunes must be recorded and considered equally with the texts, and Bertrand Bronson's *The Traditional Tunes of the Child Ballads* is the monument to ballad music. Other forms of folk poetry, such as the blues, also require the expertise of a folk musicologist, as does the whole vast body of traditional music in nonliterate societies. The Folklore Institute provides a field of concentration for ethnomusicology majors, supervised by the director of the Archives of Traditional Music, George List, who holds degrees from the Juilliard and Indiana University Schools of Music, as well as the title professor of folklore.

English literature is of course only one of the world's literatures, and any department of language and literature may harbor a scholar who perceives the connections between his literary studies and folk models. Strongly committed folklorists at Indiana University are found in the Spanish, Slavic, and Uralic-Altaic departments, and they regularly offer courses on Spanish and Spanish-American, Russian, Finnish, Turkish, and Tibetan folklore. Visiting faculty have at one time or another taught French, Italian, Scandinavian, German, Chinese, and Arabic folklore. The folklore program at Harvard University, making available the first undergraduate major in folklore and mythology in the United States, developed from the strong research interests in the Yugoslav oral epic of the Slavic department's Albert Lord. His well-known book, *The Singer of Tales*, followed the guidelines of Lord's colleague in classics, Milman Parry, who conceived the idea of illuminating the Homeric epics through study of living folk epics. One of Indiana's Folklore Fellows is a classicist who wrote his dissertation on Homer's use of folklore themes. At the University of California at Berkeley, Joseph Fontenrose, professor of classics and member of the M.A. committee on folklore, composed *Python*, a splendid study of the dragon-slayer myth that examines classical mythology through folklore concepts.

Because of the influence of the Grimm brothers on *Volkskunde*, departments of German have more often than other language and literature departments produced folklore scholars of reputation. Archer Taylor and his student Wayland Hand at once come to mind.

The teacher and researcher in folklore coming from a language department usually follows a literary approach in his handling of folk materials. In area studies programs, a looser conglomerate unit in the academic structure, folklore plays a needed role, and here it will often be taught and studied from an ethnological viewpoint. The link here is between folklore and culture. Folklore courses have been associated with all the large area programs at Indiana University: African Studies, Afro-American Studies, American Studies, Asian Studies, Latin-American Studies, and the Russian and East European Institute. Only American Studies, which every year attracts some folklore co-majors, involves a perspective neither literary nor ethnological but *sui generis*, and in my own teaching of

"American Folklore in American Civilization" I attempt a synthesis of folklore with cultural history.

Still other fields in the humanities have folklore implications. Departments of art, often called fine arts, like music departments, display a highbrow bias, but the folk too engage in graphic and plastic arts, and courses in "folk arts, crafts, and architecture" may be cross-listed by art historians. Folk drama or folk theater occasionally enters the curriculums of departments of theater and drama, although a distinction needs to be made between the regional theater guided by Frederick Koch in North Carolina and Robert Gard in Wisconsin, which is art theater utilizing local color themes, and traditional drama proper. Folk dance as an academic subject finds its way, if at all, into departments of physical education. The philosophic values in traditional folk wisdom have not noticeably attracted professors of philosophy, but at the 1971 annual meeting of the American Folklore Society a philosopher conducted a forum on philosophical problems in the theory and methodology of folklore studies. Religion, or religious studies, represents a growing department on a number of college campuses that draws on folklore in the sphere of popular supernaturalism. Courses on "Folklore and Religion" and "Folk Religions" attract students at Indiana University. Ministers, priests, and nuns, who have completed their own religious training, and indeed support themselves on the side with parish work, have enrolled in the Folklore Institute.

Younger folklorists in the United States today evince a strong orientation toward the social sciences, and their manifestos are arousing the interest of social scientists. The Social Science Research Council sponsored a conference in New York in 1967 on "Social Science and Folklore," in which a panel of folklorists faced a mixed group of anthropologists, sociologists, psychologists, and historians. Theories of social interaction, role-playing, expressive behavior, and communication systems, formulated by social psychologists and ethnosociologists, have entered the thinking of the new generation of folklorists. (See, e.g., the January-March 1971 issue of the *Journal of American Folklore* titled "Toward New Perspectives in Folklore.") Structural linguistics in particular has influenced these rising folklorists to explain folktales and other folk genres in terms of universal models. A course on "Folklore and Linguistics," taught at Indiana University by Thomas A. Sebeok, professor of linguistics and Fellow of the Folklore Institute, stimulated the subsequent work of such students as Alan Dundes and Elli Köngäs Maranda. The linguistic anthropologist Dell Hymes ignited folklore students with his concept of the ethnography of communication and, responding to their enthusiasm, he made an unprecedented move, late in 1971, from his home department of anthropology at the University of Pennsylvania across the hall to the department of Folklore and Folklife. While a graduate student in anthropology at Indiana University, Dell Hymes took all the folklore courses given by Stith Thompson.

One doctoral candidate in the Folklore Institute applied psychological theories of learning behavior to his study of the transmission of folklore in an immigrant urban family. The faculty member from the psychology department serving on his committee became himself interested in the potentialities of folklore and recommended it as one of the so-called tool-skill options for doctoral candidates in psychology in lieu of a foreign language requirement. It fell to my lot to deal with these clinical psychology majors, and while at first they viewed the unfamiliar subject with some reservations, their reading reports at the semester's end testified eloquently to their appreciation of a novel scholarship with values for their work. For an example, they saw in folk stereotyping projections of individual feelings of hostility, aggression, and frustration. The psychoanalytical school of psychologists from the days of Freud and Jung to the present have of course devoted considerable attention to the symbolism in folklore that corresponds to symbolism in dreams.

Another year I dealt with half a dozen candidates in the doctoral degree program of mass communications who had elected a minor in folklore. The quantity of folklore daily dispersed in diluted forms through newspapers, magazines, radio, television, and films is apparent to the folklorist and soon became so to these analysts of the mass culture. In effect the folk and the mass cultures feed upon and reinforce each other.

Not all is a success story. Political scientists remain largely impervious to the charms of folklore. But once a graduate student in political science, a young woman planning a field study of political organization in the black ghetto of Roxbury, in Boston, found her way to my office and asked if she could do a reading course on black folklore. After her field experience she reported back to me that she would never have been able satisfactorily to comprehend the political mechanisms of Roxbury without some knowledge of Negro traditions. But her professors laughed when she mentioned her interest in folklore. Later, on a visit to the campus of Western Kentucky University at Bowling Green, I did discover a course on political folklore being offered in the political science department. It seems that the instructor was married to a folklorist, who had contaminated him, so that he devised this course, in which students collected sayings, slogans, slurs, and popular attitudes toward candidates for public office and about political issues. The students loved the course and were astonished at their findings. At the University of Pennsylvania a professor of folklore and a professor of political science teamed up to teach "Politics and Folklore."

Geography, in its phase called human or cultural geography, extends a friendly arm toward folklore. Estyn Evans at Queen's University in Belfast and Fred Kniffen at Louisiana State University are geographers of distinction who have related their research to traditional crafts and industries and the regional distribution of traditional dwellings and implements. Before taking his doctorate in folklore at the University of Pennsylvania and joining the Folklore Institute at Indiana University, Henry Glassie studied at Baton Rouge with Kniffen, and combined his training in cultural geography and folklore to produce his original work on *Pattern in the Material Culture of Eastern United States.*

Intellectual connections exist even between folklore and the physical sciences. My colleague Dorothy Vitaliano, member of the United States Geological Survey and the wife of a geology professor, became interested some years ago in the core of geologic fact behind the legend of Atlantis. Eventually she coined "geomythology" as a term to describe the interrelations linking geology with mythology and folklore. Geomythology covers the body of legendary traditions enveloping, distorting, but sometimes recording with fair accuracy cataclysmic natural phenomena such as volcanoes, earthquakes, and typhoons. It also includes etiological folklore made up to account for land forms and other natural features which long antedate man. (Paul Bunyan made the Grand Canyon by dragging his peavy behind him when he walked across Colorado.) I published Dorothy's article on "Geomythology" in the *Journal of the Folklore Institute* in 1968 and Indiana University

Press will publish her book on the subject in which she substantiates geologic evidence for flood legends and concludes with a geo-mythological look at Atlantis.

These random examples may serve to show how folklore touches many, indeed most, academic subjects in the humanities and the social sciences. In the essays that follow I am writing not only for other folklorists but to part-time folklorists and nonfolklorists who share an interest in this endlessly fascinating field. For the past three decades I have taught, lectured, collected, studied, and administered in behalf of folklore, and along the way produced these and other writings. At times folklore has even interfered with my tennis. These pieces represent the kinds of questions asked by one folklorist and the ways in which he tries to deal with them.

For permission to reprint these articles and essays I wish to thank the following: American Folklore Society, Basic Books, *Daedalus*, Historical Society of Michigan, Massachusetts Institute of Technology Press, Mouton and Company, Otto Schwartz and Company, Rutgers University Press, and University of California Press.

Several of these essays have been reprinted in the following places. Chapter 2, "Is There a Folk in the City?," was reprinted in *The Urban Experience and Folk Tradition*, edited by Américo Paredes and Ellen J. Stekert (Austin and London: published for the American Folklore Society by the University of Texas Press, 1971), pp. 21–52. After a second printing in 1964 of *Style in Language*, edited by Thomas A. Sebeok, containing my "Oral Styles of American Folk Narrators," the M.I.T. Press issued a paperback edition in 1966, reprinted in 1968. Chapter 5, "Theories of Myth and the Folklorist," was reprinted in *Myth and Mythmaking*, edited by Henry A. Murray (New York: George Braziller, 1960), pp. 76–89, and in a Beacon paperback in 1968, reprinted in 1969. It was also reprinted in *The Making of Myth*, edited by Richard M. Ohmann (New York: G. P. Putnam's Sons, 1962), vol. I, pp. 38–50. Chapter 6, "Legends and Tall Tales," was also published in an edition of *Our Living Traditions* retitled *American Folklore* (Voice of America Forum Lectures, March, 1968), pp. 175–90. Chapter 11, "The Academic Future of Folklore," is to be published in the *Supplement* of the *Journal of American Folklore*.

Everyone puzzles over the definition of folklore, but rather than go over this ground again, in the opening essay I have tried to identify the skills peculiar to the folklorist. A novel has been defined as what a novelist writes, so folklore may be defined as what a folklorist—a professional folklorist—studies.

One of the principal skills of the folklorist is fieldwork, and, in the second essay, "Is There a Folk in the City?" I have considered fieldwork in a new setting. Folklore has customarily been associated with the countryside and the folk have been equated with the peasantry or the rural population. Today folklorists are beginning to recognize that urban centers teem with cultural traditions of the kind they have recorded in isolated communities.

Folklore has its aesthetic dimension. Why do the tales and ballads and crafts continue to intrigue their audiences and consumers? The third and fourth essays examine the folk aesthetic from the point of view of the underlying form of tales and the individual styles of tale-tellers.

The categories or genres of folklore, so fluid and elusive, are always hard to pin down, and none more so than those tantalizing terms myth and legend. Essays five, six, and seven reinterpret the concepts of myth and legend through the eyes of the pragmatic folklorist.

Folklore and history seem ill-matched disciplines, but their well-wishers on each side are finding patches of common ground. The eighth and ninth essays look at two such patches: the oral historical traditions collected by the folklorist, which may serve the historian; and the history of ordinary people, neglected by elitist historians.

Folklorists constitute an international fraternity, speaking a common language regardless whether or not they know each other's tongue. To pursue their comparative researches, they must correspond and meet and cooperate. In the tenth essay, "American Folklorists in Britain," I review the successful efforts of four folklore-minded Yankees to make contact with their British colleagues and to pursue fieldwork on British soil.

The moral of this volume of recent writings (all but two have appeared since 1968), and of my philosophy of folklore studies, is spelled out in the final essay, "The Academic Future of Folklore." In brief, folklore is a serious and sophisticated branch of learning particularly helpful in today's tormented world and should be taught on every college campus.

1 /

Techniques of the Folklorist

LAST NOVEMBER [1967] the once lean and hungry American Folk-lore Society met independently in Toronto for a crowded two and a half day session with one hundred and fifty registered attendants and participants.[1] Several carloads of graduate students drove there from distant points, and faculty members flew in from around the country on their annual free professional junket. Complaints were heard that the staging of parallel sessions prevented eager auditors from absorbing two pet topics at the same time, that the program was too concentrated and should be extended to at least three days, and that the Society was getting too large anyway to meet all to-gether. Back in 1948 this Society had also met in Toronto, but then as a tiny barnacle clinging to the American Anthropological Asso-ciation, and I delivered the final paper of our session to an audience of six, including the president and secretary-treasurer. In 1948 not a scholar in the United States held a Ph.D. in Folklore. In 1967 some thirty persons possessed such a degree, and in one week in August of that year Indiana University granted five doctorates, while eighty-five others waited in the wings for a Ph.D. or an M.A. in Folklore. A substantial number of higher degree candidates are also pursuing folklore and folklife studies at the University of Pennsyl-vania, the University of California at Berkeley and at Los Angeles, and the University of Texas. Whatever *mana* this degree confers, it

Reprinted from the *Louisiana Folklore Miscellany* 11 (August, 1968): 1–23.

does designate its holder as an accredited academic species, the folklorist, who is now part of the university scene. The programs carry such mouth-filling titles as The Center for the Comparative Study of Folklore and Mythology at the University of California at Los Angeles, and The Center for Intercultural Studies in Folklore and Oral History at the University of Texas.

Folklorists have of course made their way and their name before the advent of their own special doctorate. Among eminent contemporaries who have advanced the subject, Stith Thompson, Archer Taylor, MacEdward Leach, Wayland Hand, and Herbert Halpert took degrees in English or Germanic literature. Looking abroad, we see England as a prime example of a country where brilliant folklorists developed their new field of learning without benefit of academic chairs or higher degrees. But William John Thoms, George Laurence Gomme, Andrew Lang, and their fellows did organize a Folk-Lore Society in 1878 to identify their calling. Whether in a university, a society, an institute, or an archives, or as a spare-time writer and collector, the folklorist has, for a century and a half, asserted his individuality. How is he to be defined? Defining folklore has proved to be a task for Tantalus, but we may do better defining the folklorist, and then say that what he studies is folklore. Our premise is that he possesses a set of skills setting him apart from his departmental neighbors in literatures and languages, anthropology, linguistics, history and sociology. No one of these skills may be unique but in totality they do describe the *gestalt* of a particular kind of scholar.

FIELDWORK

When Jacob and Wilhelm Grimm set down the peasant tales of Frau Viehmannin for the second volume of their *Kinder- und Hausmärchen* in 1815, they ushered in the serious study of folklore. Two processes were involved in this encounter. Intellectuals from a learned tradition made contact with and paid respect to a spokesman for an unlettered tradition. This was an act of field recording. Beyond the writing down of the recitals of a peasant woman, and publishing them for their charm and novelty, the Grimms treated these and similar narrations as invaluable deposits of a bygone Germanic mythology whose outlines they sought to reconstruct. Collecting was thus not an end in itself but a means of obtaining data to document an hypothesis. The hypothesis of an Aryan mythological system surviving in fragmentary lore among the peasantry succumbed to new theories of evolution and dissemination, but the exponents of these schools too relied on field materials to support their views. A folklorist must understand the technique of fieldwork, even if he does not venture into the field—as Andrew Lang and Stith Thompson, for instance, never did—for his treatises rest largely upon field-collected texts and customs.

The anthropologist too considers fieldwork a basic method, and in notable instances, particularly those of Franz Boas and his illustrious students, such as Ruth Benedict, Melville Herskovits, and Melville Jacobs, anthropologists have contributed substantially to the resources of the folklorist. For many years since its founding in 1888, the American Folklore Society was sustained by anthropologists, and only very recently has the Society abandoned the practice of alternating its main offices between so-called humanistic folklorists and anthropologists. The founders of the English Folk-Lore Society, who were known as anthropological folklorists, debated vigorously over whether their field terrain embraced both savages in the jungle and peasants in the village. Today we may draw a fairly firm line between the field domain of the anthropologist, which lies outside his own culture and within a largely nonliterate, nontechnological society, and that of the folklorist, which does fall within his own civilization.

And this distinction involves a considerable difference in field method. The anthropologist is visibly the outsider, almost a visitor from another planet, perhaps conducting his interviews through an interpreter. The folklorist operates from the inside, and sometimes, as with the Gaelic-speaking collectors of Scotland and Ireland, he knows from birth the tongue of his target group. Still, no matter how close his ties to his subjects, whether by residence, as Randolph among the Ozarkers, or by faith, as the Fifes among the Mormons, the folklorist stands apart from the folk through his formal education and intellectual outlook. He recognizes, as the Victorians first appreciated, with a shock, that other cultures lie about him, cultures that the intellectuals have ignored or despised or misunderstood. Often the Victorian gentleman could communicate with representatives of these submerged cultures, of the "lower orders" as he was wont to call them, only through his house servant. The folklorist sets out deliberately to establish contacts with these tradition-oriented societies. He may, unlike the anthropologist, do his collecting fitfully and opportunistically from his home base, as did Frank C. Brown in North Carolina. But he can also set off on a quest to a terra incognita, in a mountain region, on a rugged peninsula, in an industrial city, at a state prison, where he must win friends and gain confidences among people suspicious of FBI agents, tax collectors, encyclopedia salesmen, and novel types of con men.

The mechanics of pencil and pad, tape recorder and camera, dress, and behavior is not my present concern. They have been fully treated by Kenneth Goldstein in *A Guide for Field Workers in Folklore*. It is the technique, not the mechanics, of entering into and observing hidden segments of the dominant, official civilization that marks the folklorist. Jack London made use of this technique when he donned workingmen's clothes and walked through the streets of London's East End conversing with the destitute and despairing. One need not adopt disguise, and London's motive was to obtain ammunition for his socialist criticisms of capitalist society, but in effect he opened a window into ghetto culture. Unlike the anthropologist and the sociologist, the folklorist does not survey equally and impartially the whole society or its segments. His antennae are alert for signals leading to articulate exponents of the unofficial culture, like W. H. Barrett, the Fenman discovered by museum curator Enid Porter, or Angus McLellan, the crofter of South Uist recorded by the laird of the isle of Canna, John Lorne Campbell. Put a folklorist in Vietnam and he would soon uncover stellar tradition carriers who would make the mass of Vietnamese distinctive for Americans.

Fieldwork can be tightly planned for specific objectives, such as the preparation of folklore atlases charting the distribution of a belief or observance or craft. European folklorists have published a number of such atlases, but the only equivalent in the United States is the Linguistic Atlas of America enterprise, which has produced excellent volumes plotting the boundaries of folk and elite speech patterns of the eastern seaboard, based on field interviews with selected regional speakers. But as yet American folklorists have not applied this method to other folklore genres.

Use of Written and Printed Sources

If the folklorist looks for his primary data to the text, custom, or artifact that he, or a professional colleague, has personally collected or observed, he must still employ another technique to amass the raw materials for his study. Field collecting began only in the nineteenth century, but the folklorist needs to trace traditional customs, sayings, narratives, and verse back to the beginning of the human record. Any eyewitness report of a ceremony or written remembrance of a legend may furnish him with an early dating of a currently collected item. He must consult a staggering variety and volume of printed sources, from highly visible tale collections assembled in classical and medieval times, such as the *Panchatantra*, the *Thousand and One Nights,* and the *Gesta Romanorum,* to elusive references in travel writings, chapbooks, memoirs, histories, and certain newspaper and periodical files. Even after field collecting begins, the folklorist must continue to comb the printed sources that engulf our culture and in haphazard ways trap traditional matter. In handling these sources, he must continually face the problem of determining how faithfully they report oral traditions or how accurately they render local customs. A ballad scholar attempting to unravel the influence of a broadside on the history of a ballad text and tune has problems enough, but at least he deals with only one avenue of print. What can the student of a popular outlaw tradition make of the welter of printed accounts about Billy the Kid, ranging from penny dreadfuls to sober biographies, and comprising in themselves a book-length bibliography? In his *Tall Tales of Arkansaw,* James Masterson produced an ample volume based entirely on printed folk humor. My own *Jonathan Draws the Long Bow* explored the printed sources of New England popular tales and legends.

It is also true that Benjamin Botkin has assembled his series of treasuries almost entirely from printed sources. My criticism of his treasuries is that he accepts the most disparate sources without proper discrimination or system. The folklorist must apply rigorous criteria to printed texts. Does the item in hand contain traditional motifs, is it analogous to field-collected reports, does it come from a publication close to the grass roots, does its style indicate a spoken rather than a literary manner, is the purpose of the writer to report rather than to invent? All these are questions to be weighed. The English Folk-Lore Society's series of Printed Extracts of County Folk-Lore is a model set of volumes in which the answers to the above questions all prove affirmative. They show the wealth of elusive lore to be gleaned from local newspapers, periodicals, and gazetteers. American sources seem less homogeneous. Three main suppliers for *Jonathan Draws the Long Bow* can illustrate their diversity: town histories, sporting weeklies, and *The Jonny-Cake Letters* of "Shepherd Tom" Hazard. The town histories are customarily written by local antiquaries in stodgy style but with the sound of village gossip in their ears and they transmit the corporate memory of haunted places and village eccentrics. Sporting weeklies like the New York *Spirit of the Times* and the *Boston Yankee Blade* flourished in the 1830's, '40's, and '50's and entertained readers with humorous sketches often drawn from tavern anecdotes and campfire yarns. "Shepherd Tom" wrote a series of letters to the Providence (Rhode Island) *Journal*, gathered in book form in 1880, in which he wove together a string of delicious reminiscences covering the local legends and characters of Washington County. A recipe for Rhode Island jonny-cake launched his recollections and gave his book its title. The folklorist can profitably mine these sources, but he must differentiate between their special styles and perspectives.

Would that today's newspapers and their editors maintained as close a connection with the grass roots as did the ante-bellum press! Still the daily and Sunday reams of newsprint do inescapably catch matters of interest to the folklorist, if somehow they can be culled. The journal *Western Folklore* has carried a department "Folklore in the News" to which alert folklorists send clippings about the folksong revival, unnatural phenomena, legends passing as facts, old beliefs still honored, holiday rites, and such folk newsworthy items. For a period of three years, from 1939 to 1941, I subscribed to a news-clipping service to obtain all references to Paul Bunyan, and secured, not so much texts of Bunyan tales, although some turned up, but a mountainous pile of allusions, and even pictorial illustrations, revealing the varied conceptions of Old Paul by diverse American groups, from resort promoters to myth-hungry schoolchildren to the staff of the *Daily Worker*.

TERMINOLOGY

Like every branch of the humanities and social sciences, folklore possesses its esoteric jargon, but with one vast difference: the world at large also employs the jargon of folklorists. The barrier of conspicuous terminology shielding the literary critic or the social scientist from the layman does not protect the followers of William John Thoms, who in 1846 chose "folklore" rather than "antiquariology" or "preternaturalistics" to designate his subject, desiring a "good Anglo-Saxon compound." Since then "folklore" is on everyone's lips, as are the collateral terms "myth," "legend," "fairy tale," "ballad," and sundry compounds of "folk." Much confusion arises from the everyday use of these words when the folklorist attempts to explain, or defend, his mission. Because of the general ignorance as to the serious study and international implications of folklore, the *Wall Street Journal* chose to attack fellowship grants given to Indiana University and the University of Kansas in folklore in 1961 under the National Defense Education Act, and Congress, immediately responsive, lopped a million dollars off the fellowship funds while barring folklore from further support. Certain of our foundation-wise academic friends suggested changing the name of folklore, in the same way that social scientists started calling themselves behavioral scientists when Congressmen began associating social sciences with socialism and ergo communism. This dodge appears to me to relinquish a valuable asset, for the word and concept of folklore have enjoyed an honorable history, and when used by powerful minds the term has won a respectful audience.

The precise intellectual employment of his vocabulary constitutes a key technique of the folklorist. One of the most original scholarly works in the subject is *The Science of Fairy Tales* by Edwin Sidney Hartland, and no reader will confuse his sense of "fairy tales" with bedtime stories. Meanings alter of course with historical periods, and such nineteenth century favorites as "popular antiquities," "custom and usage," "lower orders," "savages," "survivals," "sagas" (in the sense of legends), "drolls," and "disease of language" carry little, if any, impact today. Emotive terms in current fashion are "type," "archetype," "motif," "variant" and its twin or cousin "version" depending on the user), "Märchen," "Sagen," and the re-charged "myth."

Now fresh concepts are pressing for attention with shiny new, or dusted off, labels, such as "folk life" suggesting a broader dimension than the oral literature equated with "folklore." At Harvard, Lord and Bynum push "theme" and at Berkeley Dundes proposes "motifeme" as refinements for "motif," in the realm of what his colleague Bascom calls "verbal art." At Indiana University the Archives of Folk and Primitive Music has discarded its two tarnished labels and been rebaptized the Archives of Traditional Music. "Tradition" is indeed one of the most enduring and palatable terms. "Folklore is the science of tradition," Hartland once stated. Meanwhile the attempt to find an acceptable substitute for "fairy tale" continues, with "magical tale" and "wonder tale" lagging behind "Märchen," firm in sense if not in pronunciation. Kenneth Jackson has proposed "international popular tale" to replace "folktale," since all classes of society, and not just the folk, whoever they are, relate traditional stories. "Folktale" itself is usually intended to signify a fiction, even though Stith Thompson in his comprehensive volume on *The Folktale* covers the whole range of oral narratives. (As a footnote, the spelling of "folk" compounds presents a headache of its own; once when I was preparing a brochure of our Folklore Institute, the proofreader at the Printing and Duplicating Division changed my spelling of Stith Thompson's course on "The Folktale" from one to two words, according to Webster, and remained intransigent even though I pointed out that we were identifying him as the author of and authority on *The Folktale*, spelled as one word.)

European scholars have proved far more ingenious and imaginative in word coinages than the British and Americans, and they have now given us two dictionaries of conceptual terms, Åke Hultkrantz's *Ethnological Concepts*, presented from the continental point of view but restricted to English nomenclature, and Laurits Bødker's *Folk Literature (Germanic)*, offering a wealth of usages by folklorists in the Germanic languages. Bødker particularly admires the brilliant Swedish folklorist, Carl von Sydow, two of whose many neologisms have penetrated into English, *oikotype*, to designate a regional variant of an international tale type, and *memorat*, to identify a marvelous personal experience. Whole theories may be synopsized in phrases such as Hans Naumann's *gesunkenes Kulturgut* describing folklore as the cultural slag that works its way down from the elite to the folk, and the equally famous *einfache Formen* of André Jolles applied to primary forms of oral expression.

Motif-Indexing and Tale-Typing

All forms of folklore must be classified in an orderly and systematic way if they are to be analyzed and interpreted. The interrelated *Motif-Index of Folk Literature* of Stith Thompson and *Types of the Folktale* of Antti Aarne and Thompson provide one major system, with other interlocking indexes, such as Baughman's for England and North America, those of Tom Peete Cross and O'Sullivan-Christiansen for Ireland, Thompson-Balys and Thompson-Roberts for India, and a number of collateral national indexes. No proper folklorist can be untrained in these tools. Anthropologists are noticeably ill at ease in handling them, or rather, they do not handle them, and in essay after essay they depict folk narratives collected from their society as a reflector of culture traits and tensions in that society, unaware that the same tales are told at the other end of the world. Criticisms and resentments of the type and motif indexes deplore their reduction of pleasing wonder tales, fabliaux, exempla, romances, jests, and ballads to skeletal outlines, assembled, tabulated, and computerized by the practitioners of the Finnish historic-geographic method in their ambitious quest for the time, place, and form of the original text. The forbidding lists of numerals and letters make an obvious target for the uninitiated. In reviewing the England volume in the Folktales of the World series, the London *Evening Standard* captioned the piece, "one time there was an F469.1." This jeu d'esprit suggests an inside joke about the folklorists' congress, at which Stith Thompson arose and said, "Gentlemen, I wish to bring to your attention an extremely interesting new tale type, 469." He sat down to thunderous applause.

An amateur in the audience asked his neighbor the meaning of this performance. "Well, we are all such experts we don't bother to tell the tales, we just refer to their numbers." The dilettante then requested the platform and announced grandly, "Gentlemen, allow me to make known to you a startling discovery of an extraordinary folkstory, Type 1087." Complete silence greeted his announcement, and he took his seat abashed and crestfallen. "What happened?" he asked his neighbor. "Well, some can tell 'em and some can't," was the reply. This tale about folklorists is itself a folktale, attached to Bob Hope's gagwriters who amuse themselves by reeling off the numbers on the jokes in their file.

The criticism of the indexes quite misses the point that they are a means, not an end, a tool or technique, not a theory. Robert Graves had fun reviewing my *Negro Folktales in Michigan* in *Commentary* and making snide remarks on the notes packed with type and motif numbers for the purpose, he said, of charting the routes of tales under the obsolete premise of diffusionism. But tracing the migration of stories and songs is not the primary aim of the index-user. Firstly, he wishes to establish the traditional character, the family relationships, the genealogical tree, of his collected samples. In a word, is the story he had heard folklore? If so, how well known is it and in what places? To these questions the indexes provide answers. They lay out thoroughfares and side streets through the maze of collected materials. What the type index can be criticized for is an imperialistic design on the folktales of the world, which cannot all be neatly squeezed into the slots of the European tale-synopses with which Aarne began. For this reason Wolfram Eberhard and Pertev Boratav composed an independent type index of Turkish folktales.

Each genre needs its own retrieval system. Archer Taylor has made riddles logical in his analytic encyclopedia, *English Riddles from Oral Tradition*. Three hundred five ballad types were canonized by Francis James Child, and Malcolm Laws has identified *Native American Ballads* through a letter and number code. Children's rhymes are arranged alphabetically by Peter and Iona Opie in the *Oxford Book of Nursery Rhymes*. The elusive legend has been tackled by Reidar Christiansen working with Norwegian examples, in *The Migratory Legends*, and international committees are now wrestling with the problems of global legend and ballad classifications. Customs and items of material culture cannot be as readily pigeonholed as oral texts, but the Folklore Society keeps issuing volumes of British Calendar Customs, organized on the calendar year, a principle popular in Europe but not in the United States where seasonal rite and celebration are relatively subdued.

Indexing and classifying systems enable the collector to annotate his texts and field reports properly, and annotating becomes almost a separate technique. A pox on the author who strings together type and motif numbers and bibliographic references without elaboration! Notes should be readable and informative. A text without an explanatory note is the surest mark of a half-baked folklorist. The greatest of all annotations, Bolte and Polívka's five volumes of commentary on the Grimms' Household Tales, has become in its turn a celebrated and indispensable classification tool.

Archiving

The manuscript and tape archives of Europe and the United States are treasure houses for the folklorist to plumb, or perhaps they represent the labyrinthine maze of Daedalus through which Theseus must find his way in and out, grasping for a thread. Field collecting, indexing, and archiving blend one into the other. The collector often deposits his hard-won specimens in an archive for safe-keeping and greater or less availability to others, depending on the contract option he chooses. In Europe a government or university-supported folklore institute often has professional collectors on its staff who feed materials regularly into the national or provincial archive. The much less pretentious American archives have developed chiefly at universities on the basis of student collections. Archivists tend to organize their genres according to standard reference systems: tales by Aarne-Thompson, ballads by Child and Laws, beliefs by Wayland Hand's two volumes in the *Frank C. Brown Collection of North Carolina Folklore*, riddles by Taylor, games by Paul Brewster's *American Nonsinging Games* and Alice B. Gomme's *The Traditional Games of England, Scotland and Ireland*. When Stith Thompson was revising *The Types of the Folk-*

tale, he visited major archives to obtain information on the number of established tales and possible new tale types received since the previous edition in 1928, and he incorporated this data into the 1961 edition. One of his significant findings was the trend to greatly increased collecting of anecdotes and a corresponding diminution of magic tales. Sean O'Sullivan, archivist of the magnificent Irish Folklore Commission in Dublin, has written the invaluable *Handbook of Irish Folklore*, adapted from the categories of the Swedish folklore archive in Uppsala, and used by the field collectors in the Irish counties as a questionnaire guide; and he also compiled, in association with Reider Christiansen, *The Types of the Irish Folktale*, a listing of the Aarne-Thompson tales in the Dublin archive. In this kind of symbiosis the archivist, collector, and type indexer join forces.

In spite of the use by folklore archivists of certain national and international classification systems, archives do not conform to any universal model, and each is to some extent idiosyncratic. The master file rests in the brain pan of the chief archivist. Descriptions of the organization of various major archives can be found in the files of the *Folklore and Folk Music Archivist*, edited at Indiana University by George List, director of the Archives of Traditional Music. As an example of the problems confronting archives builders in the United States, we may cite the question currently under heated discussion, as to whether a collection should remain intact and be catalogued under an accession number or whether it should be distributed among the various genres already in the archive. The genre specialist will of course prefer to have all the texts of a tale, song, or custom side by side, while the ethnologically minded folklorist will argue persuasively that each collection possesses its own individuality, marked by the bias of the collector, and must be preserved as a unit. Compromises are possible, such as photocopying the collection and distributing the sheets of the copy. The accessioning of tapes presents problems quite different from those of manuscripts. Tapes must be copied to protect the originals, and they cannot be reshuffled as can paper sheets. But again procedures vary, and the Irish Folklore Commission has transcribed its tapes onto manuscripts, microfilmed the manuscripts for security, and released the tapes for fresh collecting.

At any rate the all-around folklorist must know how to make the most of the institutional folklore archives whose materials dwarf even the mountains of printed texts.

BIBLIOGRAPHY

Since the world is his province, in the sense that items of folklore can traverse the globe, the folklorist must acquire bibliographical savvy. Stith Thompson tells how when as a graduate student at Harvard in 1914 he was assigned by the great Kittredge to investigate the presence of European tales in the repertoire of North American Indians, no one in Cambridge knew about the Aarne index published in Finland four years before, in the now prestigious *Folklore Fellows Communications* series. At that time, and for long after, the Harvard faculty contained no committed folklore scholar. To enable their colleagues to keep up with the multifarious publications issued in many languages, some folklorists devote a large portion of their energies to preparing bibliographic inventories. The most monumental of these is the *Internationale Volkskundliche Bibliographie* edited from Basel, Switzerland by Robert Wildhaber with the aid of scores of collaborators around the world. Because of its formidable coverage, this work appears some years after the period it deals with. For more timely aids, there is the June issue of *Southern Folklore Quarterly* given over entirely to a classified listing of books and articles issued the preceding year. Ralph Steele Boggs conducted this bibliography for twenty-five years, and Merle Simmons is now in charge, both professors of Spanish. The SFQ bibliography has always emphasized Latin American as well as North American publications, although Professor Simmons has extended its scope to the Romance-language countries of Europe; it furnishes pithy synoptic notes for nearly every entry. *Folklore Abstracts* commenced in 1963 as a quarterly bulletin sponsored by the American Folklore Society and devoted to summarizing the contents of articles in folklore journals and periodicals of related interest. The first editor, Donald M. Winkelman, steadily enlarged the corps of abstracters, enlisting fellow degree candidates at Indiana University from countries abroad, and building up an editorial staff at Ohio's Bowling Green State University. Herbert Halpert of Memorial University, St. John's, Newfoundland, assumed the demanding editorial post in 1968. The acceptance of this responsibility by Halpert, an expert collector and annotator of oral folklore, indicates the links between fieldwork, indexing, and bibliography recognized by the folklorist. Vance Randolph is another case in point of the indefatigable collector who turned to patient exhuming of all kinds of elusive printed references for his forthcoming *Ozark Folklore, A Bibliography*. A dramatic example of the American folklorist on alien soil faced by not one but over a dozen impenetrable tongues, who unearthed and made visible nearly 7000 publications, is Edwin C. Kirkland, author of the compendious *Bibliography of South Asian Folklore*. On leave from the University of Florida as cultural attaché of the State Department in India, Professor Kirkland enlisted the aid of official translators of the National Library in Calcutta to render titles from the thirteen major languages. Since spellings are completely individualistic, and the same person may sign his transliterated name differently on different occasions, Kirkland faced formidable problems.

The folklore bibliographer has two perpetual headaches: how to classify and arrange his entries; and what to accept or reject. In his preemptive but fallible production, *A Bibliography of North American Folklore and Folksong*, Charles Haywood solved the first puzzle creditably, with his separation of the Indian from all other groups, and his subdivision of these other groups into regional, occupational, and ethnic units. But he came a cropper on his principle of inclusion, for he mixed together all kinds of writings, from local-color novels to county histories to memoirs to scholarly articles to fakelore. For expert screening of field collections and library studies, one turns to the comprehensive bibliographical lists in Aarne-Thompson or Laws or Baughman's *Type and Motif-Index of the Folktales of England and North America*, or any of the standard indexes. Here again several folklore techniques merge: bibliography, fieldwork, the making of classificatory indexes.

RELATED FIELDS

As part of his technical equipment, the folklore scholar needs to possess more than a bowing acquaintance with three well established disciplines which intersect with his own at certain key points.

Folklore and Anthropology. With cultural anthropology, a branch of anthropology unfortunately somewhat on the wane since the death of Melville Herskovits, folklorists have a natural affinity. Cultural anthropology relates the verbal, graphic, plastic, musical, and performing arts to the institutions of the society in which they function. These concepts of "culture" and "function," as used by ethnologists, enable the folklorist to transcend random collecting and place his materials within a social context. Jerome Mintz's *Legends of the Hasidim* is an example of a field study drawn from a rigidly orthodox Hasidic community in Brooklyn that applies Boasian concepts to a body of oral narratives. If Frazer is now a whipping boy, his intellectual influence on anthropologists and folklorists jointly in the realm of comparative agricultural rituals must be reckoned with in the history of ideas. The doctrine of survivals that Frazer applied to his thesis of the ritual sacrifice of the divine king was formulated by an anthropologist still highly esteemed, Edward B. Tylor, who himself made extensive use of the materials of folklore on a comparative basis. In his theory of animism in primitive religion, Tylor opened another door through which anthropologists and folklorists both pass. Today the term "folk religion" is replacing primitive religion, and applies not just to non-Christian polytheistic societies but to the underlying strata of magico-religious belief in Christianized countries. Robert Redfield's concept of the "great and little traditions" appeals to some folklorists who see in this polarity an analogy between the official and unofficial cultures.

Because the streams of folklore are continually crossing between the nonliterate societies and the blacked-out segments of advanced populations, folklore and anthropology do find a common ground. It was Boas and his disciples who collected North American Indian tales, but it was Stith Thompson who demonstrated the European examples among them, and Alan Dundes who worked out their morphology.

Folklore and Literature. Although Francis James Child began as a mathematician, he ended in the English department at Harvard and bequeathed to the history of English literature the hallowed 305 ballads that bear his name. Since his time the literary historians of England have often strayed over their boundary line into folklorist enterprises, in balladry, in medieval romance, in source studies of

Chaucer and Shakespeare. Child's eminent successor George Lyman Kittredge ventured deep into popular belief in *Witchcraft in Old and New England* and *The Old Farmer and His Almanac.*

We may define three broad relationships of folklore to literature. There are oral poetry and oral narratives of such artistic power that they win acceptance on their own merits as literature, even though these field-recorded texts lack known authors. A generation of critics have considered the dramatic tautness and tensions and eloquent phrasings of the best ballads. Milman Parry and Albert Lord have rescued orally sung south Slavic epics and conjectured that Homer's epics relied on similar processes of oral composition. *Beowulf* has been scrutinized by Robert Creed and Bruce Rosenberg as one surviving variant of an heroic folk epic. The Danish folklorist Axel Olrik in his essay on "Epic Laws of Folk Narrative" elaborated a set of aesthetic principles governing oral literature that can aid in identifying artistically superior texts. Or to put the case in reverse, I have singled out Anglo-American narratives that appealed to me for their power and intensity and found that they conform perfectly to Olrik's laws of peak tableaux, dual protagonists, and uncluttered action.

Secondly, there is literature that begins as folklore and ends as a polished product stamped with an individual genius. In this class belong the finished *Iliad* and *Odyssey,* if we consider that Homer set in writing, with selection, revision, and time for re-editing, the traditional texts of oral bards. Elias Lönnröt went further in stitching together traditional runes and charms to compose the *Kalevala.* The whole process whereby oral legends and lays cluster around celebrated champions in preliterate, seminomadic cultures and eventually arrive in written form as sagas, romances, heroic ballads, and folk epics, has been admirably treated by Hector Munro and Nora K. Chadwick in their three wide-ranging volumes on *The Growth of Literature.* Do we place here a so-called folk poet like Larry Gorman, the lumberjack minstrel of Maine and the Maritimes, who composed satirical verses within a traditional form and with traditional tunes, but aimed at the immediate objects of his ire? The West Indian calypso and Puerto Rican *plena* are similarly composed on the spot within a set metrical and stanzaic pattern. If these compositions endure and become traditional, as have the songs of Larry Gorman, collected half a century after his death by Edward Ives, they represent a process of literary creating indebted at both ends to folklore.

Thirdly, there are the famous authors who have drawn for plots and local color upon folk tradition. Again a number of gradations exist, from Joel Chandler Harris who listened to Georgia Negro folktales and reworked them with a close knowledge of their form and mood, to Longfellow who contrived *The Song of Hiawatha* at second-hand, from the notebooks of Henry Rowe Schoolcraft, and adapted these genuine materials to fit the nineteenth century sentimental stereotype of the primeval red man. Constance Rourke was the first literary scholar to illustrate the debts of a number of major American authors, among them Irving, Mark Twain, Melville, Emerson, Whitman, and Henry James, to a pervasive popular humorous lore. Other critics followed her lead, most recently and most notably Daniel G. Hoffman in *Form and Fable in American Fiction*. These critics do not distinguish between the influence on an author's imagination of folklore directly encountered, and folklore read in printed form. If he recognized this distinction Hoffman would be in a much better position to appreciate the Vermont sketches of Rowland Robinson, who deftly captured the themes and rhythms of oral yarn-spinning in a cobbler's shop. At any rate, this large area of investigation beckons the folklorist, who must at all odds have some training in literature.

Folklore and History. Few will argue about the interrelationships of folklore with anthropology and literature, but eyebrows, or even hackles, will rise at the suggestion that folklore has a common interest with history. One new development that is reducing the opposition of historians who value the documented fact and scorn the verbal rumor is the coming of age of oral history, although a large gap separates the emphasis of oral historians on the elite from the focus of traditional history, or historical tradition, upon the common folk and minority groups. But the use of the tape recorder and the personal interview to obtain remembered information now unites folklorist and historian. And there are historians, from Herodotus to Samuel Eliot Morison, who have respected traditions as a source of historical knowledge. The question of validating such traditions, which deal with events major and trivial, has perplexed scholars in a number of fields, and has attracted the attention of one active folklorist after another, although usually, like George Laurence Gomme who wrote *Folklore as an Historical Science*, they have not possessed historical training. From the other end, the historian Theodore Blegen in *Grass Roots History* contended persuasively for a reorientation of historical thinking away from the national political scene in Washington, D.C., to the towns and hamlets of the countryside. In speaking of sources for the grass roots historian, to be found in attic mementoes, diaries, and the so-called America letters and songs dealing with the immigrant experience, Blegen verged toward oral traditions. The folklorist certainly needs to understand sufficient of historical method to handle and evaluate the local legends, blason populaire, anecdotes, and reminiscences that continually pour his way.

Just as I wrote this, a graduate student in the history department at the University of California told me how he stumbled on folklore, actually through a course taken by his wife, and so discovered a means of learning about the 95 percent of the Negro population omitted from histories of the Negro. There is Gladys Fry, a recent Ph.D. in Folklore at Indiana University, with an M.A. in history, herself a black, who obtained historical traditions with a tape recorder and used them for her dissertation on the "night doctors" and other bogies feared by slaves. Two other students have completed dissertations on county folk histories in Kentucky and Ohio combining oral and written sources. Traditions may not yield precise dates but they can reveal accurate prejudices, hates, dreads, and what Thomas Browne once called "vulgar errors."

FOLKLIFE STUDIES AND THE FOLK MUSEUM

Ever since the baptizing of "folklore," the term has to some suggested artifacts as well as oral forms. At the International Folklore Congress held in London in 1891, a special exhibition featured objects connected with folklore, such as sorcerers' instruments, amulets, a harvest "baby" of straw, a forked hazel twig used in dowsing, ornaments, and carvings. The idea of a folk museum, indoor or outdoor, displaying utensils, furniture, and dwellings of an agrarian past, is commonplace in Europe and now gains headway in the United States, particularly at the New York State Historical

Society headquarters in Cooperstown. There a folk art collection, ranging from wall paintings to hay rakes, is housed in the Fenimore House, and an outdoor Farmer's Museum reconstructs a pioneer village, with handicrafts demonstrated. A master's degree may be obtained in either Museum Methods or American Folklore, administered by a resident faculty attached to Oneonta College in the State University of New York system. The doctoral program at the University of Pennsylvania in Folklore has now added Folklife to its title. In England a Society for Folk-Life Studies organized in 1963 issues a journal and holds annual meetings that attract some members of the much older Folklore Society. The terms "material culture" and "folklife" appear regularly in the current vocabulary of folklorists.

Examples such as these indicate an enlargement of the concept of folklore as oral literature to bring it more into line with the German notion of Volkskunde and the European notion of ethnology. Accordingly the folklorists of today must be familiar with techniques of folklife research, such as field collecting of material culture specimens, interviewing of craftsmen concerning their skills and markets, and distribution mapping of traditional house types and pottery designs. In his added dimension, the folklorist will perceive relationships between economic practice and folk belief, as in the "Shetland fisherman's taboo names for boat parts and fishing equipment," alluded to by Alexander Fenton in writing about "Material Culture as an Aid to Local History Studies in Scotland." [2]

History of the Study of Folklore

Folklorists properly prize the accomplishments of brilliant theoretical scholars and dedicated collectors who established the science of folklore in the nineteenth century, and drew upon the labors of still earlier antiquaries and traveler-reporters. It is such illustrious names as the Grimms, Benfey, Pitré, Afanasiev, Asbjörnsen and Moe, Sébillot, Gaidoz, Campbell of Islay, and the group I have called the "Great Team of English Folklorists"—Lang, Gomme, Clodd, Nutt, and Hartland—who sparked each other through their philosophic controversies as much as through their agreed principles. The United States too can point to earlier giants, who deserve more attention: Jeremiah Curtin, industrious collector of Irish and Slavic folktales; Charles Godfrey Leland, writer on Algonquin Indian legends of New England and gypsy lore of Europe; and Thomas F. Crane, editor of *Italian Popular Tales* and *The Exempla of Jacques de Vitry* and author of informative articles on the "external history" of the Grimms' Märchen collections. These pioneer scholars wrote classics still irreplaceable, and upon which the modern masterworks build: Stith Thompson commenced the Motif-Index with the rich treasury of references Bolte and Polívka had patiently added to the Grimms' own notes and commentaries to their household tales.

Writing the intellectual history of a field of learning and critical biographies of its eminent men and women requires a special technique of library research, value judgments, and the tracing of genetic relationships. In folklore, this kind of history has special rewards, more even than in the history of historical writing or the history of literary scholarship for tasks of the folklorist are to a large extent cooperative and collaborative and require the contributions of the living as well as the dead. The large theoretical systems of both Lang and Müller have passed, but some of their statements on folklore problems cannot be improved upon today, and they both stimulated collectors throughout the Empire.

The other side of the coin is the danger that specialists unfamiliar with the major folklore works of the past may duplicate or fail to profit from them. Archer Taylor points out how such clever scholars as J. G. Von Hahn, Otto Rank, Lord Raglan, and Joseph Campbell unwittingly repeated some of each other's formulations on the biographical pattern of the legendary hero. Because so many doors lead into the study of folklore, the history of folklore studies offers as many problems to the folklorist as does the neat archiving of the materials of folklore.

INTERNATIONAL RELATIONS IN FOLKLORE

Whatever his special interest or regional preoccupation, the folklorist who pursues his subject far enough will find his trail leading to the corners of the globe. Somehow he must gain access to the comparative materials and learn about the relevant studies that will buttress his own inquiry. To cultivate international channels of communication and contact open to folklorists is a technique in itself, and one that can afford many delights. In my own case, beginning as the most parochial of American folklorists, I have been able, after getting on the international bandwagon, to attend folklore congresses in Sweden, Germany, Denmark, France, Yugoslavia, Hungary, Belgium, Portugal, Greece, Romania, Scotland, and Argentina, as well as meet folklorists during extended stays in Japan and England. These congresses and the personal friendships that accrue are an education in themselves and productive of enterprises not otherwise feasible. The Aarne-Thompson index resulted from Stith Thompson's visit to Finland and consultation with Kaarle Krohn, the dean of European folklorists. The Folktales of the World series could never have developed, or even been conceived, without the network of international contacts made possible through the congresses and conferences of European-based societies. Now a Society for Asian Folklore has been organized, and held its first meeting in Bloomington in 1966.

What might be called the technique of international relations involves travel and visits to archives, institutes, centers, folk museums, and society meetings, reinforced by correspondence, symposia, translation projects, and publications exchanges. By such means the world-wide fraternity of folklorists maintain their intellectual bonds in the face of vast distances and hostile ideologies. A tangible demonstration of the bonds formed and the forays completed into foreign lands by American folklorists in the past two decades can be seen in the volume *Folklore Research Around the World, A North American Point of View,* which I edited in 1961 in the Indiana University Folklore Series. Europe still attracts the largest number of peripatetic fieldworkers, archives-workers, and folk-museum workers, but Asia, Africa, Oceania, and Australia too have their *aficionados.* Nor is it only senior faculty who develop overseas ties. The latest Newsletter of the Folklore Institute at Indiana University quotes correspondence from pre-doctoral students or new Ph.D.'s (some of whom have returned to their home countries) from American Samoa, North Malaita in the British Solomons, Nigeria, Ghana, Uganda, Poland, Malaysia, East Pakistan, and Thailand. Certainly one of the chief strengths of the folk-lorist in today's anxious world is his ability to locate and work with like-minded colleagues on every continent.

This paper has attempted to isolate components of the genus folklorist. Members of this genus may vary widely in their theoretical views, but they do employ a common set of techniques, or ways of examining, ferreting out, and cogitating over their materials. A number of folklorists, swayed by the computer and awed, like everybody else, by the scientific method, will wish to consider themselves hard-nosed social scientists, who draw representational models and predict the migration routes and stylistic changes of tale and song, perhaps quantifying the number of proverbs a given individual will utter in his lifetime. But even the most hard-nosed folk-lorist is at heart a humanist, attracted by the vagaries, the affability, the expressive power, and the wayward genius of tradition-directed peoples.

NOTES

1. Just to show how the Society keeps growing, this past November, 1971, the Society held a four-day meeting in Washington, D.C., with three concurrent sessions.
2. *Journal of the Folklore Institute* 2 (1965): 326–39.

2 /

Is There a Folk in the City?

NORTH UIST LIES AMONG THE OUTER HEBRIDES in the Atlantic
coastal sea, a Scottish outpost on the western edge of Europe.
When the plane from Inverness swoops down toward the airport at
Benbecula, the isle looks like a lonely crater of the moon, pockmarked with hollows and lifeless lakes, striated with mountainous
ridges, coated with vapor. A nearer view is no more encouraging.
There are no hotels, no villages, nothing but solitary crofters' stone
cottages scattered at long intervals over the empty moors. A driving rain and wind blow across the moors, stinging the face and
dampening the clothes. Trousers do not keep a press long in the
Hebrides. Roads are primitive, and cars when they meet must
jockey to find a "passing place," a widened shoulder of the road
located at intervals, because the roads are all one way, whichever
way you are going. Gaelic is the tongue everyone speaks from
birth, and English is the second language.

This is the country and here are the folk known to folklorists.
No richer tradition in the western world has been uncovered than
the Gaelic treasure found in the Hebrides. John Francis Campbell
of Islay gathered his classic four-volume *Popular Tales of the West
of Scotland* (Edinburgh, 1860–1862) from the Hebrides and Highlands. Alexander Carmichael amassed five volumes of folk blessings,

Reprinted from the *Journal of American Folklore* 83 (April–June, 1970): 185–
216.

hymns, charms, and incantations from the same area in his *Carmina Gadelica* (Edinburgh and London, 1928–1953). At the present time John Lorne Campbell, laird of the Isle of Canna, continues to mine the isles, with book-length collections from single narrators on Barra and South Uist, while his wife, Margaret Fay Shaw, has brought forth a substantial sheaf of folksongs from South Uist. Even the hoard of Campbell of Islay and his collectors is still being tapped in the twentieth century, with two posthumous volumes of folktales and the impressive cache of local historical traditions titled *The Dewar Manuscripts* (Glasgow, 1964).

North Uist and the Hebrides are the case I offer as a classic illustration of the terrain of the folklorist and the concept of the folk. I was there the end of August 1967, accompanying a collector from the School of Scottish Studies in the University of Edinburgh, John MacInnes, himself island born and raised. Although the Hebrides have been so amply collected, and although only some two thousand souls remain on North Uist, John says there are layers upon layers of tradition still to be peeled, a lifetime of work. The people of North Uist are all one; their names begin with Mac, they appear all at some point to be interrelated; they have inhabited this isle for ten clear centuries. In common they speak Gaelic, farm the land, cut peat, and tend the sheep, and they visit each other in sociable *ceilidhs* in which they recall marvelous events of yore occurring on the isle. The name of almost every locality and landmark involves a tradition. Only in faith are they divided between Catholics and Protestants.

If the remote countryside, symbolized by North Uist, has provided the questing ground of the folklorist, what business has he in the city? One ready answer is that the folklorist deals with people, and the people have left the country and flocked to the cities. While North Uist has dwindled to a couple of thousand crofters, Gary in northwest Indiana has risen from empty sand dunes in 1906 to become a metropolis of 200,000, peopled by over fifty nationalities. To Gary and its neighbor East Chicago, one-third its size, I went in February 1968, to live under field conditions. Knowing no one, I sought to form contacts and interview representatives of the dominant ethnic groups. Gary received nationwide publicity when it elected a Negro mayor, Richard G. Hatcher, on November 7, 1967, an election reflecting the rise in the city's Negro population to over 50 percent. The other major groups in Gary are the Serbian, Croatian, Greek, and "Latin," a term that includes Mexicans and Puerto Ricans. Throughout Lake County as a whole the Poles predominate. East Chicago has proportionally a smaller Negro and a larger Latin element, with its mayor, John B. Nicosia, representing an earlier, now established Italian colony. When speaking of East Chicago the commentator must include Indiana Harbor, a community within the city; before they were combined, East Chicago and Indiana Harbor were known as the twin cities. They are still physically separated by a forest of giant oil drums and installations lined along Route 20. Close connections bind the two—or three—cities, for they are all part of the steel kingdom that has sucked into its fiery vortex the manpower of many peoples. Inland and Youngstown in East Chicago and U.S. Steel and Bethlehem in Gary are the regal plants that must be fed with iron ore and coal twenty-four hours a day, seven days a week, and tended by men and women. The need for laborers in the mills is never sated. First it was met by East Europeans from every Balkan country, then by southern Negroes, then by Mexicans and Puerto Ricans brought up in truckloads and planeloads concurrently with southern whites, who streamed north from Kentucky and southern Illinois, Virginia and Tennessee, Alabama and Louisiana. "Eighty-five percent of them around here is from the South," one Kentuckian observed airily.

Such a complex of ethnic and regional groups is bound to attract the folklorist, especially when the groups involved derive from the peasant-farmer and laboring classes. Linda Dégh and her husband Andrew Vaszonyi first penetrated Indiana Harbor in the winter of 1964–1965 and again in the summer of 1967, speaking with the sizable body of emigrants from their native Hungary. They had soon realized that one ethnic group led into another, and my mission was to explore in a preliminary way these other groups. Born and schooled in New York City, living in London for three stretches totaling two years, and in Tokyo for ten months, I had experienced the world's largest cities, but never as a collector of folklore. My folklore field trips had taken me to the country towns. My present purposes were threefold: to ascertain if the folklorist could ply his trade in the city; to contrast the vitality of the traditions among the various ethnic and racial groups; and to observe the effect of life in an urban, industrial center upon these imported cultures.

Obviously a stay of twenty-three days can only begin to probe these questions. But experiences in the field can be intense and concentrated, they may yield intimate revelations into lives, experiences, hatreds, fears, and cherished symbols that one may never encounter in years of routine living. By "the field" I mean an area in which the folklorist lives completely divorced from his own usual schedule, occupation, and residence—a period in which he devotes all of his waking moments to making contacts, interviewing, recording, listening to and observing the people with whom he is concerned. In this sense I lived in the field in Gary, staying downtown in the environs of the Negro ghetto, in the now bankrupt Hotel Gary, an integrated, gloomy structure no longer patronized by middle-class travelers.

The reputation of Gary matches the sullen glow of the ever-lit furnaces in the mills, for, thanks in good part to a *Time* article, Gary symbolizes the urban jungle—crime-ridden, race-wracked, and cultureless. One's first impression driving into Gary along the endless central avenue of Broadway bisecting the city confirms the worst—particularly if the day (February 2, 1968) is rainy and drear, the surrounding countryside brown and muddy, and the roadsides deep in water. Broadway is lined with one-story joints, bars, liquor stores and increasingly crummy shops as one gets further down town into the Negro ghetto. A movie marquee reads "Greek movies on Saturday, Spanish on Sunday." Polluted air envelops the city, dust and grime cover the buildings, litter fills the alleys. Gloom, ugliness, and apprehension set the tone of Gary. Armed guards stand at the ready in every bank, and the buses cease running in the early evening because of knifings of waiting passengers. Drivers lock their car doors and sweat out the red lights. "We were held up here last month on payday at noon by four Negro gunmen, when the guard stepped out for a coffee break," a welfare agency director told me my first day in Gary. "I'm hoping to move the office away from here [16th and Broadway] soon; we're right in the midst of the pimps, queers, dope pushers, and whores. Even while I've been talking to you someone has been observing the layout." And he nervously wiped his white brow and looked at the sea of black faces.

One of the quests of this trip was to see if and how a folklorist could operate in a strange city among a number of ethnic and racial groups. To make contacts I visited Negro Baptist churches on four successive Sundays; called on Harold Malone, father of a black student of mine in Bloomington; dropped in on the International Institute of Gary, where a Serbian, a Greek, and a young black woman all introduced me to people; made the acquaintance of William Passmore, head of the Job Corps office in East Chicago, who kindly offered me a wealth of leads; looked up likely informants from student folklore collections turned in to a folklore course at the Northwest Campus in Gary; hung around the dilapidated Baltimore Hotel opposite the Inland Steel plant; followed suggestions from a trustee of Indiana University living in Gary, Robert Lucas. It was the old story of developing contacts through all likely means, chasing around town, calling people up to make appointments, trying to explain my mission. But I found persons in every group hospitable and friendly and often anxious to talk of their experiences and of life in the "Region," as this pocket of northwest Indiana is locally called. The following pages, some extracted from my field diary, attempt to convey a sense of the cultural pluralism in urban folklore.

THE NEGRO

My few weeks in Gary and East Chicago did not uncover a master folk narrator, although one may well be there. In no group indeed did I encounter a narrator of this type, though I did meet excellent talkers. Let me consider Negro tradition under the heads of proverbs, tales, voodoo, and the folk church.

On two occasions I heard northern-born, educated blacks—who had looked blankly at me when I asked about Old Marster and Brother Buzzard—employ patently Negro proverbs to crystallize an idea and drive home a thought in the course of a tense discussion. The first situation developed in the Job Corps office on Columbus Avenue in East Chicago, where I met Willie P., both of whose legs had been amputated while he was in his teens because of a spinal disease. His mother, Laura, 73, a snowy-haired fragile old lady born in Alabama, granddaughter of a slave, related to me with quavering voice and perfect command of dates the series of long hospital sieges and near-fatal operations that Willie had endured patiently and even cheerfully. The Déghs had put me in touch with Willie, who knew all the civic leaders in East Chicago and gave me every assistance. This morning Willie—boyish, studious-looking and gentle, who at times had double-dated with Mayor Hatcher—was giving a little moralizing talk to three Negro boys of fourteen and fifteen, dropouts and potential delinquents. The boys squirmed and twisted uneasily as Willie lectured them from his wheelchair behind his desk. Willie had lapsed into the soft, slurred tones that blacks frequently use with each other. He reiterated the need for them to stay in school, to train themselves for their future jobs, to learn discipline. "A hard head makes a hard bed," he said climactically.

No proverb could have been more appropriate. "Hard head" is a phrase current among southern Negroes, who use it in jocular ghost tales about revenants that return in answer to a relative's prayer but outstay their welcome; hence the comment, "Brother, that's how come you dead now, you so hard-headed." The teller explains parenthetically, "Head hard or head long means you go looking for trouble." [1] Willie summarized and capped his message with this pithy saw.

Another day I was in the Children's Public Library of East Chicago talking with Mrs. Edna W., college-educated, precise in speech, decorous in manner, a world away from Old Marster. She began speaking about the conditions of the Negro and the election of Mayor Hatcher, but in a note rarely reported. This was a note of mistrust of black aggressiveness, a fear of consequences stemming from Hatcher's election, distress at the stridency of Negro youths no longer respectful of their elders. "There are one-third of us who feel this way, but our voice won't be heard. I won't be heard in Washington." She was telling me more than she had ever told anyone. Mrs. W. was opposed to open housing. Let the whites and the blacks each live by themselves; people are not comfortable in surroundings they are not used to. "I don't want to be a fly in the buttermilk," she said. And so, to dramatize her opposition to the open-housing ordinance, so strong an article of faith to black militants and white liberals, the librarian had recourse to a Negro proverb with apt color imagery.

The tales that seemed to me so much a touchstone of Negro

folk tradition were slow in coming. At first I was the carrier and the teller. But in the course of two evenings (one in the home of the Reverend H.J., pastor of a store-front church, with an evangelist preacher and a deacon present, the other in the home of the Reverend B. D., pastor of a Baptist church, along with his deacon L.T., southerners all and steelworkers all) tales came to the surface, one triggering another. They were old favorites: "The Coon in the Box," "Dividing Soul," "Poll Parrot and Biscuits," "Why the Fox Has a Short Tail." But as I was going out the door, the Reverend H.J. thought of one entirely new to me, "The Train Going Uphill and Downhill," employing slow, drawn-out phrases for the uphill climb, and fast, chug-chug phrases for the descent.[2] Charles K. of the Gary Human Relations Commission told me a number of civil-rights stories with which he and his companions had whiled away the time during his six jail confinements for demonstrating. One was a television variant of the old Negro down South who hollers "Help!" on the radio when urged by southern governors to tell how well he is treated.[3] Another was a Negro variant of a Jewish joke about the would-be radio announcer with a dreadful stutter who claims he is the victim of bias. Civil-rights stories (the phrase is the informant's) are one segment of the southern Negro repertory which thrives and expands in northern cities.

One interview disclosed a displacement of tale tradition by book tradition, albeit not a learned book tradition. Todd R., 70, who had come from Alabama to Gary in 1922 and worked for forty years in the steel mills before retiring, remembered nostalgically the South and "country living" as the best in the world. But he told only one tale, "The Race" (Type 1074), in the shortest version I ever heard: "The rabbit and the turtle had a race; the rabbit stopped to pick berries and the turtle won." He stirred briefly to the legend of the snake and the child and said he had heard in Alabama that the girl died when her father killed her pet snake. Todd's real interest lay in reciting names, dates, and facts about Negro Americans, garnered from two battered and tattered booklets he showed me: *Afro-American World Almanac*, and *A Tribute to Achievement* issued by the Pfeiffer Brewing Company.

Voodoo or cunjer seemed at first as invisible as folktales. Harold M. took me calling on a family friend, Mrs. Katie S., a school matron born in Memphis, friendly, poised, and proper. The only element of tradition she displayed dealt with cuisine, "soul food," the Negro diet of turnip greens, chitterlings, corn bread, cabbage, sweet potatoes, which kept together bodies and souls of the colored folk in the South. The cheaper cuts and leavings of the hog and cow—neckbone, pig feet, pot licker—were nutritious. Old Marster gave them to the slaves, and the slaves throve, while the white people fell prey to rare diseases. To my question whether she liked the food of other groups in Gary, Mrs. S. replied that she enjoyed *tacos* until she heard that the Mexicans were cutting up cats for the meat. When we left her house I asked Harold M. about her husband. Andrew S. had been born in Coldwater, Mississippi, had come to Gary in 1943, and was now laid up in the hospital, claiming he had been voodooed by his son, who had given him canned corn that turned to worms.

Another voodoo case was headlined in the Chicago *Daily Defender*, the only American Negro daily, on February 20, the day I drove into its offices with Bill Passmore, who wrote a weekly column for them on East Chicago news. The city editor, Thomas Picou, a severe young intellectual, talked to me about his paper's philosophy of cohesion and adequate news coverage for the Negro. He did not have much to say about the banner headline of the day, "Possessed by 'Voodoo': Mother Charged in Triple Slaying," blazoned on the front page. The news story appeared on page three and is reproduced below.

MOTHER OF FOUR CHARGED IN "VOODOO" SLAYING

Husband, Two Aunts
Killed at Reception

By Donald Mosby
(Daily Defender Staff Writer)

A 27-year-old mother of four, who thinks she is possessed by "a voodoo lizard," was charged yesterday with killing her husband and his two aunts at a suburban wedding reception.

Held without bond is Mrs. Ruby Luckett, 107 Riverview Ave., Lockport, who, one wedding guest said, "looked as if she were in a daze," moments before she reputedly shot the trio Sunday night. Mrs. Luckett is accused of killing her husband, Peter, 29, a laborer, and his aunts, Mrs. Sadie Porter, 62, of 404 E. 72d St., and Mrs. Lisa

Harper, 43, of 118 Oak Ave., of Lockport. Luckett died yesterday in St. Francis Hospital.

According to Dixmoor Ptl. John North, the shooting deaths grew out of an argument between Mrs. Luckett and her husband in the basement of 14337 S. Honore, Dixmoor, where a wedding reception for Luckett's sister was in progress. The home belongs to Sullivan Wright, brother of the groom.

North said Mrs. Luckett shot her husband during the height of an argument and repeated the attack upstairs when she saw Luckett's aunts—Mrs. Harper and Mrs. Porter—sitting on a couch.

Luckett was shot in the chest, Mrs. Harper, in the chest, and Mrs. Porter in the head.

According to the suburban policeman, Mrs. Luckett feared her relatives were practicing some kind of "voodoo power" against her.

Mrs. Luckett was driven to Dixmoor police headquarters by some departing wedding guests, who were apparently unaware of what had happened inside the home.

According to police, Mrs. Luckett admitted shooting the trio, and handed over to police a .38 calibre revolver, believed to be the death weapon.

In court yesterday, she told a judge her relatives had put a lizard in her stomach as part of a voodoo spell and that she had to keep salt and water under her bed to satisfy the voodoo curse. Mrs. Luckett is scheduled to appear in Midlothian Court March 21.

The *Daily Defender* story called to the mind of one of my companions, Larry J., an account he had heard of a girl who voodooed the man of her desire. This man was paying her no heed, so on the advice of a girl friend she obtained two pairs of his pants and hung them up in her closet, and now the couple were living together.

For the core of Negro traditional expression, behavior, and belief we must turn to the church. Gary possesses over two hundred Negro churches. On successive Sundays I visited the First Baptist, the Calvary Baptist, and the St. John Primitive Baptist churches; these represented, in descending order, the scale of affluence, status, prestige, and denial of southern Negro culture. The First Baptist Church building was brand new, facing a pleasant park, cathedral-like in its dimensions, upper-class white in its service. Professional people attended this church—doctors, lawyers, teachers. The women vied with each other in the loftiness and dazzling colors of their hats. All was decorous and efficient; the congregation sang from hymnbooks, the minister preached with dignity, and only the faintest responses of "Amen" and "That's the truth" echoed his words. But with the Calvary Baptist Church—also in a new but much less pretentious building—the institutions of southern Negro folk religion came into view. Here was a highly personal, joking, exhorting, chanting pastor, F. Brannam Jackson, recalling the days when he was a little old barefoot boy on the bayou, and mosquitoes were so large they were called gallinippers, and when they stung you, you felt as if you had lockjaw. Here was a swaying, throbbing choir, singing without hymnbooks, reinforced by pianist and organist and the responsive congregation, spurred on by ecstatic soloists, who would interrupt their songs to cry "Shout out." In the front row sat a uniformed nurse, who sprang into action when a heavy woman a few rows back "got happy" and with other churchgoers fanned her vigorously back into normalcy.

A news item in the Gary *Post Tribune* had caught my eye, "Negro Plight Is Theme," announcing the "annual Homecoming Day" at the Calvary Baptist Church in honor of Negro history week, with a full program of service, chicken dinner, panel speakers, and a slavery-time play. The three speakers were each in his own way highly articulate and impressive. Twenty-four-year-old Bill Joiner, first Negro manager of a branch of the Gary National Bank, was modest and quiet spoken; Mrs. Nancy Brundige, an urban sociologist for the city of Chicago, was positive and direct; and Charles H. King, director of the Gary Human Relations Commission, was a performer of shattering eloquence. These were Negro intellectuals telling the Negro folk about business opportunities, historical achievements, and spiritual strengths of their race with a conviction and force deeply admired by the one white auditor. The whole day was indeed a testimonial to the facility of Negro oral expression in singing and speaking. As King said, Negroes were the greatest singers in the world because church singing was their one permitted mode of utterance. He rocked the audience with illustrations of phrases from spirituals taken in their innocuous literal sense by the slavemasters, but intended in quite specific and material ways by the singers (a matter often debated by white scholars). King made a number of effective points: that segregation began after, not during, slavery, for the slave could attend the same church as his master, even though he had to sit in the gallery (hence

Lincoln's Emancipation Proclamation was the biggest lie in American history); that the church was the center of Negro fellowship and community life, for it was the Negro's only social organization ("The Negro stays in church all day, while the white man comes for an hour and leaves; isn't that so, Professor?"); that the Baptist church was most available to the Negro, for it required no superstructure of outside authorities. In 1968, speakers were using "Negro" rather than black.

After these speeches and a comment I was called on to make, the chairs were rearranged, and an informal playlet presented, "De Lawd, the Negroes' Hope in a New Home." The scene was ostensibly laid on a slave plantation, and the appearance of members of the congregation in cotton dresses and sun bonnets, idly stroking a butter churn and a wash board, sent the spectators into spasms of laughter. Most of the action was confined to a chorus singing such spirituals as "Climbing Jacob's Ladder," "Deep River," and "There'll Be a Great Day When We All Gather Home." At the conclusion the attractive young wife of the pastor made a statement on the zeal of the performers (one had canceled a trip to New Orleans in order to be present) and the historical relevance of the drama, "I would rather be the persecuted than the persecutors." Negro church songs were often hard to follow. I asked a black friend about this, and he said he himself could not be sure of the words, since the singers picked up words listening to each other.

The Primitive Baptist Church represented still another aspect of Negro worship, the extended family unit with aspirations for autonomy. A dozen adults and a dozen children were present the two Sundays I attended, and the obese woman who led the choir of five—and supplied one daughter to the choir and five to the Sunday school—was the pastor's sister-in-law. Yet the group met in a neat, fresh-painted room in their own small building, acquired four months before for five thousand dollars. Previously they had held services in a dingy store-front up the block. Elder George M. had carpentered and plastered the new church himself. He had worked in the steel mills for eleven years and made thirty-seven dollars a day instructing crane operators, although he could neither read nor write. When I expressed surprise he called his wife, "Tell this guy how I can't read." He had been born in Arkansas and educated at Muncie Central on a football scholarship, apparently doing well in classes in spite of his handicap. He received special instruction from a white teacher at Ball State University. He had possessed the gift of preaching since he was five, being ordained by the Lord.

Handsome, athletic, still young, he preached with fervor and intensity, dipping his knees, holding a handkerchief or book to his right cheek, intoning phrases in a rising cadence with closed eyes, sometimes opening out and shaking his palms. The Primitive Baptists believed in "making a joyful noise unto the Lord" and in footwashing, which they practiced one Sunday in the month. Elder M. gave me permission to record the service the following Sunday, and asked me to play it back in church. Listening intently, he remarked, "That sounds just like country singing." Any listener would marvel at how so small a group could fill the room with song, chant, and response in swelling harmony. The elder had served as minister for five years and commented about himself, "I'm the most unlearned pastor they had, and carried them the furthest." He obtained historical references from a book his wife read to him, which he showed me, *World's Great Men of Color, 3000 B.C. to 1946 A.D.* by J. A. Rogers, published at 37 Morningside Avenue in New York.

Negro folk religion or traditional worship, as characterized in these observations, is directly connected with civil rights and urban politics. This point was ingeniously made by Charles H. King when I recorded a talk with him in his basement office in the Gary Municipal Building. King was forty-two, dark and mottled in complexion, burly in physique. His mother had been born in Boston, his father in Atlanta, and he himself in Albany. A regular contributor to *Negro Digest* with perceptive articles on the Negro church, King had shown me an autobiographical chapter of an unpublished manuscript in which he described the attempt of his father, a preacher in Harrisburg, Pennsylvania, to have young Charles "get religion" through exposure to a visiting revivalist. Charles was not converted and was painfully embarrassed. He ended the chapter by saying he later experienced religion in his own way. When I asked him how, he related an experience that had befallen him when he was eighteen as a sailor in the United States Navy on shore leave. Two shore patrolmen, southern whites, ordered him, "Boy, straighten your cap," and when he reacted too slowly, poked him in the ribs and called him nigger. King slugged one, and they dragged him off to the guardhouse and lashed him two hundred times with a belt, the buckle leaving permanent scars on his back. At his trial, the ship's captain mocked him publicly, saying, "So they called you nigger. Well what did you expect them to call you?"

After that episode King felt a need for faith, but he developed his own concept of social relevance in his ministry, employing the techniques of the southern Baptist preacher while rejecting the escapism into heavenly hopes. King pointed out that Negro civil rights leaders—and he named a string, beginning with Martin Luther King—were all former ministers. He too belonged to this sequence, having pastored for three years at Clarksville, Tennessee, and for ten years at Evansville, Indiana. Negro civil rights agitators used the same devices on the platform they had employed on the altar—the incantatory repetition (Jees-us, Jees-us), the encouragement of shouting, the emotional singing—but now it was all channeled into the specific goals of earthly recognition for the black. King cleverly illustrated the mincing, polite singing of an all-white church at Miller whose choir had practiced a spiritual in his honor the day he came as guest preacher, and his own booming, leather-lunged rendition he demonstrated to them as a corrective. "When I was finished, there were at least eight people with wet eyes." Such expertly manipulated sounds induced in the Negro congregations the mass hypnotism or cataleptic trances popularly known as "getting happy," and now black social reformers and politicians were arousing their audiences with these traditional means. King himself decried unbridled emotionalism for either theological or extremist ends, and gave me an article he had just written, "The Specter of Black Power," describing a Black Power symposium he had attended, and sharply criticized, at Howard University.[4]

An extraordinary opportunity to see a concrete illustration of King's thesis came the evening of February 14, when I found myself in a crowded basement room where the Political Alliance Club of Northwest Indiana was meeting. This was an organization for minority groups, but the members were all Negro save for one or two Puerto Ricans. A tense, chunky white woman, obviously under considerable strain, sat in the speaker's chair. This was Marion Tokarsky, now a celebrity for revealing the vote fraud attempted against Mayor Hatcher.[5] That very day she was on the front page of the Gary *Post Tribune*, in a garbled story saying the prosecutor was dropping charges against her—her punishment by the machine for her public revelations—in return for her turning state's evidence. The only other white person present was a policeman, appointed by Hatcher as part of her twenty-four-hour protection. Mrs. Tokarsky spoke a rough and sloppy English, not the clumsy English of the immigrant but the street English of the little-schooled American. She delivered her recital of the attempted vote fraud, and her decision to break with the Democratic Party machine and support Hatcher, in the form of a divine revelation.

"I am no saint," she began, "just an instrument of the Lord," and she repeated this thought at intervals. Her tale was a melodrama that would make Hollywood thrillers seem plausible. She had been a staunch Democratic committeewoman for twelve years in Glen Park, the residential center of the anti-Negro East Europeans. The machine turned against Hatcher, not because he was a Negro but because he would not do their bidding. Last July they had given her a sample voting machine with instructions on how to split the ticket and vote against Hatcher. She smuggled a sample voting machine in her shopping bag to show Hatcher, who had a picture taken of it. Democrats and Republicans alike were working to defeat Hatcher; some 5,280 names were removed from the voting rolls. Marion Tokarsky went through a period of doubt and confusion, at one time questioning Hatcher's loyalty. "I prayed as I never prayed before." The federal government flew in, and assured her she would not be involved or have to go to court.

Then one day the subpoena came. She turned over the matter all day Saturday, and at twelve o'clock Mass the Sunday before election she prayed directly to God. She explained to her Baptist audience that as a Catholic she had always before prayed to Saint Anthony or the Blessed Virgin, who could get the ear of the Lord in her behalf. But now she prayed directly. " 'God, please just give me the courage to go to court tomorrow. If I find just a few words in this missal I'll have courage.' And it was as if He had come right down from heaven." She opened the missal, and right before her eyes, in the Book of Psalms, was the word she had requested: " 'In the midst of the Assembly he opened his mouth. . . . The mark of the just man tells wisdom and his tongue tells what is right.' And I thanked God. Now I asked God to show me that Hatcher would win. 'Cause I knew I was crucified if he didn't."

Again the Lord answered her with an apt quotation.

And the next day when I went to court I didn't have to think, the words came right out of my mouth. And the defense lawyers asked me questions that I gave answers to, made them look like jackasses. So it was someone bigger than me doing it. They asked, "Mrs. Tokarsky, will you testify that a Democratic official asked you to do something illegal?" "Yes," I said, "if you'll name them one by one." "Why won't you name them, don't you know them?" "Yes," I answered, "but I don't know if you do." At that they reddened and asked two names, to which I said yes, and then they stopped. I called the mayor Sunday evening and said, "Dick, this is Marion. You know, you're going to win the election." And I read to him out of the missal. He said to me, "Ever since the primary I knew I was going to win. But this is the most glorious thing that has happened to me."

There was a good deal more in this vein. Mrs. Tokarsky was fired from her job, arrested and jailed, her children spat on, her husband, who had just renovated his gas station, threatened. But the Lord sustained her throughout. "The day that I was arrested and they put me in jail, I didn't feel one ounce of sorrow or regret. I felt elated." This was on December 29, and on New Year's Eve, alone with her children, she asked God for another message and found it in Psalms 19:13, "O Lord, you heard His voice cry to you from the temple . . . devising a plot and they will fall into it themselves."

Throughout the narration, the listeners interjected the customary responses of Baptist congregations, especially when Mrs. Tokarsky underlined her points with such precepts as "Faith can really move a mountain" and "God helps those who help themselves." At the end of her talk an elderly gentleman in the front row cried out, "That's the gospel. It should be heard all over the world." Defying all the rules, the representative of the Slavic groups in Glen Park had made common cause with the ghetto blacks. Their medium of communication was the political revival meeting, and together they saw Mayor Hatcher as blessed by the Lord in the battle against the forces of evil. Marion Tokarsky was the prophet through whom God has spoken. In recompense for her sacrifice, the black community is heavily patronizing her husband's gas station.

SERBIANS

"The Serbians live on tradition and heritage," observed one of my new Serbian friends. More than any other ethnic group in Gary and East Chicago, the Serbians do indeed cherish and abide by their Old World inheritance, an inheritance vivid and sorrowful in their minds, from the battle of Kossovo in 1389, when they sank heroically in defeat before the Turks, down to the Chetnik battles against Nazi Croatians and Tito's Communists. This is not book history but live and remembered history, as Americans rarely remember and identify with their past. Several Gary Serbs explained that orally recited history kept alive the Serbian spirit during five centuries of Turkish oppression and darkness. When the Turks blinded the learned clergy, the priests sang from memory heroic recitations of the Serbs, accompanying themselves on the one-stringed fiddle, the *gusle*, which they improvised from a stick and a strand of horsehair after the Turks confiscated their musical instruments. All the Serbs I met were proud and sad. Eighty-year-old George R., still erect and twinkling, recited emotionally a *gusle* song he had learned over seventy years before in Serbia. Thirty-one-year-old Walter T. has been in the States only since 1956, with his wife Milly (Miholjka), whom he brought over in 1963 from his native village, making sure she wasn't "brainwashed." Red-haired Milane S., a fiery Montenegrin with an LL.D., rushed at me when I came into her boss's office carrying a tape recorder and asked if I was a Communist spy; but I ended by taping her experience as a Chetnik fighter who escaped through Communist lines. Dragich B. ("Blaz"), an ex-waiter and former Chetnik, thrust his story upon me in the Chetnik-run Europa cafe. Rade R., the oak-chested leader of the mother church group in East Chicago, wept three times while recounting atrocities committed against his people in the Second World War.

These and other Serbs showed the effects of a common tradition. They shuddered at the crimes of the hated Ustashis, who allegedly had butchered two million Serbs during the last war. Walter T. gave me a booklet, *The Crime of Genocide*, published by the Serbian National Defense Council of America (Chicago, 1951), that contained shocking pictures of mutilated women and children and a decapitated priest's head held by grinning Ustashis as well as an introductory anecdote about Ante Pavelich, the Croatian Ustashi leader, exhibiting on his desk a wicker basket filled with forty pounds of human eyes. Rade R. gave me a copy of the book *Genocide in Satellite Croatia, 1941–1945* (Chicago, n.d.) by Edmond Paris, translated from the French, and documenting these horrors. I recorded eye-witness atrocities related by Walter T. and his godfather, Milos R., who had lost fifteen members of his family during the war; and by Rade and his wife, Mira, born in Novi Sad. Rade, as a Belgrade policeman, had been called to pick up the bodies of eight children floating down the Sava River with the head of their mother nailed to a board, under a sign reading, "A present from the Ustashis." Mira had seen the Hungarian troops bomb the Danube ice and push Serbian and Jewish families into the water underneath. Overwhelming bitterness against the Croatians, the Nazis, and the Communists filled their talk. The Communists especially aroused their passion, and they saw signs of communism and communist propaganda everywhere in America—among the Negroes, the hippies, the clergy.

A great split rent the solidarity of American Serbs in 1963, over the so-called mother church issue. One wing rejected the authority of the mother church in Belgrade and its edict redistricting the American diocese, whose seat was in Libertyville, Illinois. They called the opposing faction communists, and were in turn labeled schismatics. The issue resulted in bitter litigation, still in progress, and divided the Gary and East Chicago Serbs into two churches in each city. Rade represented the mother church faction in East Chicago, and he minimized the differences between Serbs and Croats, saying both fought equally with the Chetniks and Partisans. He himself had been born in Croatian Bosnia but belonged to the Serbian church. He told of Ustashis so hungry they ordered the camp cooks to fry livers of young boys. Both factions presented their case vigorously to me, and the only sure conclusion one could draw was that the most cohesive of all the ethnic groups in Steeltown had fallen into civil war.

National and folk traditions blend in the lives of the Serbian steelworkers. *Gusle* singers perform in Gary at saint's day family parties and recite the old heroic lays. Draža Mihajlovich, the Chetnik leader whom the Serbs feel was betrayed by Roosevelt and

Churchill at Yalta, is the most recent of the venerated heroes extending back to Marko Kraljevich and Miloš Obilich. The analogy between oppression under the Turks and under the Communists is often drawn. Historical plays presented in Saint Sava Church so excited emotions that members of the audience pelted the Turks, played by their own friends. George R. recited for me in Serbian the "Gusle Song" describing a renegade Serbian who joined the Turks. One day finding a *gusle*, he attempted to play it but could not, because "the *gusle* does not lie." He bent tearfully over the instrument, imploring forgiveness, and a Turk whacked off his head. In the basement of Saint Sava Church I observed a program of Serbian songs, dances, and speeches with not a word of English used. After the stage program young and old joined hands in the traditional *cola* dance to the accompaniment of two thumping accordion players.

The most striking example of Serbian cultural nationalism in Gary is the story of Bishop Varnava Nastich. He was born in Gary on January 31, 1914, the son of an immigrant barber, and was baptized Voislav in the Saint Sava Serbian Orthodox Church. As a child he excelled at *gusle* performances, and clippings refer to him as a youthful prodigy in reciting Serbian folklore and old ballads, even being taken on tour to Serbian communities in other cities. He also served as altar boy in Saint Sava Church. At the age of nine, in 1923, he left Gary with his parents, brother, and sister for Yugoslavia. His father operated the popular "American Restaurant" on King Alexander Avenue in Sarajevo. Within three or four years after their return, Voislav had won the gold medal awarded by King Alexander to the best boy *guslar*. At eighteen he undertook theological studies and graduated from the theological faculty of the University of Belgrade in 1937. Three years later he took monastic vows in the monastery at Mileshevo and changed his name to Varnava. During the war years, 1941–1945, Varnava refused a bishopric in the so-called Croatian Orthodox Church of the Nazi puppet state under Ante Pavelich. In 1945 he was ordained a priest, and in August 1947 he was consecrated a bishop. Within a year he was arrested and brought to trial by Tito's government, actually for speaking against communism, ostensibly for collaborating with the Ustashi, an infamous charge. There followed eleven years of imprisonment, harassment, surveillance, brutality, and death by poisoning, according to half a dozen informants, including Saint Sava's priest, Father Peter Bankerovich, who with others tape-recorded for me a statement about Varnava. Father Peter recalled how a telegram announcing the death of Bishop Varnava was delivered in the midst of the high celebration in church on the fiftieth anniversary of the founding of Saint Sava, November 14, 1964. He gave me a copy of the 368-page commemoration book printed in Gary in both Serbian and English, and concluded his taped remarks by reading from the communication sent by Bishop Varnava from Monastery Beocin on September 3, 1964. One paragraph reads:

"I rejoice, because your Feast is my personal feast also, for I was among the first of your Altar-boys, and I was the first one after the formation of your Church congregation to whom was given the rank of 'Chtec'—Reader—under the arch of your Church. Under the blessed heaven of your Church Community, my first formation of my physical and graceful-spiritual life sprouted." [6]

A play was written and produced in Gary in January 1965 about Bishop Varnava, "Martyr to Communism," acted in the Saint Sava Church auditorium by children, to acquaint them with his heroic life and death. I read the typescript of the play in the home of its author, Daisy Wuletich, Gary-born, who had visited the Bishop in 1961 in Beocin Monastery with her mother, born in Montenegro. Daisy had drawn from personal letters of the Bishop, from an account of the trial in the booklet *Our Spiritual Hero*, and from her personal observations. The play itself was simple fare, a first act depicting the trial, in which the bishop defied the communist judges to the cheers of the crowd, and a second act set in the hospital showing him in familiar scenes before receiving a fatal injection. Thus he talks with his uncle about the car "pesho," a Peugeot given him by the Gary church so that he could travel around the country. He writes in a letter to his Gary friends, "I realize that at any time my car can turn into a Cross for me. This is its Cross-aspect and this Cross-aspect, too, is one and not the least of the reasons for my loving it so." The car became a symbol of his persecution, for it was exorbitantly taxed by the Communists. In the play this dialogue takes place:

Uncle: How sentimental you are about the car! You take better care of it than some people do of their own children.

Bishop: My little Pesho is important to me.
Marko: How fervently you speak of your car!
Bishop: I do speak of it fervently and I love it fervently! One reason being, of course, the American-red blood in me.

In another place in the play Bishop Varnava alludes to a visit he made to the shrine of Saint Basil (Vasilije) at Ostrog in Montenegro to pray for his sick mother. Daisy and her mother, Cveta, had also visited Ostrog, and Cveta, a sickly old woman, now told in Serbian, and Daisy translated, a miracle she had heard in Tebinje, the town where she was born in 1893.

A Turkish girl in Trebinje was all doubled up. No doctor could help her. So her parents finally took her to the shrine of Saint Basil in a basket up the mountain. They left the basket there all night. And when they came in the morning she was perfectly well and straight and walked down the mountain. The basket was placed at the foot of the coffin. The girl left a necklace of gold ducats in the chapel as her gift.

Then the people asked her what kind of a doctor is this Vlasha [a derogatory term used by the Turks against the Serbs]. She answered, "No doctor, just a stiffened Vlasha." And that night when she went to bed, her body was deformed again. In the morning she found the ducats under her pillow.

She went back two or three times again but was never cured.

The Wuletichs showed me pictures of the monastery of Saint Basil carved out of the mountainside, and Cveta graphically illustrated, with sudden animation and sweeping gestures along the wall, how the Nazis had bombed all around the shrine without ever effecting a direct hit. So the modern legend of Bishop Nastich has formed a link with the historic legend of Saint Basil. There is also a connection with Saint Sava, the patron saint of children, since the play was performed by children on January 31, the birthday of Bishop Nastich and the nearest Sunday in 1965 to January 27, the death day of Saint Sava.

Another evening found me in the home of Mrs. Emily B., a first cousin of the bishop, who had in her possession boxes full of letters, photographs, clippings and memorabilia of Varnava's career. Her father had come to Gary in 1906 from a town in Montenegro near that of Varnava's father and helped lay tracks for the streetcar. Her husband Djordje had fought with the Chetniks alongside Milane Spadijer. Emily, a sad, dark haired woman of fifty-six with a slight hunchback, confided to me that Montenegro was the cradle of Serbian culture, language, and songs. Her mother was the sister of Varnava's father, who founded the Saint Sava Church in Gary, and Emily herself had taken care of the boy, a few years her junior. It was clear that the bishop's tragedy was her obsession. She showed me a photograph of Varnava—ascetic, bespectacled, talking to another bishop, with a dim figure from the Udba, Tito's secret police, in the background beside an automobile—and another of his funeral (sent her by her uncle), his body resting in a plain open casket, while the patriarch-german can be seen in white cap instead of black, an obvious mark of disrespect. Emily told of the cruel "accident" planned by the Communists in 1949 when Varnava was being taken from the prison of Sjenica to that at Srem. The guards placed the prisoners in a car on a siding, and at about 1:00 A.M. the engine rammed into it at full steam. All but eleven were killed. Varnava was thrown out of the window with both legs and one arm broken. A witness immediately telephoned his brother. However the militia put a guard at the scene of the accident, and the Udba prevented medication being given or the insertion of metal pins in his heels. Varnava was placed in an army train without mattresses or covers and taken to a hospital in Srem.

Emily and her fellow Serbs in Gary had worked ceaselessly to obtain the release and return of the bishop, through pressure on the State Department and the Indiana senators. The Saint Sava group hoped that Varnava might even succeed Dionisije as the American bishop at Libertyville. After the 1963 edict of the mother church creating three North American bishops, Varnava entered the controversy with letters supporting the anti-Communist stand of the Serbian Free Church. Emily showed me some of his letters, written in mixed Serbian and English; the English prose was eloquent and idiomatic. Varnava never lost his American spirit, Emily said; when he first went to Yugoslavia he wrote how he missed his movie idols Tom Mix and William S. Hart, chewing gum, the funny papers, and electric light switches.

Had a *gusle* song been written about the bishop? I asked Emily. She produced a three-and-a-half-page typescript, running fifty-seven lines a page, titled *Smrt Vladike Varnave*, "The Death of Bishop Varnava," composed by Milisav Maksimovich, of Cincinnati, Ohio, and dated April 3, 1965.

The mother church group with whom I met at Rade R.'s house in East Chicago promptly deflated Varnava, saying the Gary people had made a legendary figure out of hot air. It was a myth that the Communists beat him up; actually he had jumped off a train. He was not a true diocesan bishop but an assistant vicar bishop. The fact was that by his fruitless outcries he had proved an embarrassment to the Serbian Church.

In the life story of Bishop Varnava Nastich, all the elements of Serbian-American tradition fuse. He was born in Gary and died in Beocin, reversing the usual immigrant process. Letters and visitors kept his memory green in Gary. He recited *gusle* legendary songs as a youthful singer, and after his death he became the subject of a *guslar* bard. A play was produced in Gary about his martyrdom. His life and death struggle against the Communist oppressor reenacts the heroic tragedies of earlier Serbians against the Turkish tyrants. He has become a potent symbol in the fateful church issue now splitting friends and families in Gary and East Chicago.

CROATIANS (FROM DIARY)

My next appointment was with Nick E., seventy-eight, retired, a great-grandfather. He lived out in the Glen Park section beyond the Northwest Campus. Nick was in the center of organized Croatian activities; he had been president of the Croatian Fraternal Union for a dozen years and was still honorary president. Although Nick called the Serbs Oriental and the Croats Western, there was an Oriental look about his large oval face. He did not speak or volunteer readily but seemed content to answer questions. Finally he remembered a ghost story he had heard on one of his five visits to Croatia. The spark ignited when I asked him about the Serbs. Now he uttered all the counter-charges to refute Walter T.'s venom of the day before, and I got this on tape. The Serbs had assassinated Stepan Radich, leader of the Peasant Party for an independent Croatia, in Congress House in Belgrade. Serbia was trying to dominate Croatia, which had formerly held Bosnia-Hercegovina and Dalmatia, within the second Yugoslavia. The Serbs were taking over the Croatian language. Serbia took the money from Croatian factories to rebuild Belgrade at the expense of Zagreb. Croatians pay twice as much tax as the Serbians, and in Yugoslavia a friend had denied this publicly but told him privately it was true. Nick would not associate with Serbians in Gary. They were fanatic royalists for Peter, the son of King Alexander now living in Paris. Alexander was assassinated in Marseille by Croats in revenge for Radich. Serbia had taken the rich Vojvodina from Croatia. Nick showed me the "Croatian Voice," *Hrvatski Glas,* published in Winnipeg. An issue of February 10, 1968, had an article about a Croatian priest, Professor Draganovich, being kidnapped by the Serbs from Rome and taken to Belgrade, and another entitled "Separation of Croatia from Yugoslavia," all in Croatian.

As I was getting ready to leave, Nick put on records of sweet *tamburitza* music he had purchased in Zagreb, brought out two *tamburs* he had ordered from Kos Slavko, near Zagreb, and showed me large color photographs of the *tamburitzan* groups he directed, about thirty young people. They would take part in a national festival in Des Plaines, Illinois, on July 7. He rehearsed them every Friday night in the Croatian Hall and also gave lessons in Croatian. A man in Gary, Milan Opacich, made *tamburs,* but Nick could get one from Yugoslavia for $50 instead of paying $175 for one here. The name of one song on the record was "Three Days She Was Picking the Corn," and Nick said most were folksongs.

A phone call came and Nick said he had to witness the signature of the will of an old friend of eighty-two, Zlatko K., who would be dead of cancer within three months. He insisted on taking me to the house nearby. Zlatko was toothpick thin, his skin tight; he was gaunt, hollow, emaciated, hairless, but spry of mind and ready to be interviewed. He began telling of his immigrant experiences, being fired the first day on his job in a sausage factory in Chicago for stepping on a lever that sent the meat flying all over the room. An attorney arrived to draw up the will, and after the business advised me to leave, but with the understanding that if Zlatko felt in the mood I could return. Two middle-aged tearful daughters were present. (*end diary*)

Croatian tradition proved a good deal thinner than Serbian. One Croatian told me that he had married a Lithuanian and that his children were ethnic mongrels; but the Serbs remained clannish and tended to marry among themselves. The comic experience recounted by Zlatko K. belongs not to Croatian but to general immigrant lore about mishaps on first landing in America. Bessie M., of Serbian descent, related how her father ate a banana, skin and all, his first day in New York and exclaimed he had never tasted anything so horrible. A Romanian restaurant owner, John N., recounted an involved saga of his arriving in Detroit in the middle of the night with forty dollars strapped around his waist, not a word of English at his command, and waiting for the cab driver to locate a Romanian speaker. These comparable incidents, at once ludicrous and pathetic, in totality comprise one large chapter of immigrant folk history.

GREEKS

At the International Institute I met the staff member who dealt with Greek families, Mrs. Stella D., a short, matronly, worried-looking woman born in Chicago but raised in Gary and active in Greek organizations there. Her father had been born in Athens and her mother in Smyrna. As president of the local Ahepa chapter, Stella had gone to Athens for the international congress in 1964. She enumerated a long list of Greek societies and clubs in town, saying they were often organized according to the regions or islands from which people came. I asked her about the evil eye, and she responded excitedly, saying she had learned the prayer to overcome its effects from her grandmother, but indirectly, by overhearing, since the prayer could only pass from man to woman and woman to man. It was necessary to burn three cloves and repeat the prayer; when the clove sparked, the spell was broken.[7]

"I've tried it on my daughters," Mrs. D. continued.

When I was young my grandmother did it to me often. I was sick and I'd perk up right away. Grandmother told me that a horse had fallen down on the street in Smyrna because someone had put the evil eye on it, without meaning to; she said the prayer and the horse got up. In Chicago a doctor friend used to come when he was feeling low and say, "Stella, tell me the prayer," and after it was said he'd feel better right away. Three cloves should be burned and placed in a little wine glass of water. Then say the prayer, bless the water with the sign of the cross and sprinkle it around. The prayer is repeated three times, with a count, 5–10–15–20–25 and so on. [She could not utter the prayer.]

On another occasion Stella introduced me to a client of hers, Emmanuel V., a friendly, clean-featured newcomer of thirty-eight who had been in Gary only four years, joining his father who had come from the isle of Kalymnos in the eastern Aegean in 1923. Emmanuel sold sponges and worked part time in the steel mills. In halting English, with the aid of Stella, he related an event that had caused a great stir on Kalymnos.

It happened in 1908 or 1909. There was a diver named Latare, he has a big rock in his hand weighing over thirty pounds, to weight him down, and no clothes. They drop him over the side of the ship, and he goes straight down about 175 feet. And a big shark was lying on its side, and its mouth was open. Latare went right through the mouth and the rock hit the stomach. And the shark threw the man out. The man on top pulls up the rope, so Latare came up, with marks all over his back. They had a big picture of him and the fish in the city hall. The king went to see him. People paid one Italian lira to look at him. Jim Z., who came here six years ago from Kalymnos, when he was 27, saw the picture. It was a miracle, the only time it ever happened.

Emmanuel invited me that evening to the East Side Coffee House off 7th Avenue where Greek men met to play cards, talk, and have light refreshment. When I arrived, he had stepped out, and I sat conspicuously alone, eying and being eyed by the groups of dark-haired, dark-complexioned men sitting around tables reading Greek newspapers, conversing in Greek, and eating a sweet Greek pastry called *galakton baurike*. The men were all ages, in working-class clothes; women were not permitted, and one came to the door, but no further, to signal her husband. After a while the owner, Delos K., heavy-set and serious of mien, sat at my table and began conversing in passable English. Delos had been born in 1918 in Tarpon Springs, Florida, the transplanted community of Greek sponge fishermen, but lived in Kalymnos from 1921 to 1933, when he returned to Tarpon Springs and became captain of a sponge fishing boat. He moved to Gary with his brother in 1947, when some chemical killed off the sponge beds.

While we talked, Emmanuel entered and joined us. Then others crowded around, and suddenly our table was the center of excited conversation about Kalymnos, about Latare the lucky diver, about Saint Nicholas, patron saint of fishermen. A pleasant young barber, the Jim Z. who had seen the picture of Latare, counted twenty men from Kalymnos around the room. One was a famous diver, now converted into a railroad switchman, a cousin of Emmanuel, burly and impassive, and out of the conversation because he had no English. Over the mantel rested an elegant ship model called the *Kalymnos*. From somewhere in the room Jim brought a couple of prize sponges, one long and tufted and shaped like a helmet. Now Denos produced a treasured book with a torn blue paper cover showing a suited diver holding a large sponge in one hand and a claw-like instrument in the other. It was titled *Strangers at Ithaca, The Story of the Spongers of Tarpon Springs*, written by George Th. Frantzis and published by the Great Outdoors Publishing Company in St. Petersburg, Florida, in 1962. He looked through it lovingly, the others clustering around, as he pointed to persons he knew in the photographs. One was of his mother, "Eleni Georgious K., one of the first Greek beauties to come to Tarpon Springs," showing just her head. She was strikingly beautiful, with madonna-like features framed in black hair. In an emotional gesture Denos gave me the book, along with a postcard picturing a rugged peak and sheltered bay of Kalymnos.

In my notebook Denos drew a rough map of the inland coast of Florida to illustrate how in 1935 the hurricane had hit every city from Palmyra to Pensacola save Tarpon Springs.

The sponge fishermen in Kalymnos give the sponges they get on their last day to Saint Nicholas. In Tarpon Springs they say Saint Nicholas saved them from the hurricane. In 1935 my uncle, who was in the Bahamas as a sponge buyer, came to visit us in Tarpon Springs. The radio announced the hurricane coming. My uncle had had experience with the hurricane every year in the Bahamas. He called my father, "Get up and get prepared." And my father said, "Don't worry, Saint Nicholas is going to take care of that. Go back to bed." And the hurricane hit all the other cities, went out to sea about a hundred and fifty miles and came back and hit Pensacola, below Tarpon Springs.

These Gary Greeks no longer knew the *paramythia*, the old folktales with which they used to while away evenings on the sponge boats. But traditions enveloped the East Side Coffee House, conveyed in the pictures of Kalymnos, the ship model, the sponges, the true tale of Latare, and the faith in Saint Nicholas.

MEXICANS (FROM DIARY)

I was introduced to Victor L., a young, positive fellow with pockmarked skin, who promptly invited me to his Adult Citizens English class at Riley School that evening. Then I was off to William L., who had invited me to a Mexican meal when I called at 4:00 P.M. His wife, Tilly, was an attractive dark-haired girl about thirty years of age, with boys of two and four. Bill was sturdy, full-faced, serious, darker than she. Tilly did not look Mexican, except for a slight olive complexion. They were second generation but filled with tradition, or aware of it. Tilly was one of thirteen children. Her dad had come from Mexico at twenty-six, fifty-three years before, from Yuriria, Guanajauto, which she had visited, and was thankful she had been born in the States. Her mother came from Jalisco, and recalled being helped off a train by Pancho Villa. Tilly had once dated a Greek boy of means, but with the understanding that both their parents would arrange their marriages. Tilly and Bill began telling me various Mexican folklore matters: about the *mariachi*, popular singing groups with stringed instruments bringing seventy five to one hundred dollars an hour in the area; how Thomas Alva Edison was really Mexican; an account of La Llorona mixed with the female ghost of Cline Avenue, actually seen by Tilly's brother, a cab driver, who was interviewed on TV; the potato water cure of Tilly's mother to preserve her black hair and save that of her brother-in-law, which was coming out in patches. "She advised him to use water from boiled potatoes for three months." I recorded them.

Dinner was a regular Mexican meal of stew beef, yellow rice, and beans. Tilly and Bill told me that *enchiladas* and *tacos* were only used on special occasions. Everything they said I found of interest. Their church, "Our Lady of Guadalupe," in the Harbor, was having trouble keeping its parishioners, though it was the only Mexican church in town. The priests were Irish (Father Flanagan) or English (Father Meade), and when Tilly's family sponsored Father Frias from Mexico, well-spoken and handsome, the people flocked to hear him. A substantial sum was raised to send to Mexico, for a church or hospital, whereupon Father Flanagan got mad and refused to let Father Frias speak again. Tilly said that at the *mariachi* dances the "Mexican would come out" even in Americans, in the *grito*, a protracted yell. The church was losing parishioners because the younger people—and older ones—were moving out, and the Texans planned only to stay ten years and then return. Her family kept going to the old church for sentimental reasons, although they were closer to St. Mary's. Tilly remarked that the Mexicans did not stick together, as did the Serbians. Two rivals had lost out in the election for state representative to a non-Mexican, by one hundred votes. She and Bill had had to leave their Ivy Street apartment because the Serbian landlord was renting to Serbs. Pride and stubbornness were downfall traits of the Mexicans. Tilly mentioned a University of California book, *Mexican-Americans in a Midwest Metropolis*, that was so inflammatory—it described Mexican laborers being loaded into boxcars—that it could not be sold locally.[8]

After dinner I followed Bill across town to his foster mother's, around the corner from the old church in Indiana Harbor. Mrs. Tomasita G., a tiny, wrinkled, Indian-featured old lady, had been born in 1893 in Doctor Arroyo, south of Monterrey, and had come to East Chicago in 1917. Later Bill told me that she took a raw egg with garlic every morning, washed her eyes with lemon juice, had all her teeth, and had begun to wear glasses only two years before. She was a *curandera*, and her cures were based on faith. "She must be a devout Catholic," I observed tritely. "No, she's a Mormon," said Bill. "She goes to Highland to services there twice on Sunday, morning and afternoon." And not to the Catholic church next door, that Bill and Tilly drove across town to attend.

Mrs. G. had raised Bill and his three siblings, Texas-born, by herself, since he was three. When he entered her miniature apartment, he kissed her respectfully on the hand and cheek. We sat in a tiny dressing area in front of her four-poster bed, and she related cures for *susto* in Spanish, which Bill then translated. He volunteered a cure she had done for him when he was eight ("I was leery of it until then"); she had bathed him in a raw egg at night, which was cooked in the morning, and the fever gone. Another charm, involving a prayer written on paper strips and placed on four corners of the bed, drove away cockroaches. We only had a little time before the 7:00 P.M. class, which by coincidence the old lady was attending. A friend came in, a funny old gal with expressive gestures, Elisa D., from Michoacan, Mexico, and she told a comical *cuento* into the tape, a noodle tale, which Bill translated. Then we all drove off to Riley School. It turned out that Victor L. and Bill M. had gone to school and worked in the mill together. Victor pulled out of the class a grizzled Mexican, and found a classroom for us to talk in. He was Ray A. of East Chicago, born in La Barca, Jalisco, in 1901; he came to Arizona in 1921 and to East Chicago the next year. His English was fair, but he preferred Spanish. After some questioning I struck responses with La Llorona, *susto*, *brujería*, and Pancho Villa. His mother had given him a cure for *biles*, a virulent kind of *susto* causing throwing up and eventually death. A main ingredient was sour tamarind. After he left, Bill M., who had been translating, spoke of his difficulty in following the Spanish; he was just too much out of practice, although he sometimes used it at the mill or with the old folks. But in Mexico he felt at a loss. Puerto Ricans spoke very rapidly when they first came. He mentioned hybrid words, English with Spanish endings, like *watcheli*. He had learned to read Spanish by reading the Bible three times in Spanish.

Now Victor L. joined us and spoke in a very interesting and informed way about the language business and Puerto Rican-Mexican conflicts. He was the son of old Mexicans; and his sister, two years older, had had a terrible time learning English in school until her teacher told her father to speak English to her. Victor then had no trouble. He had kept up his Spanish with his parents later, in the store and in the mill. He had an A.B. and an M.A. in Education from Indiana University. His wife of four years was Puerto Rican, of a high-rank family. He had flown at Christmas time to San Juan to get parental consent, while his brothers-in-law on the island had been afraid to approach the father. A couple of aunts, who were around her constantly, were from Spain. Victor attacked a number of stereotypes: that the Puerto Ricans all had

Negro blood (his wife was a redhead, and there were plenty of blondes), that they didn't practice discrimination (there were ghettos in Puerto Rico), that they spoke so rapidly. Every other Spanish-speaking group was supposed to talk rapidly. He agreed with Bill M. that Harbor Spanish was a thing unto itself (citing a master's thesis by a Freddie Maraville), and he gave examples. He would use *autobús* in San Juan and be corrected to *huahua* and then be laughed at back home. He spoke of the warmth and hospitality of the Puerto Ricans, and also of the Mexicans. He had never expected to marry a Puerto Rican girl. Mexicans felt they could look down on Puerto Ricans because of their Negro blood. All Latins loved their mother and their country. Pride was one reason for their not learning English, and another was housing discrimination forcing them into Mexican ghettos. Two-thirds of the Puerto Ricans put their country first; they were the nationalists and territorialists. Mexicans were good workers and could take the heat in Open Hearth #2 at Inland. (*end diary*)

PUERTO RICANS (FROM DIARY)

In Gary I had an appointment with A.M. in the National Bank Building. I arrived before he did in his plush office on the ninth floor—one of the few such offices I had encountered. He turned out to be youngish, yellow-skinned, square-faced, deliberate, and slow-speaking. He was an upper-class Puerto Rican, with French and Spanish blood, he said. He had an A.B. from Northwest Campus of Indiana University and his law degree from Valparaiso University, with other education in Europe. Our conversation was halting; I asked questions and he gave slow answers. He did not see much difference between Puerto Ricans and Mexicans; the food was pretty much the same. (But Mrs. Carmen R., a Puerto Rican married to a doctor from the Dominican Republic, had given me a long list of typical Puerto Rican dishes.) Puerto Ricans were not used to cold weather when they came to Gary. Most came from the small towns, not San Juan, and had been agriculturists, but since the 1940s, under Operation Bootstrap, 185 new industries had opened in Puerto Rico. Mexicans were nationalistic; they think they will make money and return home. I began cautiously to ask him about *brujería,* and finally drew a spark. "I had a client the other day that said her husband's girl friend was trying to destroy her with the *brujería,* and that she had heard voices. They stick pins in a doll, with the person's name on it. I tried to talk her out of it." He knew of the *botánica* shop that sold herbs, seeds, candles, and *escapularios* of cotton with the Virgin or a saint on them, to use against the *brujería,* and gave me the name of a former owner, Mrs. Pilar F., who was herself accused of being a *bruja.* I asked about *susto,* and he did not know of any connection with *brujería* but called out to his secretary, a pretty young Mexican, if she knew of such a connection and was surprised to hear her say yes. He gave me a note of introduction to take to Mrs. F.

On the way out I asked the secretary, Carmen M., about *susto.* Her mother had a recipe: suspend the egg over the sick person, then place it in a glass of water, and drop in crosses made of broom straws or toothpicks, which will float. In the morning the egg may be cooked, depending on the sickness. But she had not tried it. "I don't want to get involved."

Now I decided to try Pilar, who lived in the Brunswick section of Gary, a quiet neighborhood with small homes and plots of ground between them. An enormously fat, blubbery dark woman, slightly Oriental in aspect and somewhat sinister looking, was carrying a bundle of clothing out the door. She called Pilar when I showed her my letter. Pilar was a half-sister to this one, lighter, fat but not so fat, with more regular features, open and pleasant, and speaking good English. She took me right inside and after reading A.M.'s note answered everything I asked, while trying to silence an unquenchable two-year-old, an adopted son, Carlito. She gave me an LP record of Puerto Rican music, containing traditional *plena* songs (like calypsos), and said that a local orchestra played such songs at the Puerto Rico Demo Club at birthday parties—piano, trumpet, guitar, saxophone, soloist. Yes, they made up local *plenas.* Now I questioned Pilar about her life history. She was born in 1932 in Santurce del Barrio, in a very poor section called Tras Talleres, the only child of parents who had each been married before, giving her stepbrothers and stepsisters. In 1949 she went to live with her half-brother in New York, and attended P.S. 101, at 111th between Lexington and Madison. Pilar retraced her career in close detail: a return to Puerto Rico to attend her sick mother, a course in New

York in practical nurse's training, while living with her half-brother, who was a cook's helper for twenty-five years in the Hotel Vanderbilt; a decision to move to Washington, because of unspecified trouble in her brother's family; her failure to get a nurse's position in Walter Reed Hospital because she arrived ten minutes late for the test, not knowing the Pentagon was across the Washington, D.C., boundary in Virginia; her loneliness in Washington, where there were only twenty to thirty Puerto Ricans; her job in charge of linen at the Shoreham Hotel—she was ever after soured against nursing; the return to New York, and her decision, because of the noise, to find another place where she could live with Puerto Ricans; the move to Gary in 1957, as a result of a letter from a hometown friend living there; her first income from using her fifteen-dollar jalopy to drive Puerto Ricans and Negroes daily to a clinic at Michigan City, making fifteen dollars a day by charging each $3; a move to East Chicago and a job there as typist with the city; a year in Chicago at Oak Forest Hospital; a return to East Chicago to work in politics for Mayor Nicosia on behalf of the Puerto Ricans; laborer in Inland Steel, in the tin mill; marriage in 1963; present job as jail matron, which she enjoyed. Her husband Lorenzo had worked in Youngstown [steel mill in East Chicago] seventeen years, knew no English, and even spoke Spanish poorly, but he had made $11,000 the past year as second helper in the blast furnace, where only he could speak Spanish. When it was necessary to communicate in English, he wrote messages. While we were talking, he came in, a slender, sallow man with a small mustache and a furtive look, but he offered me a cup of coffee in friendly fashion.

In all this Pilar had not mentioned the *botánica*, so I brought it up, and she looked a little surprised but giggled and spoke most openly about the whole business. So I brought in the tape recorder, and she told all her secrets to it. A.M. said I should not mention *brujería* but let Pilar bring it up, but she showed no hesitation at all in talking about the matter. "The Spanish people believe in voodoo, and they come buy herbs and take a bath in it and say it will bring good luck." There were about twenty-five *botánicas* in Chicago, and many in New York. Her own, run by her sister in East Chicago, had had to close as a result of the criticism of the churches, Catholic and Protestant. The Catholics imposed a course called *curcillistra* [*cursillo*], which cost $37 to $40 for three days, and which even her half-sister took. Pilar regarded the *botánica* as a drugstore, to sell supplies to people affected with *brujería*. While we were talking she brought out charcoal, incense, and seeds and burned them in a little dish, describing the procedure for the tape-recorder. Usually she did this Fridays at midnight, and she always stayed home Fridays (hence I had come on the right day). She said, giggling—and she giggled all the way through—that her husband told her the incense was to make him stay at home. Pilar had learned about voodoo—she fumbled for the word on the tape—from a spiritual meeting she had attended as a young girl in Puerto Rico, which she described graphically. At the end she mentioned a fly from Spain, *moscas cantareas*, black and blue, which made a z-z-z-sound, and was considered very lucky. Well, she and other *botánicas* would sell substitute flies, or substitute incense, when they couldn't get the real articles, and this led to a crackdown by the government. These articles were used to bring good luck in the numbers game; even snakes were sold, and she mentioned one good-luck snake that would curl up on the sofa. She said all this frankly into the tape. On leaving I offered to pay Pilar for the record, but she refused any money. (*end diary*)

CONCLUSIONS

A field trip of twenty-three days cannot of course answer the theoretical questions framed at the outset of this inquiry. Still from the numerous interviews and the data obtained in notebooks and on tape and in the form of donated publications and other materials, plus of course the strong impressions derived from personal observation, I put forward the following concepts of modern urban folklore. How well they will stand up after further work in the Gary-East Chicago area and to what extent they may apply in other metropolitan localities remains to be seen, but I advance them with some conviction.

1. *Paucity of Conventional Folklore.* The old familiar genres of folklore, particularly the tale and song, do not seem abundant in the city. Even jokes, the modern folktale, are forbidden in the steel mills for fear their ethnic slurs may arouse hostility. One can of

course find storytellers and folksingers in the city, and in the country village not every soul is an active tradition carrier by a long shot. But genre folklore has become increasingly displaced by other kinds of oral tradition, which deserve the attention of collectors. A good example was my evening in the Greek coffee-house, that might as well have been on the Aegean isle of Kalymnos, which indeed most of the men present claimed as their birthplace. They were eager to tell me all they knew of Greek life and lore, and other people had told me no group was so clannish as the Greeks. None could tell *paramythia,* the popular fictions with which the sponge fishermen had regaled each other in the old days and in the Old Country; yet traditions of other kinds retained a powerful hold upon them. Among the blacks and other ethnic groups I encountered a generally similar response. My closest Negro friend, Harold M., Mississippi born and bred, was exceedingly articulate but not on matters of southern lore. The steelworkers' union of which he was an official dominated his thoughts and conversation. He finally did tell me two anecdotes; one was a civil-rights joke and the other dealt with an eccentric millworker. When tales and songs are collected, as in the Polish folksongs recorded by Pawlowska and the Armenian folktales recorded by Hoogasian-Villa in Detroit, they may belong to an inactive memory culture rather than to a vigorous living growth.[9]

2. *Richness of Cultural Traditions and Personal Histories.* If the conventional genres are hard to come by, folklore, or perhaps better folk culture, is nevertheless present and pervasive. American folklorists—and this certainly includes myself—have sought for texts and largely overlooked other kinds and forms of cultural traditions less easy to report. Among the Negroes, the Baptist church is in most of its manifestations a folk institution transplanted from the South. I was told there were over two hundred such churches in Gary. The ethnomusicologist and student of folk music can have a field day analyzing the combination of choral and instrumental, country and city, gospel and rhythm elements in these church performances. For the Serbians, calendar feast days play a pivotal role in their lives, both the saints' day celebrations associated with each family and the great church holy days. In a number of ethnic societies, choral and dance groups perform regularly, such as the Croa-

tian *tamburitzan* club. On my last evening in Gary I attended a Serbian entertainment in Saint Sava Hall, the basement auditorium of the church, and saw local girl dancers, a singer, and two flailing accordionists; and finally, with the chairs cleared, a circular *cola* dance with adults and children all joining hands. The whole program was in Serbian, and one could see before one's eyes youngsters absorbing Serbian traditional song, music, and dance. To the religious and social occasions should be added the celebration of national holidays, like the Mexican one on September 16, a festal pageant with floats and a proud team of *charros*, the costumed horsemen.

Ethnic cuisine is still another flourishing form of tradition among every sizable group: the southern whites, the southern Negroes, the east Europeans, the Latins. A truck driver for Inland Steel from Kentucky discoursed rhapsodically in Mrs. Green's hotel about the heaping platters of farm fare back home. As noted above, one Negro middle-class lady from Memphis said that soul food kept the colored people from getting the rare diseases of the whites. A Puerto Rican housewife indignantly denied that Puerto Ricans had no dishes of their own to compare with those nationally publicized by the Mexicans, and she reeled off a string of recipes. The best restaurant in Gary, now enveloped by the Negro ghetto, was Greek. Ethnic restaurants tended to take on the character of social clubs. From southern hillbilly to Romanian, the people of Steel City cherished their foods.

Another dimension of folk culture to be fathomed is personal history. There are thousands of sagas created from life experiences that deserve, indeed cry for, recording. The folklorist need not worry about their relation to the oral genres. Here are precious oral narratives dealing with a series of great folk movements—from the southern states, from Mexico and Puerto Rico, from eastern Europe—and this migration should be described in terms of humanity as well as of mass statistics. No discipline other than folklore looks in this direction. Oral history is concerned with the elite, anthropology with underdeveloped countries, sociology with social organization. The personal history may well be a genre of its own, honed and structured through periodic retellings. It is at any rate a fluent oral form on the lips of a number of tellers. Several memorable life stories came to my ears with virtually no prompting. The relation by seventy-three-year-old Laura P., the frail mother of a double amputee, Bill, about the long travail and cheerful endurance of her son, fits into no known formula. It was a heart-rending account of hospitalization and surgery, despair and grief, but without particular overtones of prejudice or poverty. On reflection the history seems to belong with what Charles Keil has called the role of the Negro in America as one long sacrificial ritual. Victor L., who had come from Mexico in 1906; Edward B., who had been born in the Guiana forest; Zlatko K. from Croatia, dying of cancer at eighty-two—all launched promptly into detailed life histories. Certain incidents are clearly traditional, such as the comic misadventures of the newly arrived immigrant.

3. *The Role of the Spoken Word.* The culture of Gary-East Chicago is largely an oral culture, in the sense that talk flows freely. Television has not displaced conversation; the Book-of-the-Month Club pretensions of the middle class are little in evidence. Especially is this true for the Negro, bearing out the claims of Abrahams and Keil that the black ghetto is an auditory and tactile as opposed to a visual and literate culture, with the man of words as the culture hero. In the immigrant groups the potential man of words is often hampered by his inadequacy with English, although the desire to communicate will not be denied. I think of the long evening with Walter and Milly T. in which they conveyed all kinds of information through a limited English vocabulary. The Negro man of words appeared as preacher-entertainer, gospel singer turned preacher plus steelworker, athlete turned preacher plus steelworker, and preacher turned civil rights leader. The three superb speeches given in the Calvary Baptist Church during Negro history week, by a young bank manager, a lady sociologist, and a city official stand out in my mind in contrast to the suffocatingly dull seminar on Gary's Model City project held at Bloomington, at which professional educators mouthed their irrelevant jargon.

4. *The Role of the Book.* If this is not a highly literate society, nevertheless it is a society that greatly values special book publications for their symbolic value. In one group after another I encountered references to, demonstration of, and sometimes even the bestowal of a cherished tome. These books shared two common fac-

tors: they were far off the main stream of American publishing, often being issued with obscure imprints, and they served to reinforce cherished elements of the folk inheritance. When Chetniks spoke of their sufferings at the hands of the hated Ustashis and recorded on tape examples of atrocities they had personally beheld, they regularly alluded to and produced printed evidence to substantiate their statements, such as the pamphlet Walter T. gave me, *The Crime of Genocide*, and the book, *Genocide in Satellite Croatia*, mentioned previously. My last evening in Gary I saw Walter at the dance entertainment in St. Sava Hall, again distributing paperback books in Serbian. They were by Lazo Kostich, now living in Switzerland, and author of over fifty books documenting the atrocities that had taken the lives of two million Serbs in World War II. "He is defending my blood," said Walter simply. In the Greek coffeehouse, owner Delos K. proudly brought forth a history of the Greek settlement of sponge fishermen at Tarpon Springs, Florida, *Strangers at Ithaca*.

Another kind of book reinforcement supported ethnic pride in historical achievements customarily ignored in majority group histories. An eloquent Polish patriot in Gary with his own Polish-language radio program, T. Stan Dubiak, told me that there were 127 Polish-American organizations in Lake County. He complained about the Poles being left out of American history and triumphantly produced a volume, *Jamestown Pioneers from Poland 1608–1958*, documenting the presence of Polish colonists at Jamestown. In my interview with seventy-year-old Todd R., a retired Negro steelworker born in Alabama, I was astonished at his ability to produce little-known facts, names, and dates of black history, coupled with his dearth of folklore. Eventually he showed me two battered booklets, an *Afro-American World Almanac* and *A Tribute to Achievement*. Similarly Elder George M. in his preaching at the Primitive Baptist Church, although he could not read, relied for his impressive citations of Negro accomplishments on a book his wife read to him, *World's Great Men of Color 3000 B.C. to 1946 A.D.*

Books could be feared as well as cherished. The work of Samora and Lamanna, *Mexican-Americans in a Midwest Metropolis: A Study of East Chicago*, is a case in point. The fury it aroused in the Mexican community made the sale of the work impossible. The concept of the book in these instances is wholly different from the attitude toward books of casual book buyers and book readers. These books have a talismanic character, and they are unique, not simply titles in a library.

5. *Other Artifacts of Tradition.* If a symbolic book serves as an artifact tangibly reinforcing the traditional culture, it can be joined by many other artifacts of more than sentimental worth. These physical objects decorate the home or clubroom and fill the closets and drawers, and the ethnofolklorist should seek to inventory them. They may take the form of old country costumes for ceremonial occasions, portraits of national heroes like Draža Mihajlovich, musical instruments like the *gusle* and *tambur*, or recordings obtained from the old country. Walter T. played for me a tape recording he had made in Belgrade of a record of a Serbian folksong being played on a local radio station. In the Greek coffeehouse a ship model named *Kalymnos* and two giant sponges refreshed club members' memories of their island birthplace and occupation. As the folklorist today is enlarging his vision to include folklife, so in dealing with nationality groups he should pay special heed to the transported and imported items of material culture that help to bridge the chasm between the Old World and the New.

6. *Reinforcement.* The two preceding points lead into a related matter, the idea of reinforcement of the parent culture through continuous contacts. This concept, which I earlier suggested in *American Folklore*, contradicts the stereotype of the immigrant, northern Negro, Appalachian white, urban Puerto Rican, or Mexican as cut off abruptly and irrevocably from his traditions in an alien and hostile environment.[10] In one instance after another, in every one of these groups, the evidence accumulates as to the continuing links with the *heimat*, through visits—by the American-born as well as the foreign-born or northern-born—correspondence, bringing of relatives or mates to the metropolis, and subscription to foreign-language periodicals and newspapers. The case of Bishop Varnava Nastich is a classic example of the linkage between Europe and America, reversing the immigration pattern as the Gary-born Serb returned to Yugoslavia to become the first American bishop in the Serbian Orthodox Church and a rallying figure for Gary anti-Communists. The bishop's cousin in Gary, Emily B.,

possesses extensive files on Nastich—reams of eloquent letters, half in English, half in Serbian; photographs; and clippings from American newspapers and Serbian publications. Daisy Wuletich and her mother described to me in close detail their visit with the bishop in the monastery in Beocin. The Nastich episode of course involves high drama, but in the regular course of events the dwellers in Gary and East Chicago scheduled trips to their places of birth or those of their parents.

The effect of this intermittent but consistent reinforcement needs to be measured. Once Harold M. told me that the pastor at his church, Trinity Baptist, had noticeably reverted to southern-style preaching after a vacation in Arkansas. Further inquiry can lead to subdivisions within the transplanted cultures. The Gary Greeks meet in separate coffeehouses according to their islands or mainland communities of origin; the blacks join churches whose pastors come from their own southern states; the Croats in northwest Indiana address each other by nicknames designating the valleys and hillsides of their youth. Presumably reinforcement from these distinguishable backgrounds will show different shadings, just as dialects vary between regions.

7. *Cultural Pluralism.* The generalizations offered under the preceding headings must be countered by another generalization, that each cultural group is unique in terms of its folklore retentions and pattern of assimilation and acculturation. Negroes may look upon all white people as "Whitey," northerners may lump Mexicans and Puerto Ricans together as Latins, WASPs may speak in the aggregate of eastern Europeans, city dwellers may call all southern migrants hillbillies, and these terms themselves are revealing of cultural attitudes and stereotypes. One does not need to spend much time in the field to appreciate the considerable differences that exist between ethnic and racial groups in their degree of folk-cultural tenacity.

The Serbs and the Croats provide a good illustration, since they are usually conjoined in the minds of outsiders, and their language, although written in different alphabets, is called Serbo-Croatian. But the Serbs are much more tradition-oriented than the Croats. One reason is the Church and another is the State. The Serbian Orthodox Church unites the American Serbs—or disunites them into two warring factions in the present ecclesiastical dispute—but it at least keeps aflame their national conscience. The Croats are swallowed up in the Roman Catholic Church and will mingle more with other Catholic ethnic groups such as the Poles and Italians. Serbia has its history as an independent state and a subjugated nation under the Turks to inspire her expatriates with heroes, legends, and tragic epics; but Croatia was a province submerged in the Austro-Hungarian empire, with little historical tradition to call its own. As John Sertich put it, the Croats were tribal rather than national, never having had their own king. The legend of Bishop Varnava Nastich grew out of the Gary Serbian community and could never have developed among the Gary Croatians. This is not to deny the American Croats their ties to old country and their interest in folk music and costume, as in the *tamburitzan* ensembles. The question here is one of degree and density of cultural conservatism.

Similar contrasts came to the surface after some inquiries about differences between Mexicans and Puerto Ricans. The latter fitted more easily into Gary-East Chicago because they had already lived under the American flag. The former supposedly worked better in the steel mills because they were accustomed to heat. Mexicans wed Indians and Puerto Ricans wed Negroes. In terms of tradition, the Mexican seemed much stronger, again because of a national history as a frame of reference. Mexican ethnic cuisine has become part of the national restaurant business, while Puerto Rican dishes are unknown.

One factor in assessing cultural pluralism and its effect on folklore is the dilution that occurs, or may occur, through intermarriage. A Croat who had married to a Lithuanian said that his children had no tradition. A young Mexican woman related she had once dated a Greek boy, but with the understanding that they would never marry, for the Greeks always stayed together. Marty G., the son of a Mexican father and a southern Appalachian mother whom I recorded for a long pleasant hour, called himself a "Mexican hillbilly," but his inheritance appeared to be all on the hillbilly side. He spoke with intimate knowledge, sympathy, and wit about the "stumpjumpers," "ridgerunners," and "crackers" of the South. My own judgment, until other evidence appears, is that ethnic traditions do not blend in a mixed marriage but either cancel each other out or result in one triumphing.

8. *Ethnic Separatism.* The present urban field experience supports my previous findings in rural areas that the strong force of what I call ethnic separatism keeps the in-group folklores apart; they cannot cross into each other's zones. It is the individual who must cross into the life experience of another group to absorb the traditions of that group. Twice I recorded tales in East Chicago from Puerto Ricans married to Negro women who had never heard, and expressed astonishment at, their husbands' narrations. Puerto Ricans and Mexicans share the same language and faith, but their folklore follows different channels. The Puerto Rican *botánica* or magic herb store and Mexican *curandera* or magic healer are separate and distinct. *Susto* has special connotations to Mexicans and Mexican-Americans, who believe that *susto* is induced by some supernatural or magical means; but the Puerto Rican lawyer representing the Latin American organization of Gary and East Chicago and who knew all about the *botánica*, drew a blank on any special significance of *susto*, and was astonished to learn that his Mexican secretary did react to the word.

Folk prejudices as well as cultural inertia contribute to ethnic separatism. In a conversation with Katie S. about the soul food prized by the blacks, I thought to ask her if she had ever tried Mexican dishes. Yes, she had tried *tacos* and rather liked them until she heard they were made from dead cats. Calling on a Slovak celebrating his fiftieth wedding anniversary, I elicited no folklore but did receive one double-barreled folk hatred: "I never see a picture like mine [of his golden wedding] for a Czech; they have twenty wives, like niggers."

9. *The Urban Synthesis.* Yet if the migrant groups in Steel City never penetrate each other's folklore, or perhaps even each other's homes, they do share the environment, the living experience, and perforce the lore of their new abode. People are marked by living in Gary or East Chicago, for these are uncommon cities, just as the Upper Peninsula of Michigan is an uncommon region leaving its imprint on all its inhabitants. The pervasive themes of Gary-East Chicago binding its people into a new folk community are steel, crime, and the racial-ethnic mix.

Steel created Gary, and the great mills whose furnaces must burn twenty-four hours a day is the number one fact of life in

Gary and its environs. Some day perhaps an urban folklorist will write a "Folklore of the Steel Industry" to match Mody Boatright's *Folklore of the Oil Industry*. Meanwhile anyone can hear little stories about steelworkers, for instance about problems in communication. A Romanian crane operator worked for thirty-nine years in Inland Steel without learning English. During my stay an injured worker brought to the infirmary at Inland could not make his ailment known, although a nurse present tried speaking to him in Polish. The staff had to send back to the patient's unit to learn he was a Serb. These incidents get talked about and lay the ground for a new body of anecdotes based on the age-old motif of language misunderstanding. The human side of steel inevitably involves ethnic and racial humor and *blason populaire*. Crime stories and fears are an outgrowth of the contemporary industrial city and the Negro ghetto. Everyone is apprehensive—whites and blacks—and talk swirls around hold-ups, beatings, and murders. One of my informants, Marty G., father of seven, was murdered with his wife not long after I recorded him; no clues, no motives. Another, a Serbian priest, has since been fatally assaulted. One evening when I was interviewing a group of East Chicago Serb adherents to the mother church, one man present, a policeman, interrupted the thread of our discussion to tell about several recent crime incidents. At the time I was impatient to get back to our main topic, but now I realize that he was dealing with a central theme of Gary-East Chicago lore. One incident dealt with the refusal of a storeowner and his wife, who had just been robbed, to identify their Negro assailant, found with their goods and the owner's wallet in his car. After the suspect's release, the police officer asked the couple why they had refused to make the identification. "Well, we have to live there after you leave. Let them have a few bundles of clothes. Better than to have his friends come back and burn the place down."

A brief summary of a long evening's conversation with three southern-born Negroes, all steelworkers, may further illustrate the newly evolving urban synthesis. They were my friend Harold M., an official in a labor union; Ben D., a former professional gospel singer now preacher at the Macedonian Baptist Church; and Ben T., his former manager and now his deacon. The first half of the conversation turned on life in the South, on methods of cotton-picking, frauds in the poultry business run by Italians in New Orleans, and managing spiritual singers. During these recollections I was able to record half a dozen familiar folktales, such as "Dividing Souls" and "Why the Fox Has a Short Tail." For the second part of the evening the talk shifted to northern life, the labor unions, the Syndicate, and the political machine. Ben T. made sweeping and authoritative pronouncements: 85 percent of the people in Gary were from the South; Gary, and the world at large, were run by syndicates. Harold and he fell to comparing personalities in the unions and swapped accounts of the attempt by Democratic party forces to bribe union officials to swing votes against Dick Hatcher. Union grievance committeemen had each been given $250; half of them simply pocketed the money without acting. Louis talked at length about "snitching." Down south the black snitcher ran to Uncle Charlie, who protected him from the law, but up north the whites were the worst snitchers. The snitchers often had done the job themselves. One who was caught begged not to be sent to the "Peniten" but to the State Prison, because he knew he would be killed by the people he had snitched on. Louis ended these remarks by saying that Gary is the city of steel and that life revolved around the pay check every two weeks. Harold, a good talker but no storyteller, did think of two steel mill stories, one about an eccentric worker called "Old Man Shouting Robertson" and another about a lazy dog named Superintendent.

This full measure of talk, grossly synopsized here, suggests the shift from southern memories to northern conditions in the minds of migrants from the South, and the dominant themes of the races —petty and major crime and work in the steel plants, generating factual and finally fictional anecdotes. In the course of my sojourn I heard two fantasies in what may be an evolving legend of Richard Hatcher, the first Negro mayor of Gary. The more naturalistic ascribed to him a romance with a Jewish woman in Glen Park, which had gained him the Jewish vote, ordinarily bitterly anti-Negro. The second, propounded by a visiting television personality calling himself Psychic, held that Hatcher was actually the reincarnation of a southern white slave owner. This I heard from Harold M. Separate and divided as are the ethnic-race groups of Gary, all share participation in, and reaction to, the election of their Negro mayor. From this shared experience emerges the lore of the city.

These currents of city talk sometimes carry floating seeds of legend. On three occasions I heard the related legends of the Vanishing Hitchhiker and La Llorona, localized on Cline Avenue in East Chicago and the swampy Cudahy strip between East Chicago and Gary. A young Mexican-American, Tilly L., told me that her brother, a cab-driver, had been interviewed on television after picking up a woman often sighted and picked up on Cline Avenue by passing motorists, who found her gone from their vehicles when they arrived at the address she gave them as her destination. The newspapers had publicized the story. The related incident concerned a passionate murder of a woman in Cudahy whose wraith was frequently seen and identified by the Mexicans with La Llorona, the weeping lady-ghost mourning her lost children. An elderly but vigorous Mexican, Victor L., who narrated to me his life story for two hours without drawing breath, knew at firsthand the Cudahy murderer, a fellow-worker in the mill, and had seen his shooting of a husky man who tried to stop him the night he ran amok. Victor's son, born in East Chicago, explained that La Llorona was adapted to local events.

10. *Exceptions to Stereotypes.* A plurality of cultures exists in Steel City, going their own ways and not simmering in a melting pot. But if it is a mistake to treat all these folk cultures as equal in their rate of acculturation, it is a comparable error to treat all the individuals in the same cultural group as interchangeable parts. In the American scene—with its high mobility and unexpected juxtapositions, accentuated in urban settings—endless surprises occur. The individual breaks out of his stereotype frequently enough so that deviation itself becomes an acceptable concept.

A number of examples came to my attention in the Gary-East Chicago field trip. The most dramatic involved the Polish precinct-worker of the Democratic party, Marion Tokarsky, who broke with her ethnic, political, and religious allegiances to make common cause with the ghetto Negroes and support the Negro mayoralty candidate. Here was an unpredictable phenomenon, the Polish Catholic immigrant befriending her Negro enemies and explaining to them the supernatural-Catholic basis of her decision, to which they responded in the style and manner of the Baptist congregation. Other illustrations of deviancy can be given. The seventy-five-year-old Mexican *curandera* in Indiana Harbor, Mrs. Tomasita G., who dictated formulaic cures for *susto* in Spanish into my tape-recorder, proved to be a Mormon. On Sundays she made two trips to Highland to attend services at the Mormon church there, although the old Catholic church was just around the corner, and her foster-son and his wife came across town out of loyalty to that church, when they could have gone to a nearer Catholic church in East Chicago. The president of the Northern Indiana Political Action Alliance that Marion Tokarsky addressed was not a southern or northern Negro but a native of British Guiana, who in his youth identified with the British ruling class and looked down upon the East Indian servants on his plantation. When Edward B. came to the United States, he was astonished to discover that Negroes were second-class citizens. He had married a Negro woman from Georgia.

In the *Indiana Alumni Magazine* I read about Fedor C., who had come to America as a refugee from the Nazis and Communists, knowing no English. He had worked in the steel mills, taken courses, and become chairman of the political science department at the Northwest Campus of Indiana University. In Gary I spent an evening with Fedor and his wife Astrid and discovered that, while no fact in the magazine account was untrue, the stereotype presented was completely false. The couple were gifted and attractive intellectuals, university-trained, cosmopolitan, and sophisticated. Their life stories, which they told readily into the tape recorder, are extraordinary human documents; but they have no relation to the conventional saga of the immigrant. Again, from Victor L., Jr., I heard contradictions of the Puerto Rican stereotype, for instance, that all Puerto Ricans had Negro blood and hence would move into and marry within the American Negro community. There were indeed Puerto Rican Negro couples whom I met in East Chicago. But Victor knew whereof he spoke, for he was an Indiana-born Mexican married to a redhaired, fairskinned Puerto Rican girl, whom he had to court in the face of protective Castilian-type chaperones.

The answer to the original query, "Is there a folk in the city?" must clearly be yes. Perhaps it is best to say that there are many folk groups, who in Gary and East Chicago are becoming a city folk. But city folk are different from the country folk of yesteryear, and the folklorist exploring their ways must drastically revise his own traditional concepts of the folk and their lore. Yet the city is indeed a proper field for him to cultivate. If in North Uist, with its population decimated and a century of intensive collecting already achieved, John MacInnes can still say that he will never plumb all the layers of tradition, imagine how many lifetimes would be needed to explore the multiple folk cultures of Gary and East Chicago.

Appendix

The tangible results of this field trip—on which this paper is based—are nine tapes of twelve hundred feet played at one and seven-eighths speed and one tape of choral singing played at seven and one-half; notes on some fifty-three interviews; a diary written each evening running to ninety typed pages; and a box of books, pamphlets, leaflets, typescripts, and even a Puerto Rican straw hat and record album, given me by my new acquaintances—often books cherished and dear to them—as evidences and documents of their traditions and assertions. The interviews are divided as follows: Negro 15, Serbian 8, Mexican 7, Puerto Rican 5, Croatian 5, Greek 3, other 11. "Other" includes a Romanian couple, three Poles, two Italians, two Slovaks, one "Mexican hillbilly," and a daughter of a Sioux Indian mother and an Italian father. "Interview" is a formal word covering all kinds of meetings, sometimes with one, sometimes with several persons present, sometimes a chance encounter, sometimes an arranged appointment. Besides personal talks of some intimacy, I should also include attendance at four Negro church services on successive Sunday mornings, at a Negro choral performance, and at a program on Negro history given in Negro churches on two Sunday afternoons; a tour through Inland Steel, a luncheon-seminar and convocation lecture for and by Mayor Hatcher, for which I flew from Gary to Bloomington and back one day on the Indiana University plane; a spirited local production of "The Roar of the Greasepaint, the Smell of the Crowd," which as a review pointed out, curiously fit into the Gary milieu; and a Serbian musical program at St. Sava Church.

NOTES

1. See Richard M. Dorson, *American Negro Folktales* (New York, 1967), p. 328.
2. Compare "The Mean Boss," in ibid., pp. 156–57.
3. See "The Governor's Convention," in ibid., pp. 319–20.
4. *Sign: National Catholic Magazine* (February, 1968): 13–17.
5. *Time* 90 (November 17, 1967): 26.
6. *St. Sava Serbian Orthodox Church Fiftieth Anniversary: Our Religious Heritage in America, 1914–1964;* November 14–15, 1964 (Gary, n.d.).
7. See Richard M. Dorson, *American Folklore* (New York, 1959), p. 163, for a similar account.
8. Julian Samora and Richard A. Lamanna, *Mexican-Americans in a Midwest Metropolis: A Study of East Chicago* (Los Angeles, 1967).
9. Harriet M. Pawlowska, *Merrily We Sing: 105 Polish Folksongs* (Detroit, 1961), and Susie Hoogasian-Villa, *One Hundred Armenian Folktales* (Detroit, 1966).
10. *American Folklore,* p. 156.

3 /

Esthetic Form in British and

American Folk Narrative

WHILE THE FOLK BALLAD has won its way into the canon of English and American literature, the folktale remains as yet outside the pale. Literary histories and anthologies pay their early respects to "Sir Patrick Spens," "Young Hunting," "The Four Marys," and other illustrious specimens of English and Scottish popular balladry. Instructors in English department courses discuss stylistic and compositional elements of Anglo-American ballads to familiarize students with "leaping and lingering," the dramatic use of dialogue, dependence on commonplaces, and other techniques of the traditional ballad. Courses on the folktale are much rarer, and emphasize European and primitive rather than British and American folktales. The fact is that no one is quite sure about Anglo-American oral narratives. They suffer in contrast with the highly visible and esthetically proven ballads, so clearly and proudly a possession of the English singing world. But where are the folktales of English speakers? What are their forms, esthetic or otherwise? Do they deserve consideration from the literary historians?

Unlike the clear-cut Child ballads permeating Scotland, England, and the United States, the folktales of the three countries tell three separate stories. In his *Type and Motif-Index of the Folktales*

Reprinted from *Medieval Literature and Folklore Studies, Essays in Honor of Francis Lee Utley*, edited by Jerome Mandel and Bruce A. Rosenberg (New Brunswick, N.J.: Rutgers University Press, 1970), pp. 305–21.

of England and North America, published in 1966, Ernest W. Baughman abstracted some 13,000 tales, exclusive of the American Indian, the American Negro, and foreign-language groups in the United States and the Celtic peoples in Great Britain. Here arises the first question in our inquiry: which folktales do we include as part of English and American literature? I would unquestionably include the American Negro and exclude the American Indian, and with less assurance divide the Gaelic tales of Scotland from those of Ireland to bring Scottish traditions within the English realm. Negro storytelling takes place inside the frame of American language and civilization, but tribal Indian narratives belong to another world. Gaeldom unites the Highland and Hebridean Scot with the Irishman, but political boundaries now set them apart. Campbell of Islay presented English translations with the Gaelic texts of his famous *Popular Tales of the West Highlands* and addressed his work primarily to an English-speaking audience. The ample store of West Highland folktales contains a high incidence of the Märchen or magical fictions uncovered first by the Grimm brothers and ever since the primary object of interest for folktale scholars. Among the genres of folk narrative, the Märchen lends itself most easily to the case for esthetic form, with its firm structure of thrice-repeated episodes, its dramatis personae of peasant heroes, royal princesses, demonic ogres, and supernatural helpers, and its happy resolution of the hero's quest. But the Märchen is a rarity in England and the United States. Of all the countries of Europe, England has proved leanest in wonder tales, and consequently had few to transmit to the American colonies—although we must recognize the surprising finds in the southern Appalachians, from the 1920's on, of the so-called Jack tales. Still, Baughman's tables prove that the Märchen must take a back seat to other oral narrative forms. Even in Scotland, the balance in favor of Märchen is receding with the publication in 1964 of *The Dewar Manuscripts,* a collection of local history chronicles recorded under the supervision of Campbell of Islay but lying in file drawers for the past century.

While the narrators both in England and the United States tend to shun Märchen, their repertoires still differ noticeably from each other. English oral narratives run heavily to local legends of supernatural and spectral beings, but legends of elves and bogles are not told in the States—perhaps because, as immigrants say, half in jest, spirits cannot cross the ocean. Conversely, the lying tale or tall tale so abundantly collected in the United States is a stranger in England. Baughman arrives at a 25 percent correspondence between English and American tale types, a figure that might be stretched to 50 percent if narratives not reported from England but found in sections of the United States settled by the English are counted.

We come to the question, what are the main forms of Anglo-American oral prose traditions? and for an answer we must rely on imprecise terms: local legend, ghost story, anecdote, yarn, joke, shaggy dog, protest tale, animal and bird stories, numskull or noodle tales, dialect stories, tall tales or lies. None of these forms are sharply defined. By and large they tend to be short narratives, as opposed to long wonder tales and romances, and their characters and content often determine what names they possess. A dialect story may be told as a terse anecdote or an extended recital but it always hinges on ethnic stereotypes who speak in accents contrasting humorously with standard English. A ghost story involves a spectral experience but this may be a fragmentary report of an eerie sight or sound or a local adaptation of a hardy tale type, such as the now famous account of the Vanishing Hitchhiker. In lieu of any acceptable replacement, the vague label "legend" continues to designate the large body of believed narratives that circulate in our society. We can distinguish certain subgroups of legendary tales revolving around persons, places, or events, according to the focus of the tradition. One of the most popular species of American storytelling is the anecdote about a village or neighborhood character, and this may be called a personal legend, or legendary anecdote, or anecdotal legend.

The idea of legend involves a communally shared tradition possessed and credited by a cohesive group—geographical, occupational, ethnic. Legends are usually told in conversational and reminiscent fashion. Vance Randolph's collections of Ozark folktales take the form of breezy local legends. In spite of the wide latitude accorded the concept of legend, the word still does not satisfactorily cover all varieties of believed oral traditions. The Swedish term *memorat* denotes individual reports of encounters with supernatural creatures and is making its way into English usage. Still it does not apply to the richly detailed autobiographical stories and recollections of W. H. Barrett, the raconteur from the Cambridgeshire fens, whose wry and mordant *Tales from the Fens* bear a distant likeness to Icelandic family sagas.

Then there are jokes or jocular tales, the prime story form of our times, dispersed in town and country social circles, through the mass media, by public speakers of every hue from politicians to clergymen, and via professional and parlor entertainers. In preparing his expanded edition of *The Types of the Folktale* (1961), Stith Thompson found that the section on "Jokes and Anecdotes" had grown far more substantially than any other category. No one has yet taken the humble jest and the lowly anecdote seriously as oral art, although they surely deserve as much consideration as any other kind of folktale. Jokes seem so ephemeral, topical, and trivial that the literary and folk critic may well be excused for scorning them. But some have shown remarkable staying power, enduring from Greece of the fifth century B.C. to America of the mid-twentieth century. Athenian contemporaries of Pericles laughed at the unworldly behavior of the absent-minded pedant who vowed, after a narrow escape from drowning, that he would never go near the water until he had learned how to swim; and who cut his horse's feed daily to teach him how to live without eating, and grieved that, just as the animal was learning to do so, he died.[1]

A genre only recently baptized is the protest tale, whose humor, often grim and biting, turns on racial prejudice and social injustice. The Negro repertoire is especially rich in protest tales which mingle with better known genres such as the Br'er Rabbit fictions of speaking animals. Some humorous stories mock social protest itself, such as dialect jokes told by Jewish storytellers ridiculing excessive sensitivity to anti-Semitism.

We turn from the question of the genres of British and American storytelling to the problem of their texts. The text of an oral tale includes a good deal more than spoken words. There are facial expressions, intonations, chanted phrases, onomatopoetic sounds, gestures, bodily movements, pauses, emphases, eye contact and interplay with the audience, the use of props, noises made by banging on the table and slapping of the palms—all adding up to a small theatrical performance. The term performance is indeed now commonly used by folklorists to describe a story-telling situation. Even the electronically recorded recital conveys only a portion of the scene. Once when I was discussing the matter of textual fidelity with Vance Randolph, he admitted to some editing of his Ozark folktales, but contended that literally transcribed texts still took no account of silent intervals; and he told an illustrative tale. One time he met an Ozark friend limping, and asked the cause of the lameness. The hillman said, "I went to a dance, and a feller stepped on my foot." Pause. "He was from Chicago." Without the pause, said Vance, the written words would lose their humorous effect based on the Ozarker's disdain for the outlander from the big city.

Furthermore, any written representation of an oral tale reproduces but one variant text. Even the same speaker telling the same story varies his text with each delivery. There is no fixed text. Even the single variant is difficult to trap in print, for the exact words, including the hems and haws and confusing pronouns and incomplete sentences of transcribed oral speech need a little pruning and sprucing before they meet the reader's eye. The question is, how many small adjustments can an editor make before the text ceases to be oral? I scarcely trust my own printed texts, and go back to the field notebook or tape if I want to be thoroughly certain of the original wording.

On the other hand, the literary text is not all that definitive, what with variant editions, misprints, and censorship from authors' wives. Francis O. Matthiessen brilliantly explained the symbolic meaning of the phrase "soiled fish of the sea" in *White Jacket*, unaware that Melville had written "coiled fish of the sea." [2]

Still the point needs to be underlined that the oral text, slippery as it may be, differs wholly from a literary text based on an oral tale. The sketches in the New York *Spirit of the Times*, brought to the attention of literary historians in 1930 by Franklin J. Meine in his *Tall Tales of the Southwest*, are not folktales but sophisticated literary compositions. A writer seeking to convey the rhythms and manner of oral delivery is still a writer addressing readers. Ever since the Grimms first published their Household Tales and drew a line between the spoken and written story, collectors polishing their narratives and authors emulating village bards have crossed the line, including the Grimms themselves, and blurred the distinction. But oral art and literary art are separate productions.

The classic statement on this score was made by the eminent Danish folklorist Axel Olrik in his essay of 1909 on "Epic Laws of Folk Narrative." [3] Olrik formulated a number of principles governing oral compositions, such as the need of the narrator to present the story-line clearly and simply, even repetitively, without subtleties or subplots, since listeners had no opportunity to reread the text and ponder over its meanings. In particular he emphasized the law of concentration of character, the restriction of the characters to two strongly opposed figures, and the construction of the narrative around peak tableaux readily visualized by the audience. Olrik generalized for the European oral literature he knew best, the heroic epics, Sagen, Märchen, and ballads, and our purpose is to see how well his conclusions hold for Anglo-American forms.

TRADITIONS OF SINGLE COMBATS

With these preliminary matters of genre and text in mind, we will present three oral narratives that come from widely scattered sources but reveal common patterns of composition. The first is a portion of a Highland Scottish tradition about the battle of Culloden, collected in the 1860's by John Dewar and translated from the Gaelic by Hector Maclean.

AFTER THE BATTLE OF CULLODEN

After the day of the battle of Culloden many of the Highlanders were taken prisoners, and they were put in pens until the intentions of the Duke of Cumberland regarding them should be known. John Campbell of Mamore was General under the Duke of Cumberland on the side of King George. It was he who had the command of the Highland regiments. The Duke of Cumberland was going around to see the prisoners, and he took General Wolfe and General John Campbell with him. They were going from pen to pen, and they reached a place where there was a pen resembling a sheepfold. There were fifteen young Highland lads inside waiting for the Duke's sentence. There was a fire in the middle. One of the prisoners whom the rest called Fierce John was sitting at the side of the fire. The hand was off him a short distance from the wrist and his blood was shedding. He had a sword in the whole hand which he was heating in the fire and applying to the wound to staunch the blood. The three Generals stood for a short time observing the poor prisoner's manner of staunching the blood. Someone remarked, 'It must be that that little man has an exceedingly strong heart.' 'He, the paltry fellow!' said the Duke of Cumberland. 'It must be that Prince Charles is an exceedingly silly blockhead of a man when he took such trifling creatures for soldiers.' 'You do not estimate these men correctly,' rejoined General John Campbell. 'Although they are but little, they are as good soldiers as any in England.' 'These paltry men are not at all to be compared with the English,' observed the Duke. 'One Englishman is better than three of them.' 'Remember,' said General John Campbell, 'that these men are for a long time on bad food and without enough of it, enduring cold and hunger, and without much sleep. That would give a bad appearance to any men.' 'These men had never the appearance of soldiers,' replied the Duke of Cumberland, 'and I do not know who the devil would take the despicable creatures for soldiers.'

Although General John Campbell was on the side of the Duke of Cumberland in the battle he took it very ill to hear his countrymen dispraised, and notwithstanding that he was against the prisoners in the battle, he said, 'There are not there but fifteen young lads altogether, and although they are as tired as they are, I could choose one out of these who would fight with anyone that you could choose from any regiment under your command.'

'I will wager so many bottles of wine,' said the Duke of Cumberland, 'that you will not choose out of these anyone who will fight the Englishman that I should bring against him.' General John Campbell observed, 'I am not much inclined to hazard men's lives for wine, but wager you the men and I will wager the wine. If the Englishman shall win the fight I will pay you a dozen bottles of wine, but if the Highlander shall vanquish the Englishman, let the wager be that the Highlander and the rest who are in the pen with him shall get free leave to go home to their own place.' The Duke consented that if the Highlander won, he and his comrades should get their freedom to go to their own home.

The wager was laid, and the Duke of Cumberland sent an officer to the Colonel of a cavalry regiment which he considered the best under his command, for a man to fight a Highlander. A swordsman was got as good as they thought was to be found in the English army, and brought into the presence of the Duke of Cumberland. The English soldier was brought to see the Highland prisoners. When he saw them he was asked if he would fight one of those men. 'Yes,' said he, 'and it is my opinion that I could fight every one of them, if I got them one after the other.'

General Campbell was then asked again, if he would stand to his wager. He said he should. The wager was laid anew. Then General

Campbell went into the pen where the prisoners were and said, 'Is there any one of you at all who are here that would engage to fight with an accomplished English fencer, if all of you who are in this pen got your liberty to go home for winning victory over the Englishman?' The prisoners were silent and looked at General Campbell without saying a word. Fierce John was sitting at the side of the fire, and although the one hand was off him and the blood not yet being full stanched [*sic*], he rose and said, 'Let me to him. I will do business on him.' There was not one in the pen that did not say that he would engage him. General Campbell said, 'Take care what you are about, men! This is a weighty business. Take heed that the life of every one of you depends upon the man's hand, whichever he may be who goes to fight the Englishman. If the Englishman will kill the Highlander, every one of you here shall be put to death; but if the Highlander will win, every one of you here shall get leave to go home.' A brother of Fierce John walked a step or two apart from the rest and said, 'Let me to him. I will make use of him.' 'You are yourselves acquainted with one another,' said General Campbell, 'and I should like that you would choose the best swordsman among you.' 'I am of opinion,' remarked the brother of Fierce John, 'that I am he.' General John Campbell put it to the opinion of the rest, and that was Fierce John's brother was the best swordsman among them except Fierce John himself, who was now wounded and had also lost one of his hands; and as that was so, that they would trust the hand of his brother. It was the brother of Fierce John that was chosen for the combat.

He asked a sword, which was got for him. He was brought on level ground and the English champion was brought against him. They did not resemble each other in appearance. The Englishman was a big, stalwart man and seemingly very strong. The Highlander was but a chip of a slender, sallow stripling, very bare of flesh, but tough and brawny, and slightly under middle size. The two fencers were placed opposite each other, the word of combat was given, and the play began. The Englishman was violent at first and struck fiercely, but the Highlander sought to do nothing further than defend himself. 'You must draw up better than that, lad,' said General Campbell to the Highlander, 'much is entrusted to your hand.' 'Is it death?' said the Highlander. 'Death undoubtedly,' replied the General.

The Highlander closed up with the Englishman then, and it was but a short time until he struck him with the sword and killed him. When General Campbell saw that the Englishman had fallen, he went where the Highlander was, clapped him on the shoulder, and said to him, 'Go home now and thank your mother, because she gave you such good milk.'

All who were in the pen got leave then to go home, but the Duke of Cumberland was so full of wrath because the Englishman whom he thought to be the bravest in the whole English army was killed by a little Highlander, that he gave orders to persons of his to kill every Highlander who was found wounded in the battlefield and every prisoner who should be made after this to be hanged without mercy.[4]

This text may be called an historical legend. It derives a good deal of its dramatic power, in the first place, from its setting in history. The battle of Culloden on April 16, 1746, brought to an end the Jacobite uprising of 1745, staged by the Highland forces of Bonnie Prince Charlie, the Stuart pretender, against the royal army of George II in the last battle fought on British soil. Culloden signified the doom of the Highland cause and the extirpation of Highland culture. Anecdote, ballad, oral and written history, and documentary film all bear witness to the impact of Culloden on the imagination of Englishmen and Scotsmen. In 1964 a stirring television film of the BBC, produced by Peter Watkins, reenacted the battle scene and the desperate charge on foot of the Highland clans, whose parts were played by citizens of Inverness living close to the battle site, some themselves descendants of the survivors. Culloden is a highly charged historic name, conjuring up the final conflict of Stuarts and Hanoverians, of kilted clansmen and soldiers of the Crown, of Highland and English ways of life. It conjures up, too, the sadistic figure of the Bloody Duke of Cumberland, general of the king's army, and a heartless butcher in countless legends.

The episode of traditional history here presented thus gains considerable drama at the outset from its cast of characters, the commanders and soldiers of Culloden. It develops its own drama with the wager between the Bloody Duke and the defecting Highland general, John Campbell, who recognizes the valor of his countrymen. A classic David and Goliath duel ensues in the epic tradition of single combats between opposing champions.[5] Our sympathies are already enlisted on the side of the underdog Scots, vanquished, underfed, outnumbered, and are further moved by the injury and stoicism of Fierce John and the audacity of his small brother. In the narration the Highlander's anticipated victory is scanted, contrary to the Hollywood movie script which would have given it extended emphasis. Rather than emphasize the obvious, the narrator dwells on the Highlander's reticence and his quick dispatch of his opponent when he sees he must take his enemy's life to save those of his fellows. By contrast, the mean vengeance on other Highland prisoners taken by the Bloody Duke accords with the known character and legendary cruelty of the English general.

This selection illustrates the artistic power that oral traditional history can achieve. The action marches surely to its climax, the language is sinewy and taut (allowing for some fluff in translation), the dialogue simple and crisp, and the heroic mood of valor and honor sustained from first to last. In place of any vainglorious taunt after the Highlander's triumph, his sponsor, General Campbell, softly lauds him with a homely adage. All four protagonists fall at once into place. The Highland general and soldier duplicate each other in manly virtue as do the English general and soldier in contemptuous bluster. Cumberland and Campbell debate the merits of the Highlander in a verbal joust enacted out physically by the combatants. The heroism and tragedy of Culloden are felt from the initial prison scene through the wager, the selection of duelists, and the combat, to the final bitter order of slaughter.

In its form, this historical legend resembles other traditions in *The Dewar Manuscripts* and in clan chronicles. These oral annals are straightforward accounts of raids and feuds and tricks between rival lairds and their men, of varying length, filled with names of families and localities unfamiliar to the outsider. Frequently the sober statements are lit up with marvelous dreams and shocking acts and bizarre events. One unusual tradition describes the imprisonment of two Highlanders in Boston during the American Revolution and their rescue by a countryman they accidentally discovered, Duncan Stewart, who then himself had to flee to Britain. There Stewart encountered the Campbells whom he had saved, and they now intervened with King George III to help Stewart recover his hereditary land. The train of events is astonishing and the coincidences, escapes, and just conclusion heartwarming for a Highland audience. As a specimen of oral art it exhibits some of the same qualities as the Culloden narrative, but without achieving its tautness and tension.[6]

The second text represents a contemporary example of urban American story-telling. It was first told me on June 14, 1967, during my Harvard Thirtieth Reunion at Martha's Vineyard, by an old friend and classmate going back even to preparatory school at Exeter, William B. Gresham, Jr. "Gresh" resides at Tampa, Florida, where he is in the pest control business, and I telephoned him from Bloomington, Indiana, on June 22 to re-collect the story verbatim. He remembered his source as Tom Dowd, the traveling secretary for the Boston Red Sox, who had spoken to the local branch of the American Personnel Association at the Commerce Club in Tampa in March, 1967.

THE POOR COLORED BOY AND LEO THE LION

There was a poor little old colored boy in Jackson, Mississippi, who had just gotten his driver's license. The first day he was driving he was arrested by a motorcycle cop for speeding 25 miles an hour in a 20 mile an hour zone. The white cop hauled him before the white judge who glared down at him from high on his bench and, peering over his glasses, frowned and said, "Nigger boy, you have committed a heinous sin and a serious crime, and I am going to have to give you the maximum penalty. But I will give you a choice. You can either be hung by the neck until you are dead at 8 o'clock in the morning or fight Leo the lion in Ole Miss Stadium tomorrow afternoon at 2 o'clock."

The little colored boy thought fast, and hanging by the neck sounded awful sure, awful fatal, and awful dead. He looked up at the judge and he said, "Judge, suh, Ah chooses to fight Leo the lion." The judge said, "Take him off to the jail cell till tomorrow."

Next afternoon Old Miss Stadium was filled with 56,000 white people cheering and hollering, bands playing, the cheerleaders urging them on, because they had seen this kind of spectacle before. Two deputies brought the little colored boy out with his hands manacled behind his back. They walked him out to the middle of the field and lowered him into a hole on the 50-yard line. They filled the hole up with dirt until only his head was showing.

Then at the far end of the field where the football teams usually came in appeared a jeep hauling a lion's cage containing Leo the lion. Leo was getting anxious. They opened the cage door at the goal line and out leaped Leo. He spied the little colored head up on the 50-yard line which reminded him of his carefree days back in the jungle. He set out at full speed. By the time he reached the 40-yard line, he realized he was going too fast. He put on the brakes, and when he came to a stop his body was over the head of the poor little colored boy.

The boy looked up and right above him were the tenderest parts of Leo the lion's body. He saw his only chance, reached up with his teeth and sank them into the tenderest parts of Leo the lion.

Meanwhile the crowd was hooping and hollering and calling out, "Come on Leo, come on Leo!" But Leo the lion was in trouble. He was roaring in pain, beating his paws on the ground, thrashing his tail back and forth in agony. The little colored boy held on for dear life 'cause he knew it was his only chance.

The crowd quieted, seeing that Leo was in trouble. After a moment they realized what was going on. A hush settled over the stadium. Then a solitary voice boomed out, "Fight fair, nigger, fight fair."

The first point to observe is that the central motif of this tale exists in tradition. On a field trip in 1953 to Pine Bluff, Arkansas, located in the Mississippi Delta, I heard from a Negro the related story of "John in Alabama." In this narrative a colored man from Arkansas named John was visiting in Alabama and was informing his friends how much better the colored were treated in Arkansas, when a white man passed by, heard him, and knocked John down. John struck back, and was winning when the police arrived, arrested John, buried him in the ground up to his shoulders, and turned two bulldogs loose on him. John nodded his head so fast the "laws" stopped the dogs and told John to hold his head still and fight fair.[7]

Here is a clear example of a protest tale, and in fact it was told to me by John Courtney drinking coke in his home after I had been refused curb service by a teen-aged white girl because I had "colored" in my car. We may further note that the skillful dodger appears in the Negro but not in the white version, and that the dodger clearly belongs to Negro tradition. In still another tale type, of which I collected three variants, a Negro defies a white man to beat him up and then simply dodges his blows.

Immediately following the delivery of this paper (September 7, 1967), I was told an intermediate variant by Donald Stoddard of Skidmore College, in which the lion rushes three times at the colored boy, who the third time seizes the tender parts. Mr. Stoddard heard this in June, 1966, in Boston from a maintenance supervisor at Northeastern University.

The white text has combined the protest tale of racial injustice, recently surfacing on the American scene, with the honored American tradition of the poker-faced tall tale. Usually tall tales deal with backwoods and agricultural themes—remarkable feats of hunting and shooting, enormous vegetables, extraordinarily rich or poor soil, changeable weather. Such "windies" are amusing but lack any emotional charge. The marriage of exaggeration and protest has produced a potent offspring, a tale funny and grim, articulating the deep anxieties of a racially divided nation.

Both the protest tale and the tall tale are anecdotal in form. That is, they purport to relate actual incidents about real people in brief, conversational narrations. Supernatural beings do not enter into the dramatis personae. The protest tale characteristically makes use of irony and inversion, rather than overt social criticism, by having colored folk accept the white man's code and extend it to the point of absurdity. The tall tale too contains only natural phenomena and traps the listener by a sudden leap from the possible to the impossible. Tall tales soon become monotonous, and while they can be and are still collected today, the repetitious lies about giant pumpkins and lucky hunting shots mean little to contemporary Americans. In the above text the impulse for creative exaggeration has fastened onto new and more immediate themes. The form remains anecdotal; this is a supposedly factual incident occurring to an actual person in a specific locality, the fearsome one of Jackson, Mississippi, and introducing familiar situations: the appearance of a traffic violator before an implacable judge, a spectacle in a crowded football stadium. As blacks tell tall tales, so whites tell protest tales, and the shift from a black to a white narrator has brought an added awesomeness to the ordeal of the victim. The private incident has become a public entertainment, recalling the punitive ritual of primitive Christians thrust before the lions in the Roman amphitheater. Helpless, friendless, accused, and accursed, the poor little colored boy is the Christ-figure, reviled when he uses his last means of defense to protect himself from his would-be killers.

Platitudinous sermons delivering the message of racial injustice do not circulate among secular Americans, who consume with relish the same preachment hid in a mocking story capped with the customary joke-ending punchline. As befits the mood of the tale, the narrator maintains a solemn tone and a somber rhythm—"awful sure, awful fatal, and awful dead"—along with the deadpan mien of the older frontier Münchausens. But the laughter of this anecdote borders on tears.

In the central scene where the poor Negro boy faces Leo the lion in the football stadium, we see reenacted the single combat of heroic legend, as in the duel between Fierce John's brother and the British champion. Traditionally the hero battles not only other champions but also monsters, dragons, and wild beasts. The single combat provides one of the visual tableaux defined by Axel Olrik as narrative peaks and perfectly illustrates his law of two to a scene. What episode can more readily stir and imprint itself on a listening audience than the duel to the death between an underdog hero and a powerful ogre before opposing armies or a bloodthirsty throng?

While the Scottish tradition faithfully conveys the heroic mood of classical epic and medieval romance, the American folktale is told in a mock-heroic spirit of parody and irony. Single combats did take place in American life, although not under conditions of chivalry; the Crockett almanacs set forth encounters between Davy and assorted rapscallions of the backwoods, and in Michigan's Upper Peninsula I collected lurid descriptions of eye-gouging, groin-butting affrays between whiskey-inflamed lumberjacks in barroom melees. The third text in this group reflects the violent and reckless spirit of the Upper Peninsula. Its narrator is a Swedish immigrant, Swan Olson, who specialized in autobiographical yarns in which he outwitted and outfought highway robbers, crazed lumberjacks, and murderous tramps. Yet audacious Swan, a gentle old man of seventy-three when I met him in 1946, scarcely looked the part of the swashbuckler portrayed in the following personal narrative, which I printed in *Bloodstoppers and Bearwalkers*.

MY FIRST JOB IN AMERICA

I came from Stockholm, Sweden, when I was just confirmed, about 1890. I was seventeen. I landed at Quebec and went to Litchfield, Minnesota. I came there in harvest time, and worked for a farmer, Eric Ericson. He drank clear alcohol with a dipper. No one would work for him more than two or three days; he would go crazy and threaten to murder them, and his wife, and me.

We took some big barrels of eggs thirteen miles into town to sell for three cents a dozen. The storekeeper sold them for five cents, but Ericson could only get two cents. Well, he went into a saloon and told me to get three cents for the eggs or take them back and bury them in a hole in the manure pile. I couldn't sell them, so I went back to the saloon, and he was dead drunk—couldn't walk.

So I had a couple of fellows help me lift him up into the wagon, alongside me, and let the curved iron side hold him in place, slumped against it. So we started back, and I let the horses go as fast as they wanted to. It was a spring wagon, with springs under the seat, which fitted over the sideboards. The wagon hit a deep rut, and gave a big bump from the spring, and he went from the bloody wagon clear up in the air, and landed plunk in the bloody sluice alongside the clay road.

It took me a while to slow up and go back, and I couldn't figure out how to get him up—he was like a dishrag. So finally I unhooked one of the lines from the horse's bit and tied it under his arms, and then I went up in the wagon and began pulling him up. I got hold of him by the neck and the collar and pulled him the rest of the way. Then I put him under the bloody seat and left him there the rest of the trip.

So we got back to the farm and drove up to the front door. Then I went into his room, looked under his pillow and pulled out his gun, emptied all the cartridges and put them in my pocket. Then I went out and unhitched the team and put them in the barn. I had one harness off, and was just hanging the other up on the peg when he came in the barn holding the gun.

He said, "You son of a bitch!" and pointed the gun right in my face, and clicked the hammer—click, click, click.

Then he said, "Don't you drop? You son of a bitch."

I said, "Not for your gun or you either." Then I dropped the harness, grabbed his gun and hit him right in the mouth, and the blood squirted all over him and right in my face. I knocked out one of his teeth. He fell backwards over the doorway, and I thought I killed the bugger. I listened to his heart, heard it beat. So I got a pail of cold water from the galvanized trough and poured it over him, and he began to hiccup. Then I helped the bugger up to the house and seen him get undressed and get to bed.

94

Then I went back to the barn, after wiping off and feeding the horses. I couldn't sleep up in the attic of the log house—only two rooms in the whole place—so I slept in the barn in the hay. I slept with two blankets and a pillow, and in the morning I was covered with snakes, ice-cold snakes. They wanted my heat, so they curled up all around me, up to my neck and my face. When I'd wake up I'd take one of the bloody buggers by the tail, when his head was under my neck, and break his neck. They were slippery and cold, but not poisonous. (One time when I was pitching hay, I pulled on one's head, and he just squeezed tighter round my neck, and I had to grab his tail with my other hand.)

About three o'clock in the morning I heard a holler of "Murder" from the house. So I threw off the snakes and put some overalls on and ran up to the house. Eric was standing over his woman (his second wife—his kids ran away 'cause he said he'd kill them) with a stove handle in his hand, ready to kill her. She was lying down on the floor stretched out. He had hit her once, was going to finish her up. I grabbed the stove pipe from behind him and hit him over the head, right on the coconut, so he dropped down on the floor. Then I picked him up and put him over an Old Country chest he had in the corner (I got two of them at home—they're rounded at the top) and laid him across it on his stomach, and pushed the trunk against the wall with all my strength, so his head was caught between the trunk and the wall. Then I took the iron rod from an old muzzle-loader he had, about four feet long, and pulled it out over the barrel, and beat him with it on the hind end and the legs and all over.

The women said, "Just keep it up."

When I was finished, I was all perspired. He fell over the side of the trunk on the floor, and I picked him up and put him back in the bed.

That was Saturday night. I got up early in the morning, milked the cows, fed the horses. Then at breakfast the woman said he wanted to see me. So I went up into the bedroom, and he showed me all his bruises; he was black and blue and green.

So I said, "Well, that's what you get when you go to town. They was going to beat you up in the saloon, and I saved your life."

Then he asked me to hand him his pants. They were on the chair right alongside the bed, but he couldn't reach them, he was so weak. (He stayed in bed for a week.) And he took a silver dollar out of his pocket—they had no paper dollars then—and gave it to me for saving his life.

That was the only time he paid me all the time I was there.[8]

95

Whatever the content of fact in this narration, it is a well-told tale and a red-blooded slice of Americana. Although allegedly a personal experience, Swan's account does adhere to Olrik's laws of oral narrative. Two central characters dominate the actions, a dark villain and a shining hero, the teller himself. No subtleties obscure the plot; Olson clobbers Ericson again and again and again, but with imaginative variations. A tension persists throughout the recital, for Ericson is a madman and Swan is continually in danger. Swan knows his man and anticipates his moves, but the listener cannot, as in conventional folktales, anticipate the next episode. Throughout the story Swan plays the role of the faithful hired hand, attending to the chores and mauling Eric only under provocation. The graphic scenes move from one thrashing to another: Swan dumping Eric from the buggy, knocking him out in the barn, whaling him with the muzzle-loader as he lies draped across the Old Country chest. But Swan triumphs by wit and strategy rather than by muscle; he is the clever hero. Details of farm routine are sketched in with the precision of an archival historian. Some matters are inserted with a sure sense of their shock value: the low price of eggs, the snakes clasping Swan in the barn. A number of casual references build up the portrait of the arch villain: Eric drinks straight alcohol, has driven his children away, beats his wife, shoots at all and sundry, and never pays his help. The marvelous O. Henry ending ties together the opening visit to town with the last episode in the bedroom as the now impotent ogre rewards his sly emasculator, who triumphs intellectually as well as physically.

These three narratives come from quite unlike tellers: a Scottish Highlander, a Harvard graduate living in Florida, a Swedish immigrant in Michigan's Upper Peninsula. One story deals with a famous battle, another with an imaginary public spectacle, a third with employer-employee relations on a farm. They seem to have little in common. Yet generically, esthetically, and traditionally they all conform to the same pattern. Each is told on the plane of sober fact as a realistic occurrence. Each portrays a single combat in which the underdog hero emerges triumphant against a bully or monster. The Swiss folklorist Max Lüthi stresses the pervasive theme in folk narrative "of the defeat of the great by the small, the mighty by the apparently powerless," and cites examples:

The intelligence of the dwarfs, the stupidity of the giants, the victory of David over Goliath, of Odysseus over Polyphemus, of the clever peasant girl over the king, of Hänsel and Gretel over the witch, of the divine child over the monsters sent by his enemies (Hercules strangles Hera's serpents), the power of the Christ-child over the giant Christophorus, representing the power of the Crucified who took upon himself the form of a servant, the power of God in meek and lowly guise—all this testifies to the same insight present in all types of folk narrative, fairy tales, legends, as well as in the farces and saints' legends, based upon both faith and experience, and which tells of the possible victory of the small over the great, the weak over the strong.[9]

Lüthi sees the same theme displayed in the written literature of Kafka, Thomas Mann, Rilke, Shakespeare, Goethe, and French comedies of manners, but of course in highly complex form. We may extend Lüthi's examples to American literature, folklore, and history. There come to mind the triumphs of Br'er Rabbit over the bear and the fox, clever John the slave over his Old Marster, and Signifying Monkey over the lion in Negro tradition; of Davy Crockett over b'ars, panthers, and armies of Mexicans and cannibals in frontier legend; of Jack the giant-killer in the southern Appalachians; of Ahab's conquest of the great white whale; of the perilous odyssey of Huck Finn; of Thoreau's defiance of the State; of Horatio Alger's novels celebrating the rapid rise of Ragged Dick, the bootblack; of the success stories of Ben Franklin, Abe Lincoln, Andrew Carnegie. It is the same tale of a determined underdog hero vanquishing powerful foes or subduing a hostile society.

Our three texts are variations on this theme. From disparate materials the narrators have fashioned dramatic compositions intended to be told. They have followed a construction, presented characters, and employed speech in the manner of universally successful prose traditions. These tales have not accidentally come into existence and endured by chance. They are products of individual oral artists working within a time-honored folk tradition.

Other genres of folk narrative possess stylistic and compositional elements that contribute to their traveling power and staying power. The lowliest of Anglo-American folktale forms, the anecdote of local characters, proves on closer examination to follow a fixed story line that ends with the dupe lamenting his deception at the hands of the trickster. Folktales have to fight for approval from fresh audiences at each new telling, and their long survival testifies to the persistent appeal of oral fiction.

Now that written literature is receiving such intensive and subtle analysis, perhaps more critical attention will be directed to oral literature, its precursor and constant supplier.

NOTES

1. *The Jests of Hierocles and Philagrius,* newly translated from the Greek by Charles Clinch Bubb (Cleveland: Rowfant Club, 1920. Wittol Series No. 1).

2. David Dempsey, "Refurbishing American Authors," *Saturday Review* 50 (June 10, 1967): 30.

3. In *The Study of Folklore,* ed. Alan Dundes (New York: Prentice-Hall, 1965), pp. 129–41.

4. *The Dewar Manuscripts,* I, *Scottish West Highland Folk Tales,* collected originally in Gaelic by John Dewar, translated into English by Hector MacLean, edited with introduction and notes by John Mackechnie (Glasgow: William MacLellan, 1964), pp. 233–36.

5. The relevant motif in Stith Thompson, *Motif-Index of Folk Literature* (Bloomington: Indiana University Press, 1955–58) is H 1561.2, "Single combat to prove valor."

6. *The Dewar Manuscripts,* pp. 218–24.

7. Richard M. Dorson, *Negro Tales from Pine Bluff, Arkansas and Calvin, Michigan* (Bloomington: Indiana University Press, 1958), p. 110.

8. (Cambridge, Mass.: Harvard University Press, 1952; reprinted 1972), pp. 251–54.

9. "Parallel Themes in Folk Narrative and in Art Literature," *Journal of the Folklore Institute* 4 (1967): 3–16.

4 /

Oral Styles of American Folk Narrators

SINCE FOLKLORE BECAME a field of learning in the first half of the nineteenth century, collectors have given their primary attention to the distribution and origin of texts. Especially for the folktale has the pattern set by the Grimm brothers in their *Kinder- und Hausmärchen* been endlessly repeated, a volume of collected tales, somewhat "improved" for the reading public, with the human sources suppressed. At best, an appendix will provide a bare list of names and ages of the storytellers. The great fallacy in this approach is the divorce of texts from the folk artists who alone give them life. One notable exception is Russia, where A. F. Gil'ferding (1831–1872) established the principle in folklore studies of centering attention on the *byliny* performer, and furnishing the maximum information about his biography, repertoire, and creative talent.[1] But Russian folklore science, now propagandizing the class struggle, has failed in this one commendable respect to influence Western folklorists. Rarely does an article appear in Western publications like James H. Delargy's "The Gaelic Story-Teller," singling out individual narrators for discussion.[2] We find occasional descriptions of storytellers by the excellent British folklorists of the

Reprinted from *Style in Language*, edited by Thomas A. Sebeok (Cambridge, Mass., New York, and London: Technology Press of Massachusetts Institute of Technology and John Wiley and Sons, 1960), pp. 27–51. The texts of four of the six tales in the Appendix were not printed with the original article.

late nineteenth century; Hartland discussed "The Art of Story-Telling" in general terms, and Campbell of Islay gave pleasing detail about his Highland bards.[3] Recently Bowra in his lucid examination of *Heroic Poetry* devoted considerable attention to techniques of composition and presentation used by folk poets in scattered cultures who recite verse narratives of stirring adventure.[4]

The fact remains that folklorists have only incidentally and sporadically concerned themselves with problems of folk-narrative style. Archer Taylor has said that we know less about the structural details than about almost any other aspect of the folktale.[5] Stith Thompson in surveying our knowledge of folktale style reported mainly on problems still to be studied.[6] Olrik's general laws of epic style are one positive accomplishment and appear to cover all forms of oral narration: the oral tale is simply told, it contains no subplot, it opposes a good and an evil character, it contains much repetition, two persons only appear in a scene, the weakest character triumphs.[7] When it comes to any discussion of individual storytelling styles, however, Thompson must turn to the Russian folklorist Azadovsky and his analysis of three principal types of raconteurs: the specialist in the obscene, the precisionist anxious to relate every detail of the tradition accurately, and the embroiderer who fills in the structure of the tale with the realism and pathos of everyday life.[8]

Anthropologists have infrequently looked at myths and songs of nonliterate peoples for their qualities of style as well as their ethnographic content. Boas, for all his concern with tales as a mirror of culture, did call attention to their formal and esthetic elements.[9] His student Reichard analyzed "The Style of Coeur d'Alene Mythology" in terms of plot, action, motivation, characterization, and stylistic devices, although she used only two informants and admitted that the Coeur d'Alene were not especially adept storytellers.[10] Usually the anthropologists comment on general characteristics of tribal style rather than on the creative role of individual narrators. One difficulty, of course, for the anthropological student of style is the translation barrier.[11] In my own fieldwork with bilingual Ojibwa, Potawatomi, and Sioux, I have collected fluent English narratives in which the Indian storytellers act as it were as their own interpreters. In such texts, however, we should study acculturated rather than native style. This field experience strengthened my conviction that only certain gifted individuals, whether Indians or anyone else, are the storytellers, and hence that oral style should be considered individually as well as tribally.

The American folklorist faces a considerably different field situation from that of the European folklorist or the anthropologist. They confront a unified culture where storytelling is ritually formalized and transmits a stable body of narratives which furnish cultural sanctions and aesthetic satisfactions.[12] American civilization has produced informal yarns and anecdotes and tall tales and personal experiences, rather than elaborate creation myths or heroic sagas or night-long wonder tales. We cannot speak of *the* culture but rather of a score of ethnic, regional, and occupational subcultures which form the chief targets of the folklorist. Storytellers and folktales are less easily spotted in the United States than in Europe or among nonliterate cultures. Are jokes and anecdotes folktales? Can a true storyteller flourish among the mass media? Yet the very complexity of American civilization makes possible a broader inquiry than is possible in a simpler culture. We can search out storytellers who represent a wide variety of folk groups, from tradition-directed pockets to other-directed societies in American life.

Two younger American folklorists, Jansen and Ball, have recently published provocative papers on the problem of folk style. Jansen asks for a distinction between folk aesthetic and art aesthetic, and for proper recognition of the artistic folk performer above his ordinary fellows who merely remember or half-remember.[13] In view of the vital living context of folk narration, Jansen even suggests a classification of verbal performance, based on the degrees of casualness and formality in the storytelling situation.[14] Ball continues this plea with a demand for good collecting of good performers, to portray in full dimension the "dynamic relationship among style, story, teller, audience, and culture." The culture, the tale, and the teller each contribute to the style of a given text.[15]

Folk aesthetic does indeed differ from art aesthetic, but still a student of oral narration can borrow some concepts from literary criticism. He, too, is scrutinizing a text and considering its qualities of structure and language. However, the texts he handles are not composed by their speakers or singers, and they do not possess a constant form. The text is in continual flux, even when repeated by the same narrator. Yet the gulf is not so enormous as it appears; literary texts too undergo revision, the folk narrator like an author composes within a tradition, and folklore and literature continually feed each other themes and plots and characters and phrases.[16] A crucial difference lies in the audience; the writer writes for a private reader, the teller speaks to visible listeners. Before he sets his creation in type, the author can prune and polish and perfect, but the narrator delivers his piece as the words pour from his mind, and even though he may have told the tale often, when they are literally recorded many imperfections appear—false starts, circuitous sentences, tangled grammar. Such faults little affect the response of the listening circle, for the speech of the first-rate folk narrator is fresh, clear, and vivid, and the flaws that may vex the pampered reader vanish in the excitement of the living text. An added physical dimension enters into the elements of folk style; the narrator employs voice and body as well as words to dramatize his text. Facial expression, hand gestures, intonation and inflection, and the whole human presence mold the recitation. The audience, too, conditions the performance, and so do external factors of time and place. The critic of folk style must necessarily also be the collector-observer, and if he invites others to discuss the style of his narrators, he is bound to furnish facts about the manner of their delivery, along with the texts of their tales.

NARRATORS IN THE FIELD

In the present paper I propose first to discuss the styles of seven folk narrators from whom I have collected sizable bodies of tales, and who reflect five storytelling traditions within American civilization. They include two Southern-born Negroes whom I met in Michigan, J. D. Suggs and John Blackamore,[17] two Yankee lobster fishermen from Maine, Jim Alley and Curt Morse; and from Michigan's Upper Peninsula, a Polish immigrant and a Swedish immigrant who had worked as miners, lumberjacks, and farm hands, Joe Woods and Swan Olson; and an auto mechanic of French-Canadian background, Burt Mayotte. All qualify as outstanding narrators, from a folklore collector's point of view; they told tales fluently and graphically. For each I will give some biographical and repertoire data and discuss a characteristic text.

The Narrators. James Douglas Suggs was my number-one informant. In the course of my visits to him in 1952 and 1953 in Calvin, an all-Negro farming township in Cass County, Michigan, he related 170 folk narratives and sang a score of folksongs. Sixty-five years old when I met him, Suggs had grown up in northern Mississippi and roamed widely about the country in various occupations. Although only a day laborer with ten children to feed at the end of his life, he possessed uncontrollable high spirits and delighted in talk and company.

John Blackamore was thirty years old when I found him in Benton Harbor, Michigan, in 1952, where he had lived for nine years after moving north from Kentucky and Missouri. He was adapting himself successfully to Northern business ways, working in a foundry, driving his own truck, and renting rooms. Stolid and burly, he gave no outward appearance of possessing the narrative gift, and yet he could recite lengthy stories for hours on end.

In the little town of Jonesport and neighboring Machias high upon the Maine coast I met two raconteurs in July, 1956, who had spent their lives as lobstermen in the coastal waters. James Alley at seventy-six scraped out a living knitting heads for lobster traps, shucking clams, and delivering papers. He lived on a tiny road known as Alley's Lane where a number of related Alley families had moved from Head Harbor Island in the bay nearly half a century before. James had low status in the community and was not known as a storyteller. But I found him sensitive and sharp-minded and an inexhaustible fountain of anecdotal tales.

By contrast, the reputation of "Uncle" Curt Morse as a humorist and a character had spread through the county. Although he lived at the end of a country road in Kennebec overlooking a scenic cove, he spent every afternoon lolling along the main street of Machias, the county seat five miles away, and he frequently visited in Jonesport, where indeed I first met him. Curt at seventy did a little clamming, but principally he enjoyed his local fame as wag and entertainer. Curt had never left Maine.

Joe Woods migrated to the United States in 1904 at the age of twenty-one, from Csanok, province of Galicia, in Austrian Poland, where he was born Joseph Wojtowicz. He had traveled through many of the northern states, working in the woods and on the harvest, but he lived most of his years in Michigan's Upper Peninsula where the iron mines offered fairly steady work. Mine dampness gave him rheumatism, and he was invalided from 1930 to 1936, in the state mental hospital at Newberry. This fact may have led to local talk of his being a teller of crazy stories, the scent that led me to him in Crystal Falls in 1946, and back again in 1947. But I found him perfectly clear-headed and a narrator of well-known European tales.

Swan Olson also came from the Old Country, in his case Sweden. I met him accidentally in a barbershop in Negaunee in the Upper Peninsula, where I heard him recounting an incident about being served fly pie. Though a gentle old man of seventy-three in 1946, Swan bristled with experiences of his life in America, working on farms, in lumber camps, and down in the mines. He still worked, as mason, plasterer, bricklayer, and carpenter. At seventeen he had left Stockholm, in 1890, and taken his first job in Litchfield, Minnesota.

Burt Mayotte was born in Michigan but retained his French-Canadian identity. One branch of his family had come from Alsace-Lorraine. His grandfather was a pioneer in Keweenaw County, the lonely finger of the Upper Peninsula thrusting into Lake Superior and a preserve for French-Canadians come down from the lumber-woods of Quebec. Burt was an auto mechanic at Sault Ste. Marie when I met him in 1946, a wiry, energetic youngish man under forty.

Traditions. 1. The Southern Negro tradition of Suggs and Black-amore is more casual than Negro recitation in the West Indies, where the formal style of African storytelling persists. There we find, say in Beckwith's collection from Jamaica, ending formulas and cantefable structure (songs included within the tales), which are only fragmentarily preserved in the United States. The animal tales so prevalent in the West Indies cross over to the mainland, but they blend with tales based in slavery, supernatural experiences borrowed from the Whites, American anecdotes and tall tales, and European folktales. In spite of these diversified sources, a corpus of Southern Negro tales can be recognized; the same tales are collected again and again from Negro storytellers. This wide range of story materials permits different selections of content by individual tellers. For instance, one informant may specialize in brief, punch-ending jests, and another may indulge in extended, circumstantial relations.

2. European immigrants coming to the United States have brought with them the fictional folktales made famous by the brothers Grimm and known as Märchen or fairy tales. These complex and elaborate tales of wonder, adventure, and magic possess substantial structures and special stylistic features. The long tale will often be divided into equal and symmetrical episodes—say in the Cinderella-type narratives where the three sisters perform identical tasks in succession—which are sometimes linked by interrogations addressed to the listeners. Märchen furnished entertainment for the unlettered peasantry of medieval Europe, and deal with kings, castles, treasure, ogres, witches, and lucky youths of low birth. Joe Woods provides a case, rarely recorded by collectors, of the immigrant relating Märchen in his new tongue. Although the Celtic people of Ireland and Scotland have a wealth of fairy tales, the English are nearly barren of Märchen and contributed few to America.

3. Along the Maine coast, where an isolated Yankee stock gains a bare living from the lobsters, herring, and clams in the coastal waters, a homogeneous culture rich in folklore persists. A good deal of indigenous American yarnspinning flourishes here, drawing its materials from supernaturalism of sea and land and the humor of native character. The tall tale, the local anecdote, the marine legend abound, and specialists can be found for each vein. Here the natural requirements of storytelling under American conditions shape the style, rather than inherited narrative conventions. These requirements are keyed to the informal, gregarious group; hence the tale must be relatively brief, conversational, topical, and pointed toward laughter or shock. Even Old World plots, when they turn up, will be trimmed to this mold. Curt Morse and Jim Alley yarn within this tradition.

4. In the Upper Peninsula of Michigan a special form of hu-

morous dialect story has developed from the close proximity of foreign-born and native-born Americans. The sons of the immigrants mimic the daily mistakes in grammar, pronunciation, and vocabulary made by adults forced to acquire English as a belated second tongue. At the same time they ridicule the cultural shock and mishaps of the newcomer, who becomes a stock fool character. In the Peninsula several types of comic dialect are found, chiefly the French, Finnish, and Cornish, and secondarily the Swedish and Italian, reflecting the nationality groups of the area. Each neighborly town in the Peninsula vaunts at least one "dialectician" of repute, who entertains at lodge meetings and church socials, and most of the American-born Peninsularites can tell at least a few dialect jokes. Walter Gries, a well-known mining company executive, has told his dialect stories throughout the state in after-dinner speeches and at high school graduations. The linguistic features of each dialect are based on the relation of the parent tongue to English and the common mistakes that ensue when a speaker of that language attempts to master English. Mimetic ability is at a premium, and this extends to facial expression and hand gestures. Length, however, may vary from a two-line joke to an adventure of several thousand words. Dialect stories appear throughout the United States wherever a nationality group lives in close contact with American-born generations. Danish dialect tales have been recorded from Ephraim, Utah, in the Southwest the Spanish-Mexican dialect blossoms, in Pennsylvania the German, in big cities the Jewish.

5. The stories of Swan Olson are not usually classed as folktales. They purport to be accurate autobiographical experiences, albeit of a hair-raising nature. As oral narratives they interest the folklorist, and they appear to represent a pattern of storytelling especially fertile along the frontier, or in communities like the Upper Peninsula with frontier characteristics. Here exists a society reminiscent of Heroic Age cultures, where individual strength and daring are the admired virtues, and heroes boast of their feats. In the Peninsula I encountered other autobiographical saga men like Swan, whose derring-do, physical prowess, and violent humor echo *The Narrative of David Crockett*, which rests on an oral, heroic, autobiographical base. The successful personal saga evokes belief, suspense, and admiration. On examination its episodes show resemblances to tall tales and hero legends.

Individual Repertoires and Delivery. Suggs told me about 170 narratives during my visits with him over the course of two years.[18] They covered every theme of modern Negro tale telling: speaking animals (23), Biblical and moral lessons (14), Old Marster and clever John (10), hoodoos and fortune telling (11), spirits and hants (10), social protest (5), exaggeration (15), Irishmen (5), preachers (13), humorous anecdotes (10), with a scattering of migratory fictions, folk history, and supernatural beliefs not easy to classify. In his varied life he had worked for a year with a touring "minister" (minstrel) show and still retained some instinct of the stage performer. Suggs possessed an infectious good humor and ebullience, which spilled over into his narration; he talked with animation and gusto, and laughed from tip to toe at his jest, or mine. Yet he had his somber side, too, and spoke of occult mysteries with solemn conviction. Whichever kind of tale he related, he projected himself completely into the situation, sometimes changing from third to first person in the course of the relation, as he identified himself with the chief actor. His animation compensated the northern listener bothered by his thick Mississippi Delta dialect. A sweeping range of inflection enabled Suggs to simulate the shrieking woman at revival meeting with a high-pitched electric shout, and in a breath he was back to the rumbling tones of the preacher. Telling a personal experience with a ghost train, he conveyed the mood in short, staccato sentences with his volume turned low. Two special features of a Suggs rendition were his tendency to recapitulate the tale, or its final episodes, in a swift, excited summary immediately upon its completion; and his inclination to moralize upon the story, sometimes even adding an incident from his own personal knowledge which confirmed the lesson of the piece.

John Blackamore told me 29 tales during the same period I was collecting from Suggs.[19] They included humorous animal, Old Marster, and Irishmen and preacher narratives, but no supernaturalism. His texts are exceptionally long, a good deal longer than usual variants of the same tale type. Several of his stories reach 1800 words, a remarkable length for American Negro texts. Blackamore will take a short anecdote familiar in the Negro repertoire and clothe it with panoramic detail of daily life. Up in the North this storytelling style no longer holds an audience, and a few of his buddies left the room in boredom while he was dictating to me. But in

Charleston, Missouri, he used to indulge in all-night sessions. Black-amore delivered his meaty narratives in monotone, with no attempt at inflection. Unlike other of my gifted black informants, he seemed to lack any singing ability and recited the story of Billy Lion and Stagalee, which is customarily sung as a ballad, in rhyming couplets. He knew his texts faultlessly and dictated them to me with never a miscue.

Joe Woods related eighteen tales to me during my two visits in 1946 and 1947.[20] Besides Märchen (6), he told satirical jests of priests and Jews (5), one heroic and one local legend, one novella, a comic Devil and a comic fright tale, an exaggeration, and an unusual true story, all of obvious European origin. The length of his longest Märchen, over 3000 words, is not surprising since Märchen are extended adventure stories, although we rarely encounter full-bodied examples in the United States. Woods claimed seven languages ("Polock, Russian, Croatian, Bohemian, Serbian, Slavish, English") and had narrated his fictions and jests in Polish and Slavish to his countrymen in the mines and the lumber camps. In recounting them to me in English, his errors of pronunciation did not hamper the ease of his delivery. After reading the artificial language of fairy tales in children's books, I was relieved to hear his fresh, colloquial, idiomatic speech. He was obviously a practiced craftsman, knowing his involved plots faithfully and presenting them confidently. He handled dialogue with great ease, spaced his incidents in natural paragraphs, and carried his story line forward with clarity and directness.

In one collecting session in a tavern that lasted from 9 P.M. to 2 A.M., Swan Olson reeled off to me half a dozen sensational experiences that had befallen him in the northwoods country.[21] The episodes seemed sharp and clear in his mind, and he told each one as a unit, although all were connected as segments of his autobiographical saga, and they even repeated each other. He had two accounts of whipping his boss Eric Ericson, two of driving off robbers, two of mine mishaps. The violence of the stories contrasted oddly with Swan's gentle demeanor and ascetic features; his head swung continually from side to side from age, and he doddered when he walked. Contrary to popular belief, old people are not necessarily good informants, who must all possess keenness of mind and lucidity of speech. An old man's reminiscences may prove unbearably tedious, rambling, and disjointed. But Swan wasted never a word; he had searched out the spectacular incidents of his life in America and arranged them into neat episodic shockers. What influences had shaped his style, in the absence of any conventional form of saga tale, could only be conjectured, but this kind of storytelling based on personal adventure and exploit flourished in the Upper Peninsula, and men of the woods, mines, and lakes relished matching such experiences.

During a three-week stay in Jonesport, Maine, I saw Jim Alley nearly every day, and by the time I left he had narrated 143 tales (only 4 of them published so far) into my tape recorder.[22] Many of these were brief Irishmen jokes, which turn up with astonishing frequency in the Negro South, the Kentucky mountains, and the New Jersey piney woods. But he also knew a store of anecdotes about odd local characters, several Old World comic tales which he also told anecdotally, and supernatural legends of the Jonesport area. Although Jim uttered his tales with great assurance, none of his kinfolk and townsmen thought of him as a storyteller, except one neighbor woman whom he habitually visited to pour out his troubles. Alley had household problems, usually looked severe and troubled, and was easily offended. He gave forth his stories positively, almost raspingly, whereas his older brother Frank spoke soft and low. Stories came to his mind easily enough if I triggered him off with a tale of my own, or if Frank were on hand to prime his memory, and once under way he kept stimulating himself in an endless flow. He preferred the pithy, compressed, economic anecdote and indeed never gave me a narrative longer than 500 or 600 words. His authoritative air and humorless mien made one think of a very seedy professor delivering a lecture, rather than of a storyteller of the folk regaling his cronies.

On the other hand, the name of Curt Morse was given to me immediately I reached Jonesport and inquired for storytellers. Everyone knew Uncle Curt. I met him accidentally when he visited a home in Alley's Lane, much in character, being the worse for beers, with a couple in tow who screamed with laughter at his every word. Curt lived for his audience and was constantly on display, exuding gags, tall tales, comical expressions, and jocular pieces. He eventually gave me 61 narratives, nearly all humorous, save for one local legend and some heroic exploits of Barney Beal, the strong man of Beal's Island.[23] Curt had done a stint on Gene Hooper's Cowboy Show that toured through Maine, been publicized in the county newspaper, and owned a reputation he felt compelled to maintain. Hence Curt played for the laugh with a showman's touch. Nevertheless he knew his countryside and its legends faithfully and had stories a-plenty about the old characters, the witch Sal Joe, and a wild man of the woods called Yo-ho. He made more out of a tale about a local character than did Jim Alley, adding descriptive details of appearance and behavior and smaller jokes along the way to build up the yarn. Frequently he inserted himself into comic personal experiences, thus extending his role as funnyman from storyteller to protagonist. In such narratives as the description of his trip, riddled with mishaps, to Aroostook County to dig potatoes, he played a comic counterpart of Swan Olson's hero.

Two meetings with Burt Mayotte, one quite brief, yielded five dialect stories, four in French and one in Finnish.[24] His prize narrative, "Paree at the Carnivalle," he claimed to have composed from his grandfather's retelling in broken English of Burt's own misadventures at a carnival. This ran to 1200 words, and his version of the immigrant's first visit to a baseball game, a dialect favorite, was even longer. As *raconteur* for the Allouette singers, the local French-Canadian club of Sault Ste. Marie, Burt held a semiprofessional status, evident in the poise and ease with which he delivered his pieces. In the act of reciting he stimulated the *Canadien* with darting eyes, nervous twists of head and shoulders, and gesticulation of hands, all adding up to a spasm of physical activity that suggested the befuddled, excitable Gallic character of his tales. Burt's phrases fell into a rhythmic beat as he poured forth the story, the French nasal intonations providing neat upswings on which to pause. The vibrancy and lilt of his speech further animated the narration. All five of his texts portrayed a scene—a carnival, a ball game, a hunting trip—and even an ignorant Finnish cop giving a city speeder a ticket took on the dimensions of a little tableau. Furthermore, he set several of his recitations in a frame of straightforward prefatory remarks that explained the situation and the background quite astutely.

The Tales. 1. "The Farmer and the Snake" (J. D. Suggs)[25] is a version of the tale known in the Aarne-Thompson Type-Index[26] as "The Ungrateful Serpent Returned to Captivity," Type 155, and Motif J1172.3.[27] This was one of Aesop's fables and has enjoyed worldwide currency. It is reported from Europe, Africa, India, China, Indonesia. Joel Chandler Harris has it in *Nights with Uncle Remus.* In one common subtype the serpent is returned to the original position from which he was rescued by a third animal called in as judge.

Suggs gives the story a realistic setting on a Southern farm. Accurate details are included: the reason for the farmer's plowing, the appearance of the snake. The factual background sharpens the comic fantasy of the talking snake; the tale is given matter of factly as an actual occurrence. A Br'er Rabbit influence appears, as Suggs personalizes the snake, calls him Mister, and puts idiomatic conversation in his mouth. Suggs's range of intonation proved especially effective in the dialogue parts, where he simulated the snake's whining pleas and the farmer's dubious tones. His plastic voice conveyed the initial pity of the farmer, the sternness of the deceitful snake, and the final resignation of the fatally bitten farmer. This is a moral tale, and Suggs always seized on the moral for a personal footnote. In this instance he gives an illustration from his own knowledge documenting the moral, just the sort of application to human conduct that Aesop was suggesting. The story of Dan Sprowell is more than half the length of the folktale and is told in a different manner. There is no narrative structure, but a sequence of astonishing facts with cumulative impact. Suggs ends the piece with racy phrases— "he was as crooked as a barrel of scales"—and a character judgment that brings him back to the moral of the folktale. No conflict develops between Dan Sprowell and some particular individual who befriends him, although Uncle Jack Suggs might have played the farmer to Sprowell's snake. The two sections are, however, meant to stand together; the fiction and the reality enhance each other, and their union is a mark of narrative imagination and moral insight.

2. "Coon in the Box" (John Blackamore)[28] is usually told in a dozen sentences or so, even by Suggs. It is one of the most popular Southern Negro tales in the Old Marster cycle. Actually the Negro tale is one episode extracted from a European story complex known as "Doctor Know-All" (Type 1641), in which a poor peasant

named Crab (Cricket, or Rat) purchases a doctor's garb, pretends to be omniscient, and manages through luck to detect thieves. He is then put to the test to divine what is hidden under a dish and says "Poor Crab!" in despair; he has guessed right. In the American Negro form the colored man always refers to himself as "coon." Blackamore takes the initial idea, that the clever slave has a reputation for uncanny wisdom, and gives it depth and dimension by the logical device of having Jack hang around his master's quarters and eavesdrop. Next Blackamore fills in the script with three examples of the sort of thing a field hand might very well hear his master talk about in connection with the next day's farming chores. The incident where Jack's boss bets with a rival planter he sets in a council meeting, to introduce the skeptic Carter. Other Southern Negro tales contain scenes where masters put their best slaves to the test, and in the final episode Blackamore strokes this in with a crowded barbecue gathering for the backdrop. He ends the tale with a formula couplet, a convention disappearing from modern Negro narratives. The milieu and cast of characters are drawn from young Blackamore's life in the new South: Old Boss and Jack the handy man replace Old Marster and John the clever slave from plantation times; crackers talk at a council meeting; Jack knows the tractor and fertilizer of the modern farm. Blackamore relies on no oral effects of intonation: for instance, he states that Jack answered his boss "rather slowly," where Suggs would have actually dragged out the words with exaggerated slowness. He does employ considerable dialogue, between Old Boss and Jack, and Old Boss and Carter. Blackamore's talent lies in the supplying of elaborate details of everyday life to clothe the story outline.

3. "The Rich Landlord and the Poor Shoemaker" (Joe Woods)[29] has enjoyed considerable distribution in Europe, where it is commonly known as "The Master Thief" (Type 1525). Like Doctor Know-All, it appears as one of the Grimms' household tales but is a good deal longer, containing four or more distinct adventures in which the clever thief steals possessions of the lord who has commanded him to attempt the thefts. Woods refers to each thieving episode as a "proposition" and gives six thefts: of dogs, bull, wife's sheets, wife's ring, stallion, and finally abduction of the priest. No doubt this division into similar episodes, characteristic of Märchen, assists in the considerable feat of memorization; the nar-

rator need keep firmly in mind only the six objects stolen. One of the problems encountered by the collector is seen in Woods' refusal to tell me completely the proposition involving the theft of the wife's ring, which took place in her bedroom. Earlier he apologized for another indelicate incident, saying that was how he had heard the story. Oral tales are invariably expurgated when presented to any large reading public. One stylistic device in this tale, employed as a connective between the episodes, and commented on by Thompson[30] as a convention of Märchen, is the direct question addressed to the audience: "Why can't they find the shoes? The shoemaker has picked them up when he hang up the dummy"; "Well, what's shoemaker going to do? Is he going to steal that horse?"; "Can you guess what he gonna do, that priest, with the minister?" Woods ends with his own salty moral, but in other tales he uses a formula ending. He reproduced plaintive, subdued, and angry tones. Frequently he omitted the bothersome prefaces of "He said." Often oral narrators inject "say" several times during one quoted conversation, to indicate the speaker is still talking, and they experience trouble too with personal pronouns, repeating "he" instead of the personal name, so that the reader of the text becomes confused. Woods steers clear of these blemishes with a clear, straightforward story line. Although he follows the plot of the tale type consistently, he uses his own muscular and pungent language to tell the story. The action moves forward swiftly. Yet Woods paints in a detailed setting, describing the barn scene minutely, setting down precisely all the objects and trappings involved in the shoemaker's machinations. The effect of realism is enhanced by his asides, emphasizing the typical European style of the barn and the life and death power of the lord over the peasants as remembered by his grandmother. Although his accent was thick and his pronunciations often incorrect, Woods never floundered or groped for a word. The total effect was one of complete control over a complicated text.

4. "My First Job in America" (Swan Olson) [31] differs from the preceding tales in that it does not belong to a definitely known folktale type and does not even qualify as a folktale, since it purports to be a true personal experience. Often, however, folktales will be told in the first person, and were more of these autobiographical sagas collected, we might find the same motifs and

themes reappearing. In any event, since this is an oral narrative by a folk narrator, it does interest the folklorist. This account has the symmetry of a folktale, with its series of separate but parallel episodes, in which the brutal Eric Ericson gets severely mauled: plopping in a ditch, getting knocked down with his own gun, being smashed with the stove pipe and whaled with a ramrod. The unsavory character of Eric is demonstrated regularly, to create a satisfaction in the listener at all this mauling. Eric is introduced as a wild man drinking straight alcohol and abusing his family; we see him again drunk in a bar, trying to shoot Swan with no reason; we find him in the act of beating his second wife; we are told he never paid his hired men. In addition to the major sensations there are minor matters to startle the listener, such as the cheapness of eggs at two cents a dozen, and the snake bedfellows in the hay loft. Finally there is the beautiful O. Henry climax, with Eric rewarding the man who had pummeled him all through the preceding day. The smaller touches of realism, like the description of the Old Country chest, and the statement that only silver dollars then circulated, contribute to the effect of authenticity. But the tautness and coherence of the piece, combined with the heroic role of Swan, and the evidence of other similar tales related by him—although not so fully rounded—indicate elements of composition here. Even if it all happened, the narrator must select, arrange, describe, connect the parts. If Swan had been retelling the narrative since 1890, repetition could have perfected it in the course of half a century; and if he had begun to relate it as a septuagenarian reminiscence, his memory could have clutched the feats of other saga men. He used no verbal tricks of intonation to heighten his tale, but let it speak for itself.

5. "The Duck Hunt" (Burt Mayotte)[32] is a tall tale in dialect. Actually it combines three episodes that could be told separately. The first incident, of a Frenchman on a raft or boat who says in the morning, "Bah gosh, we ain't here, we seven miles from here," is widely told as an independent anecdote about the simple *Canadien* who twists phrases comically. The second and third actions belong to the pervasive American tall-tale tradition of remarkable hunting and shooting. The Motif F638.3, "Man is waiting for bird to fall that he had shot eight days before," is also known in India. Two humorous figures, here Joe and Curley, frequently occur in dialect stories, under various names, as a pair of comic foils who speak to

each other in mangled English and match each other's oddities. Mayotte employs a framework to introduce them and carry on the narrative between comic incidents, but suddenly he switches from the role of objective narrator speaking perfectly good English to the dialectician who is telling about Joe and Curley in their own *Canadien* speech. This switch comes immediately after a rather literary phrase, "with grave aplomb," which provides a rhythmic lilt to end a sentence and suggests the sober appearance of the Frenchmen, thus intensifying the ludicrousness of their behavior.

The humor of dialect is present throughout. Instances are the use of aspirated h's before consonants, homemade synonyms ("Two-pipe shoot-gun" for "double-barreled shotgun"), nonsense construction ("nobody see some more ducks"), and *Canadien* expletives ("maudit," "sapré"). Although obviously farcical, the tale remains true to the local culture; the place names and manner of duck hunting and reference to the *chantier* are all accurate, and the French-Canadians do exist and perform in a way to invite mimicry and caricature. This tale, like all of Mayotte's, relies considerably on verbal effects, both of dialect and rhythm; the sentences are broken into unit phrases with clear pauses in between, making almost a singsong: "So we h'all go hinside / han' Joe cook de pan*cake* / han' heverybody h'eat." "You know / Cur*lee* / Hi'll have haim / for his neck." Some creative writers employing the French-Canadian *habitant* speech, like William Henry Drummond, have chosen verse as a vehicle for dialect humor, to capture the verbal rhythms.

6. "Clever Art Church" (Jim Alley)[33] is not a single tale but three independent anecdotes told about the same local wag. Anecdotes of local characters comprise a large section of American folk narrative but have never been seriously collected or systematically studied. Art Church was an actual person, but the tricks he played are similar to those credited around the country to locally celebrated pranksters and fastened onto the Yankee in the newspaper humor of the 1830's and 1840's. The first trick belongs to the theme of the literal contract based on a double meaning. Uncle Josh took "best part" to mean most, but Art pointed out that the two sticks of hardwood were indeed the best part of the cord he sold Uncle Josh. The next supposedly true happening, where Art is asked to lie and says he has no time because so-and-so has just had an

accident and he must get a doctor—which is a lie—is an international folktale attached to various American yarnspinners, such as Gib Morgan, the tall-tale bard of the Pennsylvania oil fields.[34] The third anecdote is a variation on the Yankee trick to outwit a creditor. Alley presents the meat of the brief stories without trimmings or elaboration, to achieve the terse, pithy quality that gives the anecdote—as distinct from a casual yarn with deliberate build-up—its impact.

Direct, idiomatic dialogue in each anecdote sharpens the pace and gives a sense of immediacy, as if Jim himself had been there as witness. Quoted indirectly, the dialogue would lose its bite. Each little tale ends with a statement of chagrin by the dupe. This seems unnecessary in the hardwood story, which could stop with Art's triumphant explanation of the literal sale, but the triumph is sharpened by having the last word a lament from Art's victim. Brief as they are, the anecdotes contain a certain amount of repetition: the phrase "the best part of it was hardwood" in the first; "I ain't got time" in the second; and the parallel utterances and actions of Art and McFall in the third. These repetitions give form to the anecdote; they impress salient points on the listener unfamiliar with the personalities or the situation, who could easily lose the sense of the rapid-fire tale, perhaps hinging on a wordplay, if his attention were not arrested and riveted to the key idea. Alley's positive, even authoritative, delivery contributed to the success of the anecdotes, which become blurred and confused if the speaker falters or stumbles. In a long story a lapse can be picked up without much damage.

7. "The Horse Trade with Bill Case" (Curt Morse),[35] told as a personal experience, falls within an honored cycle of American trickster yarns dealing with horse trades. The formula requires that a trade be agreed on and a sorry animal be fobbed off by a Yankee sharper, who adds insult to injury in his subseqent explanation. Here Curt makes himself out to be the Yankee, projecting himself into the story according to his wont. Jim Alley would simply relate the comical saying or deed of the character Bill Case, but now attention is shifted from comical Bill Case to crafty Curt. Curt elaborates the yarn with incidental humor, as in the reference to Bill and his sisters being "rolled-oat eaters," and the graphic description of Bill's nose. Like Alley, Morse salts the story

with natural-sounding dialogue, not only between the traders but also between Bill Case and his sister, and he too ends the tale with a wry comment by the dupe. A humorous vocal effect in the present piece is Curt's reproduction of the snuffling whistle that punctuated Bill Case's speech, formed probably by a sharp intake of breath through a slightly open mouth. Curt used his throaty voice and timbre for doleful and lugubrious inflection.

Both verbally and structurally Curt contrives a continuously humorous piece. Bill Case himself is a comical-appearing and sounding character; he has a humorous exchange with Curt, and another with his sister, and then finally comes the jest of the second swap. Humorous improvisation is by now instinctive with Curt; when he was listening to a playback of another tale he had told about an eccentric hermit, he was surprised to hear himself say the hermit could play "The Mocking Bird" on his violin "so real that you'd have to take a stick to keep driving off the birds from the strings." In the course of narrating his yarns Curt can easily insert gags and comic expressions which he repeats regularly in his everyday banter.

Do these seven folktale texts, selected by the personal taste of the collector from the vagaries of his own field encounters, show any common stylistic features? One point that had escaped me until they were placed on the dissecting table is their plentiful use of dialogue. The tale becomes fresher, livelier, and clearer when natural conversation is introduced, and avoids a tedious and confusing trait of some folk narratives, the ambiguous use of indirect quotation.

Throughout their stories the speakers avoided garnishment with literary words and highbrow allusions. Although only three of the seven narratives purported to be true—and these contain highly dubious points (Olson, Alley, Morse)—each teller gave his story the maximum appearance of reality, through use of background detail, internal conversation, personal comments, and earnestness of delivery. This earnestness comes from an act of identification with a protagonist of the tale: Suggs with the trusting farmer against the snake and the confidence man; Blackamore with the handy man against the cracker bosses; Woods with the shoemaker thief against the rich landlord; Swan with his own role as hired man against maniacal Eric Ericson; Mayotte with the comical

Frenchmen against the alien Yankees; Alley with clever Art Church against his dupes; and Morse with himself as a shrewd Yankee trading against Bill Case. There is conflict in the tales, sometimes merely a lighthearted battle of wits in the serious business of swapping and trading (Morse, Alley), and again a grim struggle between landowner and serf (Blackamore, Woods, Olson) cloaked in comic sparring. Whether in fairy tale, saga, or jest, the tellers are committed to their tales and communicate their passion and sympathy.

These texts do conform to Olrik's laws for oral narrative. They are simple and unsubtle, they pit together a good and a bad character, and they contain repetitions, even the short anecdotes. But these laws, binding as they seem, still permit considerable play to the talents of individual folk artists.

LINCOLN AS FOLK NARRATOR

The approach suggested here for analyzing the oral style of superior folk narrators has been applied to living storytellers encountered in the field. Now I shall try it on Abraham Lincoln. From the wealth of Lincoln material we find far more data on storytelling style and repertoire than exists for most folktale tellers of the present day. Lincoln biography fully accepts the fact that Lincoln was an engaging and masterful raconteur, and numerous observers, acquaintances, and friends have described his delivery and written down his texts. In his own lifetime the daily press and Abe Lincoln jokebooks circulated around the country endless yarns, sayings, and witticisms attributed to him, many of them apocryphal. Enough, however, are authenticated, by reliable authorities, so that we can recognize Lincoln tales. Carl Sandburg's six-volume biography pays special attention to the yarns and sayings and skillfully weaves them into the life.[36] In spite of all the attention given Lincoln as humorist and narrator, no one has seriously analyzed his relation to folk tradition. I am convinced that the evidence proves Lincoln to be an artistic folk narrator and performer on the order of Suggs and Curt Morse and Jim Alley.

Background. Lincoln grew up in Kentucky, Indiana, and Illinois after the first wave of pioneers had opened the country, when farmers were beginning to break the soil and settle the land. He was born in a log cabin in Kentucky, moved after seven years, in 1816, to Little Pigeon Creek in southern Indiana, and in 1831 trekked 200 miles west to New Salem on the Illinois prairie, where a dozen families had founded a town. Here in Illinois he made his permanent home and traveled around the state as a circuit lawyer, gossiping and swapping tales in taverns. Lincoln grew from what folklorists like to call a folk background, a setting in which the formal instruments of learning have scarcely appeared and society is much influenced by time-honored beliefs, word-of-mouth reports, and the natural environment. In time, of course, other influences played upon Lincoln. By the mid-nineteenth century the earlier currents of frontier humor were being submerged by a new breed of professional funny-men writing in urban newspapers—Petroleum V. Nasby, Artemus Ward, Orpheus C. Kerr—and Lincoln read and repeated their manufactured jokes. But the stock of humorous tales on which he drew most frequently and intimately came from his youth on Indiana and Illinois pioneer farms. He said that his best stories came from country folk.[37]

Delivery and Repertoire. Most persons raised in the midst of a folk tradition never become expert folktale narrators. Only certain individuals with the flair and the relish to remember and perform the tales are themselves remembered for such talent. Lincoln said that he always recalled every story he heard and admitted that he was a mere "retailer" of yarns—a valuable clue to their folklore nature. Witnesses have testified to his enrichment of a story with mimicry of characters and acting out of parts; he reproduced a stutterer's peculiar whistle between syllables (like Curt Morse), gyrated his arms and legs in accompaniment to the text, and twanged in dialect. Under the spell of the tale his melancholy countenance glowed with animation and he seemed transformed, almost handsome. At the Capitol he was soon recognized as a champion yarnspinner.[38] "His favorite seat was at the left of the open fireplace, tilted back in his chair, with his long legs reaching over to the chimney jamb. He never told a story twice, but appeared to have an endless repertoire always ready, like the successive charges of a magazine gun." [39] One

observer stressed the dry chuckle, the gesture of rubbing the hand
down the side of the long leg, the gleam in the eye.[40] Lincoln tre-
mendously enjoyed relating his fables. "I can't resist telling a good
story," he said. Once he got up in the middle of the night to rouse a
sleepy friend and tell him a yarn that was tickling him irresistibly.
When he met another tale teller he responded immediately with a
matching yarn—again a sure sign of the folk raconteur. An office
seeker topped Lincoln's parable with a splendid folk yarn of his
own, whereon Lincoln promptly gave him the job. He appreciated
the painter Conant for one especial tale he borrowed himself, and
he would introduce him as the author of "the Slow Horse story." [41]

John Hay guessed that Lincoln knew a hundred stories. Any
such surmise is problematical. Sandburg lists 135 in the index to *The
War Years* and gives a score more in the less well-indexed *Prairie
Years*. Beyond a doubt Lincoln possessed an extraordinary repertoire rarely equaled by folk narrators currently being recorded in
the field.[42] He specialized in the humorous anecdotal yarn, "neither
too broad nor too long," said Horace Porter. His texts are fuller
than the brief anecdotes of Jim Alley, but pointed and concentrated
on a single incident so that they never wandered off into a rambling
yarn, in the fashion of Mark Twain's garrulous talkers.[43] Apparently
he adapted his stories to differing situations, and variants appear for
certain ones, in distinction to separate versions of the same yarn
recorded by different bystanders.

The Tradition. The particular folk tradition represented by Lincoln is not immediately clear. He does not belong to the backwoods
vein of Davy Crockett that branched through the Kentucky and
Tennessee canebrakes in the early years of the nineteenth century,
producing tall tales of bear hunting and Indian fighting and melees
between boasting bullies. The scene of Lincoln's stories is the
prairie farm, not the forest clearing; the setting is in cornfields and
country stores, not in the isolated cabin. His aphorisms and expressions grow from pioneer farm life and concern hogs and ploughs,
blacksmiths and circuit preachers. Crockett is the solitary hunter,
tangling with occasional eccentrics who penetrate to the backwoods, like Yankee peddlers or uncouth squatters. Some backwoods anecdotes do turn up in Lincoln's repertoire, but few, and
they are told *on* degenerate log cabin families, rather than *by* the

intrepid backwoodsman, as in Crockett's yarns.[44] Lincoln comes a stage later than the Kentucky hunters and Mississippi keelboatmen who pioneered the West and brought forth hero legends of Crockett and Mike Fink. His folk are farmers. Folklorists have collected surprisingly few farm tales, considering the importance of America's agricultural past and present. Therefore we cannot find many variants to Lincoln's farm stories, but they bear all the internal marks of folktales. Several choice examples follow.

> And this reminds me [Lincoln's dream of death] of an old farmer in Illinois whose family were made sick by eating greens. Some poisonous herb had got into the mess, and members of the family were in danger of dying. There was a half-witted boy in the family called Jake; and always afterward when they had greens the old man would say, "Now, afore we risk these greens, *let's try 'em on Jake. If he stands 'em,* we're all right." Just so with me. As long as this imaginary assassin continues to exercise himself on others I can stand it.[45]

> The glib representations of one military report, concealing disgrace and defeat involved, reminded Lincoln of the young fellow who shouted at the plowing farmer, "I want your daughter!" The farmer went on plowing, merely shouting over his shoulder, "Take her," whereupon the youth stood scratching his head; "Too easy, too durned easy!" [46]

> "R[aymond], you were brought up on a farm, were you not? Then you know what a *chin fly* is. My brother and I . . . were once ploughing corn on a Kentucky farm, I driving the horse, and he holding the plough. The horse was lazy; but on one occasion rushed across the field so that I, with my long legs, could scarcely keep pace with him. On reaching the end of the furrow, I found an enormous *chin fly* fastened upon him, and knocked him off. My brother asked me what I did that for. I told him I didn't want the old horse bitten in that way. 'Why,' said my brother, 'that's all that made him go!' "
> "Now," added Lincoln, "if Mr. C[hase] has a presidential *chin fly* biting him, I'm not going to knock him off, if it will only make his department go." [47]

> They [United States Marshals] are like a man in Illinois, whose cabin was burned down, and according to the kindly custom of early days in the West, his neighbors all contributed something to start him again. In his case they had been so liberal that he soon found him-

self better off than before the fire, and he got proud. One day, a neighbor brought him a bag of oats, but the fellow refused it with scorn. "No," said he, "I'm not taking oats now, I take nothing but money." [48]

Some of Lincoln's yarns are recognizable folktales. Mrs. Vallandigham, wife of the Copperhead leader, said she would never return to Ohio except as wife of its governor, a statement reminding Lincoln of a story about a candidate for the county board in Illinois who told his wife on election morning that she would sleep with the township supervisor that night. After the returns came in, she dressed up to sleep with the victor, her husband's rival. I heard the same anecdote told on an unpopular old fellow in Munising, Abe Artibee, during a field trip I made to upper Michigan in 1946.[49] An odd horse tale of Lincoln's dealt with a balky animal traded off by its owner as good for hunting birds; it squatted in the middle of a creek, and the owner called out to the dupe: "Ride him! Ride him! He's as good for fish as for birds." [50] This popped up in recent years in the cycle of "shaggy dog" stories and was told me in pretty much the same form as this by a colleague at Michigan State University, LeRoy Ferguson, save that the horse sat on grapefruit instead of birds. A superb yarn about a blacksmith hammering a big piece of heated wrought iron into successively smaller tools and finally throwing it into the water to make a "fizzle" out of it, suggests another shaggy dog favorite about the "cush-maker," which has an early variant.[51] The boy sparking the farmer's daughter who is chased by her father with a shotgun and outruns a rabbit falls into the tall-tale theme of fast runners who outrace ghosts and rabbits.[52] The tearful deathbed reconciliation of Old Brown with his sworn enemy, to be voided if the sick man recovers, is told the same way by Shepherd Tom Hazard in his recollected traditions of South County, Rhode Island.[53] Lincoln used the anecdote to express his feelings at having to release the Confederate envoys Mason and Slidell to Great Britain. Hearing of a young brigadier general who was captured by the Confederates with his small cavalry troop, Lincoln said, "I can make a better brigadier any day, but those horses cost the government $125 a head." So does a Maine sea captain mourn the loss of a couple of dories over that of one sailor and a couple of "Portygees," and a Michigan lumbercamp boss is pleased that a lumberjack rather than a teamster's horse is killed by a falling tree.[54] Commenting on Douglas's scrap with Buchanan over slavery in Kansas, Lincoln told of the backwoods wife who found her husband in a savage tussle with a bear and cheered both on impartially: "Go it, husband, go it, bear." A Joe Miller jokebook carried this tale in 1865, and later in the century the sensitive reporter of Vermont folk life, Rowland E. Robinson, placed it in the mouth of one of his raconteurs: "Go it, ol' man, go it, bear, it's the fust fight ever I see 'at I didn't keer which licked." [55]

Individual Style. As Sandburg remarks, Lincoln's talk was salted with new American words and twists of speech soaking into the language. Lincoln had the gift—as does Harry Truman—for employing the homely barnyard metaphor and earth-drawn proverb to nail his point. "Small potatoes and few in a hill" he said of a signal rocket that fizzled out. Of the Gettysburg address he fretted to Ward Hill Lamon, "Lamon, that speech won't scour," using a figure of speech derived from mud sticking to the mold board of a plow and hindering its movement. "I don't amount to pig tracks in the War Department," he remarked ruefully. "As they say in the hayfields he requires a good man to 'rake after him,' " was one of his farming saws applied to a sloppy worker. From his father he gained the proverb "Every man must skin his own skunk." "Why, I could lick salt off the top of your head," he said to a short man, and of a blowhard he commented, "the only thing you could do would be to *stop his mouth with a corn cob.*" Lincoln used the comparative exaggerations still current in rural speech, and called an argument of Stephen A. Douglas as thin as "soup made by boiling the shadow of a pigeon that had starved to death." As War President he remarked: "Some of my generals are so slow that molasses in the coldest days of winter is a race horse compared to them. They're brave enough, but somehow or other, they get fastened in a fence corner, and can't figure their way out." Country words continually arrested the attention of his associates, who were startled when he asked, "My young friend, have I *bunkered* you out of your chair?" [56]

Obviously such dialect words and expressions sauced Lincoln's yarns and added a barnyard aroma to his farming stories. Here, unfortunately, the texts are at their weakest, since reporters of longer narratives would hardly remember the racy turns of phrase that stuck in their minds when used in proverbs or single utterances. Still some of the tales, like that of the rival powder merchants, convey authentic flavor of speech.[57]

Structurally the chief characteristic of Lincoln's storytelling style is his application of the yarn to an immediate political or social situation. A genius shines forth here, in the uncanny aptness of his illustrative anecdotes. As Seward and others remarked, his little tales were fables and parables of wisdom. Aesop, we know, appealed to Lincoln. The perfection of his folktale lies in its moral lesson. So in the Middle Ages did priests relate exempla to make their point. Whereas Suggs moralized on his tale after telling it, dipping into his past experiences with sinners, Lincoln broke into his story from a live situation—frequently when beset by importunate office seekers. Examples here would include most of his known repertoire, but two felicitous instances are his story of the boy hoping his captured coon would escape so that he would not have to kill it, which Lincoln told when asked what disposition he intended to make of Jeff Davis; and his anecdote of the farmer who trapped nine skunks and then let eight go because the one he killed made such a stench, given in reply to the query why he did not fire his whole cabinet and not just Cameron.[58]

The tale of "The High- and the Low-Combed Cock" can be cited to illustrate characteristic elements of Lincoln's storytelling style.[59] The political problem posed by the Kentucky Senator, how to woo the shifting factions in Kentucky, prepares the way for the President's yarn, and the moral emerges crystal-clear upon its completion. This was Lincoln's customary framework. The tale itself contains a backcountry scene from Lincoln's own folk experience, in this case a cockfight in Kentucky, and so contrasts sharply with the huffing political arena of the White House. Still fable and crisis are neatly linked, for both pertain to Kentucky, and the weaselly Squire, who hedges his bets until the winning cock is determined, symbolizes the mass of shifting Kentuckians. No doubt the original text would show racier speech, but dialect is rendered, in the Squire's quoted words. The yarn is delicious by itself, limning the shallow fraudulence of the puffed-up Squire. He resembles one of the sharpers and scapegraces whom Baldwin, Hooper, and other antebellum Southern humorists loved to portray. Much of Lincoln's humor was aimed at such solemn frauds. The narrative possesses enough detail to depict the scene and engage the listener's interest but avoids extraneous description that could overload the story and smother the moral. As Horace Porter said, Lincoln's tale was neither too broad nor too long.[60]

APPENDIX: THE TALE TEXTS

1. The Farmer and the Snake (J. D. Suggs)*

Farmer's out early breaking his land in February, he wants to get good subsoil. Well, he's plowing along, and he plowed up Mr. Snake, a great big one. Mr. Snake was in a quirl where he'd quirled up for the winter, you know; he was cold and stiff. Farmer stopped and looked at him, says, "Well I declare, here's Mr. Snake this time of year." Mr. Snake says, "I'm cold, I'm about froze to death. See how stiff I am, I can't even move. Mr. Farmer, would you put me in your bosom and let me warm up a bit? I'm cold."

Farmer says, "Noooo. You'se a snake, I can't fool with you, you might bite." He said, "No, I wouldn't bite you for nothing in the world. Do you reckon I'd bite you after you warm me up?" He talked so pitiful Mr. Farmer decided he'll warm him in his bosom. So he stoops down to pick up Mr. Snake, and puts him in his bosom. Well, he tells his horses, "Git up," gets his plow, and goes back to work.

About nine o'clock he unbuttoned his shirt, looked down in his bosom. "How do you feel, Mr. Snake?" Mr. Snake says, "I feel pretty good, I'm warming up considerably." He buttoned his shirt up, goes on and plows till about ten-thirty. Unbuttoned his bosom, looked at it, says, "How do you feel, Mr. Snake?" "Oh, I'm feeling pretty good. Ain't you feeling me moving around? I can move now." The farmer says, "Yes, I'm glad you feeling better, feeling warm." Well, he plows till about fifteen minutes to twelve. He said, "Well, I'll go down to the other end and put Mr. Snake down." He could feel him moving around quite spirited like, so he didn't bother to unbutton his bosom at all. After a while when he got near to the other end, he was going to take him out and go on to dinner. He kinda looked down and the snake done stuck his head out and

* From R. M. Dorson, *Negro Folktales in Michigan* (Cambridge, Mass., 1956), pp. 196–97.

was looking right in his face and sticking out his tongue. (A snake wants to fight then, you know, when he sticks out his tongue.) Farmer says, "Now, Mr. Snake, you said you wasn't going to bite me; you said after I warmed you up you wouldn't bite me." Snake says, "You know I'm a snake, Mr. Farmer." "Yes, but you said you wouldn't bite me." Mr. Snake said, "Now you know, Mr. Farmer, I'm *s'posed* to bite you."

So he bit the farmer in the face. The farmer goes home, tells his wife how he carried Mr. Snake in his bosom and got him good and warm; then Mr. Snake bit him. Said, "Don't care what a snake says, don't never take one in your bosom to warm him up. For when he gits warm he will bite." In the end Mr. Farmer lay down and died.

(Now you know there's people will confidence you just like that snake. Like Dan Sprowell. He was the terriblest rogue, and just as pleasant to look at, and a good worker. Dan was from Goodman, Mississippi, in Attala County. As a boy he began stealing onion sets from stores, put them in his pocket. The laws caught him, and sent him to the pen. He chopped cotton so fast they made him a trusty in three weeks, and he walked out—changed states. He worked for my Uncle Jack Suggs after he got out, for just his keep. One day my uncle was going to Memphis on an excursion. While he was gone Dan pressed the clothes of the boys and the girls and took them all. He stole a horse and buggy in Water Valley, worth about $175, and was driving some girls around, and they arrested him and was carrying him back for a trial, when a gang took him to lynch him. They was going off a piece, and Dan knocked down the fellow with the lantern and made a lunge out in the woods. They fired at a man's height and he was crawling off on his all fours, so he got away.

They arrested him for stripping a woman's clothes line. The judge asked him, "Have you ever been in the Penitentiary?" "Yes." "How long?" "Three weeks." "How long were you sentenced for?" "Three years." The judge said, "I sentence you to six years of hard labor." But in three weeks he was out again.

Yeah, he was crooked as a barrel of scales. He'd steal his own hat off his hoe, just to keep in practice. And as fine-looking a young man as you ever seen. He just loved to steal, and he'd sell for nothing. And he didn't drink either. Anybody'd fall for him. He was a snake. You put him in your bosom and he'd bite you.)

2. Coon in the Box (John Blackamore)*

Once upon a time there was a Boss had a servant on his farm, kind of a handyman. Every night this handyman, Jack, would go down to the Boss's house and listen while he ate supper, so he'd know what Boss was going to do the next day. One night when Old Boss was eating supper he told his wife he was going to plow the west forty acres the following day. After Jack heard that he goes home to bed; next morning he gets up earlier than usual, and gets the tractor out and hooks up the plow. When Old Boss come out Jack was all ready to go. So he said, "Well Jack, we're going to plow the west forty acres today." He said, "Yes, Boss, I know, I got the rig all set up." Well, Old Boss didn't think much about it. He gets on his horse and goes in there and shows Jack how he wants him to plow it up.

So the next night when Boss sits down to eat his supper Jack goes on down to his favorite spot where he could hear everything. He heard his Old Boss tell his wife that he was going to round up all the livestock for shipping. Next day Jack gets up early, and gets the Boss's horse ready that he always rides when he rounds up the livestock. When Boss comes out later, he starts to tell Jack what he's got on the program. Jack cuts him off and says, "Yes, Boss, I know, we're going to round up the livestock this morning. I got your horse all saddled and ready to go." So Boss says, "Jack, what puzzles me is, every morning when I get up you tell me what I'm going to do before I tell you." And he wants to know what's happening, how did Jack know what he's gonna do. Jack says, "Well I don't know, I just knows." So Boss says, "Well, something funny going on." Jack says "Maybe so, but I know."

So they goes on to round up the livestock, and at the end of the day Boss sits down at the supper table again. And Jack takes the same position at the window, so he can hear everything that's talked about. Boss tells his wife about he's going to clean out the stable the next day, to use the waste to fertilize the fields. So the next morning Jack was out in the stables cleaning 'em out, before Old Boss was up. Boss eats breakfast and he goes on out to the barn, sees Jack busy working. So he asks Jack, "How did you know I wanted the stables cleaned out today?" Jack says, "That's all right, I

* From R. M. Dorson, *Negro Folktales in Michigan* (Cambridge, Mass., 1956), pp. 51–53.

knowed you wanted to get it cleaned out so I went and got it started so I could hurry up and get the job done." So Boss says, "Yes, that's right, but what puzzles me is how a nigger like you can figure out what I'm going to do every day before I tell you." He says, "Well that's all right, Boss, I know everything." So Old Boss shook his head and walks on up. So that night he was still puzzled at suppertime. Jack was still at the window. He listened to what his Boss was talking about. Old Boss told his wife, "Well this handyman we got around here, he's the smartest one I ever seen. Every morning I go out to tell him what to do he's already done it or he's telling me what we are going to do. And I don't know what to do about it."

So he was going up to the council next night, where the landlords have their meeting every Wednesday night to discuss their crops and problems. When Old Boss comes out of the house to go to the meeting, Jack had his rig all ready. Old Boss says, "Well thank you, Jack." And Jack says, "I hope you have a good time at the meeting, Boss." So Old Boss went on down to the meeting and he was telling the other landlords about this smart nigger he had down at his place. All the other councilmens laughed at him. But it didn't tickle Old Boss. He says, "You guys think I'm joking, but that's the truth." So one smart aleck he jumped up and said, "There ain't no nigger that smart." Everybody laughs again. So Old Boss got peeved. He says, "Well, all you crackers think it's so damn funny; I'll bet money on my nigger, 'cause he knows everything." Everybody begins to get quiet then, except this smart aleck. He says, "Well Jim, since you think so much of your nigger, I got $100,000 to say that I can outsmart your nigger." Old Boss called the bet. He said, "Now any of you other crackers in here think that's so funny and want to bet, I'll cover you too." So everybody kicks in with $100,000 apiece. When the total was counted up the bet run over a million dollars. So this Carver—that was the smart aleck—he says, "Well you can expect us down tomorrow about two o'clock, and we'll have something your nigger can't tell us about."

Old Boss went home. Old Jack was still up waiting, so he could find what's going to happen tomorrow. Old Boss went into his bedroom, and he sat down side of the bed and he commenced to telling his wife what he was doing. And he said he was going to give a big barbecue the next day, so he needed to have food and drinks ready for the crowd when they come on down. Then he went on to bed.

Next morning old Jack was still sleeping when Old Boss got up. He was making himself scarce. He knowed they had some kind of a trick for him; he didn't want Old Boss to think he was so smart any more. So Old Boss rapped on the door, said, "Jack, get up, it's day." He says, "Coming, Boss." Old Boss walks on off and went on back in the house. And Jack was so used to Old Boss getting up and he being ready for him ahead of time, he begins to prepare for the party, without the Boss even telling him. When Old Boss come out, he says "That's right, Jack, that's right. We're going to have a big party this afternoon, and I got a lot of money bet on you." Jack wanted to know then what for he had his money bet. So Old Boss said, "Well you know—you're trying to kid me that you don't know."

When the crowd had all of them gathered around they called Jack. Jack came around slowly. Old Boss said, "Come on up, Jack, come on up, don't be bashful." So Mr. Carter, the smart aleck, he says, "Well darky, they tell me you're pretty smart around here." So Jack says, "Aw, I wouldn't say that." Old Boss says, "Oh he's just trying to be modest." Then Old Boss said to Jack, "Didn't you tell me the other day that you know everything?" So Jack stretches his head and says, "Yes, that's right," rather slowly, scared to call the Boss a liar. So Mr. Carter says, "All right, let's get down to business, we got a lot of money bet on this. And I want you to tell us what it is, 'cause if you don't, I'm going to have your head tomorrow." Then Carter he called Jim over to tell him what the surprise was, before Jack would tell them. Carter told Jim it was a box in a box in a box in that box, and in the small box was a coon. And why they had him in so many boxes was so that Jack couldn't hear the coon scratch.

And then Jack started scratching his head and trying to tell them what was in the box, although he didn't really know. So Carter asked him again, "Well Jack, what do you say is in the box?" Jack started repeating what Carter had said. He says, "In the box, in the box, in the box." And he decided that he didn't know in his mind what, so he just scratched his head and said, "You got the old coon at last." (He was using that as an expression.)

So Old Boss grabbed him and shook his hand and said, "Thanks, Jack, thanks, that's just what it is, a coon in them boxes!"

> I stepped on a piece of tin and the tin bent,
> And that's the way the story went.

3. The Rich Landlord and the Poor Shoemaker (Joe Woods)*

Once on a time a rich man wanted ride on a horse for his pleasure. And he passed shoemaker house. Window was open, so he stopped to look in to see if the shoemaker was in. Shoemaker was sitting on a bench fixing the shoes, his wife was washing dishes. Every time his wife went to the other room, he jumped outa the bench, run to the back, grabbed the bottle a whisky from under the cover (pillow), and take a snort. Then he run back to the bench. And five minutes after that, he do the same thing, when his wife was not there.

So the rich man was thinking: What the dickens he do that? So he get up offa the horse and went to the house. So he says: "Good morning, master shoemaker. Can you tell me why do you that? Whenever your wife leave the room you jump up and take a snort out the whisky. Can you do that in open, when your wife is here?"

He says: "No, my lord. My wife bought whisky for me, but she won't give me. I gotta steal from her."

So lord say: "I give you proposition."

"My lord, what kind proposition you gonna give me?"

"Are you good stealer?" lord ask him.

So the shoemaker say: "Yes, my lord, I can steal anything that's in this room."

"Here's my proposition," rich man says. "I got two dogs. Watchman take care of them. If you can steal them tonight, I give you hundred ducats. Or if you can't do it, I give you one hundred lashes. That's the bargain."

And the shoemaker, he know them dogs very well. Nobody come at night except the night watchman. So he went to town, go to the drugstore, buy sleeping powder. And from butcher shop he get nice two steaks. And soaked them steaks in sleeping powder, in water. So he went to the rich man's yard, and hide himself in the bush. When night fall, watchman came and pick out chains from doghouse and go around on his night watch. So when dog was out

* From *Western Folklore* 8 (1949): 39–47.

of the doghouse, he sneaked in and put the meat in there. So, middle night, watchman come and put in dogs on chains, he gonna get supper for himself.

So when the dogs finda juicy meat there they eat 'em and go to sleep. That's all shoemaker was waiting for in the bushes there. So he had nothing to do, he stepped in, tie both dogs by the tails together, throw them over the shoulder, and carry them home. ('Cause he can't drag them—those heavy dogs.)

So what happens, the landlord wake up middle of night and think he forgot to tell watchman to guard those dogs. So he went to the watchman and he tell him, "Mike, watch the dogs tonight, 'cause I think somebody's going to steal them."

The watchman says, "No, my lord, nobody can steal them, 'cause they never let nobody to go to the yard. I'm the only one that feeds them. But I'm gonna see them right away, anyway." But when watchman went to the doghouse there was no dog there. So the watchman run outside and yell: "Tiger! Leopard!" 'Cause that was the dogs' names. But there was no answer.

So he was thinking: "By gosh, somebody steal them. But it wasn't my fault, because he didn't tell me early." So he went right away and reported to his landlord. When he come to the palace, he ring the bell, and landlord come out and ask him, "What's the matter, Mike?"

"Lord, the dogs is gone. I can't find them no place."

"I think that damn shoemaker got them." So the lord early in the morning went back to the shoemaker house, rap at the door, and the shoemaker come out and say, "What the matter, lord?"

"Are you get them?" the lord say.

"Yes, lord, I got it. I have them."

"But how the dickens you get them?"

"That's my business," the shoemaker say.

So the lord pay him the hundred ducats, in the golden money. So when shoemaker take his hands to rub the money, rich man say: "Wait a minute. We going to have another bargain. You think I gonna lose those hundred ducats. I guess not. I have three-years-old bull in my barn. You gotta steal them tonight, you get hundred ducats, if you don't you get two hundred lashes. And remember, I ain't fooling."

Then when he went home, he was figured that way: "If I leave the bull in the barn, he might stole it. I go call the two men, and at night they going to take the bull to the other village, half a mile outa his palace."

Then sometimes shoemaker was figuring himself: "If I was in that lord's place, I never keep it in that place, I transfer it." He was figuring same thing.

To go to the other place (the other farm) they have to go through the woods. So he make a dummy look like himself—mask, and piece of rope in the pocket, and one pair brand-new shoes. Then he went behind the barn, and he's sitting there waiting what's gonna happen.

At nine o'clock that night, two men come out the barn with the big bull, two rope around the ring-nose. And they started go to the other barn. So when they come to the timber, shoemaker take the shortcut, run ahead before them to the road which they gotta pass, and drop one shoes. Then wait, then run on ahead again, 'bout fifty yard, drop the other shoes. Then run 'bout hundred yard ahead, and hang his dummy. Then he run back where he drop the first shoes (now can you guess?) and he wait there.

Then coupla minutes after, them two men with the bull coming. And one said, "John, look, new shoes."

"Well," George said, "only one, but good one. Maybe shoemaker trick."

So they left the shoes and started going. Soon they's come to the other shoes.

So John says: "George, look. That other shoes make swell pair of shoes, and we left the other one behind." So John says: "George, you go ahead get the bull, and I go ahead get the other shoe, so we have swell pair of shoes."

"Oh, no. That's a shoemaker trick. If we left the bull over here, he might steal it. The hell with the shoes! We gotta look after our landlord's bull."

Then they left the shoes and started going ahead. Then 'bout hundred yards from them they had a big surprise. The Mr. Shoemaker hang up in the tree by a rope.

"Well, what happen?" George say.

"Nothing happen. He can't steal the bull, so he hang up himself. He didn't want to get lashes."

So George says: "You know, we tie up the bull, and we go steal the shoes. No use leave the good shoes in the woods, somebody take them."

So they tied the bull and run like crazy, 'cause each one wanted them pair of shoes. And they run to the edge of the timber, and still no shoes—can't find the shoes.

Why can't they find the shoes? The shoemaker has picked them up when he hang up the dummy.

So John and George run to the other end of the woods, and no shoes, no bull. So then they afraid go report to the lord. Then they run away, cause they know what happen when they report that. (You know that time of the story the lord can kill the men like they kill the dogs—they own the women, the children, everything, like slaves. My grandmother remember that yet.)

So in the morning the lord send the page to the barn, to see if the bull there. The page come back and report that George and John take the bull to the other farm. So he told the stableboy to saddle the horse, and went to the farm himself. And the lord was smiling to himself how's he going to give the two hundred lashes to the shoemaker and take the money back. But when he come to the other farm, there was no George, no John, no bull there—never was.

Then back he go to the shoemaker. Then the shoemaker have big smile on his face when he come there.

"Did you have it my bull?"

"Yes, my lord, I have [softly]. He's chewing out there in my barn."

"But tell me, how the dickens you get that bull from the two men?"

And the shoemaker says: "That's my business."

"Well," he says, "I gotta pay you." So he pull his money outa his pocket and pay the shoemaker. Happy shoemaker. "Thank you for money, my lord," says the shoemaker.

"Oh no, my friend," says the lord. "I gonna give you another proposition. Now my friend you gotta steal the sheets from my wife when I go to bed with her. And remember, three hundred lashes and money back if you don't do that."

"But lord, that cost you lotsa money if I do that."

"I don't care for money. I want to get revenge on you."

When the lord come home, he tell his wife: "Now watch my

dear, that damn shoemaker outfox me again. But I going to get even tonight."

So shoemaker think same thing, you know. "Now how am I going to get that sheets?" He went to the (what you call) game warden, and bought some gas powder, and went to the toy shop and bought a whistle—you know, like policeman whistle. He made himself like old man, take bottle whisky with him, he went to the kitchen, the lord's kitchen. And he mixed up the powder with the whisky, and treated them. Then he went to the barn and throwed that wolf meat between the cattle. Went back to the kitchen, pull up from the pocket the skin of a dead rabbit, and throw between the girls. And he put the whistle in the back quarter. And when the gas escape from the body, the whistle was blow, "Fee fo fo." (That's the story the way I heard it—I can't help it.)

Then in the barn when the cattle smell the wolf meat, they start a racket. Then he went under the window, he had some dummy what he hang up, he stick the hat right in the window. Then he rapped the window pane gently with his finger. So the lord jump outa the bed; he looked at the window; he see his friend the shoemaker. "Now I going to get you."

He jumped out the bed, take the gun and blasted it right at the shoemaker. And he heard the shoemaker fall down. So he says to his wife, "Now I got him." He run outside with his nightgown. But he heard a noise in the kitchen. "What the dickens is this thing now?" And fighting. The two girls was fighting. They find the dead rabbit skin and thought it was a baby. "Mary, you had baby." "No, Katie, you had baby."

He come there, light a match, find the rabbit. "That's a goddamn shoemaker trick."

So when he settle with the girls he went back to where he kill the shoemaker. He want to hide the body. He didn't know that the shoemaker throw the dummy into the old well. That time when he look for shoemaker, the shoemaker go in the front door to the bedroom, and was whisper to his wife: "Give me that sheets. That bugger will steal them, he didn't get kill."

She says, "Well, what you gonna do with the sheets?" He's going to hide them, so he won't have no chance to steal them that night.

Half hour after the hunting for the shoemaker in the park, he can't find him, so he's come back to his wife, in the bedroom. He say, "Are you here, my sweet?" She says, "Yes." He says: "That's funny, I know I kill him, but I can't find his body no place. So I am going lay down for a while yet. I going to wait for him, whether he come back or not."

When he touched the bare mattress, he asked her, "Where's the sheets?"

"Oh, Jesus, you just take them while ago. You told me you going to hide them."

"Sure, sure, that wasn't me, that was shoemaker. Can't you judge by the voice?"

"How can I judge by the voice? He was just whispering to me. I thought it was you."

Well, so next morning, lord going see shoemaker. The shoemaker had the answer ready: "Yes, lord, I take your sheets." So lord forget to ask him how he do that. The lord pay him the hundred ducats.

[Joe omitted a "proposition" here because he said it wasn't fit to print. I coaxed a synopsis from him. The shoemaker was supposed to steal the ring worn by the lord's wife. He hides in the bedroom. The lord and his wife make love. Then she goes to the bathroom. He knocks on the door and asks for her ring, so she won't lose it in the dark. She gives it to him. Then when she goes back into the bedroom, he climbs out the bathroom window. She asks the lord for her ring. He says he doesn't have it. "But I just gave it to you." "That wasn't me, that must have been that damn shoemaker. Didn't you know it wasn't my voice?" "But he was whispering."]

So now the last proposition was: "I don't have much more money. I got a stallion in the barn. You gotta steal him. And remember, there will be some guards to steal [watch] him. And if you don't steal him, that will be four hundred lashes, and all the money back."

"Yes, my lord, I try my best."

So, when the lord come home, he call the barn boss. Now he says: "Remember, you work long time for me. Now I tell you, you put the good guard, and you guard yourself that horse there. Take how much money you need it. Two men watch the door. One man stay on the top horse. I want another man should hold the line, the rope. And you, my friend, you stay and hold the tail."

"Okay, thank you, lord, we do that, our best."

Well, what's shoemaker going to do? Is he going to steal that horse?

He dress himself like lady, like pregnant lady. He tie big pillows under the dress. In the basket he put a ham, nice sandwiches and sausages, bottle wine, bottle whisky, dozen boil eggs. And the wine and whisky was opened. So 'bout nine o'clock at night he walk right straight to the barn, to the door. Two men was sitting by the door, and she walked right to them, and started moaning. "O my good friend, are you good Christian? My time come, I going to have a baby, and like Mary have Jesus in the manger, can I come in and have my baby on the piece of straw in the barn?" [plaintively].

So like good Christian they let her come in the barn, and they put piece of straw in the corner and coat over her so she can lay there. And she says: "Thank you, my dear friend. There is some refreshment there in my basket. On a chilly night like tonight you can warm yourself with that."

So she didn't have to tell them twice. They jumped at once at the proposition. The barn boss drop the tail and go to the basket and take a good snort. And the fellow on top the horse say, "Hey, leave some for me too" [loudly].

And the lady says: "Don't fight boys, there's enough for all of you. And the rest of you, there's some sandwiches, take a bite." So they were so happy. In half hour both bottles was empty. Then something happen. The barn boss start to rub his eyes. So the boss was started sleeping, and his helper too. So the old lady got up from the corner, make the rope outa the straw, and tie that man who is sitting on the horse to the rafter. And barn boss, he tie him to the post and put broom in his hand—he was supposed to hold tail, you know. And them two fellows who was sitting by the door, shoemaker take the wax and warm it, and put it on their heads, and stick their heads together. They're stuck together. And that man who's sit on the manger, he gives him the empty bottle. Then he open main door from inside. (In the barn in Europe there is always a main door and a side door in the back for the servants.) He take the stallion out. Then he come back in, lock the door from the inside. There was in the yard a grain house. On the ground floor was full of grain. On the top floor was empty. There was a sack of straw in the yard. He bunch him up that straw, put under the wall, make like bridge sloping. So he take the stallion and make him walk up the bridge onto the second floor, shut the door behind him, remove all the straw, then went home.

Then in the morning the lord go to the barn. First, see the two men what is sitting on the doorstep, two head bent together, sleeping. So he started horsewhip them. Men wake up, but they can't get out; started hollering, "John, let me go, let me go my hair." So one's hair was a little weaker, goes out, so they get out anyhow. The worse thing was on that man what was hanging on that rope on the rafter. Every time he whipped him he started to swing like pendulum. When he come back he nearly knock lord down with his knees. And barn boss get it worst 'cause he can't get outa the post. Lord take the broom and break the broom on him, but that was nothing. When he come to the one what had the bottle in his hand, he smelled it and said, "Aha, so that was it, that's what put you to sleep." So he cooled down little bit.

He went to the shoemaker now. "So you have my horse, huh?" he asked the shoemaker.

"Yes, lord, yes and no."

"What do you mean—'yes and no'?" the lord asked.

"Because I stole him, but he's still in your yard."

"All right, I didn't pay you money before I find out." So the lord went back and look all over—every barn, every shed, every nook, every corner, in the bushes, in the yard—no horse. For one hour they look all over, the house servants; no trace of the horse.

So he went back to the shoemaker and he say: "You lie. There is no horse in my yard. There is no place for horse in my yard."

"Lord, how much you give me if I show you where your horse?"

"All right. I give you ten ducats extra, when he's in my yard."

"Let's go."

They went right under the grain house. Shoemaker take the ladder, put against the wall, climb up, open the door, and there is the stallion.

"Nee-hayaah."

And poor lord look in his blue eyes there and can't believe himself.

"How the dickens you get him there?"

"That's my business."

"Well, how you get him down?"

"Well, it depends how much you give me."

"What, you think I gonna pay to get that horse down?"

"Oh, my lord, you forget you don't pay me the two hundred and ten ducats extra for stealing and showing you where's the horse."

So the lord take the money and pay him, one hundred ten ducats. He offer him ten ducats more extra to get that horse down.

So shoemaker say: "You gotta do that yourself. I show you how, for I don't wanna work like I work last night."

So the lord think, "I don't care for the ten ducats, but I wanna find out how he make it."

So he tell his servants to bring the bunch of straw back, make a slope. So they make that slope. So he jump on the horse and ride down. "Here's your horse, lord."

Then lord say: "My dear friend, you ruin me. I'm bankrupt." He says: "You know, I gotta friend, minister. Some way that story get out, so he gotta good laugh on me. That priest say, 'Poor ordinary man, he can outfox the learned man.' Can you fix him some way so I can get a good laugh on him?"

"Yes, lord, I can do that. Take a little time, and money. But I do that for nothing. Next week Sunday, the rich peoples make a ball, dance. Twelve o'clock, at middle night, you should be out in the dancing hall. You have there fireplace in your dancing hall, lord?"

"Yes," he said.

"So at twelve o'clock, at middle night, all the lords and ladies should sit around in a circle, and look on the fireplace. And look when miracle come."

What shoemaker going do?

On Saturday morning he hire coupla boys to catch him couple hundred lobsters (you know what lobster is?). At Sunday night, he went to the church with the bag full of lobster, and a coupla hundred Christmas candle. He open the door with a master key, lock himself in from inside, and went to the altar where there was big statue of Jesus, take the Jesus, put it on the floor behind the altar, and he's dress like Jesus and stand in his place.

Before he went on the altar, he took the lobsters out the bag, light the candles in the pincers, and they look like angels coming there—there was no light in the church.

When the priest had the signal, somebody went in the church, he went outside, seed the light in the church. He didn't know what happened. So he went to the church through the sacristy door. Then he see the thousand lights on the floor. And he heard a voice come from the Jesus' mouth. And Lord say with a voice like thunder: "Minister, you gotta come to heaven, with me, tonight, to take confessions from the poor souls."

And minister says: "O Lord, you take me dead or 'live?"

And the Lord says: "Take off your clothes, 'cause you can't wear them to heaven. Climb in the bag, I'll do the rest."

Can you guess what he gonna do, that priest, with the minister? [To wife: "You think I tell you everything. Thousand story I forget."]

So he climb in the bag, naked. Then he climb out the altar, tight the bag so the priest can't get free, remove the lobster, and put the Jesus on the altar. He take that bag on his shoulder, put the minister in, then walk with him to the lord's castle. Then he put the priest on the ground, finda two ladder, one put on top the roof, the other put against the roof. Then he look on the clock—it was five minutes to twelve. Then he went on the front door and tell the servants to call the lord, he wanna see him.

When the lord come he ask him, "Are you ready?" And the lord say: "Yes, yes, we all ready. Can you tell me what going to happen?" the lord ask him.

The shoemaker say: "No. Look and see." And went.

And before he went he told him, "Keep all the lights on, and all the ladies and guests should look in the fireplace."

So lord say: "Ladies and gentlemen, it's one minute to twelve. Exactly on twelve o'clock we going to see something extraordinary. But what, I don't know myself."

And the same time, shoemaker is climbing on a ladder up, with the bag with the minister in. Then he stop by the big chimley, cut the string down on the bag, shake the bag so the minister start sliding down the chimley to dancing room to the fireplace. And all the peoples in dancing room staring with eyes on the fireplace. And what you think is come down? First thing is come out bag, and behind is black devil. Only the devil had no tail from behind, he had it in front.

And poor minister when he see so many people staring at him, he didn't know what to do. He didn't know where he was neither. He know he wasn't in heaven. So he run to the window, jump through the window, and knock himself cold—bump his head on the frame. Even the lord didn't know who that was, didn't know he was devil, for the shoemaker didn't tell him. The lord tell his servants to clean him up. And that was the minister what was laughing at him.

So minister give all the money back to the lord what he lose to the shoemaker, to keep the secret.

That is story of how the brain work. A great many millionaire have no education you know. And many millionaires become bums.

4. My First Job in America (Swan Olson)*
See chapter 3, pages 93–95.

5. The Duck Hunt (Burt Mayotte) †
Two old Frenchmen decided to get an early start to Munoscong. They wanted to get down early, so they tied up at Brady Pier here night before. Buck season opened the next day. Curley was the first one to waken—the boat had broken loose from its moorings and drifted down to Hay Lake. "Woke up, Joe, woke up, we're not here at all, we're twelve miles from here." "What's de difference?" said Joe. "It's too dark to hunt anyting."

It was getting gray in the east. Curley said, "I see one duck myself two mile off—dee ducks he come pretty quick." So Joe said, "Get your thirty-eight feefty-five and take dee first won." No, it was too far for Curley. Then Joe said, "Hit's not too far for me. Hi'll take my two pipe shoot gun han show you how to get dat duck. Hi'll raise my gun hup high, and Hi'm take pretty good haim." He said, "Bang, bang, Hi'll shoot. Maudit, what you tink? De duck he's fall, and when Hi'll pick heem hup, he have been hit on de behin'. You know, Curley, Hi'll have haim for his neck."

The fellows told him he'd scared all the ducks away, so they might as well start cooking their breakfast before the flocks came

* From R. M. Dorson, *Bloodstoppers and Bearwalkers* (Cambridge, Mass., 1952), pp. 251–54.
† From *Journal of American Folklore* 61 (1948): 127.

in. So they went into the *chantier*, but there was no kindling. So Joe came out to get some kindling and spied more ducks but they were way up high, too high for his trusty two pipe shoot gun. He said to himself, "Joe halso have de pretty good heye, but not good henough for duck dat high." He called Curley with his thirty-eight feefty-five. Curley looked at the height of the ducks, with grave aplomb.

"Dis time Curley take de hell of a good haim. Bang, bang, he shoot. Two times he shoot some more, bang, bang, and nobody see some more ducks. So we all go hinside, han' Joe cook de pancake, han heverybody h'eat. W'en all of a suddink, she's come one hell of a noise on dee roof. Joe he's don't fineesh wid dee dish. So he says, 'Curley, you go see who's make all dat rakette.'

"Curley she's come back in, she's have dee great beeg smile on hees face. He said, 'Wat de hell do you know, Joe? Dem maudit sapré duck was high.' "

6. Clever Art Church (Jim Alley)*

DORSON: You were telling me that this Art Church was quite a fellow. Who was Art Church?

JIM ALLEY: Oh, a fella lived up Injun River.

DORSON: What was he known for?

JIM ALLEY: Well I don't know.

FRANK ALLEY: Oh he was a nice fella, clever.

JIM ALLEY: Clever.

FRANK ALLEY: As clever a fella as you ever see. But if he got it in for you, boys look out. He'd lie to you just as quick as flies.

DORSON: Didn't he play a trick on your Uncle Josh?

JIM ALLEY: Yes, he sold Uncle Josh a cord of wood and he told him the best part of it—he'd find the best part of it was hardwood. And Uncle Josh paid him for it and when he went out and looked he had just two sticks of hardwood. And Uncle Josh got after him about it and he said, "I told you the best part—the best of it was hardwood." "Well," he said, "I only got two sticks of hardwood."

DORSON: Now that that whistle has stopped blowing, perhaps you'd tell us one of Art Church's lies.

JIM ALLEY: Art Church was going downtown by Porter Cummings, and Porter hollered "Art, come in." He says, "I ain't got

* Tape recorded in Jonesport, Maine, July 10, 1956.

time." He says, "Come in long enough to tell me a lie." He says, "Well, I'm in a devil of a hurry, I ain't got time." Says, "Your father, I just come down by him and he's cut himself awful and I'm after a doctor." Well Porter jumped into his wagon—no automobiles then—and rushed up there and his father hadn't cut himself at all. And he said "The devil, he told me a lie right on the road."

DORSON: What's that one about the other time he wanted to get a receipt in full?

JIM ALLEY: He owed McFall a bill and McFall tried to git it. And he wrote him and wrote him and Art didn't pay no attention. And at last Art started from Machias and he got up Mason's Bay and he met McFall a-comin'. Art says, "I'm just comin' over to pay that bill." Well McFall says, "I'm just comin' over at your house after it." McFall's horses headed toward Jonesport and Art's headed toward Machias. "Well," Art says, "write me out a receipt and I'll pay you." He wrote him out a receipt and Art grabbed it and started his horse and McFall turned around and tried to get him, but said, "It's no use, he's got the receipt and that's all there is to it."

7. Curt Gets the Best of Bill Case in a Horse Trade (Curt Morse)*

DORSON: Who was Bill Case?

CURT MORSE: Bill Case was an old fella lived here with his sister. She was an old maid and he was old bach and they lived together. I guess they was kind of rolled-oat eaters, they'd eat sour apples and rolled oats, didn't cost 'em more than thirty cents a year to live. They was a comical pair. Fact, Bill had one of them great wide long transparent noses you look right through it. He was comical, but an awfully good old fella.

DORSON: Talked funny, eh?

CURT MORSE: Yeah he talked funny. So he says to me, he says "[sucking noise] Devil," he says, "How'll we trade horses?" he says, "[sn] I like the looks of your horse."

"Well," I says, "I don't know, I got a good horse."

Says "[sn] I got a better one."

But I said, "Before we trade I'll have to have your harness, your

* Tape recorded in Kennebec, Maine, July 13, 1956.

wagon and the hames, corn, brush, and blanket, and them six hens and that Plymouth Rock rooster."

"Well he looked at me and he says, "[sn] Want the ell off the end of the house too?""

Anyhow we hit up a trade, I guess he was kinda lazy about lookin' after the horse. Well that horse I let him have had the blind staggers. So the next day I heard him hollerin' at me to come over and see what ailed the horse, and I went over and he said, "The horse has got a shock."

I says, "Well you know, anybody's apt to have a shock." Just then his sister looked through the little hole in the barn door and she says, "William, don't you sell that Plymouth Rock."

He says, "Hallelujah [sn], you go in the house or I'll knock your devilish head off." Well anyhow, we got the horse outdoor she kinda straightened up, and he says, "[sn] Want to buy her?"

And I says, "No, I'll give you the six hens you give me yesterday for her."

And Bill says, "[sn] You bought her, bring my six hens back." I got both horses and the whole outfit for the six hens he give me. Never come to him till the next day, Bill says, "[sn] Great trader I am."

N O T E S

1. Y. M. Sokolov, *Russian Folklore*, tr. C. R. Smith (New York, 1950), p. 128. Cf. Roman Jakobson, "Commentary," in *Russian Fairy Tales*, tr. N. Guterman (New York, 1945), pp. 631–56.

2. James H. Delargy, "The Gaelic Story-teller," *Proceedings of the British Academy* 31 (1945): 177–221. Subsequent considerations of Gaelic storytellers appear in Maartje Draak, "Duncan MacDonald of South Uist," *Fabula* I (1957): 47–58; Calum I. MacLean, "Hebridean Traditions," *Gwerin* 1 (1956): 23–33.

3. Edwin Sidney Hartland, *The Science of Fairy Tales* (London, 1891), Ch. 1; J. F. Campbell, *Popular Tales of the West Highlands*, Vol. 1 (Edinburgh, 1860), Introduction.

4. C. M. Bowra, *Heroic Poetry* (London, 1952).

5. Archer Taylor, "Some Trends and Problems in Studies of the Folktale," *Modern Philology* 37 (1940): 19.

6. Stith Thompson, *The Folktale* (New York, 1946), pp. 449–61.

7. Ibid., pp. 445–56, from Axel Olrik, *Folkelige afhandlinger* (Copenhagen, 1919).

8. Ibid., pp. 451–53, from Mark Azadovsky, *Eine sibirische Märchenerzählerin* (Helsinki, 1926).

9. Franz Boas, *Race, Language and Culture* (New York, 1948), pp. 491–502. A linguistic approach and references to other stylistic studies of North American Indian tribes are given in C. F. Voegelin and J. Yegerlehner, "Toward a Definition of Formal Style, with Examples from Shawnee," in W. E. Richmond, ed., *Studies in Folklore* (Bloomington, Ind., 1957), p. 149, notes 3 to 7.

10. Gladys A. Reichard, *An Analysis of Coeur d'Alene Myths* (Philadelphia, 1947), pp. 5–35.

11. Ibid., p. 25. Reichard writes: "The story 'Cricket Rides Coyote' owes its humor to the fact that combinations of comic sounds are repeated until the story becomes side-splitting. This is only one of many examples which shows how impossible it is to carry over the spirit of the tale into a language like English, which has no machinery for the expression of such an effect."

12. Linda Dégh, "Some Questions of the Social Function of Storytelling," *Acta Ethnographica* 7 (1957): 91–146.

13. William H. Jansen, "From Field to Library," *Folk-Lore* 63 (1952), 152–57.

14. William H. Jansen, "Classifying Performance in the Study of Verbal Folklore," in Richmond, ed., *Studies in Folklore*, pp. 110–18.

15. John Ball, "Style in the Folktale," *Folk-Lore* 65 (1954): 170–72.

16. Cf. Sokolov, pp. 10–14.

17. In *Negro Folktales in Michigan* (Cambridge, Mass., 1956), ch. 2, I discussed individual styles of six Negro folk narrators, including Suggs and Blackamore. Here I wish to contrast them with narrators from other subcultures.

18. Of these, 59 have been printed in my *Negro Folktales in Michigan* and the remainder in my *Negro Tales from Pine Bluff, Arkansas, and Calvin, Michigan* (Bloomington, 1958).

19. Richard M. Dorson, "Negro Tales [of John Blackamore]," *Western Folklore* 13 (1954): 77–79, 160–69, 256–59.

20. Richard M. Dorson, "Polish Wonder Tales of Joe Woods," and "Polish Tales from Joe Woods," *Western Folklore* 8 (1949): 25–52, 131–45.

21. Richard M. Dorson, *Bloodstoppers and Bearwalkers* (Cambridge, Mass., 1952), pp. 250–57.

22. Only four of them published so far [1960], in Dorson, "Collecting Folklore in Jonesport, Maine," *Proceedings of the American Philosophical Society* 101 (1957): 270–89.

23. Four of them are printed in Dorson "Collecting Folklore in Jonesport, Maine," and six in Dorson, "Mishaps of a Maine Lobsterman," *Northeast Folklore* 1 (1958): 1–7. [Additional tales for both Alley and Morse have since been published in Dorson, "The Folktale Repertoires of Two Maine Lobstermen" in *Internationaler Kongress der Volkserzählungsforscher in*

Kiel und Kopenhagen, ed. Kurt Ranke (Berlin, 1961), pp. 74–83; and Dorson, *Buying the Wind* (Chicago, 1964), section I, "Maine Down-Easters."]

24. Dorson, "Dialect Stories of the Upper Peninsula," *Journal of American Folklore* 61 (1968): 121–28.

25. Dorson, *Negro Folktales in Michigan,* pp. 196–97.

26. Antti Aarne and Stith Thompson, *The Types of the Folk-Tale* (Helsinki, 1928).

27. Thompson, *Motif-Index of Folk Literature,* six vols. (Bloomington, 1955–58).

28. Dorson, *Negro Folktales in Michigan,* pp. 51–53.

29. Dorson, "Polish Wonder Tales of Joe Woods," pp. 39–47.

30. Thompson, *The Folktale,* p. 458.

31. Dorson, *Bloodstoppers and Bearwalkers,* pp. 251–54, untitled.

32. Dorson, "Dialect Stories of the Upper Peninsula," p. 127.

33. Tape-recorded in Jonesport, Maine, July 10, 1956.

34. Mody C. Boatright, *Gib Morgan, Minstrel of the Oil Fields* (Austin: Texas Folklore Society, 1945), pp. 29–30, Motif X905.4.

35. "Curt Gets the Best of Bill Case in a Horse Trade." Tape-recorded in Kennebec, Maine, July 13, 1956.

36. Carl Sandburg, *Abraham Lincoln, the Prairie Years,* vols. 1–2 (New York, 1927); *Abraham Lincoln, the War Years,* vols. 3–6 (New York, 1940).

37. Dixon Wecter, *The Hero in America* (New York, 1941), ch. 10.

38. Sandburg, *Abraham Lincoln, the Prairie Years,* vol. 2, p. 302; *Abraham Lincoln, the War Years,* vol. 5, pp. 61, 322, 335.

39. Sandburg, *Abraham Lincoln, the Prairie Years,* vol. 1, p. 357, quoting a newspaper reporter.

40. Sandburg, *Abraham Lincoln, the War Years,* vol. 4, p. 285, quoting English author-correspondent Edward Dicey.

41. Ibid., vol. 5, pp. 323, 329, 339; vol. 4, pp. 56–57. It was Anthony J. Bleecker who matched Lincoln with a tale of a converted Indian praying for his enemy, in order to heap coals of fire on his head and "burn him down to the stump."

42. Cf. A. K. McClure, *Lincoln's Yarns and Stories, a Complete Collection of the Funny and Witty Anecdotes that Made Abraham Lincoln Famous as America's Greatest Storyteller* (Chicago and Philadelphia, n. d.), and a modern collection of recollections, E. Hertz, *Lincoln Talks, a Biography in Anecdote* (New York, 1939).

43. Jim Blaine's story of the old ram in *Roughing It,* which never does get to the point, is a good example of the discursive yarn.

44. Backwoods stories are in Sandburg, *Abraham Lincoln, the War Years,* vol. 5, pp. 8, 328, 639–49 (a traveler in a thunderstorm asks for less noise and more light; a pioneer woman tells a Bible salesman, "I had no idea we were so nearly out"; a traveler denied food by a niggardly couple stirs up the ash cake hidden in their hearth fire).

45. Ibid., vol. 6, p. 245; a variant is in vol. 2, pp. 299–300, placed in Indiana.

46. Ibid., vol. 5, p. 328.

47. Ibid., vol. 4, p. 638; a variant follows, pp. 638–39.

48. Ibid., vol. 5, p. 326.

49. Ibid., vol. 4, p. 379; Dorson, *Bloodstoppers and Bearwalkers*, p. 160.

50. Sandburg, *Abraham Lincoln, the Prairie Years*, vol. 2, p. 300.

51. *Sketches and Eccentricities of Col. David Crockett of West Tennessee* (London, 1833), pp. 79–80. William H. Jansen reported in "The Kleshmaker" (*Hoosier Folklore* 7 [1948]: 47–50) the analogue between Crockett's story and the current shaggy dog jest. The story does not appear in Crockett's *Autobiography*. Cf. Sandburg, *Abraham Lincoln, the War Years*, vol. 6, p. 150, for a text from Horace Porter; a variant by Grant follows, pp. 150–51.

52. Sandburg, *Abraham Lincoln, the Prairie Years*, vol. 2, p. 296. Baughman cites examples of "Lies concerning speed" under Motif X1796, in *Type and Motif-Index of the Folktales of England and North America*, Indiana University Folklore Monograph Series 20 (The Hague, 1966).

53. Sandburg, *Abraham Lincoln, the War Years*, vol. 3, p. 368; told on Sylvester and John Hazard, in Thomas R. Hazard, *The Jonny-Cake Letters* (Providence, 1882), pp. 170–72, and *The Jonny-Cake Papers of "Shepherd Tom"* (Boston, 1915), pp. 165–66.

54. Sandburg, *Abraham Lincoln, the War Years*, vol. 4, p. 38; Horace P. Beck, *The Folklore of Maine* (Philadelphia and New York, 1957), p. 130; Dorson, *Bloodstoppers and Bearwalkers*, p. 197.

55. *Political Debates Between Abraham Lincoln and Stephen A. Douglas* (Cleveland, 1894), p. 263; R. Kempt, ed., *The American Joe Miller* (London, 1865), p. 207; Rowland E. Robinson, *Danvis Folks* (Rutland, Vt., 1934), p. 191.

56. Sandburg, *Abraham Lincoln, the War Years*, vol. 5, p. 321; vol. 4, pp. 472, 305, 299; *Abraham Lincoln, the Prairie Years*, vol. 1, p. 296; vol. 2, pp. 246, 293, 302; *Abraham Lincoln, the War Years*, vol. 5, p. 331; vol. 4, p. 203.

57. Sandburg, *Abraham Lincoln, the War Years*, vol. 5, p. 62.

58. Ibid., vol. 6, p. 237; vol. 4, p. 284; a variant is given in *Abraham Lincoln, the Prairie Years*, vol. 2, p. 447.

59. Text from Sandburg, *Abraham Lincoln, the War Years*, vol. 5, p. 327, "as published in the *Philadelphia Times* and other newspapers, and credited to [Colonel James Sanks] Brisbin."

60. Sandburg, *Abraham Lincoln, the War Years*, vol. 5, p. 61.

5 /

Theories of Myth and

the Folklorist

STUDENTS OF MYTH and folklore once occupied some common ground. In his often reprinted collection of essays called *Custom and Myth*, first published in 1884, Andrew Lang spelled out the relationship as seen by the anthropological school of English folklorists who so spiritedly advanced the cause of folklore science in the late nineteenth century. Two bodies of material intrigued Lang and his fellows. Around them they beheld archaic survivals among the British—and European—lower classes, in the form of village festival, agricultural rite, and household charm, so anomalous in the midst of the progressive, industrial, scientific England of the Victorian age. From missionaries, travelers, colonial officers, and the new anthropological fieldworkers they learned about "savage" myths, usages, and beliefs in remote corners of the world. The equation between peasants and savages provided "The Method of Folklore," the title of Lang's opening chapter. Savage myth embodied in fresh and vivid form the withered superstitions and desiccated rites now faintly visible in peasant customs. The folklorist could reconstruct their original full-fleshed shapes, and the prehistoric world in which they functioned, by close comparisons with the myths of primitive peoples.

These bodies of living myths further explained to the folklorist the irrational elements in myths of civilized peoples. Lang puzzled

Reprinted from *Daedalus* 88 (1959): 280–90.

over the question why classical Greece preserved in her mythology such barbarous ideas, and found his answer in the new anthropology of E. B. Tylor. Greek myths were survivals and distorted mirrors of an earlier culture when cannibalism and human sacrifice did indeed prevail. To see such customs intact in his own day, the folklorist need simply turn to the Andaman Islanders, the African Hottentots, the Australian Noongahburrahs, and similar newly exposed areas of primitive life. Now the ugly Greek myth of Cronus becomes meaningful. Cronus cruelly castrated his father Uranus, who was about to embrace his mother Gaea. A Maori myth from New Zealand gives the key, depicting Heaven and Earth as a wedded couple, Heaven lying on Earth and imprisoning their children between them. Finally one child, the forest god, forces them asunder, freeing the offspring for their godly duties over the various elements. So did Cronus secure the separation of Heaven (Uranus) and Earth (Gaea), although the Hellenic Greeks had forgotten the original sense of the nature myth.[1]

Behind this method of folklore inquiry lay an enticing theory, transferred from Darwin's biology to the young science of anthropology and thence to folklore. Lang and his coworkers, G. L. Gomme, E. S. Hartland, and Edward Clodd, all accepted the unilinear view of cultural evolution. Mankind had climbed from his simian ancestry upward to the state of polished civilization by successive stages. All peoples ascended the evolutionary ladder in exactly the same manner. The savages of today were the Victorians of tomorrow, simply arrested by local circumstance, and conversely the Victorians of the contemporary moment were the savages of yesteryear.

In his far-reaching study of *The Legend of Perseus* (three volumes, 1894–1896), Edwin Sidney Hartland engaged upon the most sweeping application of the folklore method to a single classical myth. By slicing the Perseus myth into component episodes, such as the notions of the Supernatural Birth, the Life Token, the Witch and her Evil Eye, and pursuing their appearances throughout the worldwide collections of fairy tales, sagas, and savage mythologies, Hartland was able to demonstrate the substratum of primitive ideas underlying the literary myth. In the refined versions by Ovid and Strabo, Pausanias and Lucian, coarse traits essential to the primitive saga had dropped out: the external soul of the ogre, the lousing of the sleeping hero by his maiden-lover.

Another leading member of the anthropological school, Edward Clodd, examined the relationship between myth and the new study of folklore in his *Myths and Dreams* (1885).[2] The title of a preliminary lecture expresses more completely his point of view: "The Birth and Growth of Myth, and Its Survival in Folk-Lore, Legend, and Dogma." Clodd saw in the concept of "myth" not merely the label for a narrative of the gods or the creation of the universe, but also the designation of an entire period in the stage of man's intellectual development, "a necessary travailing through which the mind of man passed in its slow progress towards certitude."[3] In this stage, prehistoric man corresponded to the child, taking dreams for reality, endowing inanimate objects with life, crediting animals with the power of speech.

While the anthropological school of folklorists depended on myths, in this broad sense, to document their major hypotheses, they were at the same time vigorously battling a rival group of myth interpreters. The philological school of comparative mythology, championed in England by Max Müller, unlocked the secrets of myths with the new key of Vedic Sanskrit. In his famous essay on *Comparative Mythology* in 1856, Müller outlined the principles governing the proper explication of myths. All Aryan tongues stemmed from the Sanskrit, which transferred to its offspring the names of gods, all referring to celestial phenomena. The basic equation lay in Dyaus = Zeus, uniting the two chief gods of the Vedic and Hellenic pantheons. Through a "disease of language," the original meanings and myths of the inherited names were forgotten and barbarous new myths arose to take their place. These myths had revolved around the sky (Dyaus) and the sun, the dawn and the clouds, and now comparative mythology could reconstruct these primary meanings buried within revolting Aryan mythologies.

So did solar mythology make its persuasive plea. Among the solarists who followed Müller's lead, George Cox outstripped all others in the sweep of his claims. Every mythical hero—from Herakles, Perseus, Theseus, Oedipus, Samson, down to Beowulf and King Arthur and the humbler heroes and heroines of the fairy tales, the Frog Prince, Cinderella, Hansel and Gretel—embodied the same solar deity or children of the dawn. One plot underlay all the primary myths and fairy tales, from the siege of Troy to the *Song of Roland*, the struggle of the sun against the powers of darkness. The sun hero battled monsters and ogres and armies, and suffered frightful trials in the nether regions, just as the sun toiled his way across the sky in the face of clouds and tempests. The gold he found at the end of his quest was the golden sunlight, and his magic swords, spears, and arrows were the sun's darting rays. All mythology revolved around the conflict between day and night.

The science of comparative mythology thus strove to incorporate into its system the narrative traditions prized by the folklorists. In leading the counterattack, Lang called repeated attention to the inner disagreements among the celestial mythologists. Müller read the dawn into his Sanskrit etymologies; others deciphered the storm, fire, the sky, raindrops, the moon. Who was right? The anthropologists also employed the weapon of ridicule, showing how readily "A Song of Sixpence" could be interpreted as solar myth: the pie is the earth, the crust the sky, the four and twenty blackbirds the hours; the king is the sun, and his money the golden sunshine.[4]

By the turn of the century the solar mythologists were fairly routed. Four years after George Cox's *An Introduction to the Science of Comparative Mythology and Folklore*, there appeared in 1885 a rival volume faithfully presenting the anthropological point of view, *An Introduction to Folk-Lore*, by Marian Roalfe Cox, whose study of Cinderella constituted the first extensive comparative investigation of a folktale. The anthropological school controlled the Folk-Lore Society and dominated its publications during the remaining years of "the great team of English folklorists." [5]

Half a century following the elaboration of Müller's theory another symbolism descended on myth and sought to annex folklore. The sun and the dawn yield to the son and the mother. A new dispensation, Freud's *Interpretation of Dreams*, replaces Müller's *Comparative Mythology*, and psychoanalysis succeeds philology as the handmaiden of myth, laying bare the secret lore of the unconscious, as Vedic Sanskrit had opened the ancient wisdom of the East. Oedipus now leads the pantheon, embracing Jocasta as heaven had formerly clutched earth. In the myths, the toiling sun and the darksome night abandon their ceaseless contention, giving way to the energetic phallus and the enveloping womb. Where light had vanquished darkness, now, in the words of Jung, consciousness triumphed over unconsciousness.[6] In the specific terms of Freud, the hero is a wish fulfillment, and the Devil personifies the "repressed unconscious instinctual life."[7] No longer are the meanings of the myths writ large in external, visible nature, but rather they are sunk deep in man's unfathomed inner nature.

The Viennese psychoanalytical school could scarcely have avoided familiarity with the German nature mythologists, and the extent of their reading is seen in Otto Rank's study of *The Myth of the Birth of the Hero*. Rank cites a shelfful of writings by the older school, disparaging them but adopting their method of interpretation. Only the symbols change. How transparent the myth of Cronus now is![8] And how appropriate that the word "incest" comes from the Sanskrit![9]

In Rank's gallery of heroes, the Freudian symbols fall neatly into place. The myth hero corresponds to the child ego, rebelling against the parents. The hostile father, projecting back his son's hatred, exposes the child in a box or basket in the water; the box is the womb, and exposure in water is known in dreams to signalize birth. (The Flood myths are thus the hero myth amplified; the Ark is the box-womb.) The fact that birth has already occurred in the myth-story is easily explained away by Freud, who finds natural acts and fantasies from the unconscious peacefully succeeding each other in dream-myths. So the mythmakers are reconstructing their own childhood fantasies. The myth proves to be the delusion of a paranoiac resenting his father, who has preempted the mother's love.

Dreams, myths, and fairy tales tell one common story, a genital-anal saga. Thread is semen, wheat is the penis, salt is urine, gold is feces.[10] Defecation is itself symbolic of sublimated or rejected sexuality. "Jack and the Beanstalk" was once a pleasant lunar myth-tale, with the moon as the bean of abundance Jack climbs to the wealth of the morning light. Now it is a masturbation fantasy, in which the beans and the stalk symbolize testicles and penis.[11] Little Red Riding Hood, erstwhile a dawn maiden, has become a virgin ready for seduction; her red cap is a menstrual symbol, and her wandering in the woods a straying from the path of virtue; the wolf eating the girl is the sex act. But beyond this simple and obvious symbolism, Fromm finds subtler meanings, a "pregnancy envy" shown by the wolf (man), who fills his belly (womb) with a living grandmother and the girl, and is properly punished when Little Red Riding Hood stows stones, the symbol of sterility, in his insides. This copulation drama turns out to be a tale of women who hate men and sex.[12]

Just as the celestial mythologists wrangled over the primacy of sun, storms, and stars, so now do the psychoanalytical mythologists dispute over the symbols from the unconscious. Formerly it was Müller, Kuhn, Preller, Goldziher, Frobenius, who recriminated; now it is Freud, Jung, Ferenczi, Fromm, Kerényi, Róheim, Reik. The shifts and twistings of symbolism can be seen clearly enough in the crucial figure of Oedipus. In the solar orthodoxy of Cox, Oedipus the sun hero defeated the schemings of the thundercloud Sphinx that hung threateningly over the city of Thebes, he reunited with his mother Jocasta, the Dawn, from whom he had been parted since infancy; unwilling to see the misery he had wrought, he tore out his eyes, meaning that the sun had blinded himself in clouds and darkness; his death in the sanctuary of the Eumenides was the demise of the sun in the Groves of the Dawn, "the fairy network of clouds which are the first to receive and the last to lose the light of the sun in the morning and the evening." [13] Oedipus was hurried irresistibly on his predestined course, just as the sun journeyed compulsively onward.

In his revelation of the Oedipus complex Freud disclosed the wish fulfillment of our childhood goals, to sleep with our mothers and kill our fathers. Yet already in 1912, twelve years later, Ferenczi has added adornments. True both to Freud and to the older philological mythologists, he accepts Oedipus as the phallus, derived from the Greek "swell-foot"; the foot in dreams and jokes symbolizes the penis, and swelling signifies erection. But Ferenczi also worked in the castration complex, represented in Oedipus' blinding himself. The eyes, as paired organs, symbolize the testicles. Oedipus mutilated himself to express horror at his mother-incest, and also to avoid looking his father in the eye. Ferenczi reads this additional motive in the reply of Oedipus to the appalled Chorus, that Apollo fills his measure of woe. Apollo, the sun, is the father symbol. Hence Oedipus, formerly the sun hero, is now son of the sun god, and thus, if both readings are accepted, has become his own father.[14]

Erich Fromm shifted the burden to a conflict between matriarchy and patriarchy, revealed in the whole Oedipus trilogy, with Oedipus, Haemon, and Antigone upholding the matriarchal order against the tyranny of Creon. Fittingly Oedipus dies in the grove of the matriarchal goddesses, to whose world he belongs. Jung, moving farther afield, is bitterly castigated by Freud for exciding the libido from the Oedipus complex, and substituting for the erotic impulses an ethical conflict between the "life task" that lies ahead and the "psychic laziness" that holds one back, clinging to the skirts of an idealized mother and a self-centered father.[15]

Fairy tales, regarded by the mythologists as truncated myths, occasion the same discords. When Müller solarized "The Frog King," first of the Grimms' *Kinder- und Hausmärchen,* he saw the frog as one more name for the sun, and worked out a derivation from the Sanskrit. People in the mythopoeic age called the frog the sun when they saw it squatting on the water. Ernest Jones, the voice of Freud, recognizes the frog as the penis. So the unconscious regards the male organ in moments of disgust, and the fairy-tale moral is the gradual overcoming of the maiden's aversion to the sex act. In the chaster, archetypal reading of Jung, according to Joseph Campbell, the frog is a miniature dragon-serpent, loathsome in appearance but representing the "unconscious deep" filled with hidden treasures. He is the herald summoning forth the child from her infantile world to the land of adventure, independence, maturity, self-discovery, and at the same time filling her with anxiety at the thought of separation from her mother. Her golden ball lost in the well is the sun, the deep dark spring waters suggest the night; so the older symbolism overlays the newer.[16]

Even in their joint commentaries on the Winnebago trickster, the contemporary mythologists differ. Kerényi sees the ubiquitous Indian scapegrace and culture hero as the phallus; Jung and Radin find in him god, man, woman, animal, buffoon, hero, the amalgam of opposites, the reflection of both consciousness and unconsciousness.[17]

Toward the new symbolism of the psychoanalytical schools, the folklorist of today takes a position similar to that held by Lang and his fellows of yesterday. The language of the unconscious is as conjectural and inconclusive as Sanskrit, when applied to myths and tales. The tortured interpretations differ widely from each other; which is right? The psychoanalysts, like the philologists, come to the materials of folklore from the outside, anxious to exploit them for their own a priori assumptions. The folklorist begins with the raw data of his field and sees where they lead him. He can admire the symmetrical structure reared by Joseph Campbell from many disparate materials, but the folk literatures that occupy him cannot all be prettily channeled into the universal monomyth.[18] The issue between contemporary mythologists and folklorists has, however, never been joined, because the one subject they could have debated, myth, has dropped from the vocabulary of folklore.

The English anthropological school of folklore did not long enjoy their conquest of the solar mythologists. Their own theory of survivals soon collapsed before the detailed field inquiries of modern anthropology.[19] Leadership in folklore studies passed to the Continent, centering in the historical-geographical technique of the Finnish scholars. Collecting, archiving, and the comparative study of branching variants became, and still are, the order of the day. In the United States a division of labor has resulted between humanistic folklorists, who would abandon the term "myth," and cultural anthropologists, who would discard the term "folklore." [20] It is no accident that the keenest review of current theories of myth has been provided by the anthropologists Melville and Frances Herskovits, who test them empirically against their field materials.[21] The collectors of folk traditions in contemporary America encounter almost all forms of traditional narrative—legend, anecdote, ghost story, Märchen, animal tale, jest, dialect story, tall tale, dirty joke, cante-fable—save only myth. The word "myth" is still flourished, say, at the mention of Davy Crockett or Paul Bunyan, but in the same fuzzy sense indistinguishable in common usage from "legend" or "folklore." [22] Cultural historians like Henry Nash Smith or Richard Hofstadter employ "myth" with the quite separate meaning of a popularly accepted cluster of images.[23]

The progress of field collecting shows that mythologists and folklorists are dealing with different classes of material. In writing on Greek gods and heroes, Kerényi prefers sacred myths of the priests and poets to the heroic saga of the folk. The folklorist exhibits just the opposite preference. Heroic saga is the very stuff of folk tradition, and the Chadwicks in their exhaustive studies have explained the formation of the folk epics in terms eminently sensible to the folklorists.[24] The hero is not the sun, or the penis, or superconsciousness, but a great warrior around whom legends gather. The gold he wins is neither sunlight nor feces, but the same legendary gold that inspires countless treasure quests in real life, among down-East lobstermen, Southern Negroes, and Western cowhands.

The Crockett tradition follows in detail after detail the Chadwicks' analysis, even given the special conditions of American history. From the frontier setting issues a Heroic Age society; Crockett is the historical figure to whom oral and written legends fasten; he undergoes adventures similar to those of all folk-epic heroes— single combats, wanderings, love affairs. He possesses famed weapons, utters fierce boasts, displays precocious strength, and meets death against great odds, like the other Heroic Age champions. His printed tales, close to their oral substratum, reveal him as a clownish hero, again in keeping with the Chadwicks' findings, but the first step in the literary process leading to epic dignity can be seen in the almanac embroidery of the tradition.[25]

The recent Disney-inspired revival of Crockett had nothing to do with the folk figure, but, like the Paul Bunyan story, was packaged by the mass media for popular consumption. These assembly-line demigods, numbering now nearly a dozen, belong to the "folklore of industrial man," as Marshall McLuhan has called it in *The Mechanical Bride*, discussing themes that are not folklore at all but "pop kutch." At the bottom of the Paul Bunyan fanfare lies the slenderest trickle of oral taletelling, and this has vanished in the sands of journalistic, advertising, radio, and juvenile-book regurgitation of Bunyan antics. Paul Bunyan has entered the vocabulary of journalism as a convenient humorous symbol for mammoth size and gargantuan undertakings, but the readings of the symbol vary widely. The lumber industry sees in him the exemplar of giant production, the *Daily Worker* finds in him the spirit of the workingman, artists extract from him the sheer brute strength of the American genius, resort promoters exhibit a big dummy to attract tourists.[26]

A recent essay claims that the rebellious youth-idol hero, a composite of Marlon Brando, James Dean, and Elvis Presley, is the lineal descendant of Crockett and Bunyan. There can be no direct connection between a hero of oral folk tradition and the idol of teen-age mass adoration, but as mass-culture heroes, Crockett and Brando shocking the dudes, Superman and James Dean hurtling through space, Tarzan and Elvis Presley grunting and grimacing, do have an affinity.[27]

Also in the domain of "pop kutch" belong the Paul Bunyan-sized treasuries of "folklore," assembled most vigorously by Benjamin A. Botkin. These bargain packages use folklore as a bright label for their miscellany of local gags, schmalz, nostalgic reminiscences, and journalistic jokes, clipped from second-hand sources, with all coarse and obscene elements excluded, and a wide geographical area covered, to insure large distribution. There is a bit of sentiment and fun for everybody in these BIG American albums.

The problems in American folklore studies today are to separate the folklore of the folk from the fakelore of industrial man, and to establish among many specialists a common ground based on the unique circumstances of American history. There is a need to secure general acceptance of scholarly procedures in collecting and reporting the raw materials of folklore. In these respects American folklorists have a good deal of catching up to do to reach the solid platform of their English predecessors. The question of myth is far afield. But when it is posed, the lesson taught by Andrew Lang still holds, and the folklorist looks with a jaundiced eye at the excessive strainings of mythologists to extort symbols from folktales.

NOTES

1. Andrew Lang, "The Myth of Cronus," in *Custom and Myth* (London, 1901), pp. 45–63.

2. London, published by the Sunday Lecture Society, 1875.

3. *Myths and Dreams* (London, 1891), pp. 5–6.

4. E. B. Tylor, *Primitive Culture* (3rd ed., London, 1891), vol. I, p. 319.

5. As I have described them in an article of that title in the *Journal of American Folklore* 64 (1951): 1–10. My discussion of the Lang-Müller controversy, "The Eclipse of Solar Mythology," appeared in the same journal, 68 (1955): 393–416, in a special symposium on myth, edited by Thomas A.

Sebeok. Titled *Myth: A Symposium*, this group of papers also appears as Volume 5 in the Bibliographical and Special Series of the American Folklore Society (Philadelphia, 1955), and has been reprinted by the Indiana University Press (Bloomington, Ind., 1958).

6. C. G. Jung and C. Kerényi, *Essays on a Science of Mythology*, trans. R. F. C. Hull (New York: Pantheon Books, 1949), p. 119.

7. *The Interpretation of Dreams*, in *The Basic Writings of Sigmund Freud*, trans. and ed. A. A. Brill (New York: The Modern Library, 1938), p. 308; S. Freud and D. E. Oppenheim, *Dreams in Folklore*, trans. A. M. O. Richards (New York: International Universities Press, 1958), p. 39.

8. Otto Rank, *The Myth of the Birth of the Hero, A Psychological Interpretation of Mythology*, trans. F. Robbins and S. E. Jelliffe (New York: Robert Brunner, 1952, 2nd ed. 1957), p. 93, note 97.

9. Ernest Jones, *Essays in Applied Psycho-Analysis*, vol. II, "Essays in Folklore, Anthropology and Religion" (London: Hogarth Press, 1951), p. 19.

10. See, e.g., Jones, "The Symbolic Significance of Salt," ibid., pp. 22–109; Freud and Oppenheim, "Feces Symbolism and Related Dream Actions," *Dreams in Folklore*, pp. 36–65.

11. Angelo de Gubernatis, *Zoological Mythology* (2 vols., New York and London, 1872), vol. I, p. 244; William H. Desmonde, "Jack and the Beanstalk," *American Imago* 8 (1951): 287–88.

12. Erich Fromm, *The Forgotten Language, An Introduction to the Understanding of Dreams, Fairy Tales and Myths* (New York: Rinehart & Co., 1951), pp. 235–41.

13. George W. Cox, *An Introduction to the Science of Comparative Mythology and Folklore* (London, 1881), p. 126.

14. Freud, *The Interpretation of Dreams*, pp. 307–309; Sándor Ferenczi, "The Symbolic Representation of the Pleasure and the Reality Principles in the Oedipus Myth," *Imago* 1 (1912), reprinted in *Sex in Psychoanalysis*, trans. Ernest Jones (New York: Robert Brunner, 1950), pp. 253–69.

15. Fromm, "The Oedipus Myth," in *The Forgotten Language*, pp. 196–231; Freud, *The History of the Psychoanalytic Movement*, in *The Basic Writings of Sigmund Freud*, p. 974. Rival psychoanalytic systems are considered in Patrick Mullahy, *Oedipus, Myth and Complex* (New York: 1948; reprinted in Evergreen Edition, 1955).

16. Max Müller, *Chips from a German Workshop* (New York, 1872), vol. II, pp. 244–46; Ernest Jones, "Psycho-Analysis and Folklore," vol. II, p. 16; Joseph Campbell, *The Hero with a Thousand Faces* (New York: Pantheon Books, 1949), pp. 49–53.

17. Paul Radin, *The Trickster, A Study in American Indian Mythology*, with commentaries by Karl Kerényi and C. G. Jung (New York: Philosophical Library, 1956). Cf. Kerényi, pp. 183–85, with Radin, p. 169, and Jung, p. 203.

18. Joseph Campbell's achievement in *The Hero with a Thousand Faces* rests on equal familiarity with folklore, psychoanalysis, literature, and theology. His brilliantly written "Folkloristic Commentary" to the Pantheon

Books edition of *Grimm's Fairy Tales* (New York, 1944), pp. 833–64, shows his mastery of folktale scholarship.

19. The psychoanalytical mythologists evinced considerable interest in the survival theory. Freud saw the savage as well as the child in adult dreams and neuroses (Ernest Jones, *The Life and Work of Sigmund Freud*, vol. II, New York: Basic Books, Inc., 1955, p. 272), and made elaborate analogies between savages and neurotics in *Totem and Taboo*. Speaking at a congress of the English Folklore Society, Ernest Jones referred to "survivals" in the individual unconscious of totemistic beliefs, corresponding to survivals in racial memory ("Psycho-Analysis and Folklore," p. 7).

20. Stith Thompson, "Myths and Folktales, in *Myth: A Symposium*, pp. 482–88; William R. Bascom, "Verbal Art, *Journal of American Folklore* 68 (1955): 245–52.

21. Melville J. and Frances S. Herskovits, "A Cross-Cultural Approach to Myth," in *Dahomean Narrative* (Evanston, Ill.: Northwestern University Press, 1958), pp. 81–122. See also the review by M. J. Herskovits of Fromm, *The Forgotten Language*, in *Journal of American Folklore* 66 (1953): 87–89.

22. E.g., Stuart A. Stiffler, "Davy Crockett: The Genesis of Heroic Myth," *Tennessee Historical Quarterly* 16 (1957): 134–40.

23. Thus H. N. Smith, *Virgin Land, The American West as Symbol and Myth* (Cambridge, Mass.: Harvard University Press, 1950); R. Hofstadter, "The Agrarian Myth and Commercial Realities," in *The Age of Reform* (New York: Alfred A. Knopf, Inc., 1956), pp. 23–59.

24. C. Kerényi, *The Gods of the Greeks* (London and New York: Thames & Hudson, 1951); H. M. and N. K. Chadwick, *The Growth of Literature* (3 vols., Cambridge: Cambridge University Press, 1932–1940).

25. I developed this idea in "Davy Crockett and the Heroic Age," *Southern Folklore Quarterly* 6 (1942): 95–102.

26. My evidence for the journalistic treatment of Bunyan is given in "Paul Bunyan in the News, 1939–1941," *Western Folklore* 15 (1956): 26–39, 179–93, 247–61. The only full scholarly treatment is by Daniel G. Hoffman, *Paul Bunyan, Last of the Frontier Demigods* (Philadelphia: University of Pennsylvania Press, 1952).

27. Robert S. Brustein, "America's New Culture Hero," *Commentary*, 25 (February, 1958): 123–29. Leo Gurko considers the muscle-bound quality of American mass heroes in "Folklore of the American Hero," in *Heroes, Highbrows and the Popular Mind* (Indianapolis and New York: Bobbs-Merrill Co., 1953), pp. 168–98.

6 /

Legends and Tall Tales

In GENERAL USAGE the word "legend" implies an exaggerated and colorful account of an event. Legend in this sense differs from historical fact and is indeed disdained by historians. The folklorist attaches a more specific meaning to legend and regards legends with keen interest, for they form one of the staple categories of his subject. To him a legend is a traditional oral narrative regarded as true by its teller and by many members of the society in which it circulates, but containing remarkable or supernatural elements that follow a pattern. The folklorist recognizes these elements as part of the great floating stock of themes and motifs in constant circulation among the peoples of the world. Legends, or *Sagen*, stand in contrast to fairy tales or Märchen, the German terms brought into wide usage by the Grimm brothers. While the Märchen collected by Jacob and Wilhelm Grimm are well known in English translation as *Grimms' Fairy Tales*, the Sagen also collected by the Grimms have never been translated into English. The reason seems to be that Sagen are too local and episodic for the general reader, while the fictional Märchen, with magical adventures and well-constructed plots, command wider interest.

In the United States, folklorists have paid relatively little atten-

Reprinted from *Our Living Traditions*, edited by Tristram Potter Coffin (New York and London: Basic Books, 1968), pp. 154–69. The Note on Sources is new material.

tion to collecting or defining the legend. In Japan, for instance, collectors have printed many books of local legends, but not a single book of orally collected American legends has been published. The older works of Charles M. Skinner, *Myths and Legends of Our Own Land* (1897) and *American Myths and Legends* (1903), represent the first attempt to report in any systematic way on the regional legends of the United States, but Skinner, a newspaper writer, provided no sources and presented the narratives in a literary style attractive to read but clearly far removed from the original words. Skinner seems to have discovered his most authentic legendary traditions along the Atlantic seaboard in various printed sources, but as he moved into the Midwest and the Far West he depended increasingly on collections of Indian tales, which he called myths. (A myth differs from a legend by being laid in ancient or prehistoric times and dealing with gods or other sacred beings.) More recently, Vance Randolph has published four volumes of Ozark folktales that seem much like legends. They customarily begin: "One time there was . . . ," in contrast to: "Once upon a time . . . ," which was used for the same plots by an earlier generation of storytellers in the southern Appalachians. There is a world of difference between these two introductions, for the first leads into a world of reality and the second into a world of fantasy. The most adroit rendering of local legendary traditions is *The Jonny-Cake Papers* of Shepherd Tom Hazard, set in Washington County, Rhode Island, and written in 1880.

Legends deal with persons, places, and events. Because they purport to be historical and factual, they must be associated in the mind of the community with some known individual, geographical landmark, or particular episode. Many or all of the members of a given social group will have heard of the tradition and can recall it in brief or elaborate form. This is indeed one of the main tests of a legend, that it be known to a number of people united by their area of residence or occupation or nationality or faith. These groups keep alive and pass along legends of heroes and badmen, of local visitations from demons and goblins, and of miraculous interpositions in battles and plagues. Printed sources such as town histories and newspaper feature articles often reinforce the spoken tradition. Let us look at these three main kinds of legends.

The personal legend may deal with a nationally famous statesman, an obscure eccentric, a celebrated outlaw, or a high-society wit. It can be divided into the heroic legend recounting the extraordinary feats of a superman, the saint's legend describing the miraculous cures of a holy man, and the anecdotal legend repeating the clever sayings and odd actions of a comical man.

In the formative years of the United States, pioneer and frontier conditions of living put a premium on the qualities of physical strength and stamina required for clearing the forests and erecting homesteads. Village tales reported remarkable feats of lifting and carrying that verged on the fabulous and incredible. In my *Jonathan Draws the Long Bow: New England Popular Tales and Legends,* I have brought together some of these strong-man anecdotes. They tell of titans lifting an 800-pound anchor, a 1,600-pound stone, a log thirty-five feet long and nearly a foot square, and barrels of molasses and cider. Once in a while a known incident can be recognized, as in the account of Joe Montferrat of Woonsocket, Rhode Island, credited with raising his plow from the furrow to point a direction to an inquiring passer-by. This feat is also ascribed to Old World folk heroes and to other figures in America, such as farm boys being recruited for college football teams.

Some of these locally renowned strong men achieve a reputation that extends to neighboring communities. As the stories about them accumulate, they take on the character of a whole cycle of legends, comprising a folk biography. This process is observable in the case of Barney Beal of Beal's Island on the Maine coast, who made his living lobstering and fishing. Barney died in 1899, but all the coast and island folk from Portland to Calais know the name and some of the exploits of Barney and, in 1956, I recorded a number of tales they continue to tell about him. Barney is certainly a real enough person, and I was shown an old tintype of him, standing like an oak alongside his little son, who stood on a chair beside him and reached only to Barney's waist. In the half century since Barney's death, caused by overstrain from pulling a fifteen-foot fishing dory over the sea wall, the tales have continued to grow, and some contain international folklore motifs, such as the following tape-recorded story of how Barney overawed the bully of Peak's Island:

Esten Beal:

Yes, I've heard that story told many a time, that he went into Peak's Island to get water for his fishing vessel. And the bully of

Peak's Island met him on the beach and challenged him to a fight. So he told him that as soon as he filled his water barrel why he would accommodate him. So he went and filled his water barrel. And they used to use these large molasses tierces for water barrels. So he brought the water barrel down on the beach, and he said, "Well," he said, "I guess before we start, I'll have a drink of water." So he picked up the water barrel and took a drink out of the bunghole, set it down on the beach, and the bully of Peak's Island walked up, slapped him on the shoulder, and he says, "Mr. Beal, I don't think I'll have anything to do with you whatever."

Whereas the legend of the strong hero emphasizes his physical prowess, the legend of a saint concentrates on his spiritual power. In the Middle Ages, the peasantry in Europe tended to locate the divine energies of the church in their local saint, to whom they prayed for assistance and to whom they ascribed their miraculous deliverances. Immigrants coming to the United States in the nineteenth and twentieth centuries brought with them their faith and loyalty to their village saint, and collectors have obtained saints' legends in profusion from Greek and Italian families now making their permanent home in America. The scene of these legends is the Old Country. They may describe how a Greek town was saved from attack by the Germans when St. Haralampos caused a fog to blanket the town, or how St. Anthony led an Italian girl to a sweetheart when she threw the saint's image out the window in despair and hit a young man who became enamored of her. But among the Mexicans of Spanish descent living in Texas and New Mexico, the saints' legends are laid in the New World. The healer of Los Olmos, as Pedro Jaramillo was popularly known throughout south Texas, where he first settled in 1881, effected so many wonderful cures that Mexican families placed pictures and statues of him in their homes beside those of canonized saints. Many stories are told of his cures, which customarily required some action to be performed nine times, such as drinking a bottle of beer for nine consecutive days while taking a bath.

On the frontier, Johnny Appleseed, who was born in Massachusetts in 1774 but spent his mature years planting apple orchards in the Midwest, has taken on the character of an American saint. Himself a Swedenborgian mystic, he is pictured in the guise of a primitive Christian tramping the back country barefoot, wearing a garment made from a coffee sack with a mush pot on his head, accepting the hospitality of frontier families to whom he read his religious tracts. Wild animals and Indians recognized his spiritual nature and allowed him to pass among them unharmed. Yet this conception of Johnny Appleseed seems to bear little relationship to the actual person, who was a rough, hearty fellow married to a Choctaw Indian woman.

The third type of personal legend, the comic anecdote, pervades American life. Anecdotes fasten on eccentric local characters in every country town, drawing their humor from traits of cunning, knavery, indolence, and ignorance exhibited by these odd individuals. The more or less true tales soon become mixed with apocryphal stories. New England is a special breeding ground for legends of eccentrics, due to the longer history of the region and to its settlement from the beginning in compact township units. Some examples may illustrate the main traits of local characters that furnish the humor of the anecdotes.

Stinginess, Meanness. Yankee characters, especially, display a miserly quality. The Yankee's grief at the death of a loved one is tempered by the fact he has one less mouth to feed. A Maine farmer expressed regret that his wife kicked down so many green apples when she hanged herself on the apple tree.

The family of Joe Swain, who had sent Joe on board a schooner bound for the West Indies with a load of their fowls to sell, crowded to shore when they saw the ship approach. The captain yelled out across the water, "Joe drowned." Joe's father called back, "Fowls drowned too?"

Then there was the hired man in Maine who stopped work at noon, saying he had to go to a funeral. "What a shame! Whose?" asked his employer. "My wife's," the down-Easter replied.

On his deathbed Hiram requested a piece of ham. His wife refused, saying she planned to serve the ham at his funeral.

A notoriously mean man offered his children a penny if they would go to bed supperless, then sold them nice hot biscuits at breakfast for a penny apiece.

Another miser put a piece of cheese into a glass bottle where his son could see it at dinner. One night he caught the boy rubbing the piece of bread that was his sole repast against the bottle and promptly whipped him, saying, "You can't eat bread and cheese every night!"

A similar character in Iowa, Mr. Mac, instructed his children to take long steps when wearing new shoes to save shoeleather. He pushed his car when starting it, to save gas, and told his son Willie to take off his glasses when he wasn't looking at anything, to save wear and tear. In this case the stingy man is verging on the fool.

Stubbornness. Some characters are known for their obdurate refusal to give in on an argument or concede a point, no matter what the cost. Or they may pursue a course of action in spite of all obstacles. Hazard tells in *The Jonny-cake Papers* how brothers Sylvester and John Hazard fell out and would not speak to each other for ten years. A friend interceded, and Sylvester agreed to speak first. Seeing John on the other side of the street, he yelled out, "When are you going to bring home that iron bar you stole from me, you thief?"

Finally, as Sylvester lay dying, the brothers effected a reconciliation. Sylvester gasped out, "If I recover it's off." John concurred, "Yes, I only agreed because I didn't think you had a chance."

The Mississippi River overflowed its levees in one of its periodic floods. Two of the flood refugees perched on a housetop surveying the waters below them, on which various household articles floated by. One commented to the other, "Notice how that hat seems to float back and forth in a regular line." "Oh yes," replied his companion, "that's the hired man. He said he was going to mow the yard today come hell or high water." Here a comic anecdote has merged with a tall tale.

Sometimes two stubborn characters oppose each other. Meeting on a narrow road, two travelers belligerently faced each other, each refusing to move his carriage. One opened a newspaper and began to read. The other asked, "May I read your paper when you're through?"

In similar fashion, Dan and Dunk took to sea in a boat, quarreled, and divided up their craft. Dan took the wheel, Dunk dropped the anchor, and neither has been seen since.

Ugliness. On the early frontier, the ugly man was a constant figure of fun, since so many frontiersmen were marked and scarred by fever and ague, or eye-gouging, ear-biting brawls. Johnson

Jones Hooper, one of the ante-bellum Southern humorists, wrote a sketch of a backwoodsman so ugly that flies would not light on his face; lightning glanced off him; and his wife practiced kissing the cow before she kissed him. Here again the tall-tale element enters into the character anecdote.

A current story tells of the ugly man walking home one night, when he is suddenly accosted by a stranger, who throws him to the ground, plants one knee on his chest, and presses a knife to his throat. The victim begs to know the reason for the assault. His assailant says, "I swore if ever I met a man homelier than myself, I would kill him." The prostate man peers closely into the face of the other, then sighs, "If I'm homelier than you, kill me."

The trait of ugliness is a passive attribute of the local character, but it underscores his generally unkempt or grotesque appearance.

Knavery, Rascality. The village eccentric in one role is very much a rogue, given to petty deceptions and cunning tricks. An oft-repeated story relates how the town rascal turned up in the general store, ordered a doughnut, then changed his mind and requested a glass of cider. When the storekeeper asked him to pay for the cider, he said he had exchanged it for the doughnut. Asked to pay for the doughnut, he pointed out that he had not eaten it and walked away, leaving the storekeeper scratching his head.

One widely circulated legendary trick of similar nature is told on village characters around the country who seek to obtain liquor without cash or credit. The scalawag, having filled a gallon jug half full of water, asks the storekeeper to pour two quarts of whisky, rum, or gin into his jug. Then he requests credit, which is denied him, and he is obliged to pour back the two quarts. But he leaves the store with a mixture of water and liquor in his jug.

A vagrant enters a diner and asks if he can have a few potatoes to eat with his cold meat. After he is given them, he asks for a little cold meat to go with his potatoes.

Ignorance, Rusticity. On the other side of the coin, the local character exhibits a childlike naïveté and gullibility that make him the target of tricks and an object of laughter. Ben Hooper in Wisconsin took his first train trip to Chicago. He and his wife bought a bunch of bananas from a train vendor and started to eat them just as the train entered a tunnel. Mrs. Hooper asked Ben how he liked his banana. "I et mine and just went blind," he told her.

At a funeral Ben substituted for the big-horn player. Suddenly he let out a loud blast during the dirge. When asked why, he said he had played a fly that settled on his music sheet.

Another Wisconsin character, Bluenose Brainerd, was told by his wife to lose their meddlesome cat. He took the cat such a distance into the woods that he himself became lost and had to follow the cat home.

One time Bluenose went into town and had a number of drinks with the boys. Two wags reversed the large rear and small front wheels on his carriage while he was inside the tavern. On returning home he explained his tardiness to his wife by saying that he had had to drive uphill all the way.

A Massachusetts rustic bought a salmon priced at one dollar a pound and put it in his ice chest, waiting till the price went down to twenty-five cents a pound before eating it.

Pat Casey in Colorado was asked to contribute to the purchase of a chandelier for a new Catholic church. "Sure," he agreed. "But, begorry, I wonder who you can get up here that can play it after ye git it."

Pat was also confused by the suggestion that the town council buy half a dozen gondolas. "Why not buy one male and one female?" he asked.

Clever Retorts. The tart sayings and smart rejoinders of local characters deflating the pompous and self-righteous pass into oral legend. A summer visitor points knowingly to a tree in the orchard and tells the native, "You won't get a peck of apples from that tree." The Yankee replies drily, "Y'r right, it's ash."

A character in Maine known as "Uncle Daniel" Decker was asked by a self-important summer renter how he kept the squirrels from eating his corn. "I have no outside rows," he explained.

Then there is the classic story of the native in the back country accosted by a city visitor who has lost his way. The traveler is unable to elicit any information from the rustic as to where the road leads or how far it is to the next town. All the yokel says is, "I don't know." Finally the exasperated traveler asks, "What do you know?" "Well, I know I ain't lost," the answer comes back.

A thief in Rhode Island was heard to complain, "There is a great deal stole around here on my credit."

Dying Obadiah remained the skinflint Yankee to the end. Told his coffin was too short, he commented, "Oh, I can scrooch up a little."

Degeneracy. In folklore as in real life, the village character frequently is unsound in mind and body, and so the object of sometimes cruel humor. One tale reported in Illinois, Maine, and Canada describes a misshapen and dull-witted fellow, four feet tall and nearly as wide, whose wife yoked him to the family steer to provide a second beast of burden to draw the plow. The steer broke and ran away with the wife chasing after him and whipping both ox and man. The husband called out, "God dammit, don't hit me. I'll stand."

A character in Ohio known as Temporary Thad lived alone in an unheated shack and used to beg for old newspapers, although he couldn't read. He explained that by burning the newspapers in his sheet-iron stove he could get enough "temporary heat" to change his clothes.

Laziness. A trait both regrettable and yet somehow endearing that leads to anecdotes is the shameless laziness and sloth of the local ne'er-do-well. Lazy Nathan, a Vermont character, hired a man to snore for him. A delegation called him as he was lying in his hammock to award him prize money as the laziest man in town. He asked them to roll him over and stuff the bills in his back pocket. Nathan said he was sorry he had missed seeing the sheriff's funeral that had passed by his house, but he had been facing the wrong way in his hammock.

One of the best-known American anecdotes concerns the starving man who was offered popcorn. "Is it shelled?" he asks.

Similarly, up in Maine Ab Yancey and his seven strapping sons borrow cordwood from a neighbor, then ask him to chop it for them.

Hazard recalled a Rhode Island lazy man who, told by his doctor that he must exercise, sat in his garden in his rocking chair pulling up weeds with fire tongs.

Then there was shiftless Ezra, who decided to raise hogs because they can mostly raise themselves and Cynthy could fetch the swill.

Absent-mindedness. The quality of absent-mindedness, like

that of ugliness, seems to have received more attention from nineteenth-century humorists than from those of the present time. Long sequences of absent-minded actions appear in pre-Civil War newspapers and comic almanacs. We hear of Bill Jones, who placed the bucket alongside the well and lowered himself down and was drowned.

In our own day, the college professor rather than the village crank has become the symbol of absent-mindedness. Classic anecdotes, told of several professors at different universities, including the Harvard professor of transportation, has the preoccupied pedant drive away from the gas station leaving his wife in the rest room, or taking a train back from the city where he has attended a conference, forgetting that he has driven there.

General Eccentricity. The foregoing traits by no means cover every example of odd behavior, thus the broader term, "eccentricity," is needed to account for all cases. First and foremost the character is eccentric and his legend is built upon his deviations from normal and accepted conduct. He may be an inventor of useless contraptions, such as the Upper Michigan genius who invented a crooked shade, a door that would not open, and a bottle that could not be refilled. Or he can be a persuasive entrepreneur like the Wild Rice King of Grand Rapids, Minnesota, who sold carloads of wild-rice seeds to the state of New Jersey. When they did not grow, he sold the state half a carload of mud. According to legend, the Premier of Japan wrote him to come over and teach wild-rice culture to the Japanese. Or the character may be the victim of a lifelong obsession, such as the Old Darn Man of Connecticut, who wandered the roads searching for his bride in his tattered wedding suit, or Thunder River Frank of Wisconsin, who spent seven years digging for gold revealed to him by the Divinity in a vision, and another long stretch building an ark in anticipation of a second flood.

All kinds of anecdotal legends were inspired by Uncle Boney Ridley of Macon County, North Carolina. Such stories were known as "Boneys" and they portrayed his comical mishaps and naïve mistakes. Going to the post office, he inquires for mail. "What is your name?" the postmaster asks him. "Why, you durned old fool, you, if I've got any mail, I reckon my name would be on it, wouldn't it?" sputtered Uncle Boney.

Another time a friend saw Boney at midnight leaning against a brick building writing a letter to himself, and asked him what he was writing. "How do you think I would know?" responded Boney. "I won't get it till the mail comes tomorrow."

Once Boney borrowed a quarter from his sister to get a drink in town. On his way he stumbled and dropped it, but he continued to Franklin and scratched around under the one street light there, looking for the coin. The hotel owner standing by asked Boney why he didn't look on the hill where he had lost the quarter. "It's dark up there," said Boney, "and my eyes are failing, so I better look where there is a light."

After a drinking party one night, Boney and his friend Dr. Snipe McCloud mounted the same horse. Boney fell off and remarked, "Shnipe, if I ain't the worsh mishtaken I ever wuz, I believe I heard something drap!" He remounted backward, bumped against Snipe, felt for the bridle, and said, "Shnipe, if I ain't the worsh mishtaken I ever wuz, it wuz this horse's head that I heard drap, for I shore can't find it on this end!"

On his deathbed Boney felt remorse and asked his wife Polly to pray for him. She knelt down and intoned. "O Lord, please have mercy on my poor old drunken husband." Boney remonstrated, "Oh, damn it, Polly, don't tell Him I'm drunk; tell Him I'm sick."

Place legends are connected with a locality rather than with a person. The story behind a haunted house or other haunted spot is such a legend, and when Cotton Mather wrote his *Magnalia Christi Americana* in 1702 he was able already to record well-established traditions of New England houses afflicted with spectral disturbances. Enticing accounts of buried treasure, sometimes left by Captain Kidd, along with the corpse of a murdered Negro slave whose spirit would guard the treasure, abound on the New England coast, while in the Southwest fabulous reports of lost mines keep alluring prospectors. These traditions, too, belong with place legends. Throughout many states one hears of a cliff or a mountainside known as Lovers' Leap from which two distraught Indian lovers, prevented from marrying by their tribal allegiances, jump to their doom. These Lovers' Leaps belong to a class of pseudo-legends, based on the white man's poetic misconception of the "noble savage" and promoted by Chambers of Commerce to titillate tourists.

Sometimes the name given a locality memorializes and also renews a tradition. Or a picturesque name may lead to apocryphal folk etymologies. One explanation for the naming of Gnawbone in Indiana is the poverty of the inhabitants, one of whom was seen by a passer-by to be gnawing a discarded bone for his supper. But a more prosaic version says simply that Gnawbone is a corruption of the French Narbonne, whence some of the settlers came. An example of a genuine folk tradition preserved in a place name can be seen in the legend of Yoho Cove, Maine. Here is the story of Yoho Cove as told by a retired lobsterman, Curt Morse, living on a country road near the coast:

> Cove about two mile below where I live called Yoho Cove and the old fellas years ago allus said there was some kind of wild man lived there, and all they could understand he holler, "Yoho, yoho" all the time, especially at night. So he kinda slacked off and there was some of the natives down around the shore, don'tcha know, and took kinda of a dugout canoe I call it, dug out of tree, went across there raspberryin'. Well they got about ready to come home and they heard this Yoho hollerin'—they call him a Yoho. So before they reached the boat this fella, this man, ran out and grabbed this girl and took her back in the woods with him and left the rest screechin'. So they went home, and a little while afterwards why it kinda died out, don'tcha know? They missed the girl a lot.
>
> Well they thought she was dead and about two years afterwards, or about a year and a half afterwards, they had kinda forgot about it and they was over there raspberryin' or blueberryin' again and they heard this screechin' and they look up and this girl there, their relation was runnin' and screechin' for help. So she had a baby with her chasin' along—a year old—some little year-old baby somethin' like that. And they got her in the canoe anyway, started off from the shore. And the Yoho come down on the shore and caught the baby, or took the baby, tore it apart, tore it to pieces, throwed one part at the canoe as it was leavin' and took the other part back in the woods. So it's been called Yoho Cove ever since. That's all of it that I know about. It's always been called Yoho Cove.

Folklorists know that this is a floating legend, because they have found closely similar traditions of a wild man mating with a local woman in Kentucky, Canada, and Persia.

Legends of events do of course involve persons and places, but their interest focuses on an action or a deed that excites the community. Such legends have not been well collected in the United States, because they fall between history and folklore, but the dramatic settlement and rise in power of the American people within a short three centuries has created a host of local historical legends.

The lynching of the McDonald boys in 1881 in Menominee, a town in Michigan's Upper Peninsula on the Wisconsin border, is a historical event that rapidly grew into legend. Menominee was then a rough sawmill settlement where pioneer conditions still prevailed. A feud had flared between Billy Kittson and the McDonalds that ended, after a train of ugly incidents (described in my *Bloodstoppers and Bearwalkers*), in the fatal stabbing of Billy. Two McDonalds were jailed. A group of irate townspeople took the law into their own hands, entered the jail, and seized the accused pair whom they mauled and hanged. No trial was held, but the story spread that all the ringleaders would die with their boots on. In the Catholic version, a priest had uttered this prophecy as lynchers careened down the main street with their victims.

That a lynching took place is fact. The additions that produced a legend lie in the curse of retribution—a universal motif in folklore; the ballad that commemorated the event; and the tales of the mysterious deaths that befell the lynchers. One was burned to death in his lumber yard, one tipped over in a boat and drowned, one was bitten by a rattlesnake, one was cut in two by a saw. Even those who lived longest and swore they would beat the curse died with their boots on. But the crowning proof of the presence of legend appears in a parallel event reported as taking place in Gouger's Neck, in northern California, in 1901. Bizarre deaths overtook a group of men who broke into a jail and lynched a family of half-breed ruffians. According to the townspeople, "Hell overtook 'em, every one of 'em." The folk imagination has fitted episodes into a mythic pattern.

A number of legends of supposedly actual happenings circulate in modern society—in fact, the coming of the automobile has given legend new wings. Ubiquitous urban legends deal with the ghostly hitchhiker, the maiden given a ride by a passing motorist who finds her gone when he reaches her destination, and learns from a photograph that she had died some years before; the stolen grandmother, who died while traveling with her daughter and son-in-law, and whose corpse, strapped to the roof of their car, vanished while they were in a restaurant; and the death car, offered for sale at fifty dollars because the death smell of its former owner, who had committed suicide or had been accidentally killed inside it, could not be removed. In spite of the factual reports of these cases, no one has personally seen the hitchhiking damsel, or the deceased grandmother, or the ill-smelling car. The stories are told at second-hand.

A further word should be said about the categories of American legends. They need to be considered from two points of view: that of their themes and that of their sources. We can distinguish between folk legends, popular legends, and literary legends according to whether they are known chiefly through oral tradition, through a mixture of oral and printed sources, or chiefly through print and other mass media. Barney Beal can be called a hero of folk legend because the tales told about him are distributed chiefly by word of mouth. Mike Fink in the early nineteenth century was a hero of popular legend who benefited from campfire yarns and from stories in newspapers, almanacs, and giftbook annuals relating his feats as a brawling Mississippi keelboatman. Johnny Appleseed is today a hero of literary legend, known to the public through the poems of Carl Sandburg and Vachel Lindsay, the Walt Disney film, stories of his life written for children, countless newspaper feature articles, and a United States postage stamp. But no folk groups tell legends about Johnny Appleseed today.

It should be noted that the nature of the folk hero, whether historical or mythical, has no bearing on his legend, so long as the folk believe he exists.

Already in our glance at anecdotal legends we have seen tall-tale elements appearing. Barney Beal is well on his way to becoming a hero of humorous exaggeration, and some local characters are credited with impossible performances. Still the legend and the tall tale belong to different realms, for the legend, however remarkable and fantastic, is meant to be believed, and the tall tale, however specific and solemn in presentation, is intended as a deception.

The tall tale grew naturally out of the travelers' tales that flourished in the seventeenth century when curious explorers visited the

Americas and the Far East. In their writings for the home market, the travelers intended to convey the truth, but they also wished to satisfy the thirst of their readers for marvels, in the vein introduced by Marco Polo three centuries earlier. Then, too, the travelers had truly beheld strange savages and beasts and plants and landscapes. Early chroniclers of the American colonies described a horn snake which struck a locust tree with its venomous tail and caused it to wither within eight hours; bears who slept during the whole winter, sucking their paws for nourishment; a tulip or poplar tree so large that a settler lived inside one with his house and furniture; an oyster as big as a ship's cabin; a whirlpool at the mouth of the Mississippi that swallowed up every craft on the river and even the river itself.

These and similar wonders were written down as true travelers' tales in colonial times, but by the nineteenth century these marvels are being told as tongue-in-cheek tall tales. A jestbook of 1808 contains a piece called "The Diverting Club" which describes a liars' contest, the institution that has stimulated the competitive telling of unlikely stories. One raconteur related the wondrous incident of the Split Dog, which ran into a sapling and cut himself in two, whereupon the owner patched him together again, but in his haste placed two legs up and two down. Thereafter the dog proved a tireless hunter, for when weary on the first set of legs he flipped over onto the other two. This has proved one of the most popular American windies.

The most celebrated of all made its first appearance in print in the United States in *The Farmer's Almanack* for 1809. It was titled a "Wonderful Story related by George Howell, a mighty Hunter, and known in that part of the country where he lived by the name of the Vermont Nimrod." Howell reported how he had with one lucky shot brought down a deer, a sturgeon, a rabbit, three partridges, and a woodcock, while honey was oozing out of the hole in the tree where the bullet had lodged. This feat would be duplicated many times throughout the nineteenth and twentieth centuries, and we can trace the tale through printed sources up to the field collections of recent times. It is an international folktale, identified by the number 1890, *The Wonderful Hunt* in Antti Aarne and Stith Thompson's *The Types of the Folktale*, but particularly cherished by American sportsmen and backwoodsmen.

The free-and-easy masculine society of the frontier and the back country relished tall tales of hunting, fishing, changeable weather, fast-growing crops, mythical animals, and the reversal of natural laws. Before the Civil War the daily and weekly press often printed tall tales and humorous anecdotes, and a type of journalistic fiction, customarily referred to as the humor of the Old Southwest, drew themes and characters from this folk humor. In the figure of Davy Crockett, born on the Tennessee frontier in 1786, elected to Congress in 1827, and killed at the Alamo in 1836 defending the mission fort against the Mexicans, the currents of tall-tale humor and anecdotal legend mingled and produced a comic legendary hero. Davy was both a storyteller and a subject of stories; he was both an eccentric character and a superman. In these respects he differed from other personalities in American folklore, who tend to be either the teller of tall tales or the subject of local anecdotes. On a field trip to Maine in 1942 I collected a number of tall tales, including "The Wonderful Hunt," from Slick MacQuoid, who at one point took me to see the town character, old John Soule, a wisp of a man. Slick told windies about Old John, saying he was so light he always carried a rake on his shoulder to keep from floating off the earth, and that once when Old John was shingling his roof, he sailed twenty feet into the air and Slick had to lasso him to bring him down. But Old John himself told no stories.

The comic legend of Crockett is known to us through a series of humorous almanacs that entertained readers from 1835 to 1856. There is good evidence that these almanac tall tales did derive from oral stories told in barrooms, general stores, hotel lobbies, and other meeting places. In the case of such twentieth century tall-tale heroes as Paul Bunyan, the giant lumberjack of the north woods, and Pecos Bill, the giant cowboy of the Southwest, the evidence points to only a slender thread of oral folk legend underneath the literary and mass-culture adornments. Lumberjacks tell very few yarns about Paul Bunyan and cowboys very few about Pecos Bill. The incentive to write about these whimsical titans has come from authors sensing a market—mainly a children's market—for fiction about made-up American gods and heroes. From the folklore viewpoint, these accounts are neither genuine legends nor genuine tall tales.

A NOTE ON SOURCES FOR ANECDOTES OF LOCAL CHARACTERS

Folklorists as yet have done little specific collecting of the local character ancedote, and stories of these eccentrics must be culled in large part from a miscellany of printed sources: town histories, comic almanacs, newspapers, grass-roots authors, and various fugitive publications. One article in a folklore journal recognizing the genre is Levette J. Davidson, " 'Gassy' Thompson—and Others: Stories of Local Characters," *California Folklore Quarterly* 5 (1946): 339–49. Davidson deals with personalities of Colorado mining camps; the Pat Casey cycle is on pp. 344–48. The *Journal of American Folklore* has brief reports on local characters by Malcolm B. Jones (62, 1949: 190–91), "New England Tales," giving three family traditions about miserly fathers current in Essex County, Massachusetts; and by Kenneth W. Porter, who was led by Jones's note to print five "Thrift and Abstinence 'Scotch' Stories" about stingy Mr. Mac of Iowa in the *Journal of American Folklore* 63 (1950): 467–69. The same journal also carried talc variants, chiefly reprinted from Illinois town histories, of the character who yokes himself with an ox; see Jesse W. Harris, "Substituting for the Off Ox," *Journal of American Folklore* 60 (1947): 298–99.

Three essay reviews by Bartlett J. Whiting, the Harvard medievalist conversant with comic yarns in his state of Maine, call attention to local characters. In "Folklore in Recent Maine Books" and "Folklore in Recent Maine Books II," *Southern Folklore Quarterly* 11 (1947): 149–57 and 12 (1948): 211–23, he comments, among other works, on the books of John Gould, *Farmer Takes a Wife* (New York, 1946) and *The House that Jacob Built* (New York, 1947), and R. E. Gould, *Yankee Storekeeper* (New York, 1946) and *Yankee Drummer* (New York, 1947), all of which are filled with Maine anecdotes. See especially "Queer Characters" in *Yankee Storekeeper*, pp. 134–41; a version of the man yoked with the ox is here. The farmer rueing his wife kicking off green apples when she hung herself is in *Farmer Takes a Wife*, p. 70. In his review of B. A. Botkin's *A Treasury of New England Folklore* in *Western Folklore* 7 (1948): 396–406, Whiting alludes to "the meanest man in Maine" theme (p. 401) and tells the story of the hired man who asked for time off to go to his wife's funeral.

In his series of little booklets issued by the Wisconsin Folklore Society, Charles E. Brown brought together anecdotes about two characters of some notoriety, in *Bluenose Brainerd Stories* (Madison, Wis., 1943), 6 pages, and *Ben Hooper Tales* (Madison, Wis., 1944), 5 pages. An even smaller booklet, containing two pages of print and bound in wallpaper, by Erasmus Foster Darby, presents the anecdotal cycle of *Temporary Thad* (Chillicothe, Ohio: private press of Dave Weber, 1955; reprinted from Columbus, Ohio, *Sunday Dispatch Magazine*).

Representative local histories recognizing characters are William Little,

The History of Weare, New Hampshire, 1735–1888 (Lowell, Mass., 1888), "Peculiar People," pp. 588–90; and Gideon T. Ridlon, *Saco Valley Settlements and Families* (Portland, Me., 1895), pp. 411–16 (stories of Uncle Daniel Decker). The cycle about Uncle Boney Ridley of Macon County, North Carolina is set down by Judge Felix E. Alley in *Random Thoughts and the Musings of a Mountaineer* (Salisbury, N. C., 1941), pp. 498–504. Actual conditions of degeneracy breeding anecdotes are described by Clarence Webster in his account of the incestuous Gull family in *Town Meeting Country* (New York, 1945), pp. 84–89, 223–28.

In my *Jonathan Draws the Long Bow* (Cambridge, Mass., 1946, repr. New York, 1969), I discuss some of the New England characters preserved in printed sources and cite some variant anecdotes. See pp. 11–12 (Old Grimes of Hubbardston, Mass.); p. 100 note 6 ("Father" Moody of York, Me.); pp. 233–37 (Holman Day's ugly, absent-minded, and mean Yankees; absent-minded stories from nineteenth century comic almanacs are on pp. 235–36, and the "Fowls drowned too?" anecdote, from *The American Joe Miller* for 1839, on p. 236); p. 248 (George Wasson's rustic Yankees); and pp. 255–56 (Walter Hard's lazy and rascally Yankees; the Senator Lodge story, from *Cosmopolitan* 49 [July, 1910, p. 275] is on pp. 256–57).

A work *sui generis*, Thomas R. Hazard's personal recollections of south Rhode Island local lore, *The Jonny-Cake Letters* (Providence, R. I., 1882), is strewn with anecdotes of characters. Stories of Sylvester and John Hazard are on pp. 170–72. In two lively articles in *Proceedings of the Vermont Historical Society*, Robert Davis has rescued twentieth century characters locally celebrated for their laziness and foolishness; see "Some Characteristics of Northern Vermont Wit," n.s. 5 (1937): 330–31 (lazy Nathan), and "Heroic Buffoon," n.s. 7 (1939): 3–12. Anecdotes from an earlier period of a "singular genius" known as "Johny [sic] L—" (he who put the salmon on ice until the price went down before eating it), are in "An Original Joker Down East," New York *Spirit of the Times* 15 (May 3, 1845). A columnist for the *Antigo* (Wisconsin) *Daily Journal*, Fred Burke, compiled an unusual anecdotal saga in "Thunder River Frank Was One of Early County Characters" (undated clipping in my possession, from 1940's). Two anecdotes of old John Soule that I collected in Wilton, Maine, are in my "Maine Master-Narrator," *Southern Folklore Quarterly* 8 (1944): 280.

The magnificent *Ozark Folklore, a Bibliography* by Vance Randolph (Bloomington, Ind., 1972) points the way to a number of Ozark local characters whose anecdotes are deposited in diverse publications.

7 /

How Shall We Rewrite

Charles M. Skinner Today?

CONSIDERATION OF American folk legends should begin with the clever volumes that Charles M. Skinner, once a correspondent on the *Brooklyn Eagle*, published at the turn of the present century. Folklorists have paid him no heed, perhaps because we have done so little with the legend and, too, because he was so frankly the popularizer. Still we must admire the scope of his enterprise that led him to set forth 266 narratives in regional clusters in the two volumes of *Myths and Legends of Our Own Land* in 1896 and to follow these with 171 more, traversing the same terrain in the two volumes of *American Myths and Legends* in 1903. Between these he sandwiched in an 1899 swatch of 78 Caribbean and Pacific traditions, hard upon the imperialistic gains accruing from the Spanish-American War, in *Myths and Legends of Our New Possessions & Protectorate*. We can admire also his limpid Hawthornesque prose, evoking tinted landscapes and dark deeds in little masterpieces of mood painting. Meanwhile, we are vastly irritated by the suppression of all sources and almost all clues to sources. Yet Skinner knew his public and gave them what they wanted: pretty tales cloaking the American hills, coasts, rivers, and prairies with romantic associa-

Originally published in *American Folk Legend, A Symposium*, edited by Wayland D. Hand (Berkeley, Los Angeles, London: University of California Press, 1971), pp. 69–88. The whole original article extended to page 95. Reprinted by permission of The Regents of the University of California.

tions culled from a past skimpy by European standards but approaching a respectable three centuries in his day.

Operating by instinct, Skinner did grasp part of the concept of American legend. He understood what we might call "Legends on the Land," in paraphrase of George R. Stewart's much later book, *Names on the Land*. The course of American history, from its colonizing footholds through its westward march to the Pacific, had left in its wake local events remembered in tradition. Regional cultures and the moving frontier thus are acknowledged as regulating elements in legend-making. Not of course that Skinner indulged in any overt theory. But he provided brief prefaces indicating that he had a fair idea what he was up to and felt, if not misgivings, some sense of responsibility. "The bibliography of American legends is slight," he wrote in 1896, "and these tales have been gathered from sources the most diverse: records, histories, newspapers, magazines, oral narrative—in every case reconstructed." [1] He adds that he has devoted so much time to the pursuit of these materials that he believes they are reasonably complete. But seven years later he retracts this claim in the preface to a second series, and alludes to "many stories, poems, and essays that have for their subjects these transmitted by unverified histories." [2]

From whence these legends? One indication of provenance is geographical; they are linked to places. The first of the four volumes, and the first section of the second volume, deal with the Middle Atlantic and New England states, leaving less than half the total contents for the South, the Central States and Great Lakes, and the Rocky Mountain and Pacific states and territories. The balance shifts in the second series (which is not divided by regional headings, although the tales are presented in the same geographical arrangement), with the Southeast wedging into the first volume, and the second commencing with Mississippi. As he moved West where the pickings were leaner, Skinner had to rely increasingly on Indian tales, and the vignettes cease to represent the coagulating lore of white settlements. Yet even with his overdone Indian narrations he sought out those rooted in the soil. "Many are the legends that account for the presence of Indians on this continent," he noted, "but few of these traditions have any interest of locality." [3]

It is this feeling for locality, for the terrain of the vast, varied American continent, that gives much of the power to Skinner's editions. He sensed, what folklorists have often commented on, the connection between topography and legendry, and his prize specimens illustrate the close linkage. Thus he introduces "The Walled Herd of Colorado" with one of his deft word pictures.

> In a lonely part of Colorado, seventy-five miles northwest of Meeker, famed as the scene of the deadly revenge of the Utes for the faithlessness of our government, is a valley five miles long by three in width, completely environed by rocks about six hundred feet in height that actually overhang in places. . . . The Yampa (or Bear) River rushes past the lower end under arching crags, so that there is an abundant water supply. In no way could one reach the valley alive unless he were lowered by a rope or could descend in a balloon or a parachute.[4]

Here is an arresting natural formation, symbolic of the rugged West, and set in the historical frontier with an allusion to an Indian uprising. The legend then tells of a fleeing Mormon group who with their stolen cattle were stampeded over the cliffs into this sequestered valley, where only the last to fall survived, thanks to the cushion of dead beasts beneath them. A thousand head of cattle supposedly now roam this valley, "Lower Earth" as the Utes called it, secure from bears or mountain lions, and harmed only by an occasional hunter who fires on them wantonly from the cliffs.

In his attachment to place, Skinner necessarily foreswore those kinds of legends not strongly affixed to the soil, particularly those of celebrated persons who did not stay put. So strong was his urge to localize that, coming across "A Travelled Narrative," as he properly called it, he set it in a crossroads grocery store in Rutland, Vermont, simply to give it a specific home among numerous claimants.[5] This story stands out as a unique example in Skinner's repertoire of the antebellum Yankee trickster yarn so popular in the periodical press of the 1830's, 1840's, and 1850's; there is a text in my *Jonathan Draws the Long Bow* from the *Spirit of the Times* of January 23, 1841, credited to the New Orleans *Picayune*,[6] with the same plot of a Vermont storekeeper who spies a hanger-on filch a pound of butter and pop it under his hat and exacts revenge by seating the fellow close to the stove and detaining him until the butter oozed over his face and clothes. Skinner speaks of the prank as "formerly common in school-readers, in collections of moral tales for youth, and in the miscellany columns of newspapers." He had, of course, access to hundreds of such jocularities, but the wonder is that he included even one, for Yankee and frontier humor were not his style and furthermore, as he recognized, these new strains of American comedy did not anchor in special localities so much as in regions. In another Vermont legend, from Cavendish, roguishly titled "Yet They Call It Lover's Leap," [7] Skinner does make the connection between local landmark and Yankee understatement. In typical fashion, he describes a sheer, rugged precipice over which fated lovers might well have jumped, but for once it was an unromantic farmer who lost his footing while quarrying rock and was saved from a jellied end by landing on a projecting table of stone directly beneath; all he called up to his companion was, "Waal, I ain't hurt much, but I'll be durned if I haven't lost my jack-knife." "Ask any good villager thereabout to relate the legend of the place and he will tell you this," recommends Skinner in a rare reference to oral sources. These examples need stressing because they are so uncharacteristic of the wild, somber, mournful mood that Skinner delights in; all his other Lovers' Leaps are dead serious.

Accompanying the firm sense of place is an equally definite sense of time. The legends occurred in the receding past, beyond the memory of living man, "for the past is ever more picturesque than the present." [8] Colonial and Revolutionary times best suit Skinner. He clearly relishes the Puritan era and the Dutch days of New Netherland. The Indians always loom large in his pages, both in relation to the white man in the early days of settlement, and in their own historical and mythological traditions. Most of the nineteenth century he eliminates; legends originate in the American Revolution but not, for his readers, in the Civil War. Tales of the Gold Rush and the forty-niners are suppressed in favor of creation myths of the western Indians and an occasional miracle reported by a Catholic priest in New Spain. When he does allude in one or two instances to the Civil War, the scenes are far from the main fields of battle. A longish involved legend, "Spell Tree of the Muskingum," [9] tied to Tick Hill in Federal Bottom on the Muskingum River in Ohio, concerns a spectral scare put into the local farmers by a Confederate guerrilla named Jim Crow. "The gallant defense of the Bottom is still recounted at the cross-roads grocery, but it is not included in the official records of the war." [10] Every once in a

while Skinner will bring traditions up to his own time. "The Barge
of Defeat" [11] deals with a spectral vessel loaded with gigantic dancing Negroes seen on the Rappahannock River in Virginia shortly
after the Civil War, prior to a Democratic party meeting at Rappahannock. Next day the Democrats were defeated at the polls,
chiefly by the Negro vote, and again in 1880 and 1886 the sight of
the ominous vessel preceded a Republican victory. In addition
Skinner mentions the appearance of the Virgin in 1889 in Johnstown, Pennsylvania, on the occasion of the celebrated Johnstown
flood, for the purpose of protecting her image in the local Catholic
church.[12] He speaks of a cursed treasure in Columbia City, Oregon,
dating from a mutiny in 1841 on a Spanish ship that came to
harbor, and continuing through a spiritualist seance to uncover the
loot forty years later, until the search was abandoned in March,
1890, when one of the diggers went mad.[13] Spirits in the air, said by
the red men of Tishimongo, Indian Territory, to presage disasters,
were seen in May, 1892, by John Willis, a United States marshal
hunting horse thieves.[14] These are rare excursions into the near-
present for Skinner, who by and large holds to his self-denying ordinance that traditions must have weathered a century or more, and
acquired an aura of the remote and impalpable.

Even with elements of space and time thus defined, Skinner still
possessed some range of choice, but he imposed other limiting factors in determining the subject matter of his legends. They should
involve the tragically romantic, the supernaturalistic, and the moralistic, preferably in conjunction. Romantic is here meant literally,
as the blighted romance of star-crossed lovers. An endless array of
ill-fated swains march across Skinner's pages: the couples may be
Indian, or Spanish, or Indian and white, or Tory and patriot, or
English and American, or French and American, or highborn and
lowborn. Much of the time a jealous third party seeks to wreak
vengeance on his rival. Skinner appears happiest when one lover
dies, through foul play or mischance, and the other goes witless and
pines to an early death. Where he dug up all his enamored pairs will
probably remain an unfathomed mystery. The net effect is to make
the path of true love in America appear unbearably tortuous and
leading only to a memorial cliff, or cave, or pond where one or both
of the tormented duo met their untimely end. He himself comments
in one such affair, "As so often happened in Indian history, the re-

turn of these lovers was seen by a disappointed rival." [15] Not that he was unduly sentimental; deriding the excessive sentimentalities of Susannah Rowson's *Charlotte Temple* and Chateaubriand's *Atala*, he shows no qualms in relating the sadistic punishments inflicted on an adulterer by a grieving husband. In "A Trapper's Ghastly Revenge," a hunter and trapper of Coxsackie on the Hudson, Nick Wolsey, returns to his cabin one day to find his babe beheaded and his Indian wife witless. She dies within two days. The trapper requests from the tribe the jealous Indian who has committed the deed, and forces him back to the cabin.

> Tying his prisoner to a tree, the trapper cut a quantity of young willows, from which he fashioned a large cradle-like receptacle; in this he placed the culprit, face upward, and tied so stoutly that he could not repress a groan of horror as the awful burden sank on his breast. Wolsey bound together the living and the dead, and with a swing of his powerful arms he flung them on his horse's back, securing them there with so many turns of rope that nothing could displace them. Now he began to lash his horse until the poor beast trembled with anger and pain, when, flinging off the halter, he gave it a final lash, and the animal plunged, foaming and snorting, into the wilderness.[16]

Nick Wolsey left his cabin never to return, but passersby were said to hear the steed crashing through the woods along the Hudson and the Mohawk to the accompaniment of curses and maniacal laughter. This requital seems harsh enough, but Skinner presents a still more ghoulish variation on the theme—and in reading his legends one has a continual sense of *déjà vu*, or perhaps more accurately *déjà lu*, as the same episodes recur with different nomenclature. In "Riders of the Desert," a Spanish trader betrays the trust of Ta-in-ga-ro (First Falling Thunder) who has been living happily with his wife Zecana (The Bird) in the Colorado foothills. Zecana, bereft of reason, plunges a knife into her bosom. When Ta-in-ga-ro catches up with the Spaniard, he strips him, ties him naked with wooden thongs astride a wooden saddle on a half-trained horse, and then binds Zecana's corpse to him face to face. Ta-in-ga-ro follows him on his own mount, watching the Spaniard alternately sweat from the sun and bleed from the cords, shiver from cold at night and moan from hunger at day, until he was forced to eat the flesh of The Bird. When the Spaniard at length went mad, Ta-in-ga-ro lashed the horse into the plains, where the ghost riders yet wander.[17] This revolting torture should be counted on the credit side of Skinner's ledger, showing that he was not wedded simply to the picturesque, the pathetic, the scenic, but could stomach, and perhaps even savor, a brutal legend.

Crowding the unlucky lovers in the legend books are gibbering ghosts. Skinner's ghosts usually gibber—one of his favorite words —at the scene of a murder or suicide, and they fail to assume the personal and nonmalevolent roles we find in modern collections of ghost stories. It is not the ghost story as such that interests Skinner, but the haunted spot that serves as reminder of a gruesome or macabre happening. Throughout the legends he strives to create an atmosphere of the unearthly, whether he deals with the Great Spirit of the Indian tribes, Indian wizards, colonial witches, or recluse alchemists who make magic, or the fevered visions of ordinary mortals who behold apparitions and hear uncanny sounds. Thunderous reports from the heavens, exploding blue lights, midnight revels of spectral hordes, and shimmering mists that take on human forms continually adorn the legends and engender some suspicion as to how much is tradition and how much is atmosphere. When Skinner has definite supernatural materials to work with, as in his exposition of "Salem and other Witchcraft," [18] he is particularly effective in conveying the sense of foreboding and awe that clung to hags scattered throughout New England. One surmises that Skinner yearned for the lower mythology and demonology so available in Europe, and he made a few gestures toward vampires, werewolves, and Indian fairies and mermaids, but for the most part he relied on the prevalent if less exotic English ghost, witch, and devil to carry the burden of his supernatural needs. One of his most striking legends recounts the sighting of a phantom train at Marshall Pass, Colorado, twelve thousand feet above the sea, barreling down upon a real enough train.[19] But this is a lone departure from his antique ghosts.

A strong moralistic tone pervades the legends and raises them above the level of the merely picturesque. Pride is humbled, courage rewarded, faith upheld, faithlessness punished. They are in good part cautionary tales whose message is writ clear. The patriot farmer's son who joins the British redcoats and kills his father unwittingly atones for the acts of parricide and treason by trampling his uniform in the dust and spurring his horse off a cliff.[20] A fisherman's son on Cape Cod braves the rolling surf to rescue a storm-tossed British ship on Thanksgiving eve of 1778 and leads the hated foe to shore; the captain sups at the father's table next day in amity.[21] Fairplay, Colorado, enjoys its name in memory of an incident when Bob Lee, a miner's son, pointed a gun to shoot his partner, Luke Purdy, who had gotten Bob's sister in the family way; Bob asked for fair play and a gun of his own, and went on to say that he had struck it rich and meant to do right by Rosie. Now Luke asks for fair play, and all three lived happily ever after in Fairplay.[22] While Skinner gives nothing as hackneyed as the cherry tree legend about Washington, he does offer several pieces portraying the commander-in-chief of the Continental Army in a manly and gentlemanly light. As a young officer with Braddock's troops, George chased a rascally half-breed from the cabin of the damsel Marion, and tarried under her roof while she nursed away his fever. He promised to return, and did, only to find her cabin in ashes, but he kept until his own death a brown tress folded in a paper marked "Marion, July 11, 1755." [23] Another maiden, a Tory's daughter betrothed to an American soldier at Valley Forge, saves Washington's life when he stays at their dwelling for the night. The Tory stabs his guest as he sleeps, only to discover next morning that it is his daughter, who has deliberately switched bedrooms with the general, whom he has killed. We recall Type 1119, "The Ogre Kills His Own Children," wherein the bogeyman murders his own offspring with whom the hero has changed beds.[24] Even Indian polytheism is condemned. Because the red men honored lesser gods instead of the one Master of Life, signs of heavenly anger ruffled the waters of Lake Initou, Massachusetts, and the game and fish fled. A spirit told Chief Wakima in a vision to pray to the Great Spirit instead of permitting his medicine men to indulge in their follies. As a sign of his goodwill, the Great Spirit sent a giant swan to the lake whose wings covered all the tribe assembled there in boats; when the swan left, an island arose in the lake, since called the Swan.[25]

These examples could be almost indefinitely expanded, but the point is clear enough that Skinner selected his legends with a view to reinforcing Christian morality and Yankee patriotism.

Sooner or later we must come to the question of Skinner's sources. If he is to be taken with any degree of seriousness, we need assurance that he has dredged up and not dreamed up these legends, and dealt with them fairly. On this score we can to some extent be set at ease. A number of well-established American folk traditions appear in his pages in versions that, allowing for Skinner's deft style, convey their story justly. Here are "The New Haven Storm Ship," sighted in the air by a throng of Puritans in 1648 and reported by John Winthrop and Cotton Mather; "The Windham Frogs," that notorious business of thirsty frogs who startled the Connecticut villagers from their beds thinking Indians were attacking; "Micah Rood Apples," whose red centers betray the murder of a peddler in the orchard of farmer Rood in Franklin, Connecticut, in 1693; "General Moulton and the Devil," commemorating the pact that Jonathan Moulton made with Satan in Hampton, New Hampshire, to sell his soul for all the gold his Sable Majesty could pour down the chimney into Moulton's boots—whereon the wily Yankee cut off the soles of his boots; "The Leeds Devil," the monster that rampaged the New Jersey piney woods until it was exorcised by a minister in 1740 for a hundred years, reappearing duly in 1840 and seen as late as 1899. These and other hardy traditions had taken firm root in the American soil, and we can judge pretty well where Skinner plucked them. In my own researches for *Jonathan Draws the Long Bow* I came across a number of early printings of these and other legendary narratives available to him. For instance, a long lineage of sources lies behind his telling of "Passaconaway's Ride to Heaven,"[26] the wizard chief of the Merrimacs, sometimes identified with the missionary Saint Aspenquid, and credited with many marvels. As early as 1635, the transient colonist William Wood reported in *New England's Prospect* the Indian's belief in "one Passacannawa that he can make the water burn, the rocks move, the trees dance, metamorphize himself into a flaming man," with other like wonders.[27] Two years later Thomas Morton echoes the report in his *New-English Canaan*. The town histories of Barnstead, Concord, Manchester, and Warren, New Hampshire, and Kennebunkport, Maine, published between 1837 and 1872, referred to the shaman. Whittier wove Passaconaway into his extended poem "The Bridal of Penacook." For the strange phenomenon of "The Gloucester Leaguers,"[28] the spectral force of French and Indians that plagued Cape Ann throughout the 1690's, Skinner could have had recourse to Cotton Mather's *Magnalia Christi*

Americana of 1702, Niles's "History of the Indian and French Wars," and the 1860 town history of Gloucester. Among the possible accounts of Moll Pitcher that Skinner could have tapped were stories about the fortune-telling witch in the *American Comic Almanac* for 1837, in the *Granite Monthly* for 1879, in the *Life, Letters and Wayside Gleanings for the Folks at Home* that Mrs. Bathsheba H. Crane published in 1880, and in the town history of Brookline, New Hampshire. Certain prominent landmarks, like the White Mountains of New Hampshire, have continually attracted montane biographers of lore and legends, before and since Skinner's day, and he would have had no trouble securing his choice sheaf of traditions associated with "The White Mountains," [29] from such a work as John H. Spaulding's *Historical Relics of the White Mountains*, published in 1855.

One obvious source to which Skinner sometimes points, and which even he could not readily conceal, is literature. Some literary treatments of what might or might not have been bona fide traditions did undeniably give an impetus to subsequent tradition. He levies upon Hawthorne for colonial legends of the Province House in Boston, the Maypole of Merrymount, and the Gray Champion; upon Longfellow for Evangeline and the courtship of Myles Standish; upon Irving for Rip Van Winkle, the Devil and Tom Walker, and the legend of Sleepy Hollow (titled "The Galloping Hessian"); upon Whittier for the ghost-vessels of the "Palatine" and the Dead Ship of Harpswell, and Skipper Ireson's Ride; upon Susannah Rowson for Charlotte Temple. Skinner recognizes the potency of literature and the arts in establishing legends in the popular imagination. He begins his series by stating forthrightly, "The story of Rip Van Winkle, told by Irving, dramatized by Boucicault, acted by Jefferson, pictured by Darley, set to music by Bristow, is the best known of American legends." As to the tradition behind Irving, he does not speculate. In utilizing Hawthorne's *The Scarlet Letter*, he does refer to the "alleged foundation" behind the romance in charges of adultery which two of his parishioners leveled against the Reverend Hanserd Knollys of Dover, New Hampshire; and similarly he presents a legend of cursed pirate's gold supposed to have suggested "The Gold Bug" to Poe.[30] One wonders why Skinner did not follow the trail of local-color writers in the South and West leading to local traditions. An incident in the Miami Valley, Ohio, when a soldier fleeing Indians in 1791 hid in a deep hollow oak, there to perish until a cyclone tipped over the tree and revealed the skeleton inside, along with a pitiful diary of eleven days, leads Skinner to remark how the novelist James Payn had used such an episode in *Lost Sir Massingberd*. Hearing of the skeleton in the tree, Payn complained against "Nature's acts of plagiarism." [31]

Reconstructing Skinner's sources is probably a hopeless and unprofitable venture, but one comes away with a grudging respect for his legend-books as a source in themselves. Tucked away in a passing reference within his extended account of "Lost Mines" is the name of Packer, the prospector of San Juan County in Colorado supposed to have eaten his comrades during a hard winter, a name revived recently on the national news media when the students of the University of Colorado changed the name of their cafeteria in his honor, or dishonor.[32] Mary Richardson in Calvin, Michigan, told me how her father in slavery times belled a buzzard, which then flew in distress from North Carolina to South Carolina; Vance Randolph knows the tradition in the Ozarks, and Ira Ford in *Traditional Music of America* (1940) speaks of a hoodoo buzzard with a tinkling bell heralding an epidemic of typhoid fever, and he supplies a fiddle tune that simulates the sound of the bell. But Skinner antedates these reports with his own of "The Belled Buzzard" that settled in Roxbury Mills, Maryland, shortly after the Civil War and, spoiled by the feasts from that carnage, would thereafter eat only human flesh; its bell foretold some disaster that would enable the bird to gratify its appetite.[33] The pseudo-Indian Nebraska legend of the salt pillar, so suggestive of the biblical story of Lot and so cleverly unraveled by Louise Pound, has a version, which apparently she missed, in *Myths and Legends of Our Own Land*.[34] For the murdered peddler cycle, Skinner offers, besides the Micah Rood apple, the gruesome tale of "the crab-clawed Zoarites" of upstate New York, who bore the deformities on their hands and feet which their forebears had caused to a hapless peddler; the ghost of a Hebrew peddler dispatched in 1853 near Lebanon, Missouri, which, seven years later, shocked his murderer into suicide; and the haunting of Orleans Cross-roads, Maryland, until the ghost of the peddler slain there was laid by branches thrown on his grave.[35] In short, Skinner's compilations are not to be overlooked when one traces histories of American folk legends.

Still we recognize at the same time how much must have been omitted. He is wanting particularly in the field of the post-Revolutionary historical folk legend. One example that he does include suggests the possibilities. This is "The Escaped Nun," dealing with the notorious burning of the Ursuline convent in Somerville, Massachusetts, in 1834 by neighbors outraged by rumors of disobedient nuns walled alive, Protestant girls seduced by priests and critics sealed in dark dungeons. When Sister Mary John fled the convent and spread these stories, a mob broke in and set fire to the building. This ugly chapter in what historian Ray Billington has called *The Protestant Crusade* usually receives passing mention in general American histories, and it belongs squarely in the middle ground between historical fact and fictional folklore where traditional prejudices, bogies, slanders, and horror tales flourish. Skinner recognized the genre, saying "this story of the convent has already become a tradition rather than a history." [36] We would vastly prefer that Skinner had substituted more of these mainstream American legends for his interminable Indian romances and myths.

At the end of both of his two-volume editions, Skinner departs from his strictly geographical scheme to pursue topical themes, still related to the land but crossing state lines. In these, perhaps his most interesting and forward-looking sections, he glances at Buried Treasure, Lost Mines, Snakes and Sea-Serpents, Storied Cliffs and Waters and Trees and Mountains, with special attention to Captain Kidd and the Wandering Jew. "Every Western State has its lost mine," he observes, "as every Atlantic State has a part of Kidd's or Blackbeard's treasure." [37] Commenting on "How Some Places Were Named," he remarks, in appropriate folkloric vein, that the classical names affixed by scholars to towns and cities have far less appeal than the "Doodletowns that are indigenous to the soil." [38] And he allows himself some humorous etymologies of New Jersey towns. "We are entitled to have doubts when we are told that Beatyestown is Irish; that Boilsville was named in commemoration of Sufferin' Job Hitchins, who stood it as long as he could and then died there; that six of the most ancient settlers named Feebletown for themselves, just before they shuffled off the coil." [39] This rather unexpected light touch is best displayed in the one entry that departs from places, on "Deadheads," "Crackers," "Hoodlums," and "Panhandlers," although here too he ties their origins to Mich-

igan, Georgia and Florida, and San Francisco. "Hoodlum" is supposed to have originated with rowdies, drifting to California after
the Gold Rush, who gained their name from the misspelling of the
name of their leader, the bully Muldoon, by a San Francisco newspaper editor, who spelled the name backward, but slipped in an *h* for
an *n*.[40] In Mitford Mathews's *A Dictionary of American English on
Historical Principles*, entries for 1871 and 1881 associate "hoodlums" with San Francisco, although not with Muldoon. Mathews
lacks the anecdotal origin Skinner gives for deadhead.

> In the first half of the nineteenth century a new toll-road was built
> out of Detroit, replacing a rough plank-road leading to Elmwood
> Cemetery. As the burial-ground had been laid out before the toll-
> road was created, and a hardship was involved in refusing access to it,
> the owners of the road agreed to let all funeral processions pass free.
> A physician of the town, Dr. Pierce, stopping to pay his toll one day,
> remarked to the gate-keeper, "Considering the benevolent character
> of my profession, I ought to be allowed to travel on this road without
> charge."
> "No, no, doctor," answered the toll-man; "we can't afford that.
> You send too many deadheads through, as it is."
> The incident was repeated, caught up all over the country, and
> "deadhead" is now colloquial, if not elegant English.[41]

This kind of anecdotal legend, so characteristic of the American
scene, is, regrettably, quite out of character for Skinner, but here
too, as in other matters, he surprises us with an occasional deviation.

We have one last series of questions to consider about Skinner's
legend-books: the extent to which he consciously recognized folkloric patterns. More specifically, how aware was he of the migratory legend, or of the folktale that assumes the guise of a unique
local event, or of variant versions? As his terminal essays show, he
certainly perceived some of the recurrent themes in American land-
scape legendry. Sometimes he also indicates a sensitivity to traditional narratives, and alludes to likenesses of Endymion and Diana
among the Ojibways, and to the "Helen of a New-World Troy"
among the Zuñis and the Wintus; a New York Dutch tradition
makes him think of the Hat Rogue of the Devil's Bridge in Switzerland; he rejects a relationship between the lost tribes of Israel and
the northern Indians on the basis of flood legends, but sees other
analogies, for instance between biblical patriarchs and the medicine

men.[42] Once he remarks drily on "Folk-lorists who take their work very seriously" interpreting Helen as a moon myth because her name means "shining," as if the siege of Troy never took place.[43] This solitary acknowledgment of the swirling controversies in folklore theory places Skinner on the side of the euhemerists, as we might expect from a dealer in physically based legends. The question of variation did not seem to disturb him, and every once in a while instead of synthesizing a narrative he sets down the options. Under the caption "Various Grindstone Hill," he relates distinctive Indian, Yankee, Irish, and French-Canadian explanations for the odd-shaped hill on Maine's Penobscot River.[44] (To the Indian, it was a moon peopled with imps that Melgasoway shot down from the sky; to the Yankee, a wizard's conjuration to enable mowers to sharpen their scythes; to the Irish, the wheel of a barrow on which a "stout fellow" was pushing a monument up to the North Pole; to the *habitant*, the devil's response to a lusty oath of a captain of French troops marching to reinforce Montcalm in Quebec, who swore that he wished it would rain grindstones and harrowteeth.) He gives two forms of the celebrated legend of the tribal suicide of the Biloxi. In one, the remnants of the Biloxi, besieged by the Choctaws, march into the Pascagoula River in Mississippi. In the other, a postcontact version, the Biloxi, who have willy-nilly accepted Catholicism, hear a mermaid singing atop a mound of the Pascagoula waters; they encircle the mound, entranced, and the waters recede and drown them. A dying priest, taking the blame on himself for this pagan lapse, declared that if a fellow clergyman would row to the spot in the bay where music was heard in the deeps, and drop a crucifix at midnight on Christmas, he could save the souls below, at the cost of his own life.[45] While not pausing to speculate on these discrepancies, Skinner did recognize that some geographically separated legends showed closer community than variants in the same locale, and he treats "Besieged by Starvation" under one head, although he discovered places in three different states where Indian forces made their last stand on rock formations since associated with their lost cause.[46] By and large, origins did not concern the adroit legend-spinner, yet he does cite as "an example of the way in which legends sometimes grow" the case of No-Head Pond, about which Thomas Nelson Page wrote his story "No Haid Pawn." Fed by underground springs, the pond seemed to have no source, and the blacks on Page's plantation attributed its existence to a headless ghost.[47] As for the reverse process, where the itinerant tale finds a congenial roost, Skinner sometimes perceived its workings. In the account of farmer Lovel capturing six Indians with the old trick of knocking out a wedge in a cleft log they were holding (Type 38), he observes that Lovel, for whom Lovel Mountain in New Hampshire is named, must have read ancient history to be so prepared.[48] On the other hand, while he uses the title "The Singing Bones" for a graphic rendition of Type 720, *My Father Slew Me, My Mother Ate Me,* and ends it with the terse statement, "A Louisiana negro legend," he gives no indication of its folktale nature.[49] Skinner introduces dialogue of a literary turn of phrase particularly ill suited to his characters and develops a personality conflict between the hard-pressed husband and evasive wife in the manner of the short story rather than the folktale. In one apocryphal legend, Skinner invents a place called Lonetown, New Jersey, as the setting of what he concedes is a "quip of long endurance" that might indeed have originated in the courts of Egypt or the caves of the Stone Age. It is the plaint of the stranger in town—the towns vary—who was sentenced to death by hanging or six months in Lonetown. After a spell in Lonetown, he publicly admits the error of his choice.[50] This kind of prank on the reader, revealed in the final paragraph, reveals Skinner in a lighter moment that he could not indulge in more than once or twice without destroying his reader's faith, but it does show his alertness to migrating legends, and even his willingness to give them a little push. His open-mindedness on origins appears in his observation on Lovers' Leaps, that "while in some cases the legend has been made to fit the place, there is no doubt that in many instances the story antedates the arrival of the white man."[51] Occasionally, he lets drop provocative generalizations on the matter of American legendry, such as the view that American witches for all their magic live in poverty compared to their European counterparts, or the perception of an odd recurrence of assaults on people and their homes by "imps of darkness"—this latter comment as a preface to the poltergeist legend of the George Walton house in Portsmouth, New Hampshire.[52] We must however score him down for alleging that "ghosts cannot abide factories, locomotives, breweries and trolley-cars."[53]

On the mechanism of legend transmission, Skinner again has

little to say, but here too he suddenly surprises us by declaring that the school and college around Bryn Mawr and Haverford have kept alive the traditions and superstitions of early Pennsylvania settlers. Somehow Skinner does not seem the man to appreciate the vitality of collegiate lore. He then proceeds to tell the undergraduate legend of "The Man With the Skates," anticipating such current dormitory horror legends as "The Pickled Hand" and "The Hook." In this earlier prototype, one student accidentally throttles another, and in panic clothes the corpse with overcoat and hat, ties skates to its feet, and drops it through a hole he breaks in a frozen pond. The coroner returns a verdict of accidental death by drowning, but each night thereafter the killer hears a dragging, shuffling sound, and sees his victim climb over the transom. On the third night the killer is found dead, with finger marks on his throat.[54]

Further to his credit, Skinner did recognize and give space to what we might call the impostor legend. One longish narrative concerns a scamp named Ransford Rogers who came to Morristown, New Jersey, in 1788 and organized the local citizenry to seek for Kidd's treasure on Schooley's Mountain, selling them shares in the enterprise in return for his guarantee to lay the guardian ghost, which turned out to be Rogers himself.[55] The whimsical and even irreverent manner in which Skinner relates this and some other traditional escapes—such as Captain Kidd's unintentional bequest of a magic gold tooth to a Dutch goodwife[56]—provides a welcome change of pace to the romantic tragedies, even if they seem too lighthearted for genuine legends. In his boyhood in New England, Skinner tells us, in an unexpected confidence, he had once played the poltergeist himself, until rudely apprehended by the "unpopular gentleman" whose house he was plaguing.[57]

What progress have we made since Skinner? The answer would seem to be, surprisingly little. Field collections of American folk narratives have pleasantly multiplied since the 1920's, but the legend remains still pretty much an orphan, ill defined, poorly collected, unheralded—I was about to say unsung. One looks hopefully through the major field books—Frank C. Brown, Vance Randolph, Emelyn Gardner, Leonard Roberts—and finds small pickings. The Legends of Texas in the Publications of the Texas Folklore Society offer mostly retold texts on trite themes. An example of what appears to me a representative American place legend is the account of Everlasting Water at High Knob, Kentucky, in Leonard Roberts's *South from Hell-fer-Sartin*. There is a literal, and dramatic, text told by Felix Turner, 60, of Burning Springs, Clay County, Kentucky, of how an old Baptist preacher, denied the use of a well by his brother-in-law, prayed on a dry bank by his home for God to send him everlasting water. After three tries the section of a hollow black gum tree he had cut down overflowed with water.

> And it's never failed since. And they's been sawmills, cattle watered out of it, and they've never been able to sink that one foot down in that gum. And that happened at High Knob, Kentucky. That's a true fact now. And I can find you twenty different old men and old women that will swear to the facts of that.[58]

Here are combined the ingredients of the oral folk legend, as opposed to the well-publicized mass media legend: a remarkable local happening, accepted as fact, with an identifiable motif at its core (D1766.1, "Magic fountain produced by prayer"), a specific locale, and a general knowledge by the community of the episode. What we would like, however, are the statements of the score of persons to whom Felix Turner refers. A local legend, to my thinking, can never be accepted in one text, for the proof is on the legend collector to demonstrate that it pervades the social group. We are not dealing here with folktale variants, but with awareness of the tradition, perhaps in something like entirety, more frequently in fragments. Consequently, there arises a publishing problem: how are these fuzzy bits and pieces to be presented? My answer is, just as they are told, without any attempt at reconstructing a synthetic —truly a synthetic—narrative. The publishing outlet will have to be, and should be, a scholarly monograph. Vance Randolph once told me that he had collected many tales of so local and disjointed a nature that he never attempted to print them. Charles Neely did set down eighteen narratives he called "Local Legends" in *Tales and Songs of Southern Illinois*, and they ring true because they are formless, filled with local references, personal and anecdotal, and not particularly interesting as story stuff. But they are rich in the stuff of human experience in a backcountry setting, with their accounts of wolf and panther scares; the self-strangling of a hog thief;

the escape of a Confederate sympathizer who kissed a pretty girl on his way out the window; the execution during the Civil War of a government informer by a group of deserters, at lonely Dug Hill, thereafter said to be haunted; the recovery of a stolen horse with the aid of a herb doctor. Neely was on the right track.

On the basis of my earlier paper, "Defining the American Folk Legend," and the present review of Skinner's two series, I would like to throw open for consideration the following general propositions.

1. *American folk legends belong in large part to a different universe from the Sagen of the Old World.* The fairies, trolls, nissen, and sea-spirits of Christiansen's *The Migratory Legends*, or the *kappa, tengu, oni,* and fox-demons of my *Folk Legends of Japan*, have no counterparts in the United States. Skinner sought to cover the American land with legendary associations like those in Germany and Japan, chiefly on the basis of Indian spirit-beings, but this scheme simply does not work in America. Indian mythology, or legendry, does not carry over into American life. American legends begin with colonization.

2. *Many American folk legends can be divided into three large divisions:* those connected with the land and with communities, according to Skinner's premise; those attached to legendary individuals, whether strong heroes, badmen, healers, saints, characters, or celebrities; and those involving experiences alleged to have occurred to a given individual but connected with many persons in different places. These three classes of traditions, while all falling under the head of believed narratives, are so dissimilar that perhaps they deserve distinguishing labels. Category one covers events of local history that have struck the imagination of the townspeople; from my fieldwork in upper Michigan, I think of the Lynching of the MacDonald Boys in Menominee, How Crystal Falls Stole the Courthouse from Iron River, and Pat Sheridan's Speech at Escanaba. Category two covers cycles of legendary anecdotes, such as those about the Three Nephites, or John Darling, or Barney Beal, or the Healer of Los Olmos. Ballad heroes like John Henry may actually not be heroes of prose legends. Political figures in the United States have never attained the legendary status, say, of Mexican leaders like Emiliano Zapata and Pancho Villa. A character may

sometimes be local, or he may belong to an occupation or profession, like the late Stephen Visscher, professor of geography at Indiana University, and the subject of jovial anecdotes among his colleagues in Bloomington and in the national fraternity of geographers concerning his niggardly habits, such as retrieving the Sunday *New York Times* from his neighbor's garbage can, or attempting to cart his mother-in-law's corpse across the state line from Indiana to Kentucky to save a burial fee. Category three covers floating single-episode legends, like the Vanishing Hitchhiker, the Stolen Grandmother, the Dead Cat in the Package, the Hook, the Killer in the Back Seat, the Graveyard Wager, and the Death Car. These are usually told as second-hand memorats, and this genre is represented in four of the eighteen "Folk Legends of Indiana" in the first issue of *Indiana Folklore* (1968). The same tradition may of course take a "free floating" or "bound place" form, in the words of de Caro and Lunt commenting on the unusual legend in that issue of "The Face on the Tombstone," but a decision can be rendered as to its basic emphasis; in that case, involving the theme of the ineradicable likeness on the stone, the element of place predominates.

3. *Other categories of American legends are required to deal with urban, ethnic, and Negro traditions.* Immigrants, slaves, and city dwellers bear a different relation to the land from the direct possession and cultivation of farmer-settlers; they are often, as John Higham has titled his history of immigration, *Strangers in the Land.* We are only beginning to investigate the folklore of cities, but one omnipresent city legend, sinister and foreboding, and defying any existing classification, is already visible, that of the Mafia or the Syndicate. Ethnic societies frequently cherish legends and heroes of their homelands, which they renew and reinforce by visits and artifacts. Negro narratives of slavery and postslavery atrocities and terrorism, such as the bogey of the night riders uncovered by Gladys Fry, also transcend the simple categories of place and person.

4. *Regionally limited depth collecting is needed to excavate historical or community place legends.* Our model here can be the *Folklore of Adams County, Illinois,* by Harry M. Hyatt, who turned up eleven thousand beliefs and memorats within an area of ten square miles around Quincy. The current enterprise of one folklorist, to write his brethren for the most popular legend in their

respective states, will simply perpetuate mass-culture pseudolegendry. Besides we need more than legend texts; we need their ethnographic, historical, and psychological settings.

5. *American folk legends should be published with a maximum of variant texts and annotation, and with no attempt to appeal to the general reader.* Social scientists have gently warned us about succumbing to the intrinsic appeal of our materials at the cost of scientific detachment. The legend issue of *Indiana Folklore* moves in the direction of scholarly faithfulness.

6. *In speaking about American folk legends, we will have to differentiate between the forty-eight contiguous states and other territory flying the American flag.* Here too Skinner has anticipated us. The cultural history of Hawaii, Alaska, Puerto Rico, Guam, American Samoa, and other odd islets deviates so widely from the story of colonization and the westward movement that we will have to look at their legends with different binoculars.

7. *The vitality of American folk legends is directly related to the epochs of American history.* Times have changed since Skinner's day; the population has doubled, and its ways are profoundly altered by the automobile, airplane, radio, television. But times had changed before Skinner's day. Legends that he revived had already lost their force, and legends that he excluded were in full vigor. In a society as dynamic as that of the United States, legends continually grow and wither, to be embalmed in tourist books and brochures. Any presentation of American folk legends should take into account these temporal periods.

NOTES

1. Charles M. Skinner, *Myths and Legends of Our Own Land*, 2 vols. (Philadelphia and London: J. B. Lippincott, 1896), I, 5. (Hereinafter cited: *Own Land.*)

2. Skinner, *American Myths and Legends*, 2 vols. (Philadelphia and London: J. B. Lippincott, 1903), I, 5.

3. Ibid., II, 146.

4. Ibid., II, 122–23.

5. Ibid., I, 54.

6. Richard M. Dorson, *Jonathan Draws the Long Bow* (Cambridge,

Mass.: Harvard University Press, 1946), pp. 89–91, "A Melting Story."

7. Skinner, *Own Land*, I, 225–26.

8. Ibid., I, 257.

9. Skinner, *American Myths and Legends*, II, 49–54.

10. Ibid., II, 54.

11. Skinner, *Own Land*, II, 71.

12. Ibid., II, 210.

13. Ibid., II, 292–93.

14. Ibid., II, 237–38.

15. Skinner, *American Myths and Legends*, I, 86.

16. Skinner, *Own Land*, I, 45.

17. Ibid., II, 197–200.

18. Ibid., I, 226–38.

19. Ibid., II, 192–95.

20. "Parricide of the Wissahickon," *Own Land*, I, 162–64.

21. "The Revenge of Josiah Breeze," *Own Land*, I, 269–72.

22. "Fairplay," *American Myths and Legends*, II, 116–20.

23. "Marion," *Own Land*, I, 180–81.

24. "A Blow in the Dark," *Own Land*, I, 153–55.

25. "The Swan of Light," *American Myths and Legends*, I, 83–85.

26. *Own Land*, I, 212–13.

27. Dorson, ed., *America Begins* (New York: Fawcett World Library, 1966), p. 285.

28. *Own Land*, I, 238–41.

29. Ibid., I, 215–20.

30. Skinner, *American Myths and Legends*, I, 49–52, "The Confession of Hanserd Knollys"; cf. II, 292–94.

31. Ibid., II, 248.

32. Ibid., II, 318–19.

33. Ibid., I, 274–75; Dorson, *Negro Folktales in Michigan* (Cambridge, Mass.: Harvard University Press, 1956), pp. 46, 207.

34. Skinner, *Own Land*, II, 186–88, "The Salt Witch."

35. Ibid., I, 63–65, "The Deformed of Zoar"; ibid., II, 182–83, "How the Crime Was Revealed"; and Skinner, *American Myths and Legends*, I, 275–78, "Stick Pile Hill."

36. Skinner, *American Myths and Legends*, I, 59.

37. Ibid., II, 301.

38. Ibid., II, 228.

39. Ibid., II, 223.

40. Ibid., II, 215.

41. Ibid., II, 212–13.

42. Skinner, *Own Land*, II, 119; ibid., II, 219; Skinner, *American Myths and Legends*, II, 195; Skinner, *Own Land*, I, 38; Skinner, *American Myths and Legends*, I, 194.

43. Skinner, *American Myths and Legends*, II, 195.

44. Ibid., I, 15–19.

45. Skinner, *Own Land*, II, 90–92, "Last Stand of the Biloxi."

46. Ibid., II, 203–4.

47. Skinner, *American Myths and Legends*, II, 266.

48. Skinner, *Own Land*, I, 207–8, "A Chestnut Log."

49. Skinner, *American Myths and Legends*, II, 33–36.

50. Ibid., I, 238–40, "The Lonetown Mystery."

51. Skinner, *Own Land*, II, 318.

52. Skinner, *American Myths and Legends*, I, 270; Skinner, *Own Land*, II, 305.

53. Skinner, *American Myths and Legends*, I, 226.

54. Ibid., I, 260–64.

55. Ibid., I, 224–34, "The Spooks of Schooley's Mountain."

56. "The Golden Tooth," *American Myths and Legends*, I, 176–86.

57. Skinner, *Own Land*, II, 310.

58. Leonard Roberts, *South from Hell-fer-Sartin* (Lexington: University of Kentucky Press, 1955), p. 173.

8 /

The Debate over the Trustworthiness

of Oral Traditional History

THE RELIABILITY of oral traditional history is one of the most controversial and even inflammatory questions to perplex humanists and social scientists. It has raged since Euhemerus in the fourth century B.C. argued that the gods of the myths were deified heroes of history. Under the allegorical and symbolical interpretations of myth prevailing from classical times on, euhemerism became a dirty word, until nineteenth century anthropology brought fresh new materials into the discussion.

During the last century the contretemps has divided historians, anthropologists, classicists, psychologists, folklorists, mythologists, literary scholars, and theologians. Ethnologists in the field, historians in the library, and psychologists in the laboratory have presented their conflicting evidence on the accuracy of oral genealogies, the trustworthiness of verbal report, and the vagaries of memory.

The issues of traditional history were cogently defined and formulated for the modern period by Alfred Nutt, the English publisher and folklorist and Celtic scholar. In two papers, "Problems of Heroic Legend" (1892), and "History, Tradition, and Historic Myths" (1901), Nutt tended to take a negative view on oral

Reprinted from *Volksüberlieferung, Festschrift für Kurt Ranke,* edited by Fritz Harkort, Karel C. Peeters, and Robert C. Wildhaber (Göttingen, Germany: Otto Schwartz and Company, 1968), pp. 19-35.

history, but called for more evidence before the problems could be attacked.

These problems are: in how far heroic legend is indebted to historic fact; in what manner does it transform historic fact to its own needs; what is the nature of the portion which owes nothing to history and which we call mythic; does this portion picture forth man's memory of the past or embody his ancient imaginings of the material universe; is the marked similarity which obtains between the great heroic cycles due to a common conception of life, to descent from a common original, or to borrowing from one another? [1]

Sweeping claims have been made both assailing and upholding the validity of oral traditional history. On the one hand Lord Raglan, vociferous champion of the skeptics, denies any scrap of historical truth to traditions that have weathered a century and a half. The great folk epics, the cherished sagas, the heroic legends and ballads, even the Christ story itself, display the same mythic structure. These are stories once told about gods worshiped in fertility rites. In *The Hero* in 1937 Lord Raglan assailed the previous supporters of euhemerism in mythology and historicity in local traditions, such as George Laurence Gomme and William Ridgeway, with a broadside attack on all myths and sagas individually, and on folk-memory in general. He resorted to this strategy because the euhemerists customarily defended one hero in terms of another, saying that Siegfried was as historical as Achilles. Raglan asserted, and continued to assert at every opportunity, that savages and illiterates lacked any sense of chronology before their fathers' lifetimes, and that their orally transmitted history is compounded with absurdities and anachronisms. How can the historicists winnow out fabulous monsters and dragons and call the residue fact? If part of the narrative is fiction, why not the whole? [2]

Raglan tested and to his satisfaction disproved all claims to historical truth in traditional genealogies ("pedigrees"), in local traditions of historic events and personages, in celebrated heroes like Robin Hood, Siegfried, King Arthur, Leif the Lucky, Cuchulainn, Hengist and Horsa, Achilles. Raglan's technique is to point out inconsistencies, contradictions, lacunae, impossibilities, and transposition of names and incidents in traditional sagas and stories, and then outline the common mythological structure which unites them all.

One example of Raglan's criticism may suffice. He cites Gomme's local tradition of buried treasure in the valley of the Ribble, in Lancashire, found at Cuerdale in 1840. Tradition ascribed the treasure to the Danes. History records that Danes raided Mercia in 911. Raglan writes:

> Yet the story is demonstrably untrue. It is not merely that the *Anglo-Saxon Chronicle* gives us no reason to suppose that the fight took place in Lancashire and that the *Chronicle of Ethelword* places it on the Severn, at least eighty miles from Cuerdale; Gomme's eagerness to believe was such that it caused him to overlook a fact which he himself mentions, namely, that more than a third of the hoard consists of coins of Canute, who did not come to the throne until more than a century after the fight in question.[3]

The polemical and dogmatic nature of Raglan's work has obscured the fact that a considerable body of more or less temperate scholarship supports his thesis.

The most impressive rejoinder to the literary critics of historicity is found in the worldwide examination by the Chadwicks of *The Growth of Literature* in Europe, Asia, Oceania, and Africa. In their three solid volumes the authors view all the heroes of epic, *byliny*, and saga as truly historical and authenticated, even if legends have swelled their fame. In place of the ritual myths which Raglan sees as the source of epic poetry and traditional saga, the Chadwicks postulate an historical Heroic Age in the semi-nomadic, warring, raiding stage of cultural evolution, when oral literature flowers. By the time it is written down, a good deal of fiction has crept in, but the painstaking literary scholar can separate the historical from the unhistorical elements, and this is one of the major tasks the Chadwicks set themselves. Their recurrent thesis is unequivocally stated: "There is no doubt that many of the persons and events celebrated in stories of the Teutonic, British, and Irish Heroic Ages are historical";[4] and they advance the same claim for all the other literatures they explore.

To counter Raglan's assertion that the presence of some fictitious elements in the traditional song or saga casts doubt on the whole, the Chadwicks point out that supernatural beings and deities are customarily introduced into narratives, even in recent times, as poetic convention. Thus a god appears in a folk poem about King

Haakon I of Norway; the Serbian hero Marko Kraljevich, who died in 1394, was supposed to have married a Vila.[5] The Valkyrie may derive from the women who accompanied early Teutonic and Celtic peoples to the battlefields and served as messengers.[6] Some of the supernatural monsters in the Kiev cycle of Russian *byliny* have been identified with leaders like Polovtsky fighting against the heroes of Kiev.[7]

Turning from general propositions, we will consider four especially contentious areas of debate.

I. NORTH AMERICAN INDIAN

The strongest statement against traditional history on this side of the Atlantic was made by the well known anthropologist Robert Lowie. In 1915 he published a short comment in the *American Anthropologist* on "Oral Tradition and History" objecting to the prohistorical position taken in that journal the previous year by John R. Swanton and Roland B. Dixon. In their article on "Primitive American History" they had cited a number of American Indian migration legends to fill in the picture of prehistoric tribal movements. "I cannot attach to oral traditions any historical value whatsoever under any conditions whatsoever," Lowie pronounced flatly.[8] Two years later in his presidential address to the American Folklore Society he returned to the subject to deal with the storm of protest that had descended around his ears. "Instead of being a high priest hurling anathemas against the unregenerate heathen, I found myself a prophet preaching in the wilderness, a dangerous heretic, only secretly aided and abetted by such fellow-iconoclasts as Drs. P. E. Goddard and B. Laufer." [9] Lowie accepted the psychological significance of traditional narrative—along with religious and social phenomena and archaeological specimens—in providing information about the general historical conditions of a tribal culture, but he categorically refused to concede any historical credibility to the details of the narratives. Aboriginal history was on the same level as aboriginal science, or even lower, since it depended not upon observation but selectivity, retention, and a sense of perspective. The assumption that people know best about themselves is monstrous.

The psychologist does not *ask* his victim for his reaction-time, but subjects him to experimental conditions that render the required determination possible. The palaeontologist does not interrogate calculating circus-horses to ascertain their phylogeny. How can the historian beguile himself into the belief that he need only question the natives of a tribe to get at its history? [10]

Lowie argued that primitive man cannot distinguish between a trivial incident and a major fact worthy of remembrance. With so revolutionary a fact as the introduction of the horse, the Nez Perce tradition errs seriously, while the Assiniboine connect the horse with a cosmogonic hero-myth. The Lemhi Shoshoni possess no recollection of the visit of Lewis and Clark, but do relate a mythical encounter between Wolk as father of the Indians and Iron-Man as father of the Whites. The Indian's historical perspective can be said to match that of the illiterate peasant who describes the European war from his own personal observation. As for the accuracy of migration legends, the chances are one in four (or six, if earth and sky are included) that they will guess right the direction of their travel. Even entirely possible trifling stories of wars and quarrels are now shown, by their geographical distribution, to be folklore and not fact. Therefore, ". . . as we cannot substitute folk-etymology for philology, so we cannot substitute primitive tradition for scientific history." Hence "Indian tradition is historically worthless. . . ." [11]

In the absence of written records to substantiate the testimony of oral traditions in prehistoric times or among preliterate societies, the evidence from archaeology and paleontology becomes all the more important. In a paper on "Myth and Mammoth in Archaeology" appearing in 1945 in *American Antiquity*, Loren C. Eiseley devalued Indian traditions of extinct monsters. Eiseley quoted from the study of 1934 in the *American Anthropologist*, "North American Indian Traditions Suggesting a Knowledge of the Mammoth," by W. D. Strong, who concluded that oral traditions of fossil vertebrates could never take the place of objective data and were probably mythical rationalizations based on observations of fossil bones. In the ten years since Strong's paper, the association of man with extinct animals in the New World had become accepted, but not on the "upper archaeological horizons" from which legends might have dated. [12]

Eiseley then advanced plausible speculations of his own to account for the multiplicity of aboriginal traditions in the late eighteenth and early nineteenth centuries. This was an intellectual period of discovery and exploration of the virgin wilderness by white men, who eagerly questioned Indians about large undisturbed fossil deposits, such as the one at Big Bone Lick, Kentucky, described by Thomas Jefferson. Indians responded sympathetically with accounts of these creatures. Memories of African elephants by Negro slaves may have contributed to Indian legends. "In fact, these stories seem to show a suspicious growth in numbers just at the time when white interest and enthusiasm were keenest." Eiseley dismisses the traditions as "ghostly, disembodied, and unverifiable." [13]

Writing on "Beginnings of Vertebrate Paleontology in North America," George Gaylord Simpson (quoted by Eiseley) dismissed the traditions without a qualm. "Various reported Indian legends of fabulous beasts represented by fossil bones have little ethnological and no paleontological value; the data are sparse, often untrustworthy and carry little conviction of genuine and spontaneous (truly aboriginal) reference to real finds of fossils." [14]

First-hand corroboration of Eiseley's surmise that Indians fabricated legends to please the white man is given by Thomas C. Donaldson in his personal history, *Idaho of Yesterday*. Donaldson, who held a number of public positions in the Idaho territorial government, including that of special Federal agent in charge of a North American Indian census (1890), recounts in breezy style how the Moqui-Pueblo Indians of Arizona and New Mexico invented fables to amaze the white man. Donaldson says he was present when the well known author-collector Frank Cushing visited Tesuque pueblo in 1879 and was filled full of fantasies by ragged old Pedro, talking in Moqui through an interpreter for a dollar a day. [15]

The strong anti-historical pronouncements of Lowie against aboriginal historical traditions brought equally vehement rejoinders. Swanton and Dixon, whose original article had provoked Lowie's assault, struck back vigorously. [16] Swanton countered that in all the cases he could check, supplementary evidence confirmed the tradition nine times out of ten. [17] Dixon called Lowie's statement "amazing," and held that oral tradition could be "extraordinarily accurate." [18] Goldenweiser, who now entered the controversy with a plea for "The Heuristic Value of Traditional Records," thought

Lowie's position "erroneous," and contended that traditions needed to be sifted out, to distinguish the wholly true, partly true, and wholly untrue. If a woman sees a street-car accident, should her testimony be thrown out because she believes in ghosts? Poor evidence was still evidence, and all the more valuable when no other evidence was available.[19]

Contradicting the negative judgments from archaeology of Eiseley, Frederica de Laguna wrote in *American Antiquity* for 1958 on "Geological Confirmation of Native Traditions, Yakutat, Alaska." A file report of the United States Geological Survey of 1957 indicated habitable periods of the Icy Bay Yakutat area, confirming native traditions of great antiquity. Radiocarbon dates of wood from the end moraines dated one glacial retreat about 1400, and fitted a tradition of ice receding because Atna and Eyak Indians had thrown a dead dog into a crevasse. A corroborating legend told of a village on the west shore of Icy Bay overwhelmed when the ice advanced after 1400, because some young fellows jestingly invited the ice to a feast. De Laguna concludes by saying, "Other natives' statements about the stages in the retreat of the ice in Yakutat Bay during the eighteenth and nineteenth centuries are in complete accord with geological evidence."[20]

II. POLYNESIA

In the vast oceanic reaches of Polynesia, a battle has raged over the historicity of traditions describing a canoe migration from the Society Islands to New Zealand many centuries ago. The most eloquent defender of oral traditional history, as taught and transmitted letter-perfect in the Sacred Houses of Learning, has been Te Rangi Hiroa (Peter H. Buck), who declares, "There is no comparison between the inaccurate writings of a globe-trotting European and the ancient traditions of a cultured barbarian."[21] Buck condemned as unscientific the disdain for the spoken word and veneration for the printed word. While relying on the basic veracity of the *whare wananga* genealogies and histories, Buck sought to buttress them with evidence from parallel traditions like botany, nautical science, geography, and any other scientific knowledge that could confirm points in the narrative. As one example of what he called "Cross-bearings on Tradition," Buck cited widely separated Maori and Hawaiian traditional accounts of southerly voyages to Tahiti which support each other and are confirmed by modern geographical knowledge. "Our cross-bearing is now complete. When we consider that the Maori-sailing-directions are attributed by tradition to Kupe, who discovered New Zealand in approximately the year A.D. 950, and that for nearly nine centuries they had ceased to be of practical use to the Maori, we must be struck by the fact that oral tradition has retained in a surprising manner the records of so long ago." [22]

If Buck can be expected to uphold the accuracy of his own Maori history, support from other quarters is not lacking. Roberton in papers on "Genealogies as a Basis for Maori Chronology" [23] and "The Role of Tribal Tradition in New Zealand Prehistory" [24] arranged Tainui genealogies in chronological form and cross-checked three independent narratives of Hawaiki expansion. He regarded his findings as "extremely strong evidence of the reliability as historical material of the traditions in general and of the accuracy of the genealogies in particular." [25]

On the opposing side Ralph Piddington rejects Maori traditions out of hand, likening them to the Arthurian legends, intriguing to read and revealing of cultural values, but worthless as history. In his contribution to *Essays in Polynesian Ethnology* (Cambridge, 1939, Part II), Piddington replied point by point to the powerful case presented by Te Rangi Hiroa (Peter Buck) in defense of the accuracy of his Maori oral history. Buck had quoted a Maori song to illustrate his thesis that the ancient narratives are to be interpreted metaphorically:

> I will sing, I will sing of my ancestor Kupe.
> He it was who severed the land
> So that Kapiti, Mana and Aropawa
> Were divided off and stood apart.[26]

A European could never accept this literally, contends Buck, but the poet simply intended to convey the historic fact that Kupe was the first man on record to sail between those islands and prove they were separated from the mainland. Piddington then raises the question how the metaphorical and poetic inner thought can always be correctly detected.

When Buck points out how the institution of the *whare wananga*, the sacred houses of learning, protected the accuracy of the oral traditions with severe supernatural punishments in case of *hapa*, or broken ritual, for even a single incorrect word, Piddington rejoins that similar taboos against heresy have not produced a uniform Christian dogma, even in a society with written as well as oral records to preserve its religious lore.

The pride of race that Buck invokes in support of his Maori traditional history, Piddington turns against him with the thrust that racial pride intensifies the natural human tendency to exaggeration and self-glorification. And where is the line to be drawn between poetic metaphor and miraculous phenomena? Piddington cites Buck's own reference to old Maori who believed that the islands of Matiu and Makaro were the actual petrified remains of the daughters of Kupe, who historically had once visited the islands which were then named for them.[27]

Genealogies are liable to distortions from expansion and suppression, and even the confirmation of "Cross-bearings" may simply cross-document error. A comparison of genealogical traditions from Mangaia and Rarotonga reveals a discrepancy of two hundred years, since figures belonging to the thirteenth and fifteenth centuries appear as contemporaries. Through an ingenious reconstruction, Buck reasons that the Mangaia were kept in social subjugation for two centuries by the Rarotongans, and have simply omitted that period from their legends, substituting a mythical land for Rarotonga, claiming descent of their chiefs directly from the high gods, and demoting and humiliating the Rarotonga deity Tangaroa. Accepting Buck's interpretation as correct, does not this tampering reveal the manipulation of oral history for ethnocentric ends? [28]

Piddington ultimately discards primitive "history" in favor of "probable episodes in the past," meager, scattered, and unrelated.[29]

Overviewing all Polynesian mythology and hero-cycles, the anthropological folklorist Katharine Luomala takes a median position in noting the interplay between historical and mythological narratives. She sees a patterning process influencing and conventionalizing both types of traditions, especially in the older periods. Thus "the Tongan chronicles of the first Tui Tonga are simply localized variants of the Polynesian hero-pattern. . . ." [30] Heroes like Maui and Tahaki enter the genealogies and chronicles of real families. Nevertheless, these intrusive elements can be dated, by determining at which point they appear in local genealogies, and considering how the mythical heroes act toward historical characters. "Tahaki and his relatives appear on Hawaiian genealogies about the time when contact was resumed, after several hundred years separation, between the Society and Hawaii groups." [31]

III. Icelandic Sagas

One of the chief proving grounds to test the historical content of oral narratives is provided by the Icelandic sagas, and again the disputants have ranged heatedly on opposite sides.

The folklorist Knut Liestøl in *The Origin of the Icelandic Family Sagas* (1929, translated 1930) discussed the historical core of the sagas, whose events belonged chiefly to the period 930–1030, and were written down in the period 1120–1230.[32] He used a number of techniques to test the reliability of the incidents preserved in the sagas: comparing variant examples of the same incident in different sagas, to ascertain the original oral tradition; analyzing stylistic devices of oral narration, to see which of the written sagas reveal the marks of oral style; evaluating the amount of recognizable folklore material in the sagas; considering the social conditions and historical background from which the sagas developed. The chief value of the study proves to be its close analysis of oral traditional history as a form of historical record-keeping separate and distinct from written historical records. Students of history, the argument runs, should not apply the rules of evidence belonging to documentary history in their evaluation of unwritten history.

Liestøl does address himself only to oral history among more advanced peoples. He accepts the verdict that "family traditions of primitive races" do not extend beyond more than one hundred and fifty or two hundred years, save for especially significant events, a judgment he takes from Arnold van Gennep's well-known work *La formation des legendes* (Paris, 1910). But in Liestøl's view the group memory of peoples at a higher level of civilization may be more tenacious and reliable. As an example he cites traditions of north Abyssinia collected by Johannes Kolmodin in the province of

Hamasén, where the purely oral tradition has been checked for accuracy against written sources as far back as fifteen generations. Children had family history drilled into them at home, and oral-history researchers made a practice of collecting all the traditions of their tribe. The historian of north Abyssinia, Conti Rossini, placed considerable dependence on these traditions.[33]

Turning to the Icelandic sagas, Liestøl devotes his attention first to establishing their oral nature. He concludes that the sagas do represent unbroken oral traditions committed to writing, rather than literary compositions. The monotonous style, repetition of set phrases, anacolutha, and similarity of variants all strongly indicate that the sagas were written down directly from the recitals of storytellers, and are in effect equivalent to modern field-collected texts.

As a next step Liestøl undertook to determine the degree of historical validity in the sagas. He developed a thesis to account for two opposing forces at work in reshaping orally transmitted narratives, forces which altered but did not negate the historical content.

A story which at the outset is thin, may acquire greater epic richness. It becomes fuller as dialogues are inserted and various details added. This applies to legends founded on historical fact, whether the main theme is supernatural or of a more rationalistic type. . . . If, on the other hand, the material is rich and varied from the outset, with many little points of interest, many different characters, and a number of loosely connected incidents, some important, others quite unimportant, the story will soon begin to slough off various features and assume a more schematic form.[34]

So all was not necessarily art. Axel Olrik in his persuasive paper on Epic Laws (*Danske Studier*, 1908), had presented the theory of the trinary law, or successive repetitions of three incidents, as one of the fundamental principles in the structuring of the folktales, but Liestøl, while recognizing the principle, contended that triads occur in fact as well as in superstition. Thus the tale of Knut Skraddar contains eleven triadic events within fourteen octavo pages, surely a suspiciously large number, some of which seem evidently folkloristic, e.g., the hearse-horse at Knut's funeral making three attempts to pull the coffin. Still the documentary records do support certain triads: that Knut Skraddar owned hides of land at Austegard; that he had three or more sons, one of whom was also called Knut and had in turn three sons; and that Austegard was at one time divided among three children of one of the Knuts.[35]

Then again, an individual oral historian may possess scientific and artistic qualities of the kind which distinguish the great documentary historians. In some unusual comparisons, Liestøl considers Scott and Macaulay, Trevelyan and Prescott as scientific but imaginative historians, whose powers of memory and skill at seizing upon dramatic and graphic incidents, and arranging them artistically, suggest the techniques of the Icelandic sagamen. In particular William Hickling Prescott, historian of post-conquest Mexico and Peru, as a consequence of his near blindness, was compelled to train his memory as a receptacle for storing the source materials he drew upon for his histories, and composed some sixty pages at a time in dictation, a length equivalent to a medium Icelandic saga. Liestøl sees in the sagaman Snorri Sturluson a chronicler of breadth and insight comparable to the great historians.[36] Modern conditions among literate societies do not favor the training of the historical memory, and such traditions as are remembered rapidly take the character of short anecdotes. But even in the twentieth century under appropriate conditions talented oral historians can be observed, and Liestøl describes the artistry of "a famous peasant storyteller, Svein Hovden of Bykle in Saetesdal," whom he encountered in 1923. Svein could render into lively and thrilling form accounts of contemporary events which on other lips held relatively little interest.[37] In the saga time in Iceland, this kind of talent received the tribute of society, and was especially fostered and encouraged. The society was socially and politically well advanced, and populated from a section of Norway, Telemark, known for the ability of its people to transmit heroic poetry and saga. In Iceland the units of society were close and familiar, brought together by such institutions as the *thing*, or court sittings, and local news became the property of the whole society. Even the topography supported the tenacity of the sagas, for across the flat treeless stretches the eyes of the storyteller could sweep over long distances and see sites and places mentioned in the sagas. Other checks upon historicity are found in the multiple sources of the saga, the saga being an amalgam of the reports of many observers and eyewitnesses, somewhat like the modern news report, and in the response of the audience, who from their own familiarity with the events of the saga could refute deviations or point out omissions. The saga is a told narrative and must satisfy its audience, but historical tradition differs in its appeal from the fairy tale and other folk forms; its appeal is that of scientific history.

Liestøl also discusses unhistorical elements in the sagas, such as substitution of names and incidents, magnification and enlargement of episodes, ethnocentrism, and assimilation of folklore motifs. The Norwegian folk hero of the fairy tales, Askelad, the low-born unwanted youngest son, has influenced the careers of the saga-heroes. Yet Liestøl believes that these factors can be appraised and allowance made for them by the analyst of historical tradition. As an example of a nonhistorical tradition that has preserved its stability for over a thousand years, with only a few detectable alterations, Liestøl points to the tale of "Kaiser und Abt," subject of a well-known monographic study by the eminent folktale scholar Walter Anderson. If this is true of a nonhistorical narrative, the inference is justified that an historical saga may similarly retain its basic features over the centuries. Nor is the passage of time as long as the span of years may indicate, for a storyteller who relates the tale to his grandson cuts the generations in half. "Knut Skraddar might have described events which happened around 1580 to his grandson Olav, who lived until about 1720. Hallvor Bjaai was born in 1777 and related stories to Svein Hovden, who lived until 1924." [38]

Yet Liestøl's persuasive arguments met with strong counter-blows in the analyses of Sigurdur Nordal, *The Historical Element in the Icelandic Family Sagas* (Glasgow, 1957), Peter Hallberg, *The Icelandic Saga* (translated by Paul Schach, Lincoln, Nebraska, 1962), and Theodore M. Andersson, *The Problem of Icelandic Saga Origins* (New Haven and London, 1964).

In his work Andersson summarized a series of sharp rejoinders to Liestøl by Walter Baetke in "Über die Entstehung der Isländersagas." Baetke's criticism fell under the following heads. References to oral tradition are actually literary formulas of the saga writers and so to be discounted. Even the allusions to oral variants is a stylistic device. Accurate references to local topography could easily be introduced by an Icelandic author and prove nothing about tradition. The realistic tone and style of sagas reflect not an oral epic but the literary idiom of the writer. These seemingly realistic touches camouflaged the artistic construction of the sagas which, like the French *chansons de geste* and the Arabic epics, were simply literary imitations of historical chronicles.

Andersson himself contributed to the undermining of the historicist position by pointing out the lack of necessary connection between the freeprose theory and the defenders of historical truth in the sagas. Exponents of the freeprose doctrine like Liestøl hold that the saga manuscripts reached written form after a complete development in oral tradition. In opposition, the upholders of the bookprose theory maintain that individual authors composed the sagas during a literary flowering in thirteenth century Iceland. While admitting the compelling arguments to support the existence of a powerful oral narrative art in twelfth century Iceland, Hallberg still challenged Liestøl's claims, saying that he begins with the assumptions he is trying to prove. The various stylistic features typifying oral style in the sagas—the repetition of conventional phrases, anacolutha, similarity of themes—could also be employed by the first generation of Icelandic writers who would naturally reproduce the oral idiom they knew. For an instance, Liestøl considered the frequent use of pithy dialogue in the sagas as evidence of a highly developed mode of oral history giving immediacy and color to the recital. He cited the following specimen of a realistic dialogue between the cowardly bully, chieftain Guðmundr inn ríki, and Ófeigr, who is seated next to him at table, as related in the *Ljøsvetninga saga*.

When the tables were brought, Ófeigr laid his fist on the table and said, "Don't you think this fist is large, Guðmundr?"
He answered, "Large it is."
Ófeigr said, "Do you believe there's any strength in it?"
Guðmundr said, "I certainly do."
Ófeigr said, "Do you believe it can deliver a hard blow?"
Guðmundr said, "Terribly hard."
Ófeigr said, "What kind of damage do you think would come of it?"
Guðmundr said, "Broken bones or death."
Ófeigr said, "How do you think death like that would be?"
Guðmundr said, "Very bad. I wouldn't want to die like that."
Ófeigr said, "Then don't sit in my place."
Guðmundr said, "Just as you say." And he sat down on the other side of the table.[39]

This passage appeared to Hallberg to represent a literary convention rather than a transcript of actual talk. In his phrase, it is too "finely chiseled." Liestøl's position has therefore suffered two setbacks. First, the freeprose theory he supported has lost ground to the bookprose theory advanced by the school of Sigurdur Nordal, which saw considerable influence on saga style from the Latin literary language. In Nordal's 1940 study of the Hrafnkels saga, he presented striking arguments to demonstrate that this saga, formerly considered one of the most trustworthy accounts of a native hero, devoid of exaggeration or foreign influences, was actually a highly developed literary epic. For instance, two chief protagonists, sons of Pjostarr, are never mentioned in other sagas which do mention their father, while the land supposedly theirs as chieftains was known to be already occupied.[40]

Secondly, even should the freeprose theory be countenanced, the question yet remains whether the orally transmitted sagas contain much if any history. Andersson has said flatly, "There is however no logical connection or interdependence between the view that the sagas are documentary history and the theory of oral transmission." [41]

IV. VICTORIAN FOLKLORISTS

Although products of the same intellectual background, the talented Victorian folklorists divided sharply over the issue. Edwin Sidney Hartland, author of *The Legend of Perseus*, in a closely reasoned article analyzing the accuracy of certain African traditions struck a forthright blow against oral history. Hartland's legal training is apparent in this paper, "On the Evidential Value of the Historical Traditions of the Baganda and Bushongo," printed in the journal *Folk-Lore* in 1914. His purpose was considerably broader than the refutation of claims to historicity by two African ethnologists, for in his opening comments he takes note of the creeping advance by champions of oral history during the past half century, to recapture ground long occupied by skeptical critics of Roman and Biblical history. The ethnologists were driving back the scientific historians. Hartland wrote:

With hardly any formal challenge of critical principles the attitude at least of ethnological enquirers has been somewhat changed. In many directions there has been a tendency to accept traditions not merely as giving a general indication of the direction in which the solution of problems may be sought, but as accurate in detail. And an appeal to tradition has been held to settle complicated questions of the origin of a people, the pedigrees of its chiefs and rulers, its migrations, the beginnings of its institutions and the vicissitudes of its history. When one student accepts genealogies carried by oral transmission through many centuries, another relies on stories of an indefinite past to prove the course of institutional changes, and a third takes almost at its face-value the history preserved by a close corporation of professional traditionists, and calculates the actual dates of the events as far back as fifteen hundred years, it is time for somebody to protest.[42]

Hartland speaks of special institutions among preliterate peoples, such as the *griots* of Senegal and the *Moaridi* of the Bushongo in the Congo, designed to safeguard dynastic memories of the royal families through rigorous training and secret precautions. But he distrusts these traditional narratives "locked up in the bosoms of a close corporation," and gives greater trust to public narratives in free daily circulation. In commenting on the similar Polynesian institution, Piddington agreed with Hartland's view in suspecting private aristocratic traditions, but regarded unchecked common narratives as even more untrustworthy!

The limits of historical reliability in oral tradition among African peoples were estimated at one hundred, or at the utmost two hundred years, according to Hartland, who reached this figure after surveying the near unanimous testimony of travelers, explorers, and missionaries on the ancestral poverty of nonliterate African races.

Hartland's close coworker, Alfred Nutt, displayed an increasingly negative attitude toward the historicity of tradition. He queried whether there was on record anywhere any historic myth among "barbaric peoples . . . living in an oral-traditional mythopoeic stage of culture."[43] For centuries the story of Troy was regarded as gospel truth, but now it is known to be "sheer, absolute fiction . . . destitute of any and every kind of basis, historical, racial, archaeological, or linguistic."[44] Basically Nutt doubted that storytellers commemorated collective actions of a people, such as tribal wanderings, conquests, and cultural innovations, in tales of individual heroes.

If Hartland had defected and if Nutt were wavering, there were plenty of recruits on the side of Euhemerus among the English folklorists in the energetic Folk-Lore Society founded in 1878. Writing in the *Folk-Lore Record* in 1881 on "Folk-Lore Traditions of Historical Events," Lach-Szyrma spoke from his own knowledge of the selective process of folkmemory in the West of England. Tradition clustered around Oliver Cromwell, the Bloody Assize, the Battle of Sedgemoor, and the persecution of Monmouth's followers. Yet of such important events in Cornish history as the revolt of Perkin Warbeck and the Cornish religious rebellion of 1549 against Edward VI, he could find no trace. He explained the first lacuna on the grounds of sheer forgetting when the Yorkist-Lancastrian rivalry and its ensuing bitterness died out, leaving no wounded feelings to nurse the tradition. In the second case, Cornish Methodist miners did not care to tell their children they had fought against the Reformation.[45] Tradition did not tell the whole story but it told a part. David MacRitchie in an 1891 paper on "The Historical Aspect of Folk-Lore" gave instances of verified local traditions, such as the belief of countryfolk in Wigtownshire that a cave in the vicinity had been inhabited fourteen centuries before by Saint Ninias.[46] In his own book, *The Testimony of Tradition* (1890), MacRitchie upheld folk traditions of European dwarfs with archaeological evidence from chambered mounds. York Powell in 1904, speaking on "Tradition and Its Conditions," dwelt on the traditional dramas of the Hervey Islanders, performed and remembered by hundreds of natives, which preserved such events as the visit of Captain Cook in 1777, and other historic occurrences handed down for eight generations and corroborated.[47] John Myres in his presidential address of 1926 on "Folk-Memory" developed a thesis of the power of folkmemory in such societies as the Icelandic and the Polynesian, where "family history, communal history, and regional history were matters of practical concern and common knowledge."[48] In these isolated, stable, homogeneous, orderly, and preliterate societies, folkmemory was toughest and strongest.

In the wake of the Victorians, a group of British archaeologists has avowed support for the historical basis of oral tradition. In a little volume titled *Myth or Legend?*, printing radio talks delivered over the British Broadcasting Company in 1953 and 1954, the various specialists presented generally affirmative answers to the question of the authenticity of classical traditions. Writing on "The City of Troy," D. H. Page offered evidence to substantiate the myth and reverse Nutt's vehement rejection of the epic tale as sheer fantasy. Page summarizes the accounts of excavations by Heinrich Schliemann and Wilhelm Doerpfeld, and later by Carl Blegen, uncovering seven Trojan cities.

It is at this point that myth and legend make perfect harmony: for the myth told us of a great siege and great sack of Troy about 1200 B.C.; and history, in huge walls, and skeletons of men transfixed by the spear 3,000 years ago, and relics of a citadel in flames, show us—not merely tells us—that this massive stronghold was captured and burned about that very date, and was (for the first time in 2,000 years) abandoned by civilised men.[49]

Page concludes that we can now distinguish in part between the fabric of history and the embroidery of poetic imagination, between the actuality of Troy and the enigma of the Wooden Horse.

In another script, Sir Leonard Wooley reaches a similar position on the Flood story. His excavations at Ur in southern Mesopotamia in 1929 dramatically testified to a Deluge before 2600 B.C. and the Erech dynasty, drowning the valleys of the Tigris and Euphrates Rivers. This was the flood of the Sumerian king-lists and of Genesis. But Noah and the Ark remain perplexing.[50]

COMMENTS

What are we to make out of such conflicting views and testimonies? At this stage I would suggest two sets of comments, one dealing with the circumstances and the other with the theme of the debate.

(1) First, the observer is struck by the compartmentalization of the controversy. Each discipline has examined the issue in its own terms in seeming oblivion of the similar discussion being carried on elsewhere. Lord Raglan never learned of the identical views of Lowie until Lowie's 1915 paper was reprinted in a volume of his collected writings in 1960, and not until that year did Raglan enter

the American arena in a communication to the *Journal of American Folklore*. Further, the observer notices the severity and rigidity of the opposing positions in fields so widely separated. My recommendation here is that the problem of historical tradition deserves the attention primarily of the comparative folklorist, who is accustomed to handling the materials of tradition from many different quarters. Even the Victorian folklorists never addressed themselves comprehensively to the question. The gaps between the disciplines and specialties will not be bridged by a specialist. Test cases a-plenty are ready at hand in archives and published collections for the consideration of the folklorist, although the genre of historical legend remains hazy and ill-defined. Of all the disciplines, that of the folklorist is most pertinent. Even Jan Vansina, the historian-anthropologist, in his skilful study of *Oral Tradition* (1961) speaks vaguely of "stereotypes" and makes only one fuzzy reference to Thompson's *Motif-Index of Folk Literature*.

A striking instance of patterning in the oral tradition of recent local historical events came to my attention during a field trip to northern Michigan. In 1946 I heard accounts of a brutal lynching in Menominee, a sawmill town on the Wisconsin border, which had taken place in 1881. The general outlines of the affair seemed familiar to all the townspeople, and in particular the dénouement, that every member of the lynch party, though they were never brought to trial, "died with their boots on." After a number of interviews I was able to piece together a dozen of these mysterious and violent deaths, by burning, drowning, falling into machinery, or without apparent cause, even when the victims had sworn to beat the curse.[51] The structure of this episode, which I published under the title "The Lynching of the McDonald Boys," suggested analogues, but while the motive of retributive justice is common enough, and of the curse (in Catholic versions of the lynching a priest warns the lynchers who are dragging the corpses down the main street that they will die unnaturally), I never could find a close analogue in the scanty collections of local historical traditions. Then in the summer of 1959, while participating in a joint seminar on "American Folktales" with Dean Hector Lee of Chico State College, Chico, California, an experienced collector of Western and northern California traditions, I heard him relate the counterpart. His narrative of the Lynching on Lookout Bridge, perpetuated in 1901 in the now deserted village of Gouger's Neck in northeastern California, contained the same skeletal themes: the town resentment against a family of halfbreed ruffians, their arrest, the storming of the jail, a fight and the lynching, the exoneration of the lynch party, and their macabre deaths. In the phrase of the elderly townspeople, "Hell overtook 'em, every one of 'em." One walked in front of a train, another developed a cancer of the throat, a third died from a rotting in the stomach as if he had been kicked there.[52]

Here are historical events occurring within the memory of eyewitnesses, perpetuated orally, and already taking on the common outlines of a morality tale. What will happen to the narration should it endure for another century by word-of-mouth transmission? Will the eléments presently verifiable (Calvin Hall, lynched at Lookout Bridge, was a sergeant with General George Crook during the Civil War, and has left journals of ethnological value) be replaced with more familiar names and places when the generation who knew the main actors has all died?

Visible evidence of the patterning effects of tradition upon recent historical events can be observed in oral accounts of Culloden, the last battle fought on British soil, in 1746, in which the army of George I under the Bloody Duke of Cumberland crushed the Jacobite followers of Bonnie Prince Charlie and obliterated their Highland culture. The events of the '45 have burned deeply into Highland race-memory. A narrative of "The Battle of Culloden" not known to conventional history comes to light in the magnificent compendium of Scottish local history traditions recorded for Campbell of Islay in the 1870's and only published in 1964 as *The Dewar Manuscripts*. In this stark and powerful tale, a Highland stripling taken prisoner after Culloden fights a duel for the lives of himself and his fellow-prisoners with the champion British swordsman. The Bloody Duke has wagered their lives against so many bottles of wine with General John Campbell, a supporter of the Highlanders' soldiering ability. When the lad slays his opponent, the Duke in anger orders that every Highlander subsequently found wounded on the battlefield be put to death and everyone captured be hanged.[53] (See chapter 3.)

We think of other epic single combats, such as David against Goliath, and of the folktale contrast between the ogrish Duke and the undersized hero. Yet the episode is set within the frame of a well documented battleground and well-known military figures.

Another Culloden tradition clearly reveals the grafting of an international tale type onto the skein of history. This Gaelic narrative was collected by Calum Maclean from Angus MacLellan and deposited in the archives of the School of Scottish Studies in Edinburgh. It contains Type 1281A, *Getting Rid of the Man-eating Calf*, known in northern and eastern Europe. I collected variants from a Yankee lobsterman on the Maine coast and from an elderly lady of French-Canadian ancestry in northern Michigan.[54] An unpublished Finnish-American text from Utica, Michigan has been collected by Aili Johnson. In all these American texts (but with only a suggestion in the Maine one), a preceding episode has a messenger take a bottle of the man's urine to the doctor, spill it and substitute cow's urine, and report back that the doctor has said he will have a calf (Type 1739, *The Parson and the Calf*). The ignorant man flees town, finds the boots on the corpse, and takes them with him to the farmhouse where he is given shelter. On awakening in the barn to find a new calf beside him, he thinks he has given birth and flees again, leaving the boots behind him. In the Angus MacLellan text, Type 1739 with its doltish protagonist is eliminated, and the Laird of Bernera, although forced to flee the battlefield, plays an heroic role, killing an Englishman and cutting off his legs to secure his boots.

(2) Secondly, the judgment may be offered that blanket judgments should be avoided. Tradition is not cut from one cloth. The question has been incorrectly posed. It is not a matter of fact versus fiction so much as the social acceptance of traditional history. Africanist ethnohistorians such as Ian Cunnison, Meyer Fortes, and Paul Bohannan have recently been pursuing this line.[55] They recommend that Western cultural historians discard their ethnocentric concepts of time and history and accept the African idea of historical truth in dealing with African traditions. Speaking of the Tallensi, Fortes writes, "They do not think of the lapse of time as being associated with cumulative changes in their culture or social structure but rather as a periodical or cyclical rhythm of eternal repetition. . . . There is a direct correlation between the time perspective recognized by the society and the social structure." [56]

Bohannan makes a similar point in discussing "Concepts of Time among the Tiv of Nigeria." Events and incidents in myths and legends explain the social process not the historical past. "The most common incidents all cluster about a standard situation which arises time and again in the dynamic of Tiv social process: particularly fission and fusion of lineage territories. . . ." [57] The Tiv think in terms of social space rather than time. Their genealogies are true because they correlate with the existing realities of the political structure.

These suggestions are pursued to book length in the sophisticated treatise of Jan Vansina, *Oral Tradition, A Study in Historical Methodology* (1961, translated from the French, 1965). Vansina examines in close and precise detail all aspects of the processes and functions of oral traditions in African societies. As one of his main findings, Vansina demonstrates the contrast in attitudes toward historical knowledge displayed by societies even in the same culture area. The Rwanda abounded in family and local histories while the Burundi, with their much more fluid governmental system and uncertain provincial boundaries, lacked the coherent political organization to generate oral histories. In the end Vansina states, "Each type of society has in fact chosen to preserve the kind of historical traditions suited to its particular type of structure, and the historical information to be obtained by studying these traditions is restricted by the framework of reference constructed by the society in question." [58]

This statement may well summarize the conclusions of the ethnohistorian for Africa but it will not serve the purposes of the comparative folklorist for literate societies. The astonishing historical tales related by W. H. Barrett in *Tales from the Fens* (1963) and *More Tales from the Fens* (1964) are not the product of a particular political organization, although they may be explained in part by the social conditions of the sequestered Fen country. But the political structure of the Fens is the same as for the rest of England.

All this is not to say that the quest for history must be abandoned. Some criteria can be offered for judging the historical content of traditions: corroborating testimony from archaeology, ethnology, history, geography, linguistics, physical anthropology; the support from mnemonic devices; the presence of professional chroniclers and sagamen; and continuity in the locus of transmission, as opposed to the migration of peoples and their histories. The

absence or discounting of egoistic and folkloristic elements can also
strengthen the case. While these criteria have been attacked singly,
in combination they carry weight, and evidence exists that oral tradition can lead us to the site of Troy or even, with Plato as tradition-
bearer, to the lost Atlantis.[59]

N O T E S

1. Alfred Nutt, "Problems of Heroic Legend," *The International Folk-
Lore Congress 1891, Papers and Transactions*, ed. J. Jacobs and A. Nutt
(London, 1892), p. 113; Nutt, "History, Tradition, and Historic Myth,"
Folk-Lore 12 (London, 1901): 336–39.

2. Lord Raglan, *The Hero, a Study in Tradition, Myth, and Drama*
(New York, 1937). For a recent continuation of the controversy, see William Bascom, "The Myth-Ritual Theory," *Journal of American Folklore*
[hereafter *JAF*] 70 (1957): 103–14, especially 105, citing Charles Edward
Fuller, "An Ethnohistoric Study of Continuity and Change in Gwambe Cul-
ture," Northwestern University dissertation (Evanston, Ill., 1955); Raglan,
"Reply to Bascom," *JAF* 70 (1957): 359–60; Raglan, "Myth and Ritual,"
JAF 68 (1955): 454–61; Stanley Edgar Hyman, "The Ritual View of Myth
and the Mythic," *JAF* 68 (1955): 462; Raglan, "More on Myth and Ritual,"
JAF 10 (1957): 173; Hyman, "Reply to Bascom," *JAF* 71 (1958): 152–55;
Bascom, "Rejoinder to Hyman," *JAF* 71 (1958): 155–56.

3. Raglan, *Hero*, p. 40.

4. Hector Munro Chadwick and N. Kershaw Chadwick, *The Growth of
Literature*, 3 vols. (Cambridge, England, 1932–36), vol. I, p. 133. H. M.
Chadwick first analyzed historical and fictional elements in heroic poetry in
The Heroic Age (Cambridge, England, 1912).

5. Chadwick, *Literature*, I, p. 211.

6. Ibid., 215.

7. Ibid., II, 119.

8. Robert H. Lowie, "Oral Tradition and History," *American Anthropologist*, n.s. 17 (New York, 1917): 596–99; reprinted in Robert H. Lowie,
Selected Papers on Anthropology (Berkeley, Calif., 1960), pp. 115–18.

9. Robert H. Lowie, "Oral Tradition and History," *JAF* 30 (1917):
161–67.

10. Ibid., 163.

11. Ibid., 165, 169.

12. Loren C. Eiseley, "Myth and Mammoth in Archaeology," *American
Antiquity* 11 (1945–46): 84. Strong's paper appeared in *American Anthropologist* 36 (1934): 81–87.

13. Eiseley, "Myth and Mammoth," 87.

14. G. G. Simpson, "Beginnings of Vertebrate Paleontology in North America," *Proceedings of the American Philosophical Society* 85 (1942): 132.

15. Thomas C. Donaldson, *Idaho of Yesterday* (Caldwell, Idaho, 1941), pp. 325, 326.

16. The article of John R. Swanton and Roland B. Dixon appeared as "Primitive American History," *American Anthropologist*, n.s. 16 (1914): 376–412. See especially pp. 377–80.

17. John R. Swanton's reply, *American Anthropologist*, n.s. 17 (1915): 600.

18. Roland B. Dixon's reply, *American Anthropologist*, n.s. 17 (1915): 599–600.

19. A. A. Goldenweiser, "The Heuristic Value of Traditional Records," *American Anthropologist*, n.s. 17 (1915): 763–64.

20. Frederica de Laguna, "Geological Confirmation of Native Traditions, Yakutat, Alaska," *American Antiquity* 23 (1958): 434.

21. Te Rangi Hiroa (= Peter H. Buck), "The Value of Tradition in Polynesian Research," *Journal of the Polynesian Society* 30 (1926): 182.

22. Ibid., 193.

23. J. B. W. Roberton, "Genealogies as a Basis for Maori Chronology," *Journal of the Polynesian Society* 65 (1956): 45–54. Includes tables.

24. J. B. W. Roberton, "The Role of Tribal Tradition in New Zealand Prehistory," *Journal of the Polynesian Society* 66 (1957): 249–63.

25. Ibid., 251.

26. Quoted by Ralph Piddington in his essay "The Evidence of Tradition," *Essays in Polynesian Ethnology*, ed. Robert W. Williamson (Cambridge, England, 1939), p. 285.

27. Ibid., pp. 284–86.

28. Ralph Piddington, "The History of Mangaia," *Essays in Polynesian Ethnology*, 292.

29. Piddington, "The History of Primitive Peoples," *Essays in Polynesian Ethnology*, p. 342. Other pertinent essays of his are "The Value of Historical Ethnology," pp. 344–50, and "The Positive Value of Polynesian History," pp. 350–53.

30. Katharine Luomala, "Notes on the Development of Polynesian Hero-Cycles," *Journal of the Polynesian Society* 49 (1940): 371. The whole article covers pp. 367–74.

31. Ibid., 371.

32. Knut Liestøl, *The Origin of the Icelandic Family Sagas* (Oslo, 1930).

33. Ibid.

34. Ibid., pp. 62–63, 66.

35. Ibid., pp. 77–79.

36. Ibid., pp. 118–25.

37. Ibid., p. 61.

38. Ibid., p. 203.

39. Peter Hallberg, *The Icelandic Saga*, translation, introduction, and notes by Paul Schach (Lincoln, Nebraska, 1962), pp. 59–60. The whole chapter "Oral Tradition and Literary Authorship, History and Fiction in the Sagas of Icelanders," pp. 49–69, is pertinent.

40. Ibid., pp. 67–69.

41. Theodore M. Andersson, *The Problem of Icelandic Saga Origins* (New Haven and London, 1964), p. 50.

42. E. S. Hartland, "On the Evidential Value of the Historical Traditions of the Baganda and Bushongo," *Folk-Lore* 25 (1914): 428–29. The whole essay covers pp. 428–56.

43. Nutt, "History, Tradition, and Historic Myth," p. 339.

44. Ibid., p. 337.

45. W. S. Lach-Szyrma, "Folk-Lore Traditions of Historical Events," *Folk-Lore* 3 (1881): 157–68, especially p. 159. An editor's note, p. 159, cites Sir John Lubbock's *Pre-Historic Times* (London, 1865) on the absence of traditions about recent, well-known events in savage history.

46. David MacRitchie, "The Historical Aspect of Folk-Lore," *The International Folk-Lore Congress 1891. Papers and Transactions,* ed. Joseph Jacobs and A. Nutt (London, 1892), pp. 105–6.

47. F. York Powell, "Tradition and Its Conditions," *Folk-Lore* 15 (1904): 12–23, especially pp. 19–21.

48. John L. Myres, "Folk-Memory," *Folk-Lore* 37 (1926): 28. The whole article covers pp. 12–34.

49. Denis Page, "The City of Troy," in Glyn E. Daniel, ed. *Myth or Legend?* (London, 1956), pp. 26–27.

50. Sir Leonard Wooley, "The Flood," in Daniel, *Myth or Legend?*, pp. 39–47.

51. Richard M. Dorson, *Bloodstoppers and Bearwalkers* (Cambridge, Mass., 1952), pp. 169–76.

52. Hector Lee, "The Shadows from Lookout Bridge (a television script broadcast from Radio Station KPAY, Chico, California, 9 January 1960), bound with other scripts in the series under the title "Campfire Tales of Northern California" (1959), 41, no. 13.

53. *The Dewar Manuscripts*, vol. 1, *Scottish West Highland Folk Tales*, collected by John Dewar, trans. Hector Maclean, ed. John MacKechnie (Glasgow, 1963), pp. 233–36.

54. Richard M. Dorson, *Buying the Wind* (Chicago, 1964), pp. 87–88; *Western Folklore* 6 (1947): 27.

55. Ian Cunnison, "History and Genealogies in a Conquest State," *American Anthropologist*, n.s. 49 (1957): 20–31; "History on the Luapula, an Essay on the Historical Notions of a Central African Tribe," *The Rhodes-Livingstone Papers*, No. 21 (Capetown, London, New York, 1951); *The Luapula Peoples of Northern Rhodesia: Custom and History in Tribal Politics* (Manchester, England, 1959).

56. Meyer Fortes, *The Dynamics of Clanship Among the Tallensi* (New York, 1945), p. xi.

57. Paul Bohannan, "Concepts of Time among the Tiv of Nigeria," *Southwestern Journal of Anthropology* 9 (1953): 260–61.

58. Jan Vansina, *Oral Tradition, a Study in Historical Methodology*, trans. H. M. Wright (London, 1965), pp. 170–71.

59. Possible verification of the tradition of Atlantis, identified as the Aegean island of Santorin, is discussed in John Lear, "The Volcano that Shaped the Western World," *Saturday Review* 49 (New York, 1966), no. 45: 57 ff. While attending the Congress of the International Society for Folk Narrative Research in Athens in September, 1964, I lunched with Professor Angelos Galanopoulos, the seismologist who has advanced this theory, and heard him expound his views, which are now receiving considerable attention.

9 /

History of the Elite and

History of the Folk

THESE ARE EXCITING TIMES in the historiography of American history. Individually and collectively, historians of America's past are appraising their own and their predecessors' methods, biases, and presuppositions. These examinations of history-writing that have appeared in close succession over the past half dozen years display a variety of methods and formulas themselves, and attest the lively self-interest and advanced professionalism among American history specialists. Let us have a quick look at them.

Here is a trio engineered by John Higham, who is Professor of History at Johns Hopkins University. He ushered in the new wave of historiographical interest in 1962 by editing *The Reconstruction of American History* (the only one of the dozen titles I cite that falls before the 1965–1971 period, since it connects with two other works by Higham). For this reassessment he enlisted the cooperation of ten other professional historians, each of whom surveyed and appraised the recent historical literature on major chronological topics in American history, from Puritanism, the Revolution, and the West to progressivism and America as a world power. In his opening essay Higham commented on certain trends detectable

This paper was delivered at Grand Rapids, Michigan, 2 October 1971, as the Clarence C. Burton Memorial Lecture for the Historical Society of Michigan. It was published in somewhat briefer form in the *Chronicle* of the Society, 7:4 (April, 1972): 2–19.

in the reports of his colleagues: the absence of towering leaders in the profession such as a Turner or a Beard of an earlier generation, the growing attraction of intellectual history, and the concomitant decline of economic determinism as a governing theory of historical causation. The contributors often indulged in shoptalk of the profession about notable historians of the previous and contemporary generations.[1] In spite of the range of topics, the same names recur regularly from the colonial to the modern themes, most conspicuously Parrington, Beard, Turner, Hofstadter, and Schlesinger junior.

In 1965 Higham produced his own extended and synthesized account of the same subject matter in *History, The Development of Historical Studies in the United States*, with an emphasis on the growth of professionalism among academic historians. Of particular interest is his account of the sharp clash within the American Historical Association in 1939, when Allan Nevins' proposal that the Association sponsor a popular historical magazine was rejected. Nevins eventually succeeded in launching the magazine as *American Heritage*, which, as Higham said, pleases a public but dismays the historians. Higham contends that there are a number of selective publics for whom the historian with ideas can write, without catering to the vulgus.[2] In contrast to the earlier volume, Higham traces broad currents of historical theory in the late nineteenth and twentieth centuries, under such rubrics as evolutionism, the New History, and relativism. The uneasy relationship of the historical profession to the new social sciences provided the central issue in these debates. For authors of works of history, as opposed to the philosophy of history, he employed such labels as conservative and progressive historians to give a seeming coherence to the variety of titles he felt obliged to mention.

As a kind of sequel, Higham brought together in 1970 under the title *Writing American History* nine of his essays that explored in greater depth his concerns with American intellectual history, with Turner and Beard, and with the responsibility of the historian for moral criticism. In his concluding essay on "American Historiography in the 1960's," Higham confessed to shock at the wave of protest-engendered histories suddenly emerging from radical critics.[3] Higham himself had pleaded for a development of the young historian's moral and aesthetic sense, but not in this direction. His final words, marking the end of consensus, are ". . . a general framework for understanding American history has collapsed." [4]

Three other historians have examined the Progressive school in depth. Robert Allen Skotheim concentrated on *American Intellectual Histories and Historians* (1966), recognizing the tribute given this new area by Higham and discussing a number of the same figures under the same labels. He placed Robinson, Beard, Becker, Parrington, and Curti in the progressive tradition reacting against scientific history, and grouped together Morison, Miller, and Gabriel as challengers to that reforming, pragmatic, optimistic tradition, which held sway from the beginning of the twentieth century to the end of World War II. To one like myself who studied under Morison and Miller, their designation as "dissenting historians" seems forced. Skotheim justified his category by their admiration for early New England thought and disregard for the social sciences.[5] He does acknowledge that Miller's scholarly genius raises him above neat pigeonholes.[6] Skotheim ends with the mild rejection of the Progressive school by intellectual historians writing in the 1930's and '40's. This rejection becomes much more acerb in specific critiques of the Progressives by two well-established historians, the late Richard Hofstadter and Robert E. Brown.

Hofstadter titled his work of 1968 *The Progressive Historians: Turner, Beard, Parrington.* With its preliminary chapter on the precursors of these giants and an afterword on their successors today bounding the richly annotated central essays, this book too is a semi-history of the American historical profession. Hofstadter is scrupulously fair in these marvelous portraits of the three giants of the generation past, and seems genuinely sad at the dismemberment to which he subjects them. In the end nothing is left of their reputations but charred ashes. Turner, the non-writer, lived off an early essay whose lofty uses of such terms as "democracy" and "individualism" would be riddled by critics. Beard, linked with a class-conflict interpretation of the origins of the Constitution that has melted away before the revisionists, ended his career pitied by his colleagues for his monomaniacal isolationism. Parrington, an Enlightenment rationalist in a populist age, built a monument to Jeffersonian liberalism by inventing a Rousseauistic influence on American thought and stereotyping a motley cast of characters. Having pa-

tiently and sorrowfully disposed of the Progressives, Hofstadter
turned in his epilogue to the current school of consensus historians,
notably Hartz and Boorstin, from whom he dissociated himself,
rejecting their consensus premise as explicitly as he had repudiated
the conflict premise of the Progressives. Both schemes of interpretation are too simple; they cannot stand up to what he called the "re-
discovery of complexity in American history . . . , the new awareness of the multiplicity of forces." [7]

The great contemporary of Turner, Beard, and Parrington left
unscathed by Hofstadter, the historian's historian Carl Becker,
came tumbling down before the flail of Robert Brown. A merciless
iconoclast, Brown, in *Carl Becker on History and the American
Revolution* (1970), applied to Becker the same technique he had
previously employed on Beard; he checked the sources of the historian against his interpretations and conclusions, and found glaring
discrepancies. Becker had developed in his various volumes on
American history a class-conflict interpretation of the American
Revolution, which saw two struggles, that of colonial Americans
against British imperialism and that of unfranchised patriots against
Tory aristocrats: home rule versus who should rule at home. Examining Becker's source for his figures on the small number of free-
men in Revolutionary New York, Brown found them so obviously
understated that he accuses Becker of wilful distortion.[8] To this
charge he adds the criticism that Becker, trained under Turner as a
scholarly, objective historian pursuing truth, embraced for the
major portion of his illustrious career a philosophy of history compounded of Progressivism, pragmatism, presentism, and subjective
relativism, with which he manipulated and contrived facts to persuade his audience that the evils of the past served as lessons for the
social revolution of the present that would bring a heavenly city of
the future. Becker's quotation from Voltaire, that "history is only a
pack of tricks we play on the dead" and, if it serves useful social
ends, "does not harm the dead, who had in any case tricks of their
own," Brown repeats throughout his dissection, as evidence of
Becker's own lack of historical scruples.[9] On the credit side, Brown
gives Becker points for pulling back, in the last five years of his life,
1940–45, from the reforming liberalism that drew him close to
communist doctrine and for disavowing much of his subjective relativism and cynicism of democracy when faced by the ugly real

facts of Hitler and Stalin. But Brown feels that recantation came too late with too little, and in itself did not check the Becker cult. All the glowing tributes to Becker's craftsmanship and style, from famous peers and forgotten students, with which Brown lards his text, seem to add up to a wholesale indictment of the profession. Not only did eminent fellow-historians laud Becker to the skies, but they adopted and expanded his class-conflict thesis of the Revolution. The thesis found powerful allies in Beard and the senior Schlesinger, entered the popular textbooks of Muzzey and Hockett, and persisted among later colonial historians such as Jensen, John C. Miller, and Bridenbaugh. Only at long last, Brown concludes, have the consensus historians laid it to rest and acknowledged the democratic character of Revolutionary America. But they have not yet, he feels, recognized the hypocrisy in most of Becker's work.

Two books published in 1965 grappled with the question of the central theme in American history as conceived by historians. In *Conflict or Consensus in American History*, editors Allen F. Davis and Harold D. Woodman grouped selections from major historical writers around the pivotal topics of the Revolution, the Constitution, Jeffersonian and Jacksonian Democracy, the Civil War and so on up to the New Deal and the American Character, to show how sharply historians disagreed on whether Americans were a united or divided nation. Students must have been thoroughly confused after reading Clinton Rossiter on general agreement and Merrill Jensen on class conflict among Revolutionary Americans; Charles Beard on deep-rooted divisions and Robert Brown on middle-class democracy among the Constitution makers; Parrington on the Jeffersonian-Hamiltonian schism, Morton Borden on Jefferson as compromiser; Schlesinger junior on Jacksonians versus the business community and Bray Hammond lumping Jacksonians and businessmen together as expectant capitalists; Beard seeing in the Civil War a second American Revolution and Boorstin viewing it in terms of continuities; David Potter regarding Americans as molded into one people by abundance and Michael Harrington finding them riven between the rich and the poor, the "other America." Whatever the final verdict of historians may be, one thing is sure: "conflict" and "consensus" have become clichés in the profession.

One ingenious historian did contrive a synthesis that meshed the most illustrious American historians into the fabric of American history itself. David W. Noble gave his *Historians Against History* the subtitle "The Frontier Thesis and the National Covenant in American Historical Writing since 1830," and he accomplished the tour de force of bringing Bancroft, Turner, the earlier and the later Becker and Beard, whom he treated as separate entities, Parrington, and Boorstin into one pattern. Noble used for his binding principle the Puritan idea of the covenant between God and his saints in New England, secularized in the eighteenth century by Jefferson and the founding fathers in the social compact entered into by free men to safeguard their natural rights. Each historian, in Noble's analysis, saw the American covenant fulfilled or threatened by the play of historical forces. To Bancroft the covenant was realized in the bounty of the American land; to Turner it was clouded by the passing of the frontier. Beard at first believed it was renewed by the promise of industrial progress, and later felt it had been betrayed by eastern plutocrat-interventionists championed by Franklin Roosevelt. Becker first contended for the free action of Americans to reassert the covenant with nature in behalf of progress, but later abandoned the isolationist idea of the covenant in favor of traditions and values linking America to European civilization. Parrington viewed the covenant in terms of an eighteenth century Jeffersonian America toppling before the onrush of technology; and Boorstin reaffirmed the covenant as a natural growth from the American wilderness into a satisfying urban-industrial culture. The issue, in Noble's perception, was not conflict or consensus but the covenant with nature as the basic structure of American society, whose failure or success involved historians as much as it did the covenanting community of Americans.

The domain of American historiography has even enticed an historian of the European Enlightenment, Peter Gay, who dealt with William Bradford, Cotton Mather, and Jonathan Edwards in a brief but elegant volume, *A Loss of Mastery, Puritan Historians in Colonial America* (1966). Gay promises a sequel devoted to other colonial historians. His title conveys his theme; the Puritans failed to break out of the mythical-theological cast of their history-writing and steadily went downhill, as historians and as a sainted commonwealth. To Bradford's *History of Plymouth Plantation* Gay awarded his highest marks, for its noble detachment and felicitous style, although the *History* and the colony alike petered out. Mather's *Magnalia Christi Americana* is an apologetic family and tribal history that emphasizes consensus at the expense of unpleasant conflicts, such as John Cotton's flirtation with the antinomians and the Puritan extinction of certain trespassing Quakers, episodes hastily glossed over by Mather. As for Edwards, "An American Tragedy" as Gay captions him, his posthumously published *History of the Work of Redemption* reveals how static and old-fashioned were his world-view and his conception of history. "His mind was the opposite of reactionary or fundamentalist," Gay writes. "Yet his history was both." [10] Venerating history, the few Puritan chroniclers never developed it as art or science.

Three recent history-probing enterprises involve a galaxy of Establishment historians. In *The Craft of American History*, published in two paperback volumes by Harper Torchbooks in 1966, A. S. Eisenstadt reprinted thirty-three articles from historical and other periodicals dealing with general questions of methods and values, themes and problems in the writing of American history. Some pieces had already won their own niche in the historical record, such as Higham's baptism and critique of the "consensus" school in *Commentary;* the spirited exchange between Allan Nevins and Matthew Josephson in the *Saturday Review* over whether American history of the Gilded Age should be rewritten with greater sympathy for the Robber Barons (Nevins "yes," Josephson "no"); and Schlesinger junior's eloquent *mea culpa* in *Foreign Affairs* on recognizing the untidiness of actual history as compared with the symmetry of written history, after having watched history-in-the-making at a president's elbow. Familiar names are invoked in *The Craft:* Billington sees much residual good in Turner in spite of revisionism; Hofstadter in a 1950 article is sympathetic to Beard; and in an historical survey of American history Edward N. Saveth places Turner and Beard in perspective. Other articles consider the relation of American history to the social sciences, to biography, to American Studies. The revisionists have their say: Bailyn assails the myth of the American Enlightenment and Vandiver of the Confederacy.

A second collaborative work carries the punning title *Pastmasters, Some Essays on American Historians.* In this volume, edited in 1969 by Marcus Cunliffe of the University of Sussex and Robin

Winks of Yale, thirteen experts in American history interpret eight of their contemporaries and five of their predecessors. As a gesture of Anglo-American comity, and a recognition of the rising interest in England in American history and American studies, English co-editor Cunliffe, himself a contributor, enlists four of his country-men to render appraisals. Another fillip is provided by the dual appearance of two historians as subjects and authors: Arthur Schlesinger junior writes on Hofstadter and is written on by Cun-liffe; David M. Potter lauds C. Vann Woodward and is eulogized by Sir Denis Brogan. The editors take pains to explain their selec-tion of Clio's favorites, conceding that Becker and the senior Schles-inger would have made it in a second volume, and allowing that the New Left historians are not quite ready for canonization. They dis-claim any intent to bring forth a mutually congratulatory *Fest-schrift*, on the order of Stubbs buttering Freeman and Freeman buttering Stubbs from alternate tubs, but the book has some of that flavor. The only unrelievedly negative judgments fall upon the bat-tered trio of Progressives, Turner, Beard, and Parrington, but their flaying merely contributes to the sense of harmony and consensus among the living Establishment historians. As for the other two de-ceased pastmasters, Parkman and Henry Adams, they represent brilliant anomalies outside the profession proper, and their critics, William R. Taylor and J. C. Levenson, feel no need to discredit them. Contributors are established stars or rising young profession-als.

What the professionals agree upon, as they examine each other and belabor the Progressives, is the social-scientific basis of modern historical method. Howard Lamar on Turner, Forrest McDonald on Beard, and Ralph Henry Gabriel on Parrington all point to the faulty use of sources and the drawing of large, false generalizations by these masters with feet of clay. Turner unwittingly portrayed American folk myths; Beard played the role of devil's advocate in the classroom to ignite his students and carried this role over into his writing; Parrington allowed his emotional sympathies for Jeffer-sonian liberalism to mar his esthetic and intellectual judgments. The most caustic critic, McDonald, charges Beard with "deliberately stacking the cards" and purposely misstating facts to prove his point about the economic self-interests of the supporters of the Constitution.[11] He carried over this technique of falsification, Mc-

Donald alleges, into his attack on Franklin D. Roosevelt for maneuvering the United States into World War II, under the axiom that a worthy social end justified manipulating history.

The essays on contemporary historians in *Pastmasters* all contain balanced judgments and they all distribute bouquets. Handlin is "one of the foremost historians of the common man" [12]; Hofstadter's *The American Political Tradition* was written "with brilliant freshness and economy" [13]; Potter's examination of the American character is "far more subtle and far more intelligent than Turner's famous frontier theory, making Potter one of the truly great interpreters of American history" [14]; "*The Age of Roosevelt* demonstrated Schlesinger's exceptional talent for marshaling the raw stuff of history like an impresario directing a cast of thousands" [15]; C. Vann Wodward is "a scholar of extraordinary maturity, humane understanding, breadth of mind, and capacity to combine tolerance with idealism" [16]; the work of Daniel J. Boorstin "has grown to be one of the most ambitious and persuasive of all attempts to impose on American history the vision of a unified interpretation" [17]; Samuel Flagg Bemis "has no equal among American diplomatic historians" [18]; the "brilliant" work of Perry Miller is characterized by "extraordinary sensitivity." [19] These phrases of praise should not obscure passages of sinewy criticism; only H. C. Allen's tribute to Bemis is obsequious, while in most of the essays revisionism is heaped upon earlier revisionism, extracted from the so-called monographic explosion, until one despairs of any finalities in American history. For instance, Oscar Handlin's block generalizations about the trauma of immigrant experience in America are riven by Rudolph J. Vecoli's case studies of successful Italian settlements in Chicago, but Vecoli in turn is challenged by Humbert S. Nelli with contrary evidence.[20]

Precedents exist for essays by historians on other historians, but John A. Garraty's *Interpreting American History, Conversations with Historians* (1970) is *sui generis*. Professor Garraty of Columbia University, my former colleague at Michigan State University, interrogates twenty-nine accomplished historians (although two are professors of English, one is an economist and one a sociologist) with a tape recorder, in the presence only of his charming wife Gail, who draws a sketch of each historian that adorns the volume. The edited tapes provide the content of the meaty seven hundred page book. This method follows the new technique of oral history, and it seems fitting that American historians should employ it upon themselves. Some of the pastmasters reappear here: Schlesinger junior, Hofstadter, Potter, C. Vann Woodward, with other well-known names, such as Henry Steele Commager, T. Harry Williams, Ray Allen Billington, David Donald, well fixed in the firmament, and ascendant luminaries like Bernard Bailyn. As Garraty states in his Introduction, his panel represents the Establishment of consensus historians, but he does query his interviewees on the contributions to their fields of the New Left radical historians. He has organized the volume by chronological topics, broadly conceived, so that the reader can follow generally the familiar narrative thread of events and issues, but this is no textbook, rather it is everything that a textbook is not: vivid, alive, questing, opinionated; some of the conversations, such as Commager's on American nationalism and Potter's on interpretations of American history, transcend neat boundaries of time. There is a good deal of shoptalk about the profession, and Garraty is at pains to elicit views on sensitive and controversial points of scholarship. For instance, in talking with Bailyn on the American Revolution, he inserts questions on the validity of Robert Brown's thesis that middle-class democracy existed in revolutionary Massachusetts, rather than the class society postulated by Beard. Brown's attack on Beard has never sat too well with many of his colleagues, even with those who have discarded Beard, as being somehow an attack on the credibility of the profession; Hofstadter, Schlesinger, Forrest McDonald consider his tone intemperate. (Brown himself tells of his difficulty in obtaining a publisher for his *Charles Beard and the Constitution;* the presses to whom he submitted the manuscript kept asking him, "If what you say is true, why hasn't it been published before?" He finally resorted to publishing his critique of Becker himself.) Bailyn gives a rather negative judgment on Brown, saying that his point of view is anachronistic and his method marred by "important technical errors," but pressed by Garraty, he grudgingly concedes that Brown did contribute "to some degree" to disproving the old Beardian theory of class conflict.[21]

The titles so far discussed, while they may not all reveal a sympathy with the consensus viewpoint, do betray an inner consensus. They are written by American professional historians with a strong

sense of the prestige of their guild. Their ritualistic slaying and re-
generation of Turner, Beard, and Parrington gives them a spirit of
community and an historical anchorage. Their emphases may shift
from conflict to consensus, from objectivity to relativism to moral
judgment, but they never question the classic divisions of the colonial period, the Revolution, the westward movement, the Civil
War, industrialism, and America as a world power, as the main pre-
occupations for American historians, and as the areas to cultivate
to gain fame within the fraternity.

Three recent works do however challenge the fellowship of the
guild. In *Historians' Fallacies* (1970), David Hackett Fischer employs an unprecedented technique to demolish the entire historical
profession. Instead of addressing himself exclusively to one historian and checking his sources and interpretations with infinite labor,
as does Robert Brown with Becker, Fischer administers the coup de
grâce to a host of chroniclers in a few lightning strokes by simply
finding them guilty of bias. Thus Schlesinger junior is guilty of the
fallacies of both presentism and pragmatism, in selecting facts from
the past that bear on the present, and in associating them with his
cause of New Deal liberalism. Handlin commits the fallacy of argument *ad nauseam* by rewriting the same book over and over, making immigration the central factor in American history, even to
converting Negroes into Jews. C. Vann Woodward sins with the
telescopic fallacy in foreshortening the story of *The Strange Career
of Jim Crow* to make it appear that racial segregation was a late
development in the South. He and Potter are both charged with
pro hoc, propter hoc, putting the effect before the cause, in their
theses of America as a land of security and a land of abundance;
they simply overlooked the first two centuries of American history,
Fischer declares, when people were neither secure nor rich. Hofstadter's greatly admired *The American Political Tradition and the
Men Who Made It* sins with the fallacy of the lonely fact, by
which vast generalizations about major American statesmen are
built upon single facts, while his highly praised *The Paranoid Style
in American Politics* falls afoul of the apathetic fallacy, in failing to
show the same sympathy for conservatives as for liberals. Perry
Miller's studies of Puritanism are marred by the fallacy of idealism
that leads to neglect of individual thinkers, economic and social
processes, and behavior patterns; to over-reliance on intuitive judg-

ment; and to neglect of historical setting. Morison's stress on telling a beautiful story shores up the aesthetic fallacy. And so it goes: every living and a number of dead historians of consequence are skewered sooner or later on one or more historical fallacies. To this bomb the guild has responded with anguish and ridicule. The editor of the *Journal of American History* offered me the paperback edition of *Historians' Fallacies*, just to get it out of his office. At the December, 1970, meeting of the American Historical Association in Boston, Fischer served as commentator on Handlin's lament, "History: A Discipline in Crisis," before a packed audience in the grand ballroom of the Sheraton Hotel. Bewailing the demise of sound historical writing, Handlin remarked in passing on the stupidities in Fischer's new publication, which berated Handlin for slanting history and yet could not get the titles of his books straight. In reply Fischer apologized for his inaccuracy but pointed out that both of the factual statements Handlin made in his long paper were incorrect: one an inversion of a demographic table, the other a misattribution to John Adams of the oft-quoted statement that the American people on the eve of the Revolution were divided into one-third patriots, one-third loyalists, and one-third neutralists. Fischer then went on to reiterate his accusation that in all his books, and in his present paper as well, Handlin romanticized a golden past that never existed.

The rumblings of the New Left rose to full cry in a volume of essays edited in 1967 by Barton J. Bernstein, *Toward a New Past: Dissenting Essays in American History*. Such prominent radical historians as Staughton Lynd, Eugene Genovese, and Christopher Lasch appeared among the eleven contributors, all of whom subscribed to the historiographical revolution that rejects elite history and calls for a history "from the bottom up" rather than through the eyes of "a few at the top," phrases that Bernstein in his introduction quotes approvingly from the initial essay on the American Revolution by Jesse Lemisch. Turning their guns on consensus, the radicals return to conflict, to Beard and Marx, but construe conflict in ideological terms of the power structure versus the dispossessed and inarticulate. From the Revolution through Jacksonian democracy, the slave South, the Gilded Age up to the New Deal and postwar, the essayists seek to redress the balance of elitist emphasis and interpretation. In his chapter "Beyond Beard" Lynd frankly states that his radical revisionism is spurred by the current civil rights movement, prompting him to take a fresh look at slavery in Revolutionary times, and by the "worldwide colonial independence movement," which suggested a new model for conceptualizing the Revolution and its relation to the Civil War." [22] In his review of Jacksonianism Michael Lebowitz draws a line between declining farmers and unskilled workers on the one hand and rising merchants and manufacturers on the other. Looking at the urban population of the late nineteenth century, Stephan Thernstrom gives attention to the bottom layer of society, which he finds fixed in status but fluid in membership.[23] Bernstein belabors Franklin D. Roosevelt and his liberal-historian supporters for preserving American capitalism at the expense of the forgotten man, and tars Truman with the same brush for failure to execute a liberal program; FDR could have nationalized the banking system, and Truman should not have prepared the way for Joseph McCarthy by pushing anticommunism. The message of the New Left chroniclers is clear enough; they see in liberalism and the liberal consensus historians a sell-out to and whitewash of the power elite, and they seek to bring the poor, the enslaved, and the exploited into mainstream American history.

In contrast to these spokesmen for the downtrodden who teach at excellent universities, win fellowships and grants, and publish in the professional journals and with university presses, our last revisionist talks with the fresh voice of militancy from far outside academe. Eschewing the soporific language of pedantry and the barrage of documentation that stamp the radicals as full-fledged members of the guild whose premises they oppose, Dick Gregory tells it like it is, or like he thinks it is, in *No More Lies, The Myth and the Reality of American History* (1970), a book dedicated to Women's Liberation and American Indians. His aim is to show that the standard treatises and textbooks on American history add up to a giant swindle against the red man and the black, and their surrogates, the Irish or Italian immigrant as Indian and today's college student as nigger. Dividing his book into twelve myths—of the Puritan Pilgrim, the Founding Fathers, Black Content, Free Enterprise, and so on—he subjects each to scorn as a travesty on the realities of racism, brutality, and double-dealing. Wherever possible he introduces little-known black and Indian heroes omitted from Whitey's version of the American story. Thus Billy the Kid has become the legendary bad man of the West, but Cherokee Bill, part Indian, part Negro, and part white, was "just as tough and twice as vicious." [24] Gregory ends with a comparison between the fall of Rome and the sickness of America.

How can one summarize this body of recent publications about the writing of American history? It shows a deep intensity of concern on the part of many historians about their craft. It shows an Oedipal obsession with Turner, Beard, Becker, and Parrington, who serve as continual points of departure and return. (Why is Nevins so neglected? Does no one want to read his hundred books?) It shows a haunting uneasiness about the achievement of American history, in the rejection of the earlier masters, in the swings from conflict to consensus to complexity, in the dissent of the radical historians, and in a bracing for blasts from the counter-culture, signaled in the radical caucuses at the historical association meetings and delivered in the rhetoric of Dick Gregory's diatribe.

One cause of the uneasiness, I believe, is that American historians are trapped within an elitist concept of history and do not see how to break out of the circle. Some have said as much in one or another of the volumes under discussion. Responding to Garraty's question about the contribution of the New Left historians to colonial history, Jack P. Greene conceded that they were on the right track in seeking to look at Revolutionary society from below. "We have spent so much time in the last twenty years looking at early American history from the point of view of the elite, the dominant groups, that we have tended to ignore other elements in society." [25] The editor of *The Craft of American History*, Eisenstadt, commented on the traditional character of American history writing with its emphasis on a narrative of well-known events and of great men, usually the major American presidents, and its preoccupation with political history, as in Nevins' ten volume *Ordeal of the Union* and Schlesinger junior's *The Age of Franklin D. Roosevelt*. Historians of today are also drawn, he added, to biographies of the famous and to editions of the collected papers of the founding fathers.[26] In a similar expression of dissatisfaction with "presidential history," Samuel Hays recommended a shift "from top-level affairs to grass-roots happenings." [27] The radical historians have called for "a revolution in historiographical attitudes, a rejection of elite history" based on generalizations about entire societies from the examination of a small minority at the top; and they criticize pretended revisionists who merely swap heroes of politics for heroes of business.[28]

But when it comes to rewriting American history directed at the "powerless, the inarticulate, the poor," the historians flounder. How do they get at the records of those who leave no record? Garraty pointedly asked two historians of the Negro, C. Vann Woodward and Stanley Elkins, how they could unearth sources for blacks, and in discussing historiography with Potter he queried, "Is it *possible* to write a history of the poor? Is it possible to write the history of the slaves' discontent? Do the necessary records exist, or is the history of the inarticulate masses of the past lost simply because of their inarticulateness?"[29] None had a very good answer. Potter alluded to what medieval historians were able to do with fragmentary evidence. C. Vann Woodward believed it was possible "to write scrupulously and objectively about Negroes who took part in the great themes of American history: colonization, expansion, independence, wars, immigration, urbanization," but he did not suggest how.[30] Elkins acknowledged that some black historians like Vincent Harding referred to such potential sources as "folklore, songs, religious traditions," and admitted how much luckier was an historian of slavery than an ancient historian of Egyptian peasants, but still doubted that the slave would ever come to life as fully as the immigrant.[31] Among the New Left historians, Thernstrom rued how difficult it was to get any information about the bottom of American urban society in the nineteenth century, for "dead men tell no tales and fill out no questionnaires."[32] Allan Nevins bemoaned that the "most difficult part of history to obtain is the record of how plain men and women lived, and how they were affected by the economic, social, and cultural changes of their times; the most fascinating part of history is this same record."[33] After pleading for grass-roots history, Hays could only turn to precinct voting patterns in Iowa to exemplify it, on the curious grounds that how people voted "is about as close to the grass-roots as one can get."[34]

Let me state my own view of the matter. Historians writing elite history employ the national framework for their narratives, and the dissenters who desire a redress toward grass-roots, bottom-layer history still operate with nationalist boundaries. C. Vann Woodward followed just this thinking when he said that the Negro could be brought within the great themes of American history. But this is not the history of the Negro, who has his own themes.[35] Nor is it the history of the white man. It is nobody's history, but an artificial construct based on the structure of the federal government. It does not relate to our bored students, it does not relate to the average citizen, who carries none of this history with him. It is historians' history, and even they are getting dissatisfied with it. Hays declared that the "reason that much of history is formal and unsatisfying is because the units of history we write and talk and teach about do not consist of types of human experience, thought, and behavior." The history books are preoccupied with "nominating conventions, campaigns, cabinet meetings, the administration's legislative program and its treatment by Congress."[36] How little does this heavy emphasis on politics reflect the quality of American experiences or the daily concerns of most Americans!

History of the elite I contrast with history of the folk. Folk I use in the sense of the German *Volk* and the Russian *narod*, meaning a people united with common traditions. In this sense an Indian tribe is a folk, with its own tribal history. Joseph Mathews has described this kind of "father-to-son history" as he heard it when he returned to his people, the Osages, after a ten-year interval:

> I became almost at once aware of the importance of oral history, which I have called in this book, tribal or gentile "memory," since that is what my informants believed it to be. I at first experienced a European or Amer-European impatience when, during every visit to the old men, I had to listen again, word for word, to that which had been told me before. Then suddenly it occurred to me that if there were fabrications or misinterpretations in the history I was hearing, they might be from two to three hundred years old, and the very atmosphere they bore would be of great value to me. Certainly they would not be disturbed by "new light" thrown on them. About these stories, handed down from father to son, this oral history of a people, there was, I began to note, a biblical atmosphere, but with the advantage of never having been written down. There could be no later interpretation because of religious taboo, and each word had a certain sanctity. The history was a part of them, of the informants and the tribe, and they could not be detached from their narrative as were literate Europeans detached from their written narratives.[37]

Folk history of this sort is not formalized among nontribal groups in American society, but it has its equivalent in the remembered experiences of the regional, occupational, and ethnic groups into which we all fall. This folk history is an extension of our personal history, and it belongs to us as elite history never can. The sources of folk history are both oral traditions and personal documents.

Oral history has now achieved its own professional association and its own practitioners and caretakers among historians, archivists, and curators. But oral history simply copies the formulas of elite documentary history. The big shots are interviewed. Allan Nevins draws upon oral history tapes for his biography of Henry Ford, T. Harry Williams for his biography of Huey Long. Accordingly I make a distinction between oral history, the new tool of the nationally oriented historian, and oral traditional history, a new tool for the folklorist with historical training or the grass-roots historian with folklore training. Two good examples of oral traditional history are doctoral dissertations in folklore I directed at Indiana University, a study by Gladys Fry of the night riders who terrorized slaves, and a history by Lynwood Montell of a now vanished Negro community in southern Kentucky, which he has published as *The Saga of Coe Ridge*.[38] Both Fry and Montell obtained their primary materials from taped interviews with descendants of slaves and, in Montell's case, also from white farmers and farmwives. Oral historical traditions of this sort differ from oral history in deriving from the folk rather than from the elite, and in carrying information from past generations. Folklore elements will enter such traditions, but the folklorist can recognize them, as Montell does in an appended table of motifs, and separate the kernels of history, which he checks against written and printed sources. In the United States with its relatively short history, oral traditions can span much of the distance; with later arrivals, like the immigrants, or newer settlements, as in the trans-Mississippi West, they can cover all.

Folk history is not however simply a matter of oral traditions. By history of the folk I have in mind the history of the structures in which individuals play active roles, of what psychologists call "vital circuits." This way of looking at history does not begin with the past nor with the top, but with the present and with the individual.

It is the history that belongs to each one of us. This is not state and local history, an alternative to national history which simply reduces the governmental unit but does not necessarily involve the individual any more deeply. What are these structures that involve the individual? Well, schools and colleges involve most of us. The great sports—football, baseball, basketball—absorb large sectors of the American public. Ethnic, racial, regional affiliations engender tribal loyalties, but within small groupings: not the Italians, but the Apulians; not the blacks, but blacks from the Mississippi Delta; not the Kentuckians, but the residents in the creek bottoms of Pine Mountain. The factory, the shop, the neighborhood, the family, the office, all have their histories, and a representative history of one would do service for its innumerable counterparts. But the nationalist historians never write on such themes. Arthur Schlesinger senior did make a plea for the common man as an entity in American history, but his common man is faceless, a statistic in the national count of dietary habits and clothing styles. The most persuasive tract for the humanizing of the presidential synthesis that passes for American history was written by Theodore Blegen in *Grass Roots History* in 1947, a book unmentioned in any of the historiographical works I have cited. In these works I find only one illustration of folk history, in an essay by Douglas E. Leach on "Early Town Records of New England as Historical Sources," reprinted in *The Craft of American History* from *The American Archivist*. Leach drove to the small towns of New England in quest of the handwritten township records kept by the town and city clerks to preserve vital statistics and local information, and he came up with some nuggets about the execution of Indians, regulations for the sweeping of thatched chimneys and the fencing of cornfields, and a special permit given certain farmers of Rowley for making a wolf pen. There are other sources in abundance, oral and printed, that will lead the historian to the folk of an earlier day.

One national historian did once consider the folk. In a celebrated essay, "Everyman His Own Historian," his presidential address to the American Historical Association in 1931, Carl Becker admonished his colleagues to keep in mind the history that Mr. Average Person carried with him and made use of in his daily life. "History is the memory of things said and done," and so "every normal person, Mr. Everyman, knows some history." Becker gave a homely illustration of a man who forgot which company had delivered his coal, checked the invoices, and remembered how he had switched from one company to another. Here was a personal use of history. "What then of us, historians by profession?" Becker asked. "What have we to do with Mr. Everyman, or he with us? More, I venture to believe, than we are apt to think. For each of us is Mr. Everyman too." The academic historian using documents belongs to the "ancient and honorable company . . . of bards and storytellers and minstrels" that maintained the myths of old. With more self-conscious method, he performs the same function as does Mr. Everyman when he breeds "legends out of remembered episodes and oral tradition." [39]

This is a splendid support for my thesis, save in one respect, the stress that Becker places on the written source in Mr. Everyman's need to check his memory against the coal company's ledger. An historian of the folk will employ documentary sources where possible to complement the oral tradition, as does Montell in *The Saga of Coe Ridge*, but he recognizes that traditions contain their own veracity, as reflectors of the ideas of their transmitters, and that documents are filled with imperfections, and often not available. Contemporary historians complain of the paucity of adequate records in these days of instant communication.

If historians have shown little awareness of the folk side of American history, one radical historian has discovered the American Folklore Society. Shortly before the 1970 meeting of the American Historical Association in Boston, I received a sizable manuscript from John A. Williams of the Notre Dame history department entitled "The Establishment and the Tape Recorder: Radicalism and Professionalism in Folklore Studies, 1933–68." Professor Williams explained that he had become interested in the folklore approach while doing research on miners in southern Appalachia, and he courteously invited me to reply to his paper, if I wished, which he was delivering on a panel of radical historians at the AHA. After reading his paper I decided to go and I did reply.

This paper, buttressed with many footnotes, traced the organization of folklore as a corporate discipline in the United States over the past four decades. In the '30's and '40's leading practitioners of folklore like Alan Lomax and Pete Seeger were nonacademic and leftwing. In the '50's and '60's the professors took over folklore and made it a tool of the Establishment, by toadying to the foundations and the federal government in order to obtain grants and subsidies. Williams' chief document for this charge was a letter I had written to Senator Wayne Morse in 1961, and published in the *Journal of American Folklore*, protesting the dropping of folklore from the National Defense Education Act by Senator Morse's Committee on Labor and Public Welfare. I made the point that the Soviet Union and other communist countries used folklore as a technique for propagandizing socialist ideology. Williams stated that Dorson, having thus allied himself with the Establishment, was rewarded with a renewal of the grant. In Williams' analysis, the American Folklore Society sought in the '50's and '60's to achieve prestige and status through conformism to the power structure. Thus Dorson as president of the Society proposed an oral history of the Society's elder statesmen, just as elitist historians interviewed each other in the name of oral history. Drawing a further analogy between the AHA and the AFS, Williams declared, and produced incomplete statistics to support his contention, that the number of women officers in the Society had declined over the past quarter of a century. When introducing the radical panel at the AHA, Staughton Lynd noted the paucity of women members in evidence at the American Historical Association meeting, and Williams was following this theme of the radicals that the big professional organizations were anti-feminist with their other sins.

In reply I said that Professor Williams had made a slight error of fact in his statement that the NDEA grants to folklore were renewed. He left out the word not. While Williams cited a source for the grant renewal, he did not realize that the grants were offered in 1960 and renewed for 1961, but that the barrage of criticism against the grants led by the *Wall Street Journal* came after the renewal, and led to the exclusion of folklore from the National Defense Education Act Amendment of 1961. It was this exclusion that I protested in my letter to Senator Morse, to no avail. The fallacy in the oral history illustration is that I in my fieldwork and writings, never mentioned by Williams, have always espoused the history of the folk, not the elite, while to make an interrogation of American folklorists an elitist enterprise evokes laughter bordering on tears; no learned society has been more battered and buffeted, from the *Wall Street Journal*, Senator Goldwater, and Congressman Gross on the right, and now the radicals on the left, and self-styled experts from other fields in the middle, than the poor American Folklore Society.

Far from inhibiting the careers of women, the American Folklore Society and the academic discipline of folklore have advanced them more successfully than most fields. Two of the last six editors of the Journal have been women, Erminie Wheeler-Voegelin and Katharine Luomala; one of the last three delegates from the American Folklore Society to the American Council of Learned Societies was a woman, Thelma James; the newly elected first vice-president of the Society is a woman, Linda Dégh, who won over Albert Lord of Harvard. The issue is actually a false one, since women have done conspicuously well in folklore, earning doctorates, getting faculty positions, publishing, and actively participating in the national society. There is no parallel whatsoever between the status of women in history and in folklore. At Indiana University in 1970–71 we had more women teaching associates than men. In fact the charge from the complete outsider John Williams is the first complaint I have ever heard about anti-feminism in folklore.

What is disheartening in Williams' paper is the obvious way he has sought to reinforce his own prejudices in attempting to build his case against the academic folklorists, to the neglect of their techniques and accomplishments in reaching the folk. A member of the radical panel at the AHA, Will Watson of the Massachusetts Institute of Technology, confessed in his paper on the anarchist background of the Spanish Civil War his difficulty in making contacts with Spanish radicals, because of the difference in culture, language, customs. In my response I mentioned my colleague in folklore, Jerome Mintz, then in the field in Benalup de Sidonia in southern Spain, where he had established excellent rapport with old-line anarchists. The grass-roots history of Lynwood Montell which Williams admired was done as a doctoral dissertation under my direction. Williams and his fellow radical-historians do not fathom the methods and concepts of the folklorist, from which they could benefit in their desire to penetrate to the anonymous masses. Still, if they will skew all their data to support a radical vision of a repressive America, they can of course manipulate oral sources just as Williams has twisted documents. If an historian in our time can in pursuing his bias obtain so perverted a view of reality, what will he do with a past period? Yet Williams scrupulously documented every statement he made. He quoted from my own reports as president and editor of the Society, and from files in the Folklore section of the Library of Congress. But my reports were public statements that by their nature reflected nothing of the inner turmoils of the discipline, and the files he found in Washington had little bearing on the Society's affairs. The central issue in the Society in the late fifties and early sixties was professionalism versus amateurism, and the Society polarized between Indiana University representing the academic point of view and the University of Pennsylvania which, as the seat of the Secretary-Treasurer's office, took a lenient view toward standards of membership. When Williams declares that MacEdward Leach of Pennsylvania and Stith Thompson and Dorson of Indiana led a united front of the Society in their bid for status, he is unaware that Leach and Dorson were at loggerheads, if not swords' points within the Society, and that Thompson had retired.

Why this interest of radical historians in folklorists? The two coteries share a common point of departure; they are concerned with the anonymous, inarticulate millions in American life. The New Left has discovered the technique of the tape-recorded interview with the man in the street; at the radical panel in Boston, Staughton Lynd played a tape of a factory worker recalling an episode of police brutality, and young men in the audience, apparently engaged with him in a history of the CIO in the 1930's, gave reports on problems of the oral interview, such as how to record changes in ideology of the speaker occurring during his lifetime. Interviewing the folk, using the tape recorder, the New Left historians would naturally sooner or later cross the path of the folklorists, and hope to find them allies. Speaking for myself, and I think for a good number of my colleagues in folklore, I would say that the folklorist does not link his sympathy with the folk to any ideology—radical, liberal, or conservative, communist or capitalist. The history of the folk I endorse does stand opposed to history of the elite, but not in terms of a class opposition, rather in terms of personal social structures versus an impersonal national structure.

What sources can the historian of the folk tap? There is first of all the vast reservoir of oral reminiscences, family sagas, and gossipy personal and local history that living Americans possess. In *Division*

Street America (1967), Studs Terkel, who interviews all kinds of persons on his Chicago radio and television shows, let a number of uncelebrated Chicagoans from one neighborhood talk into his tape recorder, and the transcripts lay open the minds of a cross-section of the folk. While their revelations are personal, often the attitudes, prejudices, fantasies, and world-view they express are traditional, inherited from an earlier generation. Terkel repeated this technique in *Hard Times, an Oral History of the Great Depression* (1970), save that he included celebrities among his reminiscers, and gave his interviews a specific historical slant. Terkel's books reached the best-seller lists, but only specialists will encounter the two privately printed oversize volumes prepared by Harry M. Hyatt, a retired Episcopal clergyman, from his hundreds of tapes recorded over the last thirty years from American Negroes and issued under the title *Hoodoo, Witchcraft, Conjuration, Rootwork* (1970). This work is indispensable for an understanding of the Negro and the slave mind in America. The first volume contains statements about supernatural beliefs current in the Negro population, and the second consists entirely of interviews with hoodoo doctors, the practitioners of magic. When the black historian Sterling Stuckey was asked what was the first thing he would do if he assumed the directorship of an Afro-American Studies program at Indiana University, he replied, "Teach the students about folklore." These publications of Terkel and Hyatt cover a spectrum of verbal narration from statements of personal experience and outlook to discussions of folk belief, and the whole spectrum is useful to the historian of the folk.

Another large body of source material on which he can draw is the printed counterpart of these oral forms, in personal narratives, memoirs, diaries, travel accounts, overland journals, immigrant letters, and the like. In constructing my anthologies of the seventeenth century and the Revolutionary War, *America Begins* and *America Rebels*, I drew entirely from such sources to convey a picture of the dramas of colonization and the Revolution as seen through the eyes of participants. My *Jonathan Draws the Long Bow* culled newspapers, town histories, almanacs, and similar printed matter for folklore reflecting the ethos of New Englanders from the seventeenth to the twentieth centuries.

An example of the kind of source available to the historian of the folk is a newspaper item that came to hand while I was writing this paper, captioned "Reb Russell Full of Baseball Lore." It appeared in the Indianapolis *Star* of Sunday, September 5, 1971, and set down the recollections of eighty-two year old Albert (Reb) Russell, who in 1913 won twenty-one and lost seventeen games for the Chicago White Sox. He recalled the infamous Black Sox scandal of 1919, when players of the White Sox threw the World Series, and his own refusal to the gamblers who bribed them; stars like Shoeless Joe Jackson, who played left field barefoot because he could not find baseball shoes big enough to fit his feet, and whose paychecks Reb often signed because Joe was illiterate; and Babe Ruth, who pitched his first game for the Boston Red Sox in 1914 against Reb, losing to him 1–0, and who visited Reb several times, drinking whisky in memorable quantities; Reb's sudden release by the Pittsburgh Pirates in 1922 after he spiked a fan who was heckling him; and his later years in the minors. Here is an ephemeral printed source once removed from an oral transcript, giving the personal history of a veteran athlete now forgotten, whose memories would enrich a history of the national pastime.

To his enduring credit, one academic historian, Harold Seymour, has published with the Oxford University Press two volumes of a projected trilogy on the history of baseball written from the "perspective of American history." Seymour recognizes that "Baseball, like some other aspects of our popular culture, has been badly served by history." He conceived the first scholarly account of baseball as a doctoral dissertation at Cornell, and in it he deals not with star players and winning teams but with the "workings of the baseball business and its deeper significance as an American institution." [40]

For the past two years I have experimented with a seminar at Indiana University called "The Folk in American History," in the effort to apply some of the ideas discussed here. The students have chosen topics keyed to the history of a definable group: the Irish in Indianapolis, coal miners in Kentucky, the Ottawa and Ojibwa Indians, Mexicans in the Midwest, American settlers in Hawaii, the people of Shelby County, Indiana. One undergraduate developed a paper on the youth culture in recent American history, and accompanied it with a tape of selections from rock music singers, explaining the double entendres in the lyrics obvious to members of the drug culture but unsuspected by older listeners. Where possible the students interviewed and tape-recorded folk informants, and they all used personal, grass-roots sources. In the end none complained of paucity of materials, rather the reverse.

In one session of the seminar I used myself as a model for the personal structures with which we are all associated. The structures whose histories would be meaningful to me are Exeter, the preparatory school I attended for four years; Harvard, where I took three degrees; Michigan State and Indiana Universities, where I have taught for twelve and fourteen years respectively; the American Folklore Society; and the game of tennis. This list is heavily weighted to educational institutions, but all Americans go to school and many go on to college and universities. Exeter and Harvard are elite schools, but the students who attend them are a folk, in my sense, largely unrepresented in the elitist histories of these and other schools and colleges written from the point of view of the presidents, the boards of trustees, overall educational policies, a few eminent faculty and alumni, and the growth of the physical plant. Such histories have nothing to do with the lives and thoughts of the students, and not too much to do with the faculty. One evening I took my seminar to hear one of the Patten lecture series being given on the history of Indiana by Distinguished Professor Thomas D. Clark. There were maybe a dozen of the thirty thousand students in the audience, along with a somewhat larger number of administrative officials, including one ex-president, who enjoyed it hugely. The lecture was on the presidency of William Lowe Bryan. There was no reason for students to be there, because their college lives shared nothing with the career of President Bryan beyond residence in Bloomington. After the lecture I took the seminar to the Commons for coffee and opened up the subject of college traditions, and for two hours we exchanged anecdotes of our college years with mounting excitement. A vast subterranean lore permeates the high school and college, samples of which are now represented in our Folklore Archives, and a folk history of any American college will delve into this lore.

Professor Tom Clark is an eminent historian whom I value as mentor, colleague, and friend, and he has shown considerable sympathy toward the history of the folk in such books as *The Rampaging Frontier* and *Plows, Pills and Petticoats*. But in *Indiana University, Midwestern Pioneer* he was obliged, by his mandate, to write a history from the top. Madison Kuhn inscribed my copy of his *Michigan State, the First Hundred Years*, "To one who will describe college life as it really is," a compliment I do not expect to justify, but an indication on his own part of the bounds within which he was writing the history of Michigan State University.

Let me offer a few glimpses of the student as folk. Besides the collected folklore of school children and undergraduates, one can look for personal and autobiographical statements that yield fresh viewpoints. Here is a volume of solicited reminiscences, *Exeter Remembered*, edited by a longtime Exeter teacher, Henry Darcy Curwen, who used to preside at the Saturday night movies, coach crew, and instruct in English. Most of the pieces are conventionally nostalgic, but two strike home. Humorist Richard P. Bissell, 1932, who was a class ahead of me, in three deft pages titled "Evolution" sketches the changing mores and values of three generations of Exonians: the cornball atmosphere of his father's day; the rah-rah spirit of his own time; and the disdainful air of his sons, who, when he visited them, "created an impression of bored minor State Department officials exiled to an outpost up some river in Paraguay."[41] In contrast to this wit is the impassioned "Letter to a Friend" of Sloan Wilson, '39, author of *The Man in the Grey Flannel Suit*, who in a breath of fresh air writes Darcy Curwen, ". . . I honestly hated the school, and I still remember the one year I spent there as the unhappiest year of my life. . . ."[42] Wilson affirms his passionate interest in education, and criticizes the whole philosophy of Exeter that locks seven hundred adolescent boys in a New England town under the supervision of "morose bachelors." The homoerotic tendencies and anxieties that he hints at were made the subject of the play "Tea and Sympathy" written by another Exonian, Robert Anderson. Wilson must be pleased to know that Exeter has finally gone coed. The Exeter I remember is an Exeter of awesome sexual brags in the "butt-rooms" where we were permitted to smoke, of caste-like social levels from the fraternity "smoothies" at the top to the "queers" and "fruits" at the bottom, and of masters who inspired fear or ridicule. As an instance of the gap between the elite and the folk, there is the episode that occurred in chapel the morning of the Exeter-Andover game when "Doc" Perry, addressing the seven hundred students in his customary bland, benign, peering-over-the-spectacles manner, wished the coach victory to reward the fruits of his labors. Seven hundred boys rocked in uncontrollable laughter, while Doc Perry wondered what had hit him. He did not know that "fruit" was the most loaded term in an Exonian's vocabulary, a catch-all for queer, fairy, deviant, untouchable, and unspeakable. The more sophisticated boys also savored the innuendo in "labors."

In the yet to be written folk history of American colleges, a major theme will be cheating. Sitting in a downtown restaurant in Bloomington recently, I heard a serious, pretty coed complaining to her table-mate about the extent of cheating in her classes. "If everyone cheated it wouldn't matter," she said, "but those who don't are penalized." She then told of taking a chemistry examination, in which a bright student sat in the front row while those of his fraternity brothers who had paid five dollars each took places in the formation of an inverted V behind him, so that each could copy from the one ahead. Determined to put a stop to such cheating, the instructor on another examination asked all those students having ID cards to go to one side of the room and those without them to go to the other, whereupon six students who were taking the examination for class members made a dash for the door. Such stories I casually overheard on the passing air circulate on every college campus; they grow into a folklore based on reality and fill folders in our folklore archives, and I know a sheaf of them myself.

A former professor in the history department of Michigan State University, Elmer Lyon, told me of one. During an examination he noticed a student continually opening the fob of a turnip pocket watch. Professor Lyon took a position behind the student and saw that answers were written on a paper inside the fob. He reported the student, who, being related to one of the trustees, was let off with a light reprimand. Some years later Professor Lyon happened to be in the local bank making a deposit when the auditors were inspecting the bank's books, and he recognized one of the auditors as his cheating student.

The code of college students does not allow an honest student to inform the professor of misdeeds. In an American history survey class I was teaching, word of wrongdoing reached me indirectly. A student in the back row boasted loudly that a fraternity pledge had written his book report for the course, and that this pledge was a genius; he could read any book assigned one of the fraternity members in twenty-five minutes and dash off an A report for him to hand in. A girl near this student reported the brag to a colleague of mine (whom she would subsequently marry), the colleague told me, and I confronted the student. Seeing I had him, he did not deny the charge. "I've been busy this semester," he confided to me, "and I didn't have time to do a book report, but I wish you could meet our fraternity pledge, Professor Dorson; he can read any book you assign in twenty-five minutes and write an A paper on it." "Well," I pondered, "I have been pretty busy myself and I don't have time to read the book reports, so I turn them over to a grading assistant. But I would be happy to arrange a meeting between your writer and my reader."

The classic cheating story in my annals involves a football player who signed up for my class in "American Folklore." Twelve years at Michigan State had taught me how to appeal to that particular student clientele, and in the spring of 1956 my enrollment reached one hundred ninety, even including some star athletes. This one, whom I shall call Jack Armstrong, came up to me after the first class to make sure he would do satisfactorily in the course. It was crucial, he informed me, that he pass, so that he would graduate, so that he would obtain his coaching contract at Mudville High. I assured him he need have no worries provided he come to class, find his seat, laugh at my folk jests, and write a book report on my *Bloodstoppers and Bearwalkers*. The day came when one hundred ninety reports flowed in. All but ten were typed, and these handwritten ones I struggled with last. The one hundred eighty-ninth seemed somehow familiar, and I checked it with the one hundred and eighty-seventh, to find both cited the same page references and ended with the same glowing tribute: "I thoroughly enjoyed your book, Professor Dorson, and will recommend it to all my friends."

At the next class meeting Jack Armstrong tarried after the bell, as was his wont, to check on his progress. "You copied your book report, didn't you," I said. "You mean from Merke?" he replied. I nodded. He explained that he could not afford to buy the book, but would get hold of one and write me another paper. "Too late," I said. "What will that do to the grade?" he queried. "F," I answered. Strenuously he pleaded his graduation, his coaching contract with

Mudville High. I remained adamant, and he strode off in the direction of the fieldhouse.

When I reached home the telephone was ringing, and I lifted the receiver to hear a deep voice say, "This is Biggie Munn." Clarence Biggers Munn had been brought to Michigan State by President John Hannah to develop a winning football team; *Time* magazine quoted President Hannah in 1956 as saying that when he determined to make Michigan State a first-rate university, the first thing he did was to get a coach to go out and find the eleven toughest gorillas he could locate to field a winning football team. Biggie did the job successfully, leading Michigan State to a Big Ten title and a Rose Bowl championship and getting elected Coach of the Year. He himself wrote a book about his winning ways called *Multiple Offense*.

"Are you calling about Jack Armstrong?" I asked. "Yes, he's right here in my office. What's this about his studying with other students? I always studied with other students," said Biggie.

"No, it wasn't that. He copied his paper from another student, and admitted it."

"Well, what are we going to do for this boy, after the way he has dug and scraped for Michigan State?"

"Nothing I am afraid, Mr. Munn. The game is over." I heard a sharp intake of breath, but that was the only point I scored in the next forty-five minutes as Biggie turned his multiple offense on me. He wanted to know if Armstrong could make up the course in the summer, and when I said it was not offered then, he thought that very unreasonable. I asked if he wished to compare the two papers, and he said, "No, you have a Ph.D., you must have a brain." He stressed the importance of the coaching contract at Mudville High. "We work hard for those contracts and if we don't get them it makes us look bad."

"There is too much cheating that goes on at Michigan State," I said, "and we have to take a stand on it. In my course in American Intellectual History I gave the students an assignment to keep personal diaries in the manner of Emerson and Thoreau, and almost all of them complained at the amount of cheating that went on in college."

"How long have you been at Michigan State?" he demanded. I

asked why he wanted to know. "I thought maybe you were a new-comer and didn't appreciate our traditions." Actually I had come several years before Biggie. This ignorance of my name particularly wounded my *amour propre*, as I had received a good deal of public-ity in the local press for my talks and writings on folklore, and had even been awarded a special citation by the Michigan legislature.

"You believe in ethics, don't you, Mr. Munn," I asked. "Why of course, my teams always play clean, don't they?" Finally Biggie said calmly, "I couldn't override you if I wanted to. What do you suggest?"

I suggested we bring the matter to the attention of the student's dean. After some discussion between Biggie and Jack it was decided that, physical education being in the School of Education, the dean of that school must be Jack's dean. Biggie said he would call the dean next morning.

In the morning I received a call from the dean's assistant, who said that Biggie had been on the phone with his superior for an hour. Biggie was perturbed because Armstrong was the only member of his Rose Bowl championship team who would have graduated in four years, and he was also concerned about the con-tract with Mudville High. "Why did you fail the student?" the junior dean asked. "Because he cheated," I said. "Oh, Biggie never mentioned that. In that case we will uphold your grade."

That summer my wife's older sister moved from Detroit to Mudville, and one of her sons took American history from Jack Armstrong because, according to the folkways of the American high school, the football coach is expected to teach a course and the course he teaches is customarily American history. So the contract with Mudville High was honored, although I never learned how.

This episode, which I have recounted many times, illustrates for me central aspects of American college life. There is the towering figure of the football coach, usually the best known personality on campus; the intersection of two distinct subcultures, that of the playing field and that of the classroom, which give rise to colorful college legends; the fiercely paternal interest of the coach in his players; the vaudevillian element of the instructor catering to his large clientele; the crisis point of the grade, the chief concern of college students, now acknowledged by educators as an undue cause of anxiety; and, in the background, the era of transition in which Michigan State climbed from a cow college to a big-name university. After the new football stadium was built, a new library building arose. Educators may talk and historians may write about expanding intellectual horizons and enriching curriculum content, but the student asks first, how much work is there in the course, how many examinations are there, and what grade can I expect. Once I had occasion to visit a girls' dormitory, the evening before registration in the fieldhouse for fall courses, in my capacity as a faculty associate, and I heard a senior advising panicky freshmen on procedures and cautions to observe in the fieldhouse; the new students dreaded registration as a rite of passage and frightened each other with stories of disaster, like the one of the coed who had fainted in the fieldhouse the year before when all the sections she desired were closed.

Nor are these undergraduate attitudes confined to midwestern state universities. In the summer of 1952 I taught at Harvard, and heard President James B. Conant welcome the summer session faculty one bright morning. He assured us that Harvard's standards in the summer were the same as Harvard's in the winter; Harvard was Harvard the year round; there must be no relaxing of Harvard's standards. That afternoon I went charging into my seminar on colonial American literature aflame with the message, and danced around the podium exhorting the fourteen students to give their all for research, to use the magnificent resources of Widener Library, visible through the window, the Massachusetts Historical Society in Boston, and even the American Antiquarian Society in Worcester—in short to spend their summer happily grubbing in these great repositories of colonial Americana. That evening I heard President Conant address the summer session students with a different tune. The theme now was: Enjoy yourselves, this is summertime; socialize with your fellow students in the Wednesday afternoon yard mixer and drink the free fruit punch that will be served on the steps of Widener; join in the Friday evening dances in the Union; take the buses to the beaches of the North Shore and the South Shore and the Tanglewood Music Festival; and above all, shop around to find interesting courses; don't sign up with the first one you wander into but make sure you will receive a stimulating and enjoyable classroom experience. Next day I found four students in my seminar, one an auditor, and that was my class for the summer.

When a history of American college life is written from the folk point of view, it will need to incorporate experiences of this sort, rather than quote from the minutes of the board of trustees' meetings.

It will also need to embrace the inside story of faculties, and here again is a large gap in our knowledge. The histories of departments, disciplines, and learned societies are largely unwritten. Perhaps even more valuable than the discussion of historiography in the books I originally cited is their record of the historical profession. We can expect historians to be history-minded, but what of all the other fields of learning from astronomy to zoology? The late William Riley Parker, former executive secretary of the Modern Language Association and chairman of the English department at Indiana University, had begun shortly before his death to issue a series of highly readable newsletters covering the early history of his department, and he was encouraging other English departments around the country to undertake similar histories. Such histories would contain accounts of feuding and factionalism unsuspected by the public outside the ivory tower. Recently I completed a history of the English folklore movement, which had lain in almost total darkness, although it is a vigorous and even spectacular chapter in the history of learning.

Another structure in which I am involved is the sport of tennis. There exist of course the usual illustrated histories of the game and autobiographies of famous players. One of these autobiographies, Gardnar Mulloy's *The Will to Win*, gives me a paragraph. Mulloy, who attained the number one ranking in the United States, described my first encounter with him when he was sweeping courts at Woodstock in the Catskills, and I sauntered by with my Exeter blazer and superciliously inquired who around could give me a game. For lack of other competition I finally permitted him to play with me, and was lucky to win a point! In my own span I have seen enormous changes in the sport: in dress from long trousers to shorts, in tactics from back-court rallies to the big game of cannon-ball service and smash volley, in scoring from the marathon deuce set to the tie-breaker, in organization from sham amateurism to contract and independent professionals who now battle the United States and International Lawn Tennis Federations for control of tournaments and stars. The full history of tennis, as of other sports, would encompass all aspects, not simply the stars but the role of the game in the lives of Americans, covering the social gamut from the country clubs to the public parks; the restriction of blacks and the poor; changing attitudes of spectators (today they feel the top women are more interesting to watch than the top men); the regional and seasonal factors affecting the sport; the international dimension; the relation of tennis playing to concepts of health and fitness; fashions in heroes and heroines, exemplified in Big Bill Tilden, a national idol tarnished with the charge of homosexuality, before gay liberation, and Billie Jean King, who battles for Women's Lib with her racquet.

American historians of the elite ignore Everyman's history and write continuously on the same national themes. They are revisionist in their interpretations but not in their selection of subjects. I am not suggesting that history of the elite is expendable, but that history of the folk is *not* expendable, if we are to know our personal roots, traditions, and tribal affiliations. Each person will select his or her own set of social structures for the attention of the grass-roots historian—but whatever they are, whether scholarly organizations or urban slums, they carry a history that relates to its human parts as the chronology of federal policy-making never can relate to two hundred million individual Americans. The history of the folk is the history of our own personal worlds, and deserves the attention of talented historians.

N O T E S

1. Arthur Mann says as much in his chapter on "The Progressive Tradition" in *The Reconstruction of American History*, ed. John Higham (New York: Harper and Row, Harper Torchbooks, 1962), p. 177.

2. John Higham, with Leonard Krieger and Felix Gilbert, *History, The Development of Historical Studies in the United States* (Engelwood Cliffs, N.J.: Prentice-Hall, Inc., 1965), p. 85.

3. John Higham, *Writing American History, Essays on Modern Scholarship* (Bloomington and London: Indiana University Press, 1970), pp. 166–67.

4. Ibid., p. 173.

5. Robert Allen Skotheim, *American Intellectual Histories and Historians* (Princeton, N.J.; Princeton University Press, 1966), pp. 186, 188–90, 211.

6. Ibid., p. 309.

7. Richard Hofstadter, *The Progressive Historians: Turner, Beard, Parrington* (New York: Alfred A. Knopf, 1968), p. 442.

8. Robert E. Brown, *Carl Becker on History and the American Revolution* (East Lansing, Mich.: The Spartan Press, 1970), p. 39.

9. Ibid., p. 58.

10. Peter Gay, *A Loss of Mastery: Puritan Historians in Colonial America* (Berkeley and Los Angeles: University of California Press, 1966), p. 104.

11. *Pastmasters, Some Essays on American Historians*, ed. Marcus Cunliffe and Robin W. Winks (New York, Evanston, and London: Harper and Row, 1969), pp. 133–34.

12. Maldwyn Jones, in ibid., p. 275.

13. Arthur M. Schlesinger, jr., in ibid., p. 286.

14. Denis Brogan, in ibid., p. 344.

15. Marcus Cunliffe, in ibid., p. 366.

16. David M. Potter, in ibid., p. 407.

17. J. R. Pole, in ibid., p. 210.

18. H. C. Allen, in ibid., p. 194.

19. Robert Middlekauf, in ibid., pp. 180–81.

20. Ibid., pp. 256–57.

21. John A. Garraty, *Interpreting American History, Conversations with Historians* (New York and London: Macmillan and Collier-Macmillan, 1970), pp. 85–86.

22. In *Towards a New Past: Dissenting Essays in American History*, ed. Barton J. Bernstein (New York: Vintage Books, 1969), p. 49.

23. Ibid., p. 167.

24. Richard Claxton Gregory, *No More Lies, The Myth and the Reality of American History*, ed. James R. McGraw (New York, Evanston, and London: Harper and Row, 1971), p. 145.

25. In Garraty, *Interpreting American History*, vol. 1, p. 60.

26. A. S. Eisenstadt, "American History and Social Science," in *The Craft of American History*, ed. A. S. Eisenstadt (New York: Harper and Row, 1966), vol. 2, pp. 115–16.

27. Hays, "History as Human Behavior," in Eisenstadt, ed., *The Craft of American History*, vol. 2, pp. 126, 128.

28. Jesse Lemisch, in Bernstein, ed., *Towards a New Past*, pp. xi, 4.

29. Garraty, *Interpreting American History*, vol. 2, p. 329.

30. Ibid., p. 65.

31. Ibid., vol. 1, p. 200.

32. In Bernstein, ed., *Towards a New Past*, p. 167.

33. Nevins, "History This Side the Horizon," in Eisenstadt, ed., *The Craft of American History*, vol. 2, p. 269.

34. Hays, in ibid., p. 129.

35. To develop this point would require another paper, but some glimpses of Negro historical traditions are available in my *American Negro Folktales* (New York, 1967), especially chs. 5, 6, 9, and 10. There is elitism in black history too, in the concentration on well-known figures such as Booker T.

Washington, Frederick Douglass, and W. E. B. Du Bois, and the neglect of personalities among the rank and file, such as James Douglas Suggs, whose life history I give in *American Negro Folktales*.

36. Hays, in Eisenstadt, vol. 2, pp. 128, 126.

37. John Joseph Mathews, *The Osages* (Norman: University of Oklahoma Press, 1961), p. xii.

38. Gladys-Marie Fry, "The Night Riders: A Study in Techniques of the Social Control of the Negro" (1967) and Lynwood Montell, "A Folk History of the Coe Ridge Negro Colony" (1964).

39. Becker, *Everyman His Own Historian* (New York: Appleton-Century Crofts, 1935), pp. 235, 246, 247, 252.

40. Harold Seymour, *Baseball, the Early Years* (New York: Oxford University Press, 1960), pp. v–vi.

41. *Exeter Remembered*, ed. Henry Darcy Curwen (Exeter, N. H.: Phillips Exeter Academy, 1965), p. 154.

42. Ibid., p. 27.

10 /

American Folklorists in Britain

Introduction

PROFESSORS OF ENGLISH in American universities teach both English and American literature, English universities are now showing interest in American Studies, and we might reasonably expect a comparable relationship between American and British folklore and folklorists. We think of Henry James and T. S. Eliot leaving the United States for Britain, of Auden going the other way, of Emerson visiting Carlyle, of Cooper emulating Scott, of Mark Twain lionized in London, of a thousand interrelationships. Yet, if we leave aside ballad scholarship, the histories of American and British folklore studies seem surprisingly separated. True, W. L. Hildburgh, an American who held an engineering degree from Columbia University, did become president of the Folklore Society. I frequently lunched with him in the winter of 1949–1950, when I had digs close to his near Hyde Park, and became very fond of him, but Dr. Hildburgh was indistinguishable from other Edwardian, or perhaps even Victorian, gentleman scholars, and his speciality of medieval alabasters had little to do with American folklore. Some Britishers sent papers to the International Folk-Lore Congress of the World's Columbian Exposition held at Chicago in July 1893,

Reprinted from the *Journal of the Folklore Institute* 7 (August–December, 1970): 187–219.

and in the Proceedings we find contributions from Sidney Hartland, David MacRitchie, Lucy Garnett, John Canon O'Hanlon, John Abercromby, and other active British folklorists, but, unlike its predecessor in London of two years before, this congress was an empty affair. There was in truth no well-defined American folklore movement before the first World War with which British folklorists could make contacts. Conversely, folklore-minded Americans could enter into the intellectual ferment of their well-established colleagues in the British Isles, and four of them did, in ways worthy of recall.

CHARLES GODFREY LELAND (1824–1903)

The American who penetrated deepest into the English folklore movement, and into the Victorian world of letters and culture, was Charles Godfrey Leland, best known in his own day and still faintly remembered in ours as Hans Breitmann. His more than fifty books and pamphlets include a discourse on the art of conversation, a manual on wood carving, a translation of the works of Heinrich Heine, a biography of Abraham Lincoln, an account of a transcontinental railroad trip, a record of travel in Egypt, an historical analysis of the dispute over Alsace and Lorraine, a self-help essay titled "Have You a Strong Will?," fiction, poetry, and a dozen diversified folklore works. Of them all, it was the one he least regarded, *Hans Breitmann's Party, with other Ballads* (1857), originally written as jeux d'esprit in letters to a friend and published more or less by accident to oblige a printer, that gained him his reputation.[1] It became an instant success and Hans Breitmann speedily passed into the American comic lore of ethnic stereotypes. Leland himself recognized the analogy of his German-American creation with Bret Harte's heathen Chinee and James Russell Lowell's Hosea Bigelow —the latter the closer parallel, since Hosea speaks in Yankee dialect, as Hans talks in the Germanic English of the immigrant coming to the United States after the abortive liberal revolution of 1848. Leland could lapse into his lingo—he did not consider it a dialect, but a transitional speech—at a moment's notice, as in this verse he penned in a letter from a French seaside resort, where he was badgered by officious bathing guards:

> Gottsdonner, if ve doomple down
> Among de vaters plue,
> I kess you'll need more help from me,
> Dan I shall need from you.[2]

This feeling for off-standard language that produced the Breitmann ballads gives one clue to the folklore interests and instincts of Leland. It led to his learning Romany in England and becoming a dedicated gypsiologist, and to his discovery of Shelta, the tinkers' tongue. In the way of books, it resulted in *The English Gypsies and Their Language* (1873); *Pidgin-English Sing-Song* (1876), a Chinese version of Hans Breitmann; and, with Albert Barrère, *A Dictionary of Slang, Jargon and Cant, embracing English, American, and Anglo-Indian Slang, Pidgin English, Gypsies' Jargon and Other Irregular Phraseology* (2 volumes, 1889; revised, 1897). Leland became so versatile in European languages, from his long residence overseas, that he could convert phrases between German, Italian, French, and English without a breath;[3] yet as a student in Germany he tells how he struggled with Teutonic syntax. He continually played around with patois, from Schussen, the low-German Hebrew dialect, to Irish brogue and Tuscan Bolognese.

A second general thread in Leland's folklore output was his fascination with the living informant. While not a systematic field collector, he had the knack for unearthing carriers of tradition in or near the big cities where he lived, London, Brighton, Philadelphia, Florence, or on a summer trip to Maine where Passamaquoddy and Penobscot Indians still told old myths. Leland prided himself on getting his legends first-hand, and regarded with some disdain the critical theorists who assembled for the great English folklore congress of 1891, seeing them as men of books and not of the folk. "For him it was strange people and strange coincidences all the way,—Gypsies, tinkers, witches, magic working of his Voodoo Stone," wrote his niece-biographer, Elizabeth Robins Pennell.[4] His first year in England, in 1870, he encountered Matthias Cooper, a full-blooded Romany, sleeping out of doors in Brighton, "wild" and "eccentric," and conversant with all aspects of Gypsy life. "I soon learned his jargon, with every kind of Gypsy device, dodge, or peculiar custom, and, with the aid of several works, succeeded in drawing from the recesses of his memory an astonishing number of forgotten words." [5]

In the Preface to *The English Gipsies and Their Language*, he underscored the announcement that all his material "*was gathered directly from Gipsies themselves.*" Nor was this just a matter of conventional field collecting. In a letter to his niece (April 6, 1895), he stressed the point that "There is a great difference between collecting folk-lore as a curiosity and *living* in it in truth. I do not believe that in all the Folk-Lore Societies there is one person who lives it as I do. . . . It is curious how I find such characters—it *is* like miracle—I don't seek them, they come to me in dreams." [6]

His books are full of these chance meetings with folk personalities. Writing Elizabeth from Whitby, August, 1884, he tells of drinking ale with four blithe spirits in the Luggerhead Inn that dated back to the tenth century. One of the four was "a radical mason, covered with lime, who abused the Queen, cussed the Prince of Wales, blasphemed the bishops, and chaffed the Church —I stood four pints of ale and got the ancient legend of The Luggerhead."

> "Ees, sir, it be cawd t' Looger Head. Hoondreds o' years by gone when t' caught a smoogler, ta' boorned t' vessel and t' cargoo. And wan whiles tay caught a Logger foo' of smoogled goods, and tay boorned it an' kept ta *head*, and tat day was t' foorst pooblic opened in Whitby, and tay poot t' head here and ca'ed it ta Looger hid, and then ta Looger Head. For ta smooglers was always at logger heads wit' ta Coostoom Hoose people, and thot woord Logger Head coomed fra tis very hoose." [7]

After he fled the fogs of London to the milder clime of Florence, in 1888, Leland soon found himself living in "an atmosphere of witchcraft and sorcery, engaged in collecting songs, spells, and stories of sorcery." [8] In his "prowls about Florence" he ran onto a celebrated witch, Maddalena; a photograph in Pennell's biography shows her holding cards and exhibiting the face of the "antique Etruscan." "She was from the Romagna Toscana, born in the heart of its unsurpassingly wild and romantic scenery, amid cliffs, headlong torrents, forests, and old legendary castles." When Maddalena was in Florence Leland saw her regularly and learned about her spells, philtres, invocations and legends; when she was away, she wrote him copiously about witch news.

All the folk groups whom Leland cultivated seemed to him facets of the same primitive type. The Indians, living in the fields and woods, reminded him of the Gypsies, and so did the Florentine witches, both maintaining the occult practices of an ancient past. American Negro Voodoo and its practitioners intrigued him on the same grounds, and in 1889 he began a lengthy correspondence with the Voodoo collector Mary Alicia Owen of St. Joseph, Missouri, who sent him many specimens of her Negro-Indian tales. He encouraged and advised her, obtained a publisher, T. Fisher Unwin, for her tales, which appeared in 1893 as *Rabbit the Voodoo and Other Sorcerers,* and wrote the Introduction ascribing a Red Indian origin to much African magic.

A third consistent strain in Leland's folklore work is his particular brand of survivalism. The Rye (his niece's constant and rather irritating appellation for him) was no high-flying speculative theorist or system builder, but he clearly shared the assumptions of the Victorian folklorists. In his *Gypsy Sorcery and Fortune-Telling* (1891) he quotes approvingly from a paper by George Laurence Gomme in the *Archaeological Review* (January 1890) on "The Conditions for the Survival of Archaic Customs" affirming that even in civilized countries masses of people were still in a state of savagery, unbeknownst to monarchs and historians.[9] He himself believed that the amount of magic in the world among the "lower orders," and the higher too, was as great as it had ever been, whether in the special forms of witchcraft and voodoo, or in occult creeds and practices spread among the entire population.

There is to be found in almost every cheap book, or "penny dreadful" and newspaper shop in Great Britain and America, for sale at a very low price a Book of Fate. . . . In my copy there are twenty-five pages of incantations, charms, and spells, every one of them every whit as "superstitious" as any of the gypsy ceremonies set forth in this volume. I am convinced, from much inquiry, that next to the Bible and the Almanac there is no *one* book which is so much disseminated among the million as the fortune-teller, in some form or other. That is to say, there are, numerically, many millions more of believers in such small sorcery now in Great Britain than there were centuries ago, for, be it remembered, the superstitions of the masses were always petty ones, like those of the fate-books. . . . We may call it by other names, but . . . the old faith in the supernatural and in occult means of getting at it still exists in one form or another. . . .[10]

And he is reminded of his first publication forty years earlier, a "Folk-lore book" titled *The Poetry and Mystery of Dreams* explaining dream symbolism through allusions in poetry and popular ballads. Some hack, giving no credit, turned the work into a "common sixpenny dreambook." [11]

Since the old magic did persist, even if in new bottles, it gave a clue to the nature of early man, and Leland delighted in the thought that his English gypsies and Etruscan witches preserved prehistoric systems of belief and worship. Accepting the thesis that the gypsies had made their way across the Middle East and Europe from India, he speculated that "the Dom of India is the true parent of the Rom. . . . The Dom pariahs of India who carry out or touch dead bodies, also eat the bodies of animals that have died a natural death, as do the Gipsies of England." [12] There were other likenesses: in the dancing and festival music; in death customs, such as friends preparing food for three days for the family of the deceased; in the veneration for cooking utensils. "The conclusion which I have drawn from studying Anglo-Rommany, and different works on India," he writes in *The English Gipsies and Their Language,* "is that the Gipsies are the descendants of a vast number of Hindus, of the primitive tribes of Hindustan, who were expelled or emigrated from that country early in the fourteenth century." [13] Leland did add diffusionism to survivalism in his gypsiology, and applauded Groome's description of the Romany as the true *colporteurs* of folklore, but it was the echoes of old Hindi words and ideas that pleased him most. So too, in his last phase in Florence, he reveled in the Latin survivals in modern Tuscan speech and supernaturalism, and wrote ecstatically to Elizabeth Pennell (Florence, January 1891), "*Cosa stupenda!* I have made such a discovery! . . . For I have found all the principal deities of the Etruscans still existing as spirits or folletti in the Romagna. . . . In all these cases the informer did not know the Latin name—only the *Old Etruscan.*" [14] Two months later he had finished his "great work on the Etruscan mythology and witchcraft," and in October that year he delivered a paper on his findings in London to the international folklore congress dominated by the Tylorian theory of survivals in folklore. His paper fitted in well. In the *Gypsy Sorcery* he speculated that the first stage of shamanism was a "very horrible witchcraft" which most likely once prevailed universally among savages.[15]

A fourth vein of Leland's interests that he never connected with folklore, but which the folklife enthusiasts today emphatically would, was his espousal of the industrial arts, or the minor arts, or the home arts, as he variously called them. He loved to work with wood, leather, and metal, to sketch and draw, to restore and repair the craft objects he was constantly acquiring. His writings along this line include a series of twelve *Art-Work Manuals* which he edited and in large part wrote (1881–1882), *Drawing and Designing* (1889), *Manual of Wood Carving* (1890), *Leather Work* (1892), and *A Manual of Mending and Repairing* (1896). He conceived of these skills within a theory he presented in a book on *Practical Education* (1888), and to which he devoted much time, energy, and personal funds during his four years in Philadelphia, 1880 to 1884, sandwiched in between two long term residences in Europe. Officially he held the title of director of the Public Industrial Art School of Philadelphia, and on his return to England he sought to develop the home arts movement there.

His theory rested on the principle that "a knowledge of art, or how to make one or more things, is of immense value in stimulating in every mind a love of industry." [16] He believed that interest in the minor arts helped cultivate general intelligence and an appreciation of literature. Children came from all the school districts in Philadelphia to a central schoolhouse, where volunteer teachers instructed them, and Leland himself conducted the largest class, in drawing, wood-carving, and working with metal and leather. His goal was the forming of classes in every village and town for the study of decorative work. The public school made no provision for teaching pupils the use of their hands. He dreamed of "a great future when the people of the United States, after three or four generations had been thus trained in decorative art, would become craftsmen by instinct—rivals of the artisans who decorated the Cathedral of Europe, and who made of every pot or pan a thing of beauty now to be treasured in museums." [17] In his field interviews, Leland inquired into material culture as well as oral literature. Meeting a gypsy cooper in Tottenham Court Road carrying a roll of split canes, he took him to a bar, ordered him a pint, and then a potquart of good pale ale, and another pot for a friend, "an appalling rough who had prize fighter of the lowest stamp in every feature," but in return he learned their art of splitting the cane.[18]

Fifthly, Leland organized folklore societies. He had a flair for founding clubs and relished the titles, honors, and sense of exclusiveness of such societies. One of his fondest schemes was for a London dining club, the Rabelais, which he planned in 1878 with his good friend Walter Besant to outclass all other London clubs. "Great names are our great game," he wrote candidly, and warned against "small or mediocre names" and too much "*democracy*." He raged when Browning declined and sought to "punish" him by bringing in other celebrities. "I want the Rabelais to corruscate [sic]—whizz, blaze and sparkle, fulminate and bang." The Rabelais had its day in the 1880's—it was *de rigueur* to wear evening clothes —and finally succumbed in 1889.[19] Meanwhile, with the acceleration of the folklore movement, Leland took an active part in its organizing endeavors. After his final return to England he corresponded with David MacRitchie, in 1888, on establishing a Gypsy-Lore Society, and accepted the first presidency.[20] In a letter of May 9 he agrees to the spelling of gypsy with the two y's, and the Society and *Journal* followed suit. At the First International Folk-Lore Congress in Paris on August 1, 1889, he acted as standard-bearer for Britain, writing that "it has fallen on the Gypsy-Lore Society to come to the front, and take all the honour of representing England, as the English Folk-Lore Society has not appeared at all in it!"[21] He is fertile with all kinds of ideas for invigorating his society and not serving simply as figure-head; thus he suggests a "Notes and Queries" Corner in the *Journal*, an American corresponding Society of Gypsies, and an exchange of advertisements with a London publisher specializing in occult and magical literature.

He speaks of other folklore society involvements in a letter of August, 1893, to Mary Alicia Owen from Bagni di Lucca, Italy. "Four years ago I tried hard to get the learned Count de Gubernatis to establish an Italian Folk-Lore Society. I have just received from him a letter in which he says that he has at last effected what originated with me, and we now have one of 500 members—at 12 francs or $2.40 per annum. . . . There is to be an Italian Folk-Lore Congress at Rome in November. It is odd that in precisely the same manner, I originated the Folk-Lore Society of Hungary, and was accordingly the very first member entered. And I may be said to have been, in fact I was, the very first member and beginner of the London Folk-Lore." [22] Earlier he had written that "the greatest Folk-Lore Society in the world" with fourteen subdivisions—Hungarian, Armenian, Yiddish, Gypsy, Wallach, Croat, Serb, Spanish, and so on—had been founded in Budapest in 1888 during his sojourn there, and that he was the first member nominated. [23]

Leland could be severe as well as enthusiastic about the activities of folklore societies, particularly their publications. "What the trouble is in all Folk-Lore Journals," he protested to MacRitchie, "is that those who contribute are, as a rule, timid and yet very critical old gentlemen who generally write, in the style of 'a letter to the Times,' small paragraphs in 'an other seen in the Thames' kind of foozles. It was such writing which kept the 'Gentleman's Magazine' in a dead-alive condition for about a century. . . ." [24] At this moment (February 1891), Leland was feeling blue about the coming demise of the *Journal of the Gypsy-Lore Society*, and repining that he, MacRitchie and Groome were put at menial tasks, "rather like architects kept at sawing boards." But his euphoria could never be damped for long, and he confides to his niece, in advance of the Italian folklore congress, "You have to live in the world of Folk-Lore to know what excitement there may be in it, even for a man who, after an adventurous life, has reached his seventieth year." [25] The Queen of Italy was an ardent "Folk-Lorista," and intended to be present, but a political crisis and threats of mobbing prevented her attendance. Since she was expected, a full crowd did attend, "with all the fashion and learning of all Rome"; Leland read his paper to them in Italian, and the next day he was *célèbre* and *illustrissimo* in the newspapers. [26]

At the Second International Folk-Lore Congress sponsored in London in 1891 by the Folk-Lore Society, one of the landmarks in the history of our subject, Leland took a prominent part, and his role there capped his long career in English letters and folklore, which we might now briefly review.

In 1869, after his father's death freed him from dependence on journalism for a livelihood, Leland moved to Europe for a ten year period, living chiefly in London and Brighton with side trips to health resorts on the continent. Already well known as a versatile writer of prose and verse, he entered easily and delightedly into English literary and cultural circles. He was himself an imposing figure and something of a celebrity, although he could never shake off the aura of Hans Breitmann, and his fame has dimmed alongside the giants, on both sides of the Atlantic, with whom he supped and walked. His niece gives us her impression of him on his return to the United States in 1880, noting "his unusual height, his fine head, his long flowing beard," much as she remembered them from her childhood, all comprising what she twice called a "commanding presence," but now she notices "the light in the strange blue eyes," eyes of a seer and a mystic, and she is struck by his great kindness. Conventionally dressed in formal frock coat and black tie, he talked unconventionally, with deep seriousness, on all topics except the idle and trivial, in a low, slightly monotonous voice, but "What he had to say, he said with all his might." [27] Leland observes in one place that he wrote better than he talked, but elsewhere he prides himself on his storytelling, and tells of swapping yarns with Mark Twain in a Florence hotel.

During this his first English residence he became attracted to the gypsies, and gathered the materials which appeared in *The English Gypsies and Their Language* (1873), *English Gipsy Songs* (1875), and *The Gypsies* (1882), the largest section of which was devoted to the English Romanies. In the American interim he made contact with Passamaquoddy Indians while summering in 1882 at Campobello, New Brunswick, and two years later published *The Algonquin Legends of New England*, a collection he conceived to be "a stupendous mythology, derived from a land of storms and fire more terrible and wonderful than Iceland," [28] and strangely suggestive of the Edda. His experience with the Christianized Passamaquoddy, Penobscots, and Micmacs in Maine and New Brunswick, living in the midst of a dominant white population, paralleled his encounters with the gypsies. In 1884 he left his homeland permanently. For the next seven years he resided chiefly in England, until recurring attacks of the gout forced him in 1891 to quit Langham's Hotel in London and take refuge in Italy for the rest of his life. In all he and his wife lived twenty years in hotels, a situation that pained Leland chiefly because he could not invite his friends to dinner of a Saturday evening. In his final dozen years, although physically removed from his beloved England, he retained his intellectual ties there, and sent his unceasing flow of book manuscripts to English publishers. The exciting string of folklore collections from north Italy—*Etruscan-Roman Remains in Popular Tradition* (1893), *Legends of Florence* (2 volumes, 1895–1896), *Aradia, or the Gospel of the Witches* (1899), and *The Unpublished Legends of Virgil* (1899), all came out in London, under the imprints, respectively, of T. Fisher Unwin, David Nutt (twice), and Elliot Stock, and were much better known in England than in the United States.

Leland savored the London life of literary gossip and excitement, bonhomie, wining and dining, and boon companions of intellectual distinction. He knew and met everybody, and has given us saucy anecdotes of the great names he so coveted for his Rabelais Club: how George Borrow advertised his own work on the gypsies immediately after Leland offered to dedicate *The English Gypsies* to him; how Tennyson, on the other hand, graciously accepted the dedication of *English Gipsy-Songs*, after hearing that Leland had translated one of his poems into Romany, but before Leland inadvertently stole blackberries from Tennyson's garden; of Richard Burton sending in his subscription to the *Journal of the Gypsy-Lore Society*, on learning that gypsy would be spelt with the double y; of Lord Bulwer Lytton's astonishment when Leland tells him he knows how to restore old brass salvers, and that he has written a *Manual of Repoussé*; of meeting George Eliot and wishing to chide her for depending on books about Jews instead of learning Yiddish and talking to them; of shocking the dour and contemptuous Carlyle into a broad Scots exclamation, to which Leland replied in kind, by saying that Carlyle was unduly influenced by the melodramatic. Every Sunday in 1870 (the last year of his *Memoirs*), he dined with his friends and publishers, the Trübners, and loved the sparkling fellowship. "For it was a salon, a centre or sun with many bright and cheering rays—a civilising institution!" [29] So Anglicized did he become that he even learned, in middle age, to ride to hounds.

Leland was a character, an original. He could mix with the English swells and with the "lower orders." He wrote dialect rhymes and mystical philosophy. The scholar, the poet, and the humorist were always at odds within him. His personal foibles show the same ambiguities. In a letter from Brighton of October 20, 1870, he complains about the amount of drinking in English society.

Men and women too drink all the time like topers at home, and the *average* of young ladies top off six glasses of mixed wines at dinner. I learn this from a young lady who has unlimited opportunities of judging. As for the *men*, the one who does not show the effects of heavy drinking is a great exception. There is a very pretty young married lady lives close by us, and the other day at dinner she took six glasses of wine before the fish had arrived. I was at the dinner. The amount of drinking everywhere is awful. I had to tell a lady the other day that it was easier to get a quart of wine than a drop of water in her house. And it was true. When I wanted water, the servants had to be called up and all hell set loose before the *aqua fontana* could be produced. Well, I made her a present of an American ice pitcher, but it was so handsome they stowed it away. Then I kicked up another row—and finally they quite fell in love with it, and I got my water. I am considered a miracle of total abstinence on my 11 o'clock brandy and my little quart of strong ale at dinner.[30]

Yet fifteen years later, in another letter from Brighton he gives the following anecdote about his own drinking capacities.

Some amazement was expressed that I got so much out of ‒‒ who is regarded as being rather a cantankerous crank, but Lord bless you— the man is a rich, very rich brewer. I did not know this, and when I lunched with him and took no wine, he asked me what I drank. I replied, "Nothing but ale." "What!" he exclaimed, "Ale! Would you drink ale *now?*" "Only try me," was my reply. Never did I see such admiring delight. "Will you have," he said, "mild or strong? I can give you ale a year old—two years—up to *fourteen*. Can you drink that? I have ale of which I cannot drink more than half a glass without getting drunk." "I"—I replied—"have drunk a quart of Trinity Audit and was all the more sober for it. It was done once before me, however by a man 200 years ago." So he brought out his Fourteen year old, which burns in the fire like rum. And I drank 3 half pints of it. When he introduced me to his partner, he said I was the only man he ever knew who could drink a quart of 14 year old ale. Last Sunday he took me through his Vaults and I drank and drank till he said I must not drink any more. It made him and his *Brauknecht* laugh to see me go back to finish off my tubber of the strongest. Of course, I got the L20. It was awful to see how, as soon as I merely tasted a glass, the rest was *thrown away*.

> *Brynge in goode aile, brynge us in no wine,*
> *For if thou do that, thou shalt have Crist's curse and mine!*

He sent me to the house 3 bottles of his best. I wish I could earn £20 a day by drinking enough to floor a navvy.[31]

Leland's Anglophilism and folklorism happily converged. Like the Victorian gentlemen-intellectuals with whom he mingled, he found himself increasingly drawn to the observation of curious customs and ways of humble folk. Here is a typical account of his method of fieldwork, or fieldplay as it was to him.

> I am at some pleasant watering-place, no matter where. Let it be Torquay, or Ilfracombe, or Aberystwith, or Bath, or Bournemouth, or Hastings. I find out what old churches, castles, towns, towers, manors, lakes, forests, fairy-wells, or other charms of England lie within twenty miles. Then I take my staff and sketch-book, and set out on my day's pilgrimage. In merrie England I could nowhere be a stranger if I would, and that with people who cannot read. . . .[32]

Off on his jaunts Leland never feigned a disguise but kept his gentlemanly manner and attire, as would Cecil Sharp among the southern Appalachian mountaineers. It humored him to see the consternation of the Romany when he spoke their tongue and penetrated their secrets. Finding a gypsy lad carting home a load of obviously stolen firewood, he spoke to him in Romany, gave him a hand, cautioned him against the police, and waited at his camp until the foraging mother came home, ashen to see the fine gentleman with her lad, but soon put at ease when Leland said to her in Romany, "Mother, here is some wood we've been stealing for you." [33]

English folklorists as well as the English folk pleased Leland. He mentions Max Müller trying to persuade him to give up gypsies for Red Indians,[34] and he refers cryptically to "my foe Lang," [35] although he also speaks ecstatically of Lang's laudatory review of his *Songs of the Sea* in the *Daily News*.[36] Groome, his fellow Romany Rye, was a close friend, and they went together to Cobham Fair. York Powell, Oxford Regius Professor of Modern History and then president of the Folk-Lore Society in 1904, wrote an affectionate and eloquent obituary of Leland in *Folk-Lore*. Had Leland carried his *Memoirs* beyond 1870 we would know more of his associations with the Great Team and their group, but we can surmise his activity in the Society from his role in the great London congress of 1891. He served as Vice-Chairman of the Organising Committee, and his name appears prominently in the first two paragraphs of the *Papers and Transactions* of the congress, as the intermediary from the First International Folklore Congress at Paris in 1889 designated to bring a motion before the Council of the Folk-Lore Society to hold a second congress in London. In addition he delivered a paper on "Etrusco-Roman Remains in Modern Tuscan Tradition," which elicited the comment from the chairman of the Mythological Section, Professor John Rhys, that "they had listened to a whole world of discovery" revealing "much survival of ancient beliefs." [37] In his turn Leland commented on F. Hindes Groome's paper on "The Influence of the Gypsies on the Superstitions of the English Folk," praising it but disagreeing with Groome's contention that the gypsies knew about palmistry. He was responsible for bringing another American to the congress, his protegé Mary Alicia Owen, who read a paper "Among the Voodoos" in which she discussed "conjer-stones," even one belonging to her mentor.

> The one held by our honoured Vice-President, our Romany Rye, our Oriental scholar, our world-known Hans Breitmann, our Voodoo King, was stolen from its unworthy owner, a dissipated and malicious negro, who practised on the superstitions of his race that he might live in a brutish and debased idleness. It fell into my hands. I brought it overseas to Mr. Leland.[38]

Leland's personal letters give a wholly different slant from the official transactions of the congress. He wrote to one of his publishers, T. Fisher Unwin, that his paper "caused amazement and admiration," and had provided the content of a leader in the *Times*, along with Mary Owen's paper on voodoo. Unabashedly he declared "They have certainly been the two most *sensational* papers of the Congress." [39] A letter to his niece (Oct. 11, 1891) is full of the congress, and of his own impatience with bookish folklorists and stuffy discussions.

CHARLES GODFREY LELAND TO E. R. PENNELL

Langham Hotel, Oct. 11th, 1891.
There were a hundred in the Congress, and Mary Owen, and

Nevill, and Prof. Haddon, and I were really *all* the people in it who knew anything about Folk-Lore at *first hand* among niggers, Romanys, Dutch Uncles, hand-organ men, Injuns, bar-maids, tinkers, etc. It was funny to see how naturally we four understood one another and got together. But Mary takes the rag of all, for she was born to it in wild Missouri.

There are altogether in all America only 5 or 6 conjurin' stones, small black pebbles, which come from Africa. Whoever owns one becomes thereby a chief Voodoo—all the years of fasting, ceremonies, etc., can be dispensed with. Miss Owen found one out and promised it. The one who had it would not sell it, so she—stole it! As it had always been, when owned by blacks. And then gave it to me. I exhibited it to the Congress. MacRitchie says I am also King of the Gypsies.

Day before yesterday in Congress, there was a very long, very able, and very slow paper by Lady Welby, and then dull comments. I felt that I must either burst, vamos, or let myself out. Finally, Prof. Rhys said that no civilised man *could understand* a savage or superstitious peasant—that there was a line never to be crossed between them, etc., etc. Also something by somebody about souls in animals.

Then I riz and said:—

"Mr. Chairman (this was my foe Lang), Prof. Rhys says that there is no understanding between superstitious people and us. Now the trouble I always have is *not* to understand them and be just like them. (Here Lang laughed.) I have been on the other side of that line all last winter, and I had to come back to England because Mrs. Leland said I was becoming as superstitious as an old nigger. As for souls in animals—last night at the dinner our chairman, with his usual sagacity and perception, observed that we had in the room a *black cat* with white paws, which is a sign of luck. (By the way, I myself saw her catch a mouse in behind the curtain.) Now to be serious and drop trifling. In America every association, be it a fire company or a Folk-Lore, has a *mascot*. Ladies and gentlemen, I propose that that puss be elected a member of our Society. If we cannot have a *Mascot*, at least we shall possess a *Tho-mas-cat*!"

Roars of laughter, I felt better for 24 hours after.

We all contributed folk-lore articles to our Exhibition. I had only to pick out of one tray in one trunk to get 31 articles, which filled two large glass cases. As Belle [his wife] says, she can't turn over a shirt without having a fetish roll out. And I couldn't distinguish between those of my own make and those of others. For I am so used to picking up stones with holes in them, and driftwood, and tying red rags round chickenbones for luck etc., etc., that I consider my own just as powerful as anybody's.[40]

For all his valiant endeavors and numerous publications, Leland has left little mark on folklore studies, and he has candidly given us the reason why. In the Preface to *Legends of Florence* he refers to "certain tales, or anecdotes, or jests, which are either based on a very slight foundation of tradition—often a mere hint—or have been so 'written up' by a runaway pen—and mine is an 'awful bolter'—that the second-rate folk-lorist, whose forte consists not in finding facts but faults, may say in truth, as one of his kind did in America: 'Mr. Leland is throughout inaccurate.' "[41] True, Leland could never restrain his bolting pen, as anyone who reads his marvelously chatty letters and *Memoirs* soon sees. Texts were not sacred to him; his own stories were at least as good as the ones he collected, and he inserted himself unashamedly into his books. "It was once said of a certain man that he would tell a story on less provocation than anybody that ever lived," he wrote in *The Egyptian Sketch-Book*. "I begin to believe that *that* man was I."[42] But he would also convert stories into verse, as he did with his Glooskap tales, contending that the original Indian form was poetic, and he would make poems out of bits of tradition, as in his *Songs of the Sea and Lays of the Land* (1875), which he explicitly stated was "not a folk-lore book," and hence he need not indicate his borrowings—although Nutt included it in a list of Leland's folklore publications. At the same time he strove to keep faith with his folklorist readers, and explained to them that in collecting legends of Virgil the magician, he had to prime the pump by narrating them to his field assistant. "If you want fairy-tales, take whatever the gods may send, but if you require nothing but legends of Red Cap, you must specify, and show samples of the wares demanded."[43] And his wares did come back with "important changes." It was Hans Breitmann's fate to be caught between the horns of his belletristic and his scientific impulses.

William Wirt Sikes (1836–1883)

The most substantial book of Welsh legendry in English was produced by the United States consul to Wales, Wirt Sikes, in 1880 under the misleading title *British Goblins*. Its contents are accurately portrayed in the subtitle, *Welsh Folk-Lore, Fairy Mythology, Legends and Traditions*. Where Welsh nationalists themselves had fallen far behind Ireland and Scotland in uncovering extant lore, the Yankee who had never written a folklore book and who had lived only four years in Wales came up with a rich haul of Welsh folk stuff. When John Rhys, dean of Welsh philologists, assembled his two large volumes on *Celtic Folk-Lore, Welsh and Manx* in 1901, he conveyed chiefly a negative impression of the leanness of Brythonic tradition. Rhys took much space to report that there was little to report. By contrast, *British Goblins* is packed with legend texts and descriptions of customs. The explanation is that Rhys was an inept field man, like his associates among the Great Team, who were system-builders, while Sikes talked, collected, and observed with facility, and added his own personal materials to those he amassed from printed sources, both Welsh and English. Sikes had the wit to recognize folk matter in the Cardiff *Western Mail* he read at the breakfast table as well as in the *Mabinogion*.

Born in Watertown, New York, Sikes learned the printing trade as a youth, became a journalist on Utica and Chicago newspapers, and then took over the editorship of two up-state New York newspapers. In addition, he contributed poems, tales, and sketches to newspapers and magazines in such abundance that he employed twenty-two pseudonyms. Some of his original compositions were gathered in *A Book for the Winter-Evening Fireside* (1858), when he was only twenty-two, and he wrote two novels, *The World's Broad Stage* (1868) and *One Poor Girl* (1869) that reflected his interest in the social conditions of the lower classes in Chicago and New York. After divorcing his first wife, he remarried Olive Logan in 1871, a prominent New York actress, lecturer, playwright, and author, whom he had served as business manager, and who survived him to die in a mental institution in Banstead, England, in 1909. Shortly after this marriage Sikes visited the Wiertz Museum of fine arts in Brussels, and subsequently published a pamphlet about its collection.

In June 1876 he accepted the appointment of United States consul to Wales, and rapidly immersed himself in the living and historic culture of his new residence. An inveterate walker, he came to know familiarly the villages and byways of southern Wales, and wrote up his impressions in *Rambles and Studies in Old South Wales* in 1881. That same year he also brought out *Studies of Assassination*. With his journalistic fluency, Sikes retold Welsh legends pleasantly enough, but the *British Goblins* is more than a second-hand compendium. Its special merits lie in the orderly and perceptive arrangement of the traditions, almost suggesting a subject classification; in the fresh store of orally reported tales and usages interspersed through the volume; and in the occasional comparisons the author makes between British and American folklore. On the debit side is the mixing of uneven sources, from medieval monkish chronicles to early nineteenth century Cambrian collections, with some materials not clearly specified, all jumbled with the first-hand texts, leaving the reader puzzled as to which tradition is current in what period. Sidney Hartland, who perforce relied on Sikes in constructing *The Science of Fairy Tales* (1891) and in his own writings on Welsh folklore, expressed irritation at the consul's inadequate documentation. On the whole, Sikes performs much better than folklore scholars could reasonably expect from a Johnny-come-lately. He knows his Tylor and accepts the survival theory of animistic belief and pagan rite lingering in the "superstitious prejudices" of the peasantry; he is familiar with the antiquaries, Brand, Hone, Aubrey, Scott, Baring-Gould; he recognizes the parallelisms of comparative folklore, and introduces occasional far-flung similarities culled from such works as Nicholas B. Dennys' *The Folk-Lore of China* (1876); and he has scoured the library for unusual resources, pointing with pride to the rare publications of Prophet Edmund Jones, a dissenting and credulous minister of Monmouthshire in the early years of the nineteenth century who wrote *An Account of the Parish of Aberystruth and a Relation of Apparitions of Spirits in the County of Monmouth*, a title often cited but seldom seen by writers on folklore. Thus Thomas Keightley quoted it from Crofton Croker, who had never seen the book but heard of it through a Welsh friend, and Keightley erred on the author's name and the publication date. Sikes shows himself a wily collector, and appreciates that, from Chaucer on, old people have always credited the fairy belief to an earlier generation, and to the next parish.

The consul divided *British Goblins* into four sections: "The

Realm of Faerie," "The Spirit-World," "Quaint Old Customs," and "Bells, Wells, Stones, and Dragons." If the rubrics sometimes overlap, they do designate major clusterings of tradition. The fairies and the spirits he further subdivided according to their abodes or habits: fairies of the valley, mine fairies, water fairies, mountain fairies; changelings; fairy cattle; household ghosts, familiar spirits, death portents, corpse candles. In his tracing of the consistent patterns in fairy activities Sikes anticipates Hartland's formulation of the laws of fairyland, and he seems to suggest a comparable work for "The Science of Ghost Stories." Here he virtually outlines such a treatise.

> The laws governing the Welsh spirit-world are clear and explicit. A ghost on duty bent has no power of speech until first spoken to. Its persistency in haunting is due to its eager desire to speak, and tell its urgent errand, but the person haunted must take his courage in both hands and put the question to the issue. Having done so, he is booked for the end of the business, be it what it may. The mode of speech adopted must not vary, in addressing a spirit; in the name of the Father, Son, or Holy Ghost it must be addressed, and not otherwise. Its business must be demanded; three times the question must be repeated, unless the ghost answer earlier. When it answers, it speaks in a low and hollow voice, stating its desire; and it must not be interrupted while speaking, for to interrupt it is dangerous in the extreme. At the close of its remarks, questions are in order. They must be promptly delivered, however, or the ghost will vanish. They must bear on the business in hand: it is offended if asked as to its state, or other idle questions born of curiosity. Neglect to obey the ghost's injunctions will lead to much annoyance, and eventually to dire results. At first the spirit will appear with a discontented visage, next with an angry one, and finally with a countenance distorted with the most ferocious rage. Obedience is the only method of escape from its revenge. Such is a *resumé* of the laws.[44]

For the "Quaint Old Customs" Sikes ordered his comments according to days and seasons, and rites of passage. The bells, wells, stones, and dragons all involved magical associations and local landmarks.

Field observations give zest to Sikes' work. He is in a pub at Peterstone-super-Ely, outside Cardiff; men drink tankards of ale, smoke long clay pipes, talk about crops and hard times and the prospects of emigrating to America. The consul enters the conversation, steers it into "the domain of folk-lore," and captures tales, such as the appropriate one of a helpful fairy who brought prosperity to a poor Glamorganshire farmer by instructing the farmwife to leave her candle burning at night—so the fairies could see at their work, as it turned out.[45] Another time he is in a country inn at Christmas in a little Carmarthenshire village. A scene of festivity unfolds.

After a simple dinner off a chop and a half-pint of cwrw da, I strolled into what they called the smoke-room, by way of distinguishing it from the tap-room adjoining. It was a plain little apartment, with high-backed wooden settles nearly up to the ceiling, which gave an old-fashioned air of comfort to the place. Two or three farmers were sitting there drinking their beer and smoking their pipes, and toasting their trouserless shins before the blazing fire. Presently a Welsh harper with his harp entered from out doors, and, seating himself in a corner of the room, began to tune his instrument. The room quickly filled up with men and women, and though no drinks but beer and "pop" were indulged in (save that some of the women drank tea), Bacchus never saw a more genial company. Some one sang an English song with words like these:

> Thrice welcome, old Christmas, we greet thee again,
> With laughter and innocent mirth in thy train;
> Let joy fill the heart, and shine on the brow,
> While we snatch a sweet kiss 'neath the mistletoe-bough—
>> The mistletoe-bough,
>> The mistletoe-bough,
> We will snatch a sweet kiss 'neath the mistletoe-bough.

The words are certainly modern, and as certainly not of a high order of literary merit, but they are extremely characteristic of life at this season in Wales, where kissing under mistletoe is a custom still honoured by observance. There was dancing, too, in this inn company—performed with stern and determined purpose to excel, by individuals who could do a jig, and wished to do it well. The harper played a wild lilting tune; a serious individual who looked liked a schoolteacher took off his hat, bowed to the company, jumped into the middle of the floor, and began to dance like a madman. It was a strange sight. With a face whose grave earnestness relaxed no whit, with firmly compressed lips and knitted brow, the serious person shuffled and double-shuffled, and swung and teetered, and flailed the floor with his rattling soles, till the perspiration poured in rivulets down his solemn face. The company was greatly moved; enthusiastic ejaculations in Welsh and English were heard; shouts of approbation and encouragement arose; and still the serious person danced and danced, ending at last with a wonderful pigeon-wing, and taking his seat exhausted, amid a tremendous roar of applause.[46]

And Sikes further remarks that such scenes contrast with austere religious proceedings in the churches. In another scene a peasant points out to him on a mountain top in Monmouthshire the crossroads stone under which a witch slept by day, and was said—though he himself had never seen it—to come forth by night.[47] Sikes notes with annoyance the long list of tradesmen and work-boys who applied to him for their Christmas box, an expected customary gift although he had never seen any of them.[48] He describes festive weddings he saw at Tenby and Lampeter, with flower garlands, flags and banners, evergreen arches, a brass band, fireworks and bonfires, and thousands of spectators attending the traditional ceremonies. In the village of Sketty in Glamorganshire in August, 1877, he saw a "chaining," an old custom of a chain being stretched across the street to prevent the wedding couple—in this case a groom of fifty and a bride of eighty—from passing until the chainers were "tipped." All the village was in the streets to see the unlikely couple. Their English driver, unaware of the custom, tried angrily to force the barrier, to the glee of the Welsh onlookers. As a participant observer in Welsh folk life Sikes vividly describes a narrator of ghost stories: the "excited eye, the paling cheek, the bated breath, the sinking voice, the intense and absorbed manner. . . ."[49] He adds that no one observing this physical behavior could doubt the speaker's sincerity.

An unusual aspect of *British Goblins* for the Anglo-American folklorist is the parenthetical reference Sikes offers to like matters in the United States. Traditions of the visit to fairyland by a mortal who finds time supernaturally elapsed on his return makes Sikes think of Rip Van Winkle, rendered popular by Washington Irving and Joseph Jefferson, as "an honour to the American genius,"[50] although he concedes that the Grimms and the Hartz Mountains of Germany were the likely originals. Speaking of fetishes like magic bells and wells, Sikes muses in Tylorian fashion on the childlike mind of primitive man, exemplified by the Mississippi Negro boy on his first visit north who thought snow to be salt and claimed that it bit his fingers. He also recalls the belief of Negroes along the southern seaboard in the "Jack'mun-lantern," a hideous, goggle-eyed, long-haired, bounding goblin which, like the Walsh Sllylldan and English Will-o'-wisp, led travelers into impenetrable swamps. The Fourth of July is, for Sikes, a direct echo of the Beltane rituals. "The lad who in the United States capers around a bonfire on the night of Independence Day has not a suspicion that he is imitating the rites of an antiquity the most remote; that in burning a heap of barrels and boxes in a public square the celebrators of the American Fourth of July imitate the priests who thus worshipped the sun-god Beal." [51] (Else why endanger their wooden houses?) At the same time Sikes recognizes that American life has lost "certain joyous and genial wedding customs" [52] common throughout the British Isles.

If the fairy people and magic wells did not appear on American soil, comparable notions existed. American boys rubbed their warts upon impaled toads; when the toad died, the warts shriveled.[53] This in lieu of being able to stick a pin in their warts and throw the pin down a curing well. The Pembrokeshire taboo against a female being the first to cross the threshold on New Year's morning suggested to Sikes practices of American show business.

> A superstition resembling this prevails to this day in America among showmen. "There's no showman on the road," said an American manager of my acquaintance, "who would think of letting a lady be first to pass through the doors when opening them for a performance. There's a sort of feeling that it brings ill-luck. Then there are cross-eyed people; many a veteran ticket-seller loses all heart when one presents himself at the ticket-window. A cross-eyed patron and a bad house generally go together. A cross-eyed performer would be a regular Jonah. With circuses there is a superstition that a man with a yellow clarinet brings bad luck." Another well-known New York manager in a recent conversation assured me that to open an umbrella in a new play is deemed certain failure for the piece.[54]

To Sikes' thinking American spirits exhibited characteristics very like those of their British cousins. Spiritualism as a cult originated in the United States in the nineteenth century, but old-fashioned ghosts still walked and groaned throughout New England—and Sikes referred to haunted houses in Newburyport, New Bedford,

Cambridge. As recently as 1877 a tenant was driven from his Cambridge dwelling by the spirit of a murdered girl buried in the cellar. "An American journal lately gave an account of an apparition seen in Indiana," [55] not only by the riders in the coach but by the horses, who shied in terror until the specter dissolved. Horses in Wales particularly had the gift of seeing spectral funeral processions. To an account of a mischievous spirit which upset the inmates of a house in Tridoll Valley, Glamorganshire, Sikes appended a footnote of the "latest American case" to come to his attention, reported from Akron, Ohio, in 1878, where the home of the Michael Metzlers was plagued by rappings and stone-throwings; a priest who came to exorcise the spirits was himself hit by a stone and left hastily.[56]

Besides noticing analogous folklore, Sikes indicated two other relationships between British and American traditions: the United States as a fabled land in British legend; and the transplanting of British custom and belief in America. One of his best narratives tells of an innkeeper's son in Treconshire transported to Philadelphia by the spirit of a well-dressed woman, later identified as one Elizabeth Gething who had actually emigrated from that parish to Philadelphia. The spirit took him to a fine house, and had him lift up a board, locate a box, and carry it three miles to cast into the black sea. Thereupon he was free to return home.[57] A similar circumstantial account of an overnight trip to America from Ballinskelligs, County Kerry, Ireland, told me by Tadhg Murphy in 1951, is in *Folktales of Ireland*.[58]

In evidence of migrant British lore, Sikes speaks of a banshee in Evansville, Indiana, which had appeared before the deaths of five members of an English family from Cambridgeshire named Feast. The Evansville newspaper reported the banshee's visits.[59] Curiously, Douglas Hyde heard four Irish-Americans discourse on spirits in an Indianapolis hotel—"the only time during my entire American experiences in which such a thing happened."[60] Should a folklorist living in Bloomington, Indiana, feel guilt twinges at these reports of British traditions in nearby cities?

Sikes never pulled together these scattered threads of Anglo-American folklore, but in noting them he pointed to a beckoning line of inquiry few folklorists have pursued.

JEREMIAH CURTIN (1835–1906)

A friend of the poets Longfellow and Lowell, the scientist Louis Agassiz, the ballad scholar Francis James Child, to whom he dedicated one of his folklore books, Theodore Roosevelt, who wrote a preface to his history of the Mongols, Harvard's president Charles W. Eliot, and the Polish novelist Henryk Sienkiewicz, among others, Jeremiah Curtin was himself a figure of eminence in his day, known for his translations of Russian and Polish novels and for his work in what was then called "comparative mythology." Born in Detroit of Irish stock, he moved with his family at the age of one to Greenfield, Wisconsin, near Milwaukee, where numerous German, Polish, and Norwegian immigrants had settled, and showed his extraordinary linguistic aptitude by picking up their tongues, as well as some Indian languages. After graduating from Harvard in 1863 he made contact with the Russian fleet under Admiral Lissofsky then visiting American waters, and returned with them to St. Petersburg. He spent much of the next decade in Russia, eastern Europe, and Asia, in the services of both the American and Russian governments. In the 1880's and 1890's he made several trips to Ireland in search of Gaelic lore. From 1883 to 1891 he served with the Bureau of American Ethnology in the Smithsonian Institution, Washington, D.C., and conducted fieldwork among Indian tribes. His last years were passed in Vermont writing up his accumulated materials, but he visited the Balkans and Russia again in 1903 and 1904. At that time he predicted a shift in the balance of power from the white to the yellow race. He was reputed to know seventy languages and dialects. An inveterate traveler, he lived constantly in hotels, rarely staying in one place for more than a few months, with his faithful wife as amanuensis.

Curtin's large body of published work falls into five distinct groupings: his ethnological reports of the Iroquois, Modoc, Yuchi, and Shawnee; a series of books on the Mongols, all published posthumously; his translations of Slavic fiction, including works of Tolstoy and Sienkiewicz's *Quo Vadis*, the English edition of which, in 1906, finally eased his financial burdens, selling over a million copies; three volumes of Russian and East European folklore, the one published during his lifetime being *Myths and Folk-Tales of the Russians, Western Slavs and Magyars* (1890); and his four collections of Irish folktales.

The achievement and role of Jeremiah Curtin in British, and specifically Irish, folklore studies are known but not perhaps fully appreciated. He was the first systematic and intensive fieldworker in Ireland, and the first deliberately to pursue the Gaelic myth-tellers. Unlike the resident Irish collectors who succeeded him, he had to make his way in a foreign land, although one where he had distant relatives and made fast friends. He tells of the discomforts, difficulties, and even dangers of the field in graphic chapters in his *Memoirs* on "First Visit to Ireland" (1887), "The Second Irish Period" (1891–1893), and "Sojourn in Wales and Ireland" (1899). There he explains his motivation for going to Ireland.

> For many years I had been possessed with the idea that there was a great stock of myths current among the people of Ireland, as well as many of that class of facts which throw light on the history of the human mind. Facts of value to the scientific world. I hoped that there might still remain in the minds of the people of the remote districts of Ireland many idioms useful in explaining the language of the manuscripts preserved in the Irish academy, and myths that would supplement and strengthen recorded mythology. I was going to Ireland to settle that question.[61]

So off he went to the western counties and islands, to Kerry, Galway, Donegal, to Blasket and Tory and the Aran Islands, and to northern Ireland too. Everywhere he encounters unbelievable wretchedness and poverty and brutal landlordism; one can see his passions roused in the same spirit that produced Irish nationalism. In one anecdote he relates how poor tenants pretended to bury alive a tinker, whom they hired for the purpose of shocking the old Duke of Sutherland when he came to inspect his Irish estates. The Duke was indeed shocked when his tenants informed him that they must dispose of the useless old fellow, whom they could not feed because all their money went for rent. Thereon the Duke reduced the rent ten shillings an acre. Time and again Curtin describes windowless huts with earthen floors, filled with the smell of a peat fire, roosting hens, and grunting pigs—literally pigpens—in which he was fain to collect his myths. One house in Mallow in which four pigs were eating in the kitchen was beyond even his endurance, and he took the old man outside beyond a manure pile at the back door to record his myths. "The price paid for ancient lore is not small," he remarked ruefully, and further observes, "It is not in homes of ease and wealth that ancient lore is found." [62] The search for local accommodations also continually plagues him. "Fitzgerald's hotel looked dingy and smelled musty," he lamented typically. "The food was impossible." [63] Sometimes there were no hotels. In Glen Columbkille, which he reached on a donkey-cart through wind and rain, he had to sleep in a 10 × 12 storeroom whose windows had never been opened or washed. Curtin encouraged his landlady to fry eggs in an iron kettle, her only cooking utensil. To get to Blasket Island he had to hire a canvas boat; on the return trip a heavy wind threatened to fill the craft with heavy waves and sink all aboard.

Curtin sets down vivid and amusing portraits of his myth tellers and the Irish folk who knew witches and had seen fairies. On Blasket he asked a man on crutches for Gaelic myths, and received for an answer, "I care more about getting the price of a bottle of whiskey than about old stories." Another man told him, "If you'll give me the price of a bottle of whiskey, I'll talk about stories." [64] Neither produced for him. But rarely did he draw a blank on fairy-lore. A feeble old woman petting a blind chicken in Mallow, when asked if she knew anything about the fairies, responded:

"No, but my father, who lived when fairies and witches were in Ireland, once saw a firkin of butter walking along the road. When it was near a witch's house, a squad of soldiers met it, and one of the soldiers ran a bayonet through the butter. That stopped the firkin.

"Faith, and my father saw this with his own eyes: One morning a neighbor came to our house, picked up a firebrand, and ran out with it. A man was sitting there who knew what that meant. He took a piece of burning peat and threw it into our butter firkin. If he hadn't done that, we would have been a whole year without butter. It would have been stolen from us, for it was May morning." [65]

A gentleman in Dingle, Maurice Fitzgerald, confided to Curtin that in his youth nine out of ten persons professed a belief in fairies, where only one would nowadays. Similarly a well-acquainted native asserted to him that the old myth-tellers were dead or gone to America and Australia; the language had been exterminated, and with it the old stories. Curtin proved the prophets false, with his exciting collections of complex wonder tales, *Myths and Folk-Lore of Ireland* (1890), and *Hero-Tales of Ireland* (1894). Other like narratives of the King of Erin and Finn Mac Cumhail that Curtin printed in the New York *Sun*, whose editor, Charles H. Dana, sponsored Curtin's Irish journeys by paying for his stories, were gathered and edited by James H. Delargy in 1944 as *Folk-Tales of Ireland*. Shifting from the highly structured Märchen and bardic narratives to modern traditions, Curtin also published *Tales of the Fairies and of the Ghost World, Collected from Oral Tradition in South-West Munster* (1895), resulting from a story-swapping session in a Dingle farmhouse among workmen who had seen spirits.

More than an indefatigable collector, Curtin also theorized about his materials. He speculates on comparative mythology in his introductions to *Myths and Folk-Lore of Ireland, Myths and Folk-Tales of the Russians, Western Slavs, and Magyars*, and *Creation Myths of Primitive America*, and occasionally within his *Memoirs*. While a close friend of John Fiske, the Harvard historian whose own *Myths and Myth-Makers* (1873) followed Max Müller's system of celestial mythology, Curtin chose his own direction, and did not hesitate to criticize Müller and Herbert Spencer for constructing their theories of "oblivion" and "confusion" to explain myths on the basis of personal biases and scanty sources. Müller deals with a limited and relatively late body of myths, and Spencer speaks of the confused mental processes of primitive peoples as if he has positive facts at his command. By virtue of his own extensive field researches in different parts of the world, Curtin had a unique advantage in the mythic argument. He accepted the uniformity of mythmaking patterns among primitive peoples, until cultural development produced differentiation, most pronounced in the Aryan mythology "containing myths and myth-conceptions of the loftiest and purest character connected with religions of Europe and Asia." The science of mythology should seek to explain the Aryan product by examining all the extant lower mythologies, "for the highest forms of Aryan myth-thought have beginnings as simple as those of the lowliest race on earth." [66] Gaelic myths occupied a strategic position in the spectrum of non-Aryan and Aryan mythologies. In his work with North and Central American Indians, Slavs, Mongols, and the Gaelic-speaking Irish, Curtin continually bore in mind his grand objective.

> From the wreck of ancient Keltic and Teutonic thought much has been saved on the two islands of Ireland and Iceland. With this, together with the American system and the mythologic inheritance of the Slav world in Eastern Europe, we shall be able perhaps to obtain materials with which to explain the earliest epoch of Aryan thought, the epoch which corresponds in development with the world of American creation myths. In that case we shall gain a connected view of Aryan speculation and its methods from those early beginnings when there was no passion or quality apart from a person, when symbols, metaphors, and personifications were in the distant future.[67]

Curtin would dig back before Müller's mythopoeic age into Tylor's animistic universe of prehistoric man, still preserved in certain contemporary societies that were rapidly being obliterated. He waxed bitter at the Americans who were erasing the Indian inheritance, as the English were the Irish.

So compulsive a traveler as Curtin must needs touch base on all the British Isles. He spent some months in Scotland in 1893 in Fort Williams expressly to learn Scotch Gaelic, and in Oban in a bookstore he chanced on the author of a book of Scotch myths he held in his hand. The author, James MacDougall, at first seemed suspicious that Curtin had come to take away his myths, but appeared relieved when Curtin praised his work (*Folk and Hero Tales*, 1891) as the best of its kind. In 1899 he tarried in Cardiff and took lessons in Welsh. London was a regular port of call for him, and we find him moving in some of the same circles as did Leland, dining with the publisher Trübner, meeting George Eliot. He gives us a glimpse of the English folklorist William R. S. Ralston, a withdrawn, unhappy man, with whom he shared strong interests in Russian folklore; Ralston read the manuscript of his work on early Russian history to Curtin and Fiske. Curtin was never the Anglophile of Leland's stripe, and castigated John Bull as an enemy of democracy during the Boer War. He was properly a world-man; during what he calls a few quiet months he read Hebrew and Persian, learned Cherokee, and perused straight through the twenty-four volumes of the *Mahābhārata*.[68] Endowed with a strong frame, broad cheek-bones, blue eyes, and a tawny curling full beard,[69] he was impressive in appearance as in accomplishments, and a worthy cultural representative of the United States abroad in the days before Fulbright fellowships.

Walter Yeeling Evans-Wentz (1878–1965)

One American who knew intimately and worked closely with British folklorists of the Heroic Age lived into our own day, although after his exciting first book he moved away from folklore into religious mysticism of the Orient. In that book, *The Fairy-Faith in Celtic Countries* (1911), Walter Yeeling Evans-Wentz drew together many strands of the British folklore movement, and then sought to direct it along a new path.

Evans-Wentz was born in Trenton, New Jersey, lived as a youth in California, and took his B.A. and M.A. degrees from Stanford University in 1906 and 1907. At Stanford he came under the influence of William James in psychology and pondered on the concept of the reality of the unseen. From 1907 to 1909 he studied at the University of Rennes in Brittany, receiving the degree of doctor of letters for the first draft of his *Fairy Faith*. At Oxford in 1910, where he took the research degree of bachelor of science, he shifted from a literary to an anthropological perspective. Still further work brought his opus to publication in 1911 in a formidable volume of five hundred pages. Nothing like *The Fairy-Faith in Celtic Countries* can be found in the history of British folklore, although it is firmly embedded in that history.

In the first place, Evans-Wentz undertook a comparative field study. Where conventionally the collector investigated one region, and that usually his own, the American journeyed to all six Celtic countries, Ireland, Scotland, Wales, Isle of Man, Cornwall, and Brittany, to interview peasants and intellectuals on the fairy belief. Secondly, he concentrated exclusively on traditional beliefs and folk philosophy. Märchen, ballads, proverbs, jests were not his concern. In a commentary within *The Fairy-Faith*, Douglas Hyde distinguished between the *sean-sgéal* or structured wonder tale, which he himself chiefly collected, and the formless statement of fairy belief and experience that Evans-Wentz was eliciting. Thirdly, *The Fairy-Faith* combined exhaustive field and library evidence to build its case. Unlike the books of collectors who simply presented their hard-won texts, or of theorists who never ventured into the field, Evans-Wentz exhaustively pursued every source that could illuminate the question of the fairy creed: archaeological sites that might have served for pagan religious rites and ceremonies; bardic and monastic literature offering precedents and analogies with the modern fairy creed; anthropological reports of comparative folklore demonstrating the universal recognition of spirit beings. Fourthly, Evans-Wentz advanced an original thesis of his own, the Psychological Theory, to account for the belief of mortal man in fairy creatures. Not content merely to prove, by overwhelming evidence, the fact of the pervasive fairy-faith, he raised the level of his study from an empirical, ethnological plane to a closely reasoned, metaphysical argument climaxed with a presumed proof in a residual x-factor in his evidence explicable only on the basis of the real existence of fairies. Here Evans-Wentz was allying comparative folklore with psychical research, in the manner of Andrew Lang, but carrying the argument beyond Lang's cautious claims to include the philosophical theory of William James on the subliminal consciousness, the psychoanalytical theory of Freud on the mechanism of the superego, and the psychoreligious theory of Mary Baker Eddy on the power of malignant animal magnetism. These and other modern immaterialists agreed in hypothesizing an invisible world that some men apprehended, and with which their own world overlapped.

In a short period Evans-Wentz made contact with the leading British folklorists. He read at Oxford under Robert Ranulph Marett, inheritor of Tylor's mantle and himself an ingenious expositor of a psychological theory of folklore, although from a functional rather than a psychical viewpoint. The two examiners of his Oxford paper were Sir John Rhys, whose two-volume study of *Celtic Folk-Lore, Welsh and Manx,* had appeared in 1901, and Andrew Lang, alone of the Great Team to take seriously the efforts of the Psychical Research Society, whose president he became in the last year of his life. In *The Fairy-Faith*, Evans-Wentz invited six experts in the lore of the six Celtic lands each to write an introduction to the field report, or "taking of evidence," on his particular country. Douglas Hyde, key figure in the Irish folklore movement, introduced the section on Ireland with the most substantial comment; he suspended a decision on the Psychological Theory, but was reminded of a talk in an Indianapolis hotel with four affluent Irish-Americans, all of whom told of ghostly sights in Ireland, two falling quite outside regular categories. Hyde often accompanied Evans-Wentz into the field. So did Alexander Carmichael, author of the famed *Carmina Gadelica*, who introduced the Scottish section. Rhys gave a brief summary of the main Welsh fairy-legend types as preface to the Welsh section. In addition to these inserted prefaces, Evans-Wentz also asked Andrew Lang for a special statement on "Psychical Research and Anthropology in Relation to the Fairy-Faith." [70] While underscoring the worldwide currency of the fairy belief in various forms, Lang declared that "sane and educated persons" seldom reported seeing fairies, although they frequently beheld phantasms of the dead. Evans-Wentz responded in a note[71] pressing the point, which he reaffirmed throughout his book, that fairy and spirit phenomena merged into each other and equally merited scientific attention. In citing the scholarly literature on Celtic folklore, Evans-Wentz acknowledged the achievement of Alfred Nutt, especially for his study of the Celtic doctrine of rebirth, and approved his conclusion, that the Happy Otherworld in medieval Irish mythic romances was not only pre-Christian but from the oldest Aryan epoch. Evans-Wentz had much of his own to say on the rebirth doctrine, in which he perceived a Buddhistic perception of reincarnated spirits. Cuchulainn and King Arthur could be both gods above and incarnated kings of the Celts; extant peasant legends from Lough Dur treated Charles Parnell as the reincarnation of an old Gaelic hero. The Sleeping Hero fit into this theme, and gets attached to King Arthur and Garret Fitzgerald, Earl of Desmond, who rose against Queen Elizabeth, and who rides a silver-shod white horse across the lake every seven years.

Closely bound as he was to the British folklorists, Evans-Wentz still retained his own marked individuality and bias. While partly Celtic himself, he felt an advantage in being an American, saying "I was in many places privileged to enter where an Englishman, or a non-Celt of Europe would not be." His education in the ideals of a free democracy detached him from European prejudices regrettably apparent, he felt, in Celtic countries.[72] Yet Evans-Wentz was no chauvinistic American. Reacting against the materialistic, positivistic, natural-science emphasis of his homeland, he responded warmly to Celtic seers and mystics. In his theory, he always claimed to weigh evidence as a scientist. Tylor's prehistoric animism found its strongest growth in the Celtic zones, where wild and awesome landscapes and seascapes brought man close to the elemental psychic forces of nature. All Celtdom, indeed, formed one connected mystic terrain between the poles of Carnac, in Brittany, land of the returning dead, and Tara, in Ireland, land of Faerie. At the end of his voluminous treatise Evans-Wentz has proved to his satisfaction the existence of Fairies and a Fairyland, and the validity of his own vitalistic theory of evolution. He considered other theories: the Naturalistic Theory that explained the fairy faith by the mood of the countryside; the Pygmy Theory of MacRitchie that saw in the fairies a race-memory of dwarfish people; the Druid Theory which substituted druid priests for pygmies in racial remembrance; and the Mythological Theory that beheld in the fairies the lineal descendants of an ancient pantheon. Something there might be in all these theories, but none explained where the fairy idea came from in the beginning, save only the Psychological Theory. Fairies belong to the invisible surrounding world that privileged percipients occasionally fathom.

Evans-Wentz followed the trail he had marked out in *The Fairy-Faith* by journeying to India in 1917, seeking out, as he said, the Wise Men of the East. He became a Buddhist monk and lived for three years in Tibet with Lama Dawa-Samdup until the Lama's death in 1922. Between 1927 and 1954 he edited a series of the Lama's translations of religious documents, beginning with *The Tibetan Book of the Dead*. Oxford University awarded him an honorary degree of Doctor of Science in Comparative Religion in 1931, he being the first American to be so honored. From 1923 until his death he lived in San Diego, California, corresponding with Hindu and Buddhist sages, working with the Self-Realization Fellowship, and completing his final book on *Sacred Mountains of the World*. In his will he left the mineral rights to his 5,000 acre estate to Stanford University for a chair in Oriental philosophy and religion. The *Fairy-Faith in Celtic Countries* was reprinted in 1966 with an admiring introduction by the English folklorist Leslie Shepard, and the Mystic Arts Book Club distributed it as a book choice in 1969.

CONCLUSION

What generalizations, if any, can we draw from the careers of our four American folklorists in Britain? Strongly individualistic as each was, they still share certain traits. All were uncommon Americans of unusual talents, energies, and wanderlust. Leland and Curtin lived much of their lives restlessly in European hotels; Evans-Wentz sought mountain retreats in India, Ceylon, and Tibet; Sikes, who died in Wales at 46, may well have had further wanderings before him. All possessed facility at languages, not a notable American aptitude, and Curtin and Leland were fanatic in their zest for acquiring new tongues. All wrote skilfully and prolifically on a variety of subjects; both Leland and Curtin have left us meaty, delightful *Memoirs*. None was a full-time, or even a half-time folklorist, and in these respects they resemble the Great Team with their broad range of intellectual interests. None was an academic scholar.

The strongest unifying element in the four is their love of the field, and here they depart entirely from the Great Team. All demanded and savored the personal contact with the folk bearers of tradition, and achieved unusual successes in their field interviews, before fieldwork had made much headway in Britain. At the same time all showed some interest in theory; Curtin, Leland, and Sikes within their lights followed the survivalist point of view, while Evans-Wentz advanced an original thesis to explain the fairy creed. If his psychical research places him in doubtful company, we have to concede that today he could bolster his argument with the multiple sightings of UFO's. Curiously, none worked in mainstream American folklore; Curtin and Leland concentrated on Indians. Why did these four evince no interest in the folklore of the Celts, Slavs, Italians, and Asians who had come to America? But this is a rude question; their labors were prodigious, and each entered into the spirit and added to the triumphs of the British folklore movement.

N O T E S

1. Charles Godfrey Leland, *Memoirs*, 2 vols. (London, 1893), II, 159–60.
2. Elizabeth Robins Pennell, *Charles Godfrey Leland, a Biography*, 2 vols. (London, 1906), II, 266.
3. Pennell, II, 344.
4. Pennell, II, 258.
5. *Memoirs*, II, 275.
6. Pennell, II, 379.
7. Pennell, II, 261–62.
8. Pennell, II, 309–10.
9. *Gypsy Sorcery and Fortune-Telling*, pp. xv–xvi.
10. Ibid., xvi.
11. Ibid., xvi, note; Pennell, II, 429–30, who gives the date as 1856 but believes there must have been an earlier edition.
12. *The English Gipsies*, p. 124.
13. Ibid., p. 132.
14. Pennell, II, 340–41.
15. *Gypsy Sorcery and Fortune-Telling*, p. 6.
16. Pennell, II, 105.
17. Pennell, II, 87–88.
18. Ibid., II, 273–74.
19. Ibid., II, 54–61.
20. Ibid., II, 200.
21. Ibid., II, 207.
22. Ibid., II, 367–68.
23. Ibid., II, 307.
24. Ibid., II, 210.
25. Ibid., II, 369.
26. Ibid., II, 370.
27. Ibid., II, 76–79.
28. *The Algonquin Legends of New England*, p. 5.
29. *Memoirs*, II, 236.
30. Pennell, II, 27.
31. Ibid., II, 271–73.
32. *The Gypsies*, Centenary Edition, pp. 10–11.
33. Ibid., p. 102.
34. Pennell, II, 19.
35. Ibid., II, 350.
36. Ibid., II, 378.
37. *International Folk-Lore Congress*, 1891, p. 201.
38. Ibid., 248.
39. Pennell, II, 353.
40. Ibid., II, 350–52.

41. *Legends of Florence,* First Series, 2nd ed. (London, 1896), pp. xi–xii.

42. (London, 1873), p. 156.

43. *The Unpublished Legends of Virgil,* p. 47.

44. William Wirt Sikes, *British Goblins: Welsh Folk-Lore, Fairy Mythology, Legends and Traditions,* 2nd ed. (London, 1880), pp. 148–49.

45. Ibid., 14–16.

46. Ibid., 290–91.

47. Ibid., 368.

48. Ibid., 296.

49. Ibid., 246.

50. Ibid., 89.

51. Ibid. 278.

52. Ibid., 314.

53. Ibid., 352, n. 7.

54. Ibid., 255.

55. Ibid., 171.

56. Ibid., 185.

57. Ibid., 157–59.

58. Sean O'Sullivan, *Folktales of Ireland* (Chicago and London, 1966), pp. 209–20.

59. Sikes, p. 247.

60. Walter Yeeling Evans-Wentz, *The Fairy-Faith in Celtic Countries* (n.p.: University Books, Inc., 1911), p. 26.

61. *Memoirs of Jeremiah Curtin,* ed. with notes and introduction by Joseph Schafer (Madison, Wisconsin, 1940), p. 385.

62. Ibid., 450, 457.

63. Ibid., 763.

64. Ibid., 455.

65. Ibid., 390.

66. *Myths and Folk-Lore of Ireland* (Boston, 1880), p. 27.

67. *Creation Myths of Primitive America* (London, 1899), pp. xxxv–xxxvi.

68. *Memoirs of Jeremiah Curtin,* p. 382.

69. *Dictionary of American Biography.*

70. Evans-Wentz, pp. 474–76.

71. Ibid., 476.

72. Ibid., xxviii.

11 /

The Academic Future of Folklore

WE HAVE REACHED a crucial point in the history of folklore studies in the United States. The entire academic scene is under scrutiny and review. Some critics and gloomy prophets, like Robert Nisbet in *The Degradation of the Academic Dogma*, are even predicting the end of the American university as an institution, to be jettisoned like the medieval cathedral by a society that demands relevance and involvement. Programs and departments considered peripheral are, as we all know, being eliminated; budget belts for faculty positions are being tightened; Ph.D.'s are seeking ever more elusive jobs; the so-called fat is being squeezed out of the vast plants of higher education. What are the prospects for Folklore, which by 1971 has inched its way into the tent of academe, but could easily be pushed out again? Should Folklore wage a holding battle to retain its modest foothold? Should it recognize and bow gracefully to the current austerity by seeking protection from, and absorption into, well established disciplines? Should it seek to continue its momentum of growth, and if so, in what directions and by what means and tactics? These are the questions I submit to our panel and to our Society, and I am sure they are already in your minds.

On our direction I have a firm view; on our stratagems I do not. I believe Folklore should fight unequivocally for continued aca-

Paper read before the American Folklore Society in Washington, D.C., 13 November 1971.

demic recognition. By this I mean it should seek further Ph.D. programs, undergraduate majors and minors, and additional course offerings in Folklore, throughout the American system of higher education. To spell this out more explicitly, I think we can realistically argue that Folklore belongs in every fully developed liberal arts curriculum and that every major university and many smaller ones should have a folklorist—that is, a holder of the Ph.D. in Folklore—on its faculty. I am not contending that we should strive for many departments of Folklore, for such a goal would certainly be unrealistic today, and here is where the question of strategy comes in. For if there exist, and survive, only a handful of Folklore departments, who hires the folklorist, and who cares about replacing him if he leaves?

Let me first support my credo that Folklore should push for the major, the minor, the M.A., the Ph.D., in short, the works. I have not always subscribed to this full repertoire, and had doubts until recently about the undergraduate major. Other professional folklorists have had, and may still have, doubts about the Ph.D. At any rate here are the reasons that have led to my conversion.

First, Folklore as a subject of study is extremely attractive to students, both undergraduates and graduates. It is a poor teacher indeed who cannot turn on a class that is discovering tales and ballads and crafts. On all sides I hear reports of prospering enrolments. At Indiana the number of higher degree candidates in folklore has steadily climbed over the past fourteen years from six to one hundred twenty-five; although fellowship funds have diminished, the caliber as well as the number of applicants goes up each year. In 1969–70 and 1970–71 the three main introductory courses—survey, American, folk music—have, under the spirited direction of Robert Adams, Henry Glassie, and Charles Boilès, pushed undergraduate enrolment up to two thousand a year. The success of these courses has led to a spillover into upper division offerings. At Berkeley I was able to see the enormous drawing power of Alan Dundes with the country's most demanding students who flocked into his classes to the number of seven hundred, and when I was there as visiting professor, he dragooned two hundred fifty bodies into a course of mine that was not even listed in the catalogue. Well, we live in a day when numbers count, and if Folklore pulls in students at a time when many of them complain about the sterility of college instruction, let us advertise our record loudly and clearly. Already our new undergraduate major in Folklore at Indiana University, initiated this fall, has led students to transfer to I.U. from other colleges so they can pursue this major. The Folklore Institute has just acquired a second building to handle its growing affairs. As Folklore in the universities has waxed, so has its professional organization, the American Folklore Society, prospered amazingly since the 1940's.

Second, the humanistic values in folklore studies are especially appealing in the contemporary climate of opinion. Here I am thinking not just of student reaction but of the perspectives of university faculties, administrators, boards of trustees, alumni, legislators, businessmen, and the public at large. The nation today is concerned about its underprivileged, its poor, its blacks, its Appalachian whites, its ethnics, its Indians, its Chicanos, its forgotten and left-outs. While I will not equate the folk with the "lower orders," as the Victorian folklorists were wont to do, I am ready to see, and claim, plenty of opportunities for the folklorist among such tradition-oriented groups. The frustrated scholars of Afro-American or Black Studies, for an instance, are becoming aware of the primacy of verbal traditions in the cultural heritage of the American Negro. Those who wish to comprehend more fully the thoughts of men in prison can turn to the collections of prison folklore recorded by Bruce Jackson.

This line of thought might seem to move toward the seductions of Applied Folklore, but I am not proposing that Bruce Jackson's work will avert another Attica. Greater knowledge of mankind, particularly the overlooked masses of mankind, may well aid social reformers. But I do not think reform is the business of the folklorist. He has his work cut out to justify and explain his discipline. And today he can justify it in good part through the "disinterested" pursuit of cultural truths about his fellow-man. Here I use disinterested not in the sense of without interest, but in the Victorian sense of without bias or self-serving end, as Gordon Ray has revived the term in his splendid essay on "The Idea of Disinterestedness in the University." [1]

A third reason why I believe Folklore should strive for as complete autonomy as possible is my conviction that it is a separate and independent field of learning, fully equal to the other humanities and social sciences. By any tests one can apply—the density of the scholarly literature, the specialized nature of the concepts and techniques, the international community of professionals—Folklore is a full-time academic enterprise. At one time I thought that the historian, the literary critic, the anthropologist, and perhaps any sympathetic scholar of whatever discipline could master folkloristics by listening to some shoptalk and reading some key books. After thirty years in the game I now feel that the interdisciplinary ideal is a chimera, because the professional in one field never really understands the professional in another field. He has a hard enough time comprehending the subdisciplines of his own domain. By the time the aspiring academic has taken his graduate colloquia and seminars, sweated through his qualifying examinations, consulted with his graduate advisors, attended his professional meetings, labored over his dissertation, all the time closely closeted with his peers traveling the same rocky road, he is corrupted for life; his mental muscles have atrophied, his speech patterns have coagulated, his intellectual blood stream has thickened to a slow ooze. Until his grave he will be a political scientist, a linguist, an historian—or a folklorist. His Ph.D. is irreversible. The only difference between a doctorate in Folklore and other doctorates is that nonfolklorists think they can talk about folklore. No outsider would dream of talking, say, to a sociologist in his own jargon, but because of its restricted academic status and its popular nature, Folklore can be patronized by anybody. How often have we all had the experience of Professor Smooch from the Gerontology Department, or Mrs. Curious from Suburbia, coming up to us at some social gathering and saying, "Now what is folklore?" In his innocence Professor Smooch is no different from Mrs. Curious, and even academics whose research over the years has brought them close to folkloristics never grasp the most elementary concepts. I could cite chapter and verse for the exchanges, the book reviews, the corridor comments to document these generalizations, but one will do. In a taped discussion which is being broadcast this fall over university radio stations in the series "Conversations from Chicago," Walter Blair, professor emeritus of English at the University of Chicago, was talking with me about my new book of old essays, *American Folklore and the Historian*, in which I had held up a passage from his *Tall Tale America* as an example of fakelore. "Well, Dick, people are calling you pedantic, arrogant, and dogmatic," he said with refreshing candor. "What authority do you have to tell me what liberties I can take with my materials? *Tall Tale America* is still selling, but if I did not rewrite the stories they would be pretty dull and people would not read them." Now Walter Blair has done excellent and courageous work on American humor over a long stretch of time, and flirted with folklore, as in his co-authorship with Franklin Meine of two books on Mike Fink. He would cut his throat before he would tamper with a Mark Twain text, but in his eyes folklore texts require tampering.

The walls between disciplines work for us as well as against us. Every Ph.D. in Folklore we turn out becomes a recruit to our growing guild, and whatever department he ultimately joins, he will be irrevocably branded as a folklorist. We have of course in our Society professionals from other disciplines, but they belong for the most part—and I include myself here—to the day before doctorates in Folklore became readily available.

Our future as I see it lies in the university. We have witnessed the doldrums that folklore in England has fallen into without a university base. I do not believe that support from agencies of the federal government, were it forthcoming, would ever permit folklorists to engage in the disinterested pursuit of truth. We have before us the example of the folklore gathered under the Federal Writers Project which was never published because it fell into divisive ethnic categories rather than unified all-American stuff.

So for the strategy of folklorists in the coming years, I say go all out to get entrenched in the colleges and universities. But what of the tactics? How do we maintain and expand Folklore programs and how do we place our Ph.D.'s? The two questions are interrelated, for if more courses are taught and more majors and minors developed, more Folklore Ph.D.'s will be needed.

The crux of the matter lies in the departmental structure of American universities. Departments are composed of scholars holding the Ph.D. in a common field, and they recruit new members with the same doctorate. In smaller institutions, the president may hire new faculty, but he places them in a department of their fellow-Ph.D.'s. The problem for the new doctor of Folklore, and his sponsors, is to persuade a department composed of doctors of English, or anthropology, or history, or foreign languages, or music, to give him a home. A number of such departments have taken in their token folklorist, but each negotiation represents a struggle; many institutions possess no folklorist, and too often, especially now, if the folklorist moves to a more attractive situation his vacancy is gobbled up by hungry chairmen, former colleagues, or harassed deans to use for a Milton specialist or an urban anthropologist, or it may simply vanish. There is an opening now that has not been filled for some time in a southern university with a long commitment to Folklore, although well qualified nominees have been recommended, because the departmental spokesman insists on a candidate who will publish and make his career primarily in English. Yet this candidate is supposed to edit a folklore journal and teach some Folklore. Our Ph.D.'s at Indiana, Pennsylvania, Texas, customarily have strong minors, but the hiring institutions should expect them to make their contributions in large part as folklorists, and not to disguise themselves under other hats. Our chief argument indeed is that conventional Ph.D.'s exist in abundance, but a university should be proud and delighted to have on its roster that colorful and exotic academic growth, the professor who professes Folklore.

The question then is, how do we get doctors of Folklore onto the faculties of many of the 2600 institutions of higher learning in the United States? A university organism is a strange animal, belonging to a common genus and yet with its own individual markings, in the form of presidents, provosts, vice-presidents, chancellors, vice-chancellors, deans, vice-deans, divisions, schools, institutes, committees of every hue and complexion, and with varying relationships to other units of higher education in the state or the conference or the association. And yet, in spite of all this formidable bureaucracy, effective action may take place through informal human relationships. Once when I was seeking an appointment as tennis coach in the Harvard Athletic Association, the director of intramural athletics told me he would intercept the provost next day at 12:10 P.M. on the path the provost always took from his administrative office to the faculty club for lunch, and obtain his approval en route. As dean of the graduate school at Indiana University in 1949, Stith Thompson looked with favor on his own proposal for a graduate program in folklore. He tells in his memoir how he first met the new president, Herman B Wells, in the barber shop, and there commenced an intimacy that resulted in Folklore having a strong champion in the president's office for the next quarter of a century. In these respects universities probably resemble other large business organizations; the husband of a folklorist once told me he learned of his promotion to assistant sales manager of Chevrolet in a men's room of the General Motors Building.

Recognizing that personal initiative will always play a prominent role in the developing of academic programs, we still ponder what we may do collectively as a learned society to support our cause. I suggest the following three-stage ladder as one for the panel to consider and possibly for members of the Society to adapt to their particular situations.

In the first stage, an administrative official makes the appointment of a folklorist to a liberal arts faculty where folklore is absent from the curriculum. This official, possibly a dean of the college of arts and sciences, places the assistant, associate, or full professor of folklore, with that title, in the department of the new faculty member's choice, or on a joint appointment in two departments, say English and anthropology, if he so desires, or in the department that has actively expressed an interest in acquiring a folklorist. His salary increases, tenure and promotion decisions will be recommended by the department chairman, or chairmen in the case of a joint appointment, to the dean who controls the position. Should the folklorist leave for another institution, or be released, his slot, which has never left the dean's unallocated faculty budget, will be filled again by the dean. This device ensures the preservation of the Folklore slot against departmental pressures.

Although I had forgotten about it, this was exactly the mechanism used in my own appointment at Indiana University. When Stith Thompson, whose position was in the English department, retired, the dean of faculties and the dean of the college of arts and sciences looked for a folklorist to succeed him. If Wayland Hand had come, he would have been placed in the German department. When I came, I was located in the history department.

Stage two is the mini-department. Chance or intention may bring two or more folklorists together at the same institution. No one is so lonely as the single folklorist, and he will convert a colleague or seek to bring in a peer. The two will soon begin planning an expanded curriculum. When the time seems ripe, they can propose to the administration a semi-autonomous status for themselves, under some title such as, say, the Folklore Studies Curriculum. This unit would have its own budget—and a separate budget for Folklore is the key to everything we hope for academically. In the budget would go half salaries of the two or more folklorists, whose other halves would remain in their original departments. Such joint appointments would ensure continuing relationships between Folklore and its allies, and make less drastic the new curriculum. Also in the budget could go a modest sum for library purchases, an assistant for the now burgeoning folklore archives, and a part-time secretary. The mini-department would control two or three introductory courses, which would be given a separate identifying letter, so that they will be plainly visible in the catalogue under the Folklore Studies Curriculum. More specialized upper division folklore courses can remain for the time being in their existing departments, but be crosslisted under Folklore.

For Folklore, or American Studies, or Black Studies, or any fringe program to gain academic status means simply to gain control of a budget, for faculty slots, for teaching associates, for graduate student fellowships, for library acquisitions. But Folklore can make a better case for autonomy than area programs because it is an intellectual discipline. To depend on the good will of a sponsoring department—and here I come back to my theme of the walls between disciplines—for an indefinite period invites trouble. Folklore has its friends and its enemies. Anthropology has given its fair share of support to Folklore, but I know of one anthropology chairman at a distinguished university who has killed Folklore dead; he once confided to me that a mutual friend, a professional anthropologist, had shifted his research interests to Folklore because he could not make it in anthropology. The resistance of historians to Folklore is well known. In any event, in these days of tight budgets, why should a department be asked to squeeze out a slot for an alien Ph.D.? Once the mini-department of Folklore has its own mini-budget and its own mini-curriculum, Folklore is alive in the university, breathing through its budgetary gills. It need not fear sudden erasure at the hands of a new unsympathetic departmental head or clique, and it has a chance to grow. The two or three members of the Folklore Studies Curriculum have a base from which they can operate. They can maneuver for further joint appointments with various departments; they can add to their courses as their student following increases; they can attract outside funds to add to their university budget; they can develop a folklore journal, archives, museum; they can solidify friendships throughout the university community with a faculty—and perhaps a student—advisory committee; they can strike for the minor, the major, the M.A. from a position of strength; in short, they are in business. Administratively the Folklore Studies Curriculum reports directly to the dean or his designate.

The day may come when expanding enrolment and faculty prestige make plausible the transition to stage three, a full-fledged department of Folklore. But the mini-department is not to be presented as transitional; in a number of institutions it may answer Folklore's needs over the long haul, and will not alarm administrators apprehensive of future commitments or disturb departments that retain doubts about Folklore's intellectuality. On the other hand, if the strength is there, the Folklore Studies Curriculum should certainly push for departmental status. By every criterion the UCLA program has long since passed into stage three, and it seems to me tragic that excellent and committed holders of the M.A. in Folklore there are waiting in limbo to see if the doctorate comes through.

Two objections to these ideas I have already heard voiced. One is, how will the Ph.D.'s in Folklore get placed? Well, so far they have all gotten placed. The field develops its own momentum. In the last two tough years, Indiana placed thirteen people, none with the Ph.D. completed, and all teaching, or with the expectation of teaching, Folklore. Pennsylvania has regularly placed its Ph.D.'s.

The second demurrer is, what will a Folklore concentrator do if he majors in Folklore in college and continues with it in graduate school? My own thinking is that the A.B. is quite a separate proposition from the M.A. and Ph.D., and that college students who learn about man's ways by taking courses in Folklore are not predestined to become Folklore scholars. But for those who wish to go all the way, I see no reason why they cannot, like the history or anthropology or English major, find plenty of ground to cover at each successive level. And the student who seeks three degrees in Folklore can address himself to the task of mastering foreign languages while still in college, so that he does not spend precious time in graduate school learning elementary French, German, Spanish, or Russian. He can go on to Swahili and Hindi for his Ph.D.

Assuming the reader supports in principle this three-stage proposal—an assumption I make simply to complete this argument—how does it get presented and to whom? My own instincts are against a formal Society manifesto or a committee empowered to draft a resolution, or indeed any collective action beyond the airing of the questions in this and other forums. Rather I favor individual action based on what seems to be the consensus, if one develops, of the Society's mood, or of our panel's thinking. We may as individuals gather data and publish articles, such as Ronald Baker's recent inventory of college and university course offerings and programs in Folklore,[2] to call attention to the success and promise of Folklore in higher education. Some of these articles might be gathered together as a pamphlet and mailed to university and foundation officials. The message I would like to see transmitted forcefully and persuasively in such statements is a simple one: Folklore should be taught in every liberal arts college.

NOTE

1. *The Graduate Journal* 8 (1971): 295–309.
2. "Folklore Courses and Programs in American Universities and Colleges," *Journal of American Folklore* 84 (1971): 221–29.

INDEX